The Labour Market and Economic Development of Taiwan

This book was financed by the Chiang-Ching Kuo Foundation
for International Scholarly Exchange

The Labour Market and Economic Development of Taiwan

Edited by

Joseph S. Lee

*Jing Tin Professor of Human Resource Management,
School of Management, National Central University, Taiwan*

Edward Elgar
Cheltenham, UK • Northampton, MA, USA

Published by
Edward Elgar Publishing Limited
Glensanda House
Montpellier Parade
Cheltenham
Glos GL50 1UA
UK

Edward Elgar Publishing, Inc.
William Pratt House
9 Dewey Court
Northampton
Massachusetts 01060
USA

A catalogue record for this book
is available from the British Library

Library of Congress Cataloguing in Publication Data

The labour market and economic development of Taiwan / edited by Joseph S. Lee.
    p. cm.
Includes bibliographical references and index.
1. Labor market–Taiwan 2. Taiwan–Economic policy. I. Li, Cheng, 1939–
HD5832.A6L33 2007
  331.1095124'9–dc22
                  2007001397

ISBN 978 1 84720 342 7

Printed and bound in Great Britain by MPG Books Ltd, Bodmin, Cornwall

Contents

PART III LABOUR MARKET POLICIES IN THE NEW KNOWLEDGE
ECONOMY

Contributors

Joseph S. Lee is the Jing Ting Chair Professor of Human Resource Management at the National Central University in Taiwan. Professor Lee received his Ph.D. degree in economics from the University of Massachusetts at Amherst and went on to teach in Minnesota for 22 years before returning to Taiwan in the appointment of Vice-President of the Chung-Hua Institution for Economic Research. He subsequently served as the Dean of the School of Management at the National Central University. His research interest lies in labour relations, labour market analysis and the knowledge-based economy. He has published and edited many books including *The Role of SMEs in Taiwan's Development Process*, *The New Knowledge Economy of Taiwan* (with Tain-Jy Chen), *Labour Standards and Economic Development* and *The Emergence of the South China Growth Triangle*.

Gary S. Fields is a Professor of Labour Economics and Economic Development at Cornell University. He received his BA and Ph.D. degrees from the University of Michigan and has published more than 100 books and articles including *Poverty, Inequality and Development* (Cambridge University Press), *Retirement, Pensions and Social Security* (with Olivia Mitchell – MIT Press) and *A New Look at the Developing World* (MIT Press). His fields of specialization are the theory and empirical functioning of labour markets, and changes in poverty and inequality in developing countries.

Amanda Newton Kraus is a Research Analyst and Project Director at the CNA Corporation, where she uses applied econometric analysis to inform public policy decisions in various contexts. Dr. Kraus holds Masters and Doctoral degrees in Economics from Cornell University and is currently working on analysis into the impact of national demographic and educational trends on workforce diversity in the US military and the study of the relationships between national security, state weaknesses and economic development. Her prior work has included the use of market survey data to quantify the effects of monetary and non-monetary incentives on individuals' decisions to join or re-enlist in the Services.

Christina Y. Liu is a Professor of Finance at the National Taiwan University. She received her Ph.D. degree from the University of Chicago and has since specialized in monetary theory and international finance. She has published many articles in professional journals, including Economic Letters, the Journal of Finance and the International Journal of Economics. She is currently serving as a legislator within the Legislative Yuan of the Central Government of the Republic of China.

Wei-Chiao Huang is a Professor of Economics at the University of Western Michigan. He received his Ph.D. degree from the University of California at Santa Barbara and although his current fields of specialization include labour economics and applied microeconomics, his main research interest lies in labour market issues and the analysis of seemingly non-economic human behaviour.

Chia-Wei Wang is currently a Research Associate at Accumind Consulting Inc., and a Ph.D. candidate at the University of Illinois, Chicago. His area of primary research interest lies in the analysis of public utilities.

Chung-Chi Wu is a Professor of Economics at the National Taiwan University from where he received his BA in economics. His fields of specialization are labour economics, micro-economics and industrial economics. He has served as the President of the Consumer Rights Association and as a member of the Council of Labour Affairs. Dr. Wu has published many articles in professional journals.

Feng-Fuh Jiang is a Research Fellow within the Institute of Economics at Academia Sinica in Taiwan. He received his Ph.D. from New York State University at Binghamton and specializes in research into labour economics and public finance. He has produced many publications, including *Occupational Segregation and Gender Earning Differentials: A Case Study of Taiwan*, and *Impacts of Demographic, Economic and Political Trends on Taiwan's Social Safety Net*.

Paul K.C. Liu is the Research Fellow Emeritus within the Institute of Economics at Academia Sinica in Taiwan. He received his Ph.D degree from Michigan State University and has taught at the National Taiwan University. He has published many articles on population, fertility, migration and human resource development.

Ji-Ping Lin is an Associate Research Fellow at the Centre for Survey Research and the Research Centre for Humanities and Social Sciences at Academia Sinica in Taiwan. He received his Ph.D degree in geography from McMaster University in Canada and is currently pursuing his major research interests in labour migration (both internal and international), discrete choice theory and discrete data analysis, and medical and health geography.

Ping-Lung Hsin is an Associate Professor of Economics within the Institute of National Development at the National Taiwan University. He received his Ph.D in economics from Cornell University. His major fields of research are labour economics and social welfare, areas in which he has published many articles in professional journals including *Family Structure and Fertility Behavior, The Political Economy of Public Pensions, Medical Utilization* and *Health Expenditure amongst the Elderly in Taiwan.*

Yang Shih is an Assistant Professor of Social Work at Shih Chien University in Taiwan. He received his Ph.D degree in public administration and public policy from the National Taipei University and his current research interest lies in social security, social welfare and social insurance schemes.

Chao-Yin Lin received her Ph.D degree from the London School of Economics and Political Science and is currently an Assistant Professor of Social Work at the National Taipei University. Her field of specialization lies in social policy and social welfare, a field in which she has published many articles including *The Development of National Health Insurance in Taiwan: Lessons for Abroad,* and *An Analysis of the NHI Uninsured Population in Taiwan.*

Mei Hsu is a Professor of Economics at the National Taipei University. She received her Ph.D degree from Duke University and has since pursued her specialized fields of labour economics, health economics, industrial economics and family economics. She has written many articles for publication in international journals including *Time Series Wage Differentials in Taiwan* and *Labour Productivity of Small and Large Manufacturing Firms: The Case of Taiwan.*

Foreword

From 1949 right through to the mid-1990s, Taiwan was enormously successful in its efforts towards economic development; indeed, so impressive was the island's overall performance that the World Bank subsequently dubbed the phenomenon the 'Taiwanese Economic Miracle', a term which has since been often repeated. Some years ago, in their efforts to share the Taiwanese experience of economic development with policymakers and scholars of economic development in other countries, Professor S.C. Chiang, the late President of the Chung-Hua Institution for Economic Research (CIER), and Professor Dwight H. Perkins, the former Director of the Harvard Institute for International Development (HIID), signed an agreement to undertake a joint project involving the compilation of five volumes aimed at recording the experiences of economic development in Taiwan, with the project being funded by an extremely generous grant from the Chiang-Ching Kuo Foundation for International Scholarly Exchange (CCK Foundation). In setting up this project, it had originally been intended that it would be a collaborative effort, in every sense of the word, between researchers within these two institutions; however, collaborative efforts between scholars separated by thousands of miles were never going to be easy, and it was most unfortunate that after the completion of the first two volumes in the series, the HIID ceased to exist as an independent body in Harvard University; thus, the completion of the project became the sole responsibility of the CIER.

This volume, *The Labour Market and Economic Development of Taiwan*, is the final book in the series. The first volume, *Industrialization and the State: The Changing Role of the Taiwanese Government in the Economy, 1945-1998*, which was written by Li-Min Hsueh and C.K. Hsu from the CIER, and Dwight H. Perkins from the HIID, was published in 2001 by the HIID. The second volume, *Taxation and Economic Development in Taiwan*, which was written by Keh-Nan Sun from the CIER, and C.Y. Kuo and Glenn Jenkins from the HIID, was published by the John F. Kennedy School of Government at Harvard University in 2003. With the subsequent disbandment of the HIID as an independent body, the third volume, *Taiwan's Economic Development and the Role of SMEs*, edited by Joseph S. Lee and Chi Schive from Taiwan, was published in Singapore, by Graham Brash Pte Ltd., in 2003. The fourth volume, *The New Knowledge Economy of Taiwan*, edited by Tain-Jy Chen and Joseph S. Lee, was published in the UK, by Edward Elgar, in 2004. This concluding volume, *The Labour Market and Economic Development of Taiwan*, which is again edited by Joseph S. Lee, explains the reasons for the extremely impressive performance of Taiwan's labour market prior to 1996, and the factors leading to its deterioration since then.

In presenting this final book of the five-book project sponsored by the CCK Foundation, we must offer an apology for the considerable delay in preparing the last of these volumes for publication. This delay was, however, brought about by major changes, on several occasions, to some of the important people directly involved in the coordination of the production of these five volumes. We are extremely grateful to the CCK Foundation for the financial and moral support provided throughout this whole project. The support and patience given to this project by the past Presidents of the CIER, Professor Tzong-Shian Yu, Professor Chao-Cheng Mai and Professor Tain-Jy Chen, is also greatly appreciated.

We dedicate this book to the late Professor S.C. Tsiang, the founder of the CIER, who was later to become the Chairman of the Board of Trustees at the Institution. Indeed, as noted earlier, it was he who initiated this entire project, but sadly, he was unable to witness its successful conclusion. We would like to express our enormous appreciation to Professor Tzong Shian Yu, another key founding member of the CIER, and, as noted above, a former President of the Institution. Special thanks are reserved for Professor Joseph S. Lee, a former Vice-President of the CIER, who, despite having already completed his term and responsibilities at the institution some considerable time ago, stepped in to oversee and coordinate all of the remaining volumes, right through to the completion of the entire project. His efforts are greatly appreciated. Thanks also go to Ms. Emily Chang for her tireless efforts in coordinating the production of this final book throughout the rather protracted period of its compilation. Finally, we would like to express our sincere appreciation to Mr George Okrasa, our consultant English editor, for his outstanding patience, excellent editorial assistance and skilful compilation, not only of this volume, but also of the three previous volumes, to camera-ready state.

C.A. Ko
President
Chung-Hua Institution for Economic Research

Preface

How could it be that Taiwan's labour market, which had worked so well for several decades, could possibly have experienced such massive deterioration over recent years? This is a question which should be of significant interest and importance to public policymakers and scholars alike, because the answer may well help to shed some light on the current debate as to whether excessive regulation is harmful to the efficient operation of the labour market; that is, whether such excessive regulation can actually lead to a rise in unemployment and a general decline in the economic growth rate.

Part I of this book begins with an introduction, Chapter 1, by Joseph Lee, in which he provides a general overview of labour market flexibility and employment in Taiwan in the pre- and post-1996 periods. Gary Fields and Amanda Newton Kraus then go on to explain, over the subsequent three chapters, what it was that enabled the Taiwanese labour market to maintain such outstanding performance prior to 1996. Their analysis begins in Chapter 2, 'Taiwan's Changing Employment and Earnings Structures', where Gary Fields adopts a 'pseudo-cohort' analysis to demonstrate that the performance of the Taiwanese labour market was actually at its most efficient between 1980 and 1992, as evidenced by the low unemployment rate, the rapid improvement in the employment mix and the rapid rise in earnings for all workers. He also demonstrates that over the same period, workers were able to migrate rapidly from the low-productivity sectors to the high-productivity sectors and were thereby able to achieve considerable improvements in both their income and their living standards. Fields stresses that all of this was made possible as a result of the highly integrated nature of the labour market.

In Chapter 3, 'Education and Taiwan's Changing Employment and Earnings Structures', Fields and Kraus demonstrate that between 1980 and 1992, not only did the wage rates for skilled and unskilled workers rise almost in tandem, but that wages rose at similar rates for workers across different industries. They tackle the question of how this phenomenon could occur when there was such a sharp rise in the educational attainment of the workforce as a whole. Given such rapid expansion of the educational system and, as a result, the rapid rise in the supply of skilled workers, one might expect to see a narrowing of the wage gap between skilled and unskilled workers. However, such narrowing of the wage gap did not occur in Taiwan, largely because of the highly integrated nature of the labour market, which provided skilled workers with opportunities to accept low-skilled work if the labour market conditions were not so good, and then shift back to more highly skilled work when labour market conditions improved; as a consequence, the wage gap between skilled and unskilled workers remained quite stable.

Based on the above findings, in Chapter 4, Gary Fields goes on to develop an integrated multi-sector labour market model which aims to provide explanations for the high performance level within the Taiwanese labour market prior to 1996. As he points out, in a highly integrated labour market, with the expansion of certain sectors (and the corresponding rise in the demand for labour within the industries in those sectors) workers are drawn away from the declining sectors and into these expanding sectors. There is, however, no decline in wage rates within the declining sectors; indeed, they can actually rise. This is essentially because there is a requirement to raise the wage rates within the declining sector in order to resist labour piracy from the expanding industries, whilst also raising the productivity of those workers that are retained within such declining industries. Essentially, it was the 'hands-off' labour market policy approach adopted by the government prior to 1996 that permitted the formation of the highly integrated labour market which subsequently provided Taiwan with the flexibility required to achieve such efficient operation. This, in turn, produced low unemployment, a rapid rise in income levels and constant improvements in the working conditions of all workers.

The chapters in Part II of this book move on to a discussion of the factors contributing to the deterioration in labour market performance in Taiwan in the post-1996 period, targeting three fundamental factors as the main contributors to such deterioration in performance.

Firstly, there has been a rapid shift in the industrial structure in recent years – from 'employment-friendly' industries to those that were less friendly; that is, from the various labour-intensive industries to the high-tech industries, such as integrated circuit (IC) producers – which, although involving enormous amounts of investment, actually created very few jobs. This shift in the industrial structure had the effect of placing Taiwan in a situation of 'jobless' growth, a condition whereby the economy continued to grow but there was little growth in the number of jobs being created.

Secondly, the recent globalization of the Taiwanese economy has rendered it much more sensitive to the outside world; consequently, greater flexibility was required of the labour market if it was to be able to adjust rapidly to the changes in the outside world. Unfortunately, the response by the government to such globalization of the economy was to adopt a much more interventionist approach, imposing not only increasingly invasive regulation on the labour market, but also excessively high standards. However, not only did this impose greater rigidity upon the Taiwanese labour market, it also imposed higher direct labour costs on Taiwanese employers, as compared to their counterparts in other Asian newly industrialized economies (NIEs).

Thirdly, the globalization of the Taiwanese economy has extended the labour market beyond national borders. This is largely because, as growing numbers of employers were relocating their production facilities abroad in search of lower labour costs, at the same time, their employees were being sent from Taiwan to operate their overseas subsidiaries. Globalization essentially led to the government demonstrating its greater willingness to open its borders and permit foreign workers to come into Taiwan as a means of relieving the island's shortage of unskilled labour.

All these changes created the need for greater flexibility in the Taiwanese labour market – including greater deregulation – so as to cope with the rapidly changing global economy. This has brought about a need for expansion, by the government, of the island's vocational training system in order to provide the necessary assistance for much larger numbers of employees to gain new abilities which are now prerequisites if they are to adjust appropriately to the rapidly changing labour market conditions. Such expansion of employee training programmes can also help management to gain greater flexibility in the everyday use of their human resources.

The first of these factors, the changing industrial structure and its impact on Taiwan's employment, is addressed in Chapter 5, 'Cyclical Employment Changes in Taiwanese Industry', by Christina Liu, Wei-Chiao Huang and Chia-Wei Wang. Adopting the approach of Groshen and Potter (2003), they divide all industries in Taiwan into four categories: (i) structurally growing industries, within which employment continues to rise regardless of any increase or decrease in the economic growth rate as a whole; (ii) pro-cyclical industries, within which employment rises when there is an increase in the economic growth rate, but declines when there is a corresponding decline in the economic growth rate; (iii) structurally declining industries, within which employment declines regardless of any increase or decrease in the economic growth rate; and (iv) counter-cyclical industries, within which employment declines when there is an increase in the economic growth rate, but rises when there is a decline in the economic growth rate.

The authors demonstrate that the rate of change in the industrial structure was quite slow during the 1970s and that in that particular period a large proportion of unemployed workers were to be found in the category of cyclical unemployment; thus, through the implementation of appropriate monetary and fiscal policies, it was possible to get the economy back on track and to put unemployed workers back into work in their old jobs, or in similar jobs. However, the globalization of the Taiwanese economy since the late 1990s hastened the rate of change in the industrial structure of the island; consequently, increasing numbers of unemployed workers were now being found in the category of structural unemployment, comprising of those workers whose skills and knowledge had become obsolete. Such unemployed workers therefore had little chance of returning to their previous jobs. In 2002, for example, only 15 per cent of all unemployed workers were cyclically unemployed, with the remaining 85 per cent being structurally unemployed; thus, economic recovery programmes had become totally ineffective in terms of helping the majority of the unemployed to regain employment, and other programmes, such as training and retraining programmes, were now necessary in order to resolve the growing unemployment problem.

The authors also show that during the 1980s, most of the industries within the manufacturing sector, such as the textiles, clothing, rubber and plastics industries, were employment-friendly industries; in the late 1990s, however, the composition of the manufacturing sector was shifting more towards the chemicals industries and other industries which, as a result of their greater capital intensity, were less employment-friendly. Under such conditions, economic recovery or expansion programmes would have little impact on unemployment because any expansion of these industries would generate only a small number of jobs, as can be seen in late 1990s, a time when the same rate of economic growth generated much fewer employment opportunities. Thus, simply maintaining the economic growth rate at a high level was, by itself, no longer sufficient; the government would also need to identify and promote these employment-friendly industries, so that greater numbers of good quality jobs could be created for the island's citizens.

In Chapter 6, 'Industrial Change and Structural Unemployment in Taiwan', Chung-Chi Wu argues that the high unemployment rate in the post-1996 period was caused by the paradox of a simultaneous labour surplus and labour shortage. During the late 1980s and early 1990s, although there were rapid changes going on in the island's economic structure – along with increasing numbers of firms within the manufacturing industries relocating to Southeast Asia and mainland China in search of lower labour costs – those workers who were being displaced could easily find alternative jobs within the service and construction industries, where skills requirements were low. However, by the late-1990s, the service sector, which had previously been a major absorber of the surplus labour coming out of the manufacturing sector, had become saturated and unable to absorb any more surplus workers from this sector. Meanwhile, given that it was mired in recession, the construction sector was unable to play a similar role, in terms of absorbing the surplus labour from the manufacturing sector.

In recent years, despite the somewhat limited numbers of jobs being created within the high-tech and knowledge-intensive service industries, new jobs have, nevertheless, been created in other sectors, such as finance and banking; however, these jobs require high levels of education and training, qualifications which the newly displaced workers from the manufacturing sector do not have. Although there was some expansion in higher education during the latter part of the 1990s, the type of education being provided was not designed to meet the needs of these displaced workers; thus, the expansion of the education system at that time was unable to play the same role that it had played in the 1970s and 1980s, in terms of providing the workforce with the sort of flexibility required to rapidly adjust to the new technologies and the new environment that were being created. Had the expansion of the educational system in the 1990s not been limited to four years of college, university and postgraduate studies, but instead, to technical schools, junior colleges and recurrent adult education, then the education system may well have been able to better accommodate the needs of the displaced workers in Taiwan. This would have simultaneously ensured that the workforce was rendered more flexible, whilst also addressing the imbalance in the overall demand and supply of labour.

In Chapter 7, 'The Deterioration in Employment: Regional Unemployment Dynamics', Feng-Fuh Jiang and Paul K.C. Liu investigate both the impact of labour legislation and the importation of foreign workers in the 1990s in an effort to determine whether such policies resulted in impeding the efficient operation of the labour market in Taiwan. Although the most comprehensive labour law, the Fair Labour Standards Law (FLSL), was enacted in 1984, it had little, if any, adverse effects on the operation of the labour market at that time. This was because its enforcement agency, the Council for Labour Affairs (CLA) was not established until 1987. Furthermore, even after the establishment of the CLA, the law was not seriously enforced, partly because of the lack of staff members to conduct large-scale inspections, and partly because the jurisdiction of the law was limited at that time to the agricultural, manufacturing, transport, construction and utilities sectors, whilst other sectors, such as trade, services, finance and banking, were excluded from its jurisdiction. It was not until 1995 that the coverage of the FLSL was extended to include the trade, services and finance sectors, with the extension of the overall jurisdiction of the FLSL eventually being completed in 1998. Moreover, the CLA also became much more vigorously involved in enforcing the law after 1996, largely as a result of the pressure exerted by the opposition parties. Clearly, therefore, in the post-1996 period, the law may have begun to have a much greater impact on the operation of the labour market in Taiwan. Jiang and Liu also point out that although demographic factors were the major cause of differences in unemployment throughout the region, the level of enforcement of the FLSL, as well as the proportion of foreign workers within the local workforce as a whole, were important determinants of the differences in regional unemployment. In other words, they argue that with regard to the reduced flexibility of the Taiwanese labour market and the higher overall unemployment rate, the two most important contributory factors were the FLSL and the introduction of foreign workers.

The question therefore arises as to why the government opened its doors to foreign workers in the early 1990s and what impact this has had in Taiwan on the labour market as a whole. With the increasing development of the Taiwanese economy, the educational attainments of the workforce have also become correspondingly higher, and, as a result of their higher educational attainment and higher incomes, the island's citizens have become less willing to accept the difficult, dirty and dangerous (3D) jobs. Thus, starting in the early 1990s, Taiwan began to experience an acute shortage of low-skilled labour. In 1992, in an effort to relieve this labour shortage, the government enacted the Employment Services Act which, thereafter, would officially allow the admission of low- skilled foreign workers into Taiwan. The trade unions and other organizations were, however, strongly opposed to the admission of these workers, largely because, in their opinion, such foreign workers would displace native workers and hence cause higher unemployment amongst lower-educated native workers.

Although it has been pointed out in a number of empirical studies, including Liu (2004), Wu (1995), San (1996) and Hsu (1997), that foreign workers do have a 'substitution effect' on native workers, and thus, that the 300,000 foreign workers imported into Taiwan contributed to the higher unemployment rate in the post-1996 period, other studies have nevertheless argued that foreign workers are restricted to acute labour shortage industries and 3D jobs, the types of jobs that native workers are unwilling to accept; in other words, that foreign workers and native workers are engaged in segregated labour markets. Thus, it is suggested that they did not substitute for each other in the early 1990s (Lee, 2004).

Nevertheless, Joseph Lee goes on to point out, in Chapter 8, that this situation has changed in recent years as a result of several new developments in government policy on foreign workers, the first of which was the change in the minimum wage policy in 1997. Prior to 1997, foreign workers had been protected by the same minimum wage legislation as native workers; however, in that year, the CLA issued a new order which permitted employers to count 'room and board' and certain other foreign worker expenses as an integral part of the minimum wage, hence widening the wage gap between foreign workers and native workers. As a result, employers were provided with new incentives for hiring low-cost foreign workers as direct replacements for their more expensive native workers. Secondly, ever since the late 1990s, there have been increasing numbers of foreign workers running away from their 'official' employers – designated by the government to fill vacancies in those industrial sectors that were suffering from acute labour shortages – and finding other employers who were keen to hire them, not because of any labour shortage within their particular industrial sector, but because of the low costs involved in hiring such illegal workers. Thirdly, the government has been permitting the entry into Taiwan of growing numbers of foreign healthcare workers ever since the late 1990s; however, since these workers are not subject to the minimum wage regulations, they receive, on average, barely half of the wages of comparable native workers in the healthcare sector, thus rendering them a further source of cheap labour in Taiwan. Given that the costs of hiring these workers is so low, some employers are not actually hiring them to undertake healthcare work within their homes at all, but are instead assigning them to work in family-owned shops and factories. Finally, Taiwan has recently experienced dramatic increases in the numbers of illegal foreign workers entering from neighbouring countries in Southeast Asia and from mainland China. Most of these illegal immigrants are not necessarily working for employers who are encountering any specific labour shortage, but are instead being welcomed by unscrupulous employers simply because of their low costs. Joseph Lee therefore argues that the influx of foreign workers in recent years no longer represents a means of supplementing native workers, as originally intended by the government, but that such workers are now actually displacing native workers in certain sectors. He therefore concludes that some of the responsibility for the rise in unemployment amongst native workers in Taiwan is attributable to certain sections of the foreign workers entering into Taiwan.

This substitution effect of foreign workers is also broached by Ji-Ping Lin in Chapter 9, 'Involuntary Job Turnover in Taiwan, 1996-2000'. The availability of cheap foreign workers reduced employers' incentives to take the 'high road' of a more sophisticated, competitive strategy. Such a strategy would necessarily involve the introduction of advanced management systems alongside high-performance human resource management techniques, as well as increased R&D effort and the production of high-valued products. Lin argues that these employers are instead choosing to take the 'low road' of a low-cost competitive strategy. Amongst all unemployed workers, not only had there been a dramatic increase in the share of workers who had become involuntarily unemployed since 1997, but it had also become increasingly difficult for them to regain suitable employment, largely as a result of the increasing rigidity of the labour market and the ready availability of foreign workers. Employers therefore preferred to hire more foreign workers if they were available, since the labour costs involved in hiring such foreign workers were much lower than those for native workers.

Preface xix

Furthermore, as Lin shows, foreign workers are more willing to put in overtime work than native workers, thereby increasing the overall flexibility of employers. Lin also demonstrates that involuntary unemployment is more common within the manufacturing sector, particularly amongst males, older and less-educated workers, and that when involuntary unemployed workers are reemployed, they usually have to settle for lower-paying jobs, or jobs with a lower job title than in their previous role, whilst their counterparts (voluntarily unemployed workers) tend to move upwards, with both higher job titles and pay levels.

Most governments in market economies will tend to adopt both passive and active labour market policies as a means of effectively tackling the problem of high unemployment. Passive labour market policies include the extension of unemployment benefits to longer periods, expanding the eligibility standards for receipt of unemployment benefits and increasing the amount of benefits paid to the unemployed, whilst active labour market policies include employment services, training for the unemployed, retraining for workers subjected to mass layoffs, training for youths, wage and employment subsidies, public works, self-employment assistance and micro-enterprise development. The chapters in Part III of this book investigate some of the major passive and active labour market policies adopted by the Taiwanese government as a means of tackling the continuing rise in unemployment. These policies have included employee training programmes and the unemployment insurance programme, along with direct job creation programmes, such as the island's Public Service Employment Programme.

In Chapter 10, 'Employee Training Programmes and Sustainable Employability', Joseph Lee and Ping-Lung Hsin carry out an examination of employee training programmes in Taiwan, in terms of their effectiveness in enabling those workers in employment to achieve sustainable employability and those who are unemployed to get back into gainful employment. They also examine whether workers who have become discouraged by current labour market conditions, including those who may have completely dropped out of the labour force, are provided with the necessary skills and abilities to enable them to re-enter the labour market. They find that such programmes are not very popular in Taiwan, with only 14 per cent of the workforce having ever participated in any form of employee training; indeed, they reveal that only 13 per cent of all establishments in Taiwan had ever offered training courses to their employees. However, as Lee and Hsin reveal, employers are not alone in their lack of interest in employee training, since employees themselves have not demonstrated any particular desire to participate in such programmes. This does, however, appear to be mainly because most of the existing training courses are either poorly designed or have little relevance to the needs of either employers or employees. Furthermore, it appears that, in the case of most of the training programmes, no appropriate evaluation mechanisms have been put in place; government officials are therefore unable to assess the effectiveness of these training programmes, whilst employees, in turn, have no adequate information upon which to base their decisions as to which programmes may be capable of meeting their needs. Lee and Hsin argue that in order to ensure that such employee training programmes can become an effective tool for helping workers to achieve sustainable employability and to avert the risk of unemployment, the government needs to establish appropriate mechanisms by which employers' input can be solicited on the initial design of training programmes, as well as the evaluation of the effectiveness of such programmes. The government has recently taken steps towards establishing national systems for both occupational standards and training programme evaluation, as well as the establishment of a learning passport system; these are clearly steps in the right direction.

Ever since the late 1990s, as the unemployment rate has grown inexorably higher and displaced workers have been experiencing increasingly longer periods of unemployment, the issue of unemployment has become a real social problem for the island. In response, the government carried out a revision of the Labour Insurance Act in 1999, adding an additional section within the Act directing the payment of unemployment benefits to all unemployed workers who had previously subscribed to the island's labour insurance scheme. However, such revision was obviously inadequate, simply because the law covered only a small proportion of employees within the private sector. In 2003, the government therefore enacted a totally independent Employment Insurance Law, which, in addition to providing unemployment benefits to a much wider range of employees, was also intended to provide unemployed workers with employment counselling and vocational training services; thus, the government had signalled a shift away from its previous passive policy towards a much more active approach in dealing with unemployment.

In Chapter 11, 'Employment Insurance and Unemployment in Taiwan', Yang Shih examines the effectiveness of the newly established employment insurance programme, in terms of whether it has been successful in providing appropriate assistance for unemployed workers through unemployment benefits, employment counselling services and vocational training opportunities. He points out that, in terms of the provision of unemployment benefits, the programme appeared to be adequate, given that 97 per cent of all unemployed persons who were eligible under the unemployment insurance system were in fact receiving unemployment benefits. However, Shih also suggests that there are inadequacies in the employment insurance programme, in terms of the provision of relevant labour market information for the unemployed, as well as the training and job placement services provided.

Put simply, the programme continues to represent an unemployment programme as opposed to an employment insurance programme, and has failed to provide both the unemployed and those at risk of future unemployment with the necessary employment counselling services and vocational training opportunities that were integral elements of the service provision originally intended by the government. Shih therefore calls upon the government to place greater emphasis within the law on the provision of such vocational training and employment counselling services both to those who are already unemployed and to those workers faced with an uncertain future in their current jobs, with the potential of joining the ranks of the unemployed.

An evaluation of the effectiveness of the Public Service Employment Programme (PSEP) in Taiwan is provided by Chao-Yin Lin and Mei Hsu in Chapter 12. During the 1997 Asian financial Crisis, South Korea had adopted a public service employment programme as a means of tackling soaring domestic unemployment. It was largely as a result of the success of the South Korean experience that the government in Taiwan introduced its own PSEP in 2002, in an attempt to bring down the Taiwanese unemployment rate to a manageable 4.5 per cent. Lin and Hsu find that the PSEP has had some positive effects on the workforce, particularly in terms of increasing the social capital of certain unemployed workers and bringing them back into the mainstream of society, thereby avoiding the marginalization of such workers by the poor economic conditions. However, they also find that the PSEP has several negative effects on employment, the most important of these being the 'narcotic effect', which refers to the effect that participation in the PSEP can have on those involved once they get into the programme. Some unemployed workers can develop a desire to stick to the jobs provided by the programme, jobs which are supposed to be temporary in nature, and as a result, may refuse to look for permanent gainful employment. One additional negative aspect of the PSEP is its low placement rate, part of which is again created by the fact that some workers have no real desire to find alternative jobs. Furthermore, these types of programmes can only be used as a means of solving short-run unemployment problems; they are not appropriate for solving such problems in the long run. Lin and Hsu therefore conclude that in order to make Taiwan's PSEP more effective, the government must establish appropriate means of correcting these negative effects.

To summarize, the authors contributing to this book demonstrate that the main reasons for the efficient operation of the labour market prior to 1996 were essentially the high degree of integration within the Taiwanese labour market and the lack of institutional interference. Although a substantial number of labour relations laws had been put in place, such laws had never really been vigorously enforced. The highly integrated labour market, the freedom from institutional interference and the rapid expansion of the educational system had together provided Taiwan's labour market with the necessary flexibility to deal with the ever-changing economic conditions at that time. However, since the 1990s, as Taiwan was becoming increasingly globalized, changes in the island's economic structure also became necessary, as well as the recognition of the need for constant upgrading, so as to enable Taiwan to continue to compete with other countries in the international markets. The changes in the island's economic structure, along with the opening up of the Taiwanese labour market to foreign workers, have revealed a need within the labour market in Taiwan for greater flexibility that would enable it to rapidly and effectively adjust to such changes. Unfortunately the response to these changes by the government has been to introduce greater legislation and greater intervention, including the expansion of the coverage of the FLSL, the new working hours provisions, the Massive Layoffs Act, the Equal Gender in Employment Act and the new Pensions Law. Together, these pieces of legislation have actually resulted in increasing the inflexibility of the labour market in Taiwan.

The original design of the island's foreign labour policy was aimed at limiting foreign workers to those industries in which there were acute labour shortages, thereby creating a segregated market for foreign and native workers; thus, it was never intended that one could substitute for the other. However, in the mid-1990s, changes took place in the government's policy on foreign workers. Employers were subsequently permitted to count some of their expenses, such as 'room and board', as part of the minimum wage paid to these foreign workers. When taken together, the increasing numbers of foreign household maids and healthcare workers within the labour market, along with illegal workers, missing foreign workers and foreign spouses, have brought about a change to the initial concept of the government's foreign worker policy, since the temporary nature of these workers was originally a key element of the foreign workers programme. The new direction policy on foreign workers in Taiwan has inadvertently made such workers a source of cheap labour, which, in turn, has led to the displacement of certain groups of native workers. In order to avoid the adverse effects arising from native workers being displaced by foreign workers, the government needs to implement policies aimed at re-establishing the temporary nature of the foreign workers programme.

In attempting to tackle the growing problem of unemployment, the Taiwanese government has recently adopted much more active labour market policies, such as employee training programmes, wage subsidies and other such policies, including direct employment creation programmes; however, none of these can be regarded as having had any major successes. Further deregulation of the labour market and the education system are required in Taiwan, along with the upgrading of the current vocational and employee training systems.

These are all important and necessary steps which need to be taken if the Taiwanese labour market, and the workforce in general, are to achieve the level of flexibility required to cope with the current high unemployment situation, and thereby, to create more decent jobs for workers in Taiwan.

In conclusion, this book represents the last of this series of publications on economic development in Taiwan. We sincerely hope that this book, along with the four other volumes of the series, will help readers in both industrialized and developing countries to gain some insights into many of the factors that have led to Taiwan's successful development over a period in excess of half a century. It is also our sincere wish that the overall process of economic development in Taiwan may provide some valuable lessons for other developing countries, so that they might take advantage of some of the successes that have been achieved on the island, whilst avoiding some of the pitfalls that have since followed.

Joseph S. Lee
Jin Ting Chair Professor
National Central University

PART I

Employment Development in a Flexible Labour Market

1 Labour Market Flexibility and Employment: An Overview

Joseph S. Lee

INTRODUCTION

Over the past half century, in its continued pursuit of excellence in economic development, Taiwan has clearly achieved levels of success that have been the envy of many of the world's newly industrializing economies (NIEs). Taiwan has succeeded in developing itself from a closed and rather backward economy dominated by agriculture, into a modern, open, globalized, democratized and industrialized economy; and indeed, in more recent times, there have also been very clear signs emerging that the government in Taiwan is placing increasing emphasis on transforming the island into an ultra-modern knowledge-based economy.

Although the underlying factors contributing to such outstanding economic performance are wide-ranging, including, for example, macroeconomic and political stability, market-friendly institutions and policies, human capital accumulation, export-oriented industrialization policies and the successful development of the island's labour-intensive industries, it nevertheless appears that the labour market institutions in Taiwan have received far less attention than they would seem to have deserved. Indeed, the four most notable publications – Galenson (1979a), Ranis (1992), Mai and Shih (2000) and Chen and Lee (2004) – which have provided the most comprehensive documentation of Taiwan's economic development over a quarter of a century, have nevertheless neglected to provide separate chapters on the role of the labour market in Taiwan. Clearly, however, the labour market does play an extremely important role in determining both the economic growth rate and the level of employment within any given economy.

If we compare many of the studies on the differences between economic performance in the US and in many of the countries of the European Union, there is general consensus that the higher economic growth rates and lower unemployment rates within the US over recent years are mainly attributable to

3

the greater flexibility and more relaxed regulatory structure prevailing within the US labour market. Conversely, the stricter employment protection legislation on hiring, firing and wage structures which prevail within the labour markets of the European economies, along with the rather generous social welfare systems, including long-term entitlement to unemployment benefits at inordinately high levels, are generally regarded as being responsible for the contrasting lower economic growth rates and higher unemployment rates within these economies. Such policies are seen as major contributors to the inflexibility of the European labour markets, particularly in terms of their inability to fuel job growth and to respond appropriately to the rapid changes in economic conditions within the newly-globalized world economy (Osterman, 2001; Auer, 2005; Siebert, 2005).

It was once noted by Alan Greenspan, former chairman of the Board of Governors of the US Federal Reserve, that the greater flexibility of the US labour market, particularly with regard to the ease with which redundant workers can be laid off, ensures that US employers are much more inclined to close down less profitable facilities and to switch their valuable resources to projects and products that are more competitive and profitable. This has ultimately led to the greater competitiveness of the US economy as compared to the economies of the European Union; indeed, those studies in which such comparisons have been undertaken have generally concluded that within the highly-competitive globalized economy, the US industrial relations model works much better than the European model (Houseman and Abraham, 1993; Belot and van Ours, 2000; Block et al., 2003; Blanchard, 2004; Daniel and Siebert, 2004; Botero et al., 2004; Saint-Paul 2004a).

It was demonstrated by Scarpetta (1996) that the generosity of the welfare system within an economy (essentially with regard to the ready availability of unemployment benefits) has a positive correlation with rising structural unemployment. He presented strong evidence to show that the extensive periods of entitlement to unemployment benefits in the 1990s, along with the extremely high levels of such benefits, accounted for 3.0 to 5.0 per cent of the unemployment differentials in Demark, Belgium, France and the Netherlands. Scarpetta also noted that the 5.0 per cent increase in unemployment benefits in Spain was ultimately responsible for the subsequent 3.0 per cent rise in structural unemployment throughout the country. Conversely, however, in an examination of the labour market reforms which had taken place in Colombia during the early 1990s, Kugler (2004) found that the resultant reductions in dismissal costs for employers, along with the subsequent increase in the turnover of workers (particularly amongst the younger and better-educated workers), was responsible for 10.0 per cent of the overall reduction in unemployment during the whole of the period under examination.

Unfortunately, given the diversity of the conclusions drawn by the above studies, there has also been considerable disagreement with many of their reported findings. Notable amongst the various critics, Bertola (1990), Freeman (1994), Bertola and Ichino (1995), Nickell (1997), Siebert (1997), Nickell and Layard (1998) and Esping-Andersen and Regini (2002) were all keen to point out that many of these studies tended to suffer from problems relating to the selection of both the data samples and the methodologies adopted; hence, they raised serious questions as to the validity of many of the conclusions drawn within these studies. It has also been argued that these studies have generally failed to include any examination of the interaction between labour legislation and the labour market institutions, thus rendering their findings inconclusive. Some of these critics point out that, although Austria, Demark, Ireland, Norway, Sweden and the Netherlands all have high employment protection legislation standards, they nevertheless enjoy both high economic growth rates and low unemployment rates (Bertola et al., 1999; Baker et al., 2004; Eichhorst and Konle-Seidl, 2005). Furthermore, it had earlier been pointed out by Scarpetta (1996) that whilst strong job protection alone does not directly cause high unemployment, if it is combined with generous unemployment benefits and uncoordinated bargaining, then this will generally lead to higher structural unemployment.

In essence, therefore, whilst there is no clear, decisive evidence available to prove any direct link between employment protection legislation and unemployment, there does, nevertheless, appear to be some general agreement on the proposition that high employment protection levels do have some impact on the overall distribution of unemployment; one needs only to consider the higher unemployment levels often found amongst women, minority groups and younger workers. It is for this very reason that in April 2006, the French President, Jacques Chirac, signed the controversial 'First Employment Contract' Bill, a bill which was to have permitted employers to dismiss any employees under the age of 26 years with no requirement to state any reason for such dismissal. Clearly, the sole purpose of the bill was to increase management flexibility, with the ultimate aim of reducing, to a more acceptable level, the extremely high unemployment rate (12.2 per cent) which currently prevails amongst younger workers in France. However, President Chirac quickly recognized the need to withdraw this bill once the strength of the protest amongst such workers, as well as trade unionists, became apparent.

It was also recently announced that along with the total overhaul of the healthcare system, Chancellor Angela Merkel of Germany was considering similar proposals to strip away many of the laws protecting employees against dismissal in order to achieve greater flexibility within the German labour market, with the ultimate aim being to achieve higher economic growth. However, the very brief period of existence of the 'First Employment Contract' Bill in France may well have provided a strong signal that the high or low labour standards within any particular country are determined, to some extent, not by the whims of policymakers, but instead by the country's social and cultural background, particularly with regard to the origin of its legal system.

Thus, within the US, the UK, Canada, Ireland, Australia, Hong Kong and Singapore, each of which have legal systems rooted in common law, there is a tendency for less regulation of the activities within the labour market as a whole. In contrast, France, Germany, Japan, South Korea and Taiwan, the legal systems of which originated in civil law (and which therefore have a tendency to rely much more upon statutes and codes), will also tend to impose much greater regulation on the activities taking place within their respective labour markets. It would seem quite clear, therefore, that there is no one model that is suitable for adoption by all countries, since the adoption of such models is bedevilled by interactions between the law, enforcement of the law, culture, the social welfare system and various other relevant institutions in specific countries. What has become increasingly apparent, however, is that the roles formerly played by the origin of the legal system within a country, the prevailing economic conditions within that country, and indeed, the will of the presiding government, may now be assuming positions of much lesser importance.

Much of the analysis of the relationship between labour market regulation and prevailing unemployment levels has been carried out within Western industrialized economies, with the various studies tending, in particular, to present a contrast between the conditions prevailing within the US economy and the economies of Western Europe. Unfortunately, with the notable exceptions of the examinations of Latin America and Columbia, respectively undertaken by Heckman and Page (2000) and Kugler (2004), much less consideration has been given to the prevailing labour market conditions within the developing economies.

It is nevertheless argued that the deregulation of the labour market has much greater importance for such developing economies than for those economies within which industrialization is already well established, largely because the imposition of higher standards and a stricter regulatory framework within the developing economies is much more likely to lead to greater non-compliance with the relevant legislation, and thereby to the expansion of the informal sector. As such, a stronger regulatory framework could well produce exactly the opposite effect to that originally intended by the government (Kugler, 2004). Taiwan is not a developing economy, but a newly-industrialized economy (NIE), much like those of Hong Kong, South Korea and Singapore; nevertheless, its situation lies in between that of a developing economy and a well-developed Western industrialized economy. For this reason alone, a study of the current situation in Taiwan may prove to be very useful, simply because, as an Asian NIE, Taiwan is appropriately representative of an area within which no such studies have yet been carried out.

The efficient operation of the Taiwanese labour market played a pivotal role in the Taiwanese 'economic miracle' (Galenson, 1979b; Lee, 1980; Fields, 1992), with observers from other developing countries greatly admiring the readiness of Taiwanese workers to rapidly migrate, for example, from the lower-paying agricultural sector into the higher-paying industrial and service sectors, from low-productivity self-employed and unpaid family work to high-productivity and high-income 'paid employee' work, and from the lower-paying blue collar jobs to the higher-paying professional, technical and clerical jobs. These moves have ultimately resulted in the incessant and rapid rise of the wages and earnings rates of various groups of workers over the past four decades (see Chapter 4 of this volume and Fields, 2004).

Policymakers within other developing economies have also demonstrated their eagerness to determine the reasons why the labour market in Taiwan was able to operate so efficiently, over such a protracted period, and why the island was able to maintain virtually full employment throughout that period. Unfortunately, however, in the years since 1996 it has become clear that Taiwan's labour market is no longer operating as efficiently as it had been in the past; indeed, all of the available indicators now point to a general decline in the Taiwanese labour market. The rise in the unemployment rate, for example, which began in 1996 and which has continued steadily since then, reached a record high of 5.2 per cent in 2002. Furthermore, the economic growth rate, the rise in real wage rates, improvements in the occupational mix and improvements in income distribution have all experienced significant slowdowns over the same period; indeed, in some cases, they have essentially ground to a halt. Attempts have been made by various government officials to blame the recent global recession for the rapid deterioration in both the economic conditions and the high level of unemployment in Taiwan; however, this argument is hardly convincing, since many of the other Asian NIEs, such as South Korea, Singapore, Malaysia and mainland China, all of which are subject to the same adverse external environmental conditions, have nevertheless seen considerable improvements in their economic performance in the post-1996 period, thus demonstrating their ability to maintain higher economic growth rates and lower unemployment rates.

Taking South Korea as an example, in 1998, whilst the unemployment rate in Taiwan was still below 3.0 per cent, the rate in South Korea was 7.0 per cent; however, by 2004, the rate had fallen to just 3.5 per cent in South Korea, whilst in Taiwan it had grown to 4.4 per cent. In terms of economic performance, South Korea lagged behind Taiwan with per capita gross domestic product (GDP) of US$11,237 in 1997, whilst Taiwan's GDP stood at US$13,411; by 2004, however, South Korea had surpassed Taiwan, with per capita GDP of

US$14,144, whilst GDP in Taiwan had risen only marginally to US$13,529 (Yoo, 2005; DGBAS, 2005). South Korea has, therefore, clearly outperformed Taiwan over recent years, relegating Taiwan into fourth position amongst the 'four little dragons'.

A number of questions therefore arise as to what it was that undermined Taiwan's economy over recent years, in what ways the former efficiency of the island's labour market has been affected, and how we might be able to identify the major factors contributing to the contrasting performances within the labour market in Taiwan in the pre- and post-1996 periods. Liu (2000) pointed to the rapid growth in labour market regulation, along with the importation of foreign workers, as the two major contributory factors. If this is the case, then the flexibility of the Taiwanese labour market has clearly been lost as a result of the increasing intervention into, and regulation of, the island's labour market by the presiding government. Determination of this issue is of considerable importance, not only for the benefit of Taiwan's future economic development policy, but also within the whole debate on labour market flexibility and employment on a much wider scale. Virtually all of the prior studies on labour market regulation and employment have involved comparisons of the employment situation between highly regulated and less-regulated economies, or comparisons between the unemployment situation within various economies in their pre- and post-deregulation periods, with no studies having thus far examined the effects on employment stemming from higher labour market regulation.

The main aim of this book, therefore, is to examine those factors which are seen as having been major contributors to the efficient operation of the Taiwanese labour market prior to 1996, and those factors that may have contributed to the deterioration in the island's labour market performance in the post-1996 period. Such a study could help to shed some light on the current debate on the rigidity of the labour market vis-à-vis the flexibility of the labour market as a key determinant of the high or low unemployment rates and economic growth rates within any given economy. It is also hoped that the experience of Taiwan over recent years will provide some important and valuable lessons for other NIEs.

THE DETERIORATING PERFORMANCE OF THE TAIWANESE LABOUR MARKET SINCE 1996

Declining GDP Growth

During the earlier stages of its rapid economic development, Taiwan's GDP growth rate was particularly high, and remained so for a significant period of time. As Table 1.1 shows, although the island's GDP growth rate already stood at an average of 7.0 per cent between 1981 and 1985, this nevertheless grew even further, to 8.5 per cent, between 1986 and 1990; this was mainly due to the two periods of recovery from the 1983 and 1985 energy crises. There was, however, a subsequent slowdown in economic growth between 1996 and 2000, during which the GDP growth rate narrowed to 5.4 per cent, followed by a further significant reduction, to just 3.6 per cent, between 2001 and 2004. Thus, from an average of about 8.0 per cent prior to 1996, economic growth in Taiwan has shrunk significantly, to less than 4.0 per cent, in the post-1996 period.

Rising Unemployment

With the exceptions of the two energy crises of 1983 and 1985, Taiwan was extremely successful in achieving virtually full employment throughout the 1970s, the 1980s, and even the first half of the 1990s, with the island's unemployment rate remaining below 2.0 per cent; however, this picture has been constantly changing ever since 1996, with the rate climbing continuously and eventually reaching a historical high of 5.2 per cent in 2002. Although the unemployment rate did fall slightly in 2004, to 4.5 per cent, this was mainly due to the implementation of the Public Service Employment Programme (PSEP), a temporary programme which was destined to last for just one year; on completion of the programme, in 2004, unemployment was expected to once again return to its previous high level. According to recent economic forecasting undertaken by the Council for Economic Planning and Development (CEPD) Taiwan's unemployment is likely to remain at 4.0 per cent until 2015 (CEPD, 2005).

However, the 4.5 per cent unemployment rate in 2004 also understates the true situation because, during the post-1996 period, there was a rapid fall in the labour force participation rates amongst prime-age males. As Table 1.1 shows, between 1981 and 1995, the average labour force participation rate for males was 74.66 per cent, but this fell to 69.37 per cent between 1996 and 2004, a decline of 5.29 percentage points. The fall in labour force participation rates amongst this group was caused mainly by the stagnation of the Taiwanese labour market, with many workers being unable to find jobs and subsequently moving to mainland China where the demand for highly educated professional workers, particularly managerial workers, was now much higher. However, since these workers are commuting between Taiwan and mainland China, when the labour force census survey is carried out, their families will often report them as neither working nor seeking work in Taiwan; thus, they are classified as non-participants in the labour force. It is currently estimated that there are between 600,000 and one million of these Taiwanese workers currently employed in mainland China.

Table 1.1 Key economic indicators for Taiwan

Key Indicators	1981-1985	1986-1990	1991-1995	1996-2000	2001-2004	1981-1995	1996-2004
GDP Growth Rate (%)	6.90	8.50	7.00	5.40	3.60*	7.80	3.80*
Unemployment Rate (%)	2.31	1.91	1.56	2.78	4.79	1.93	3.68
Duration of Unemployment (weeks)	19.6	20.00	17.4	22.34	28.91	19.00	25.13
Annual Increase in Employment (%)	2.72	2.21	1.78	0.97	0.78	2.20	0.88
Annual Rate of Increase in Private Sector Employment (%)	3.00	3.60	2.53	1.96	1.48	3.04	1.74
Pay Increases (%)							
Manufacturing	7.36	11.68	8.13	3.72	0.98	9.18	2.50
Construction	8.26	11.04	7.47	1.98	-0.61	8.97	0.83
Trade	6.06	11.41	6.71	2.98	0.38	8.20	1.82
Transportation	7.48	10.13	8.74	3.67	0.10	8.87	2.08
Finance	7.51	11.21	7.15	2.22	2.36	8.70	2.28
Professional and Scientific	10.49	11.67	5.96	3.26	-0.29	9.29	1.68
Participation Rate (%)							
Male	76.24	74.80	72.94	70.43	68.04	74.66	69.37
Female	41.39	45.49	44.97	45.81	46.89	43.95	46.29

Note: * Figures for GDP growth rate are currently available only up until 2003.

Sources: GDP data is taken from CEPD (2005); employment data is taken from DGBAS (various years), *Manpower Utilization Surveys.*

Lengthening Duration of Unemployment

It is quite clear that not only has Taiwan experienced a continuous rise in the overall unemployment rate since 1996, but that there has also been a significant increase in the average period of unemployment. The average unemployment duration in 1980, for example, was 14.8 weeks; thereafter, the average period lengthened continuously, albeit slowly at first, to about 17.2 weeks by 1995, but thereafter by a significant margin, with the average unemployment period subsequently rising to 29.4 weeks by 2004. This greater duration of unemployment can also be seen from the declining share of short-term unemployment amongst all unemployed workers vis-à-vis the increasing share of long-term unemployment.

For short-term unemployment (periods of unemployment of less than four weeks) the share rose slightly, from 33.43 per cent of all unemployed workers in 1980 to 34.08 per cent of the total in 1995; however, since then, it has shrunk continuously, to 20.61 per cent by 2004. Conversely, for long-term unemployment (periods of unemployment of more than 52 weeks) the share rose from 6.53 per cent of all unemployed workers in 1980 to 9.86 per cent of the total in 1995; thereafter, long-term unemployment began to rise more rapidly. By 2004, it was accounting for an alarming 18.34 per cent of all unemployed workers (Table 1.2).

Table 1.2   Unemployment duration periods in Taiwan, 1980-2004

Year	1-4 Weeks	5-13 Weeks	14-26 Weeks	27-52 Weeks	≥53 Weeks	Average No. of Weeks
1980	33.43	27.09	15.48	17.47	6.53	14.8
1985	28.79	28.68	16.98	15.19	10.36	19.2
1990	32.29	28.05	22.12	11.18	6.36	14.8
1995	34.08	28.14	15.26	12.67	9.86	17.2
1996	26.63	29.72	20.13	13.60	9.92	20.5
1997	23.68	31.51	19.75	14.75	10.19	21.4
1998	25.06	29.78	21.19	13.57	10.41	21.8
1999	23.70	23.97	21.40	19.93	10.91	22.5
2000	22.36	24.60	20.47	18.30	14.27	23.7
2001	21.68	23.70	22.13	18.40	14.09	26.1
2002	19.03	23.50	19.66	19.05	18.77	30.3
2003	18.46	21.05	20.73	18.74	21.01	30.5
2004	20.61	22.89	19.66	18.50	18.34	29.4

Source: DGBAS (various years), *Manpower Utilization Surveys.*

Declining Employment Growth

Within any given economy, a rise in unemployment does not necessarily indicate that there is any worsening of the overall labour market conditions, since such a rise may simply be an indication that the available workforce is expanding more rapidly than the increase in new jobs; unfortunately, however, this has not been the case for Taiwan. Within the Taiwanese economy as a whole, although the rate at which new jobs were being created had remained particularly high (at over 3.0 per cent) between 1981 and 1985, this rate nevertheless subsequently began to decline steadily, to 2.21 per cent between 1986 and 1990, and still further, to 1.78 per cent between 1991 and 1995, thereby revealing a continuous decline in the creation of new jobs between 1981 and 1995. Nevertheless, the situation subsequently became even more severe; indeed, job creation as a whole has fallen to just 0.88 per cent in the post-1996 period.

There was also a discernible decline in the overall share of new jobs being created within the private sector. During the 1980s and the early 1990s, the annual rate of increase in paid employment within the private sector had stood at over 3.00 per cent, which, at the time, was well above the national average; however, this subsequently fell to 1.96 per cent between 1996 and 2000, and still further, to just 1.48 per cent between 2001 and 2004. Clearly, therefore, there has been a rapid and rather alarming fall in the rate of creation of new jobs (more specifically, good jobs) within the private sector in the post-1996 period (Table 1.3).

Table 1.3   Employment growth rate, by occupations, 1981-2004

Unit: %

Occupations	1981-1985	1986-1990	1991-1995	1996-2000	2001-2004	1981-1995	1996-2004
Administration	2.24	6.40	2.24	−1.12	2.09	3.72	0.31
Professional	4.84	6.76	3.24	4.08	4.47	4.96	4.26
Technicians and Assistants	4.34	8.94	6.85	3.53	2.76	6.88	3.19
Clerical	4.56	5.31	5.84	3.22	1.88	5.29	2.62
Sales and Services	4.61	2.48	1.37	2.97	1.94	2.69	2.52
Agricultural	0.91	−3.75	−2.18	−5.07	−3.47	−1.86	−4.36
Production	2.09	1.39	0.41	−0.33	−1.14	1.24	−0.69
Total	2.72	2.21	1.78	0.97	0.78	2.20	0.88

Source: DGBAS (various years), *Manpower Utilization Surveys.*

Slowdown in Improvements in the Occupational Mix

By examining the growth rate in the occupational mix, we can also obtain some measurement of the rate of improvement in the overall quality of employment. Prior to 1996, Taiwan had succeeded in maintaining its annual growth rate in professional, technical and clerical employment at a particularly high level; indeed, between 1981 and 1995, the average annual increase in the availability of these good jobs was 4.96 per cent. However, there was also a subsequent fall in this measure in the post-1996 period, albeit only slightly, to 4.26 per cent.

It is, however, very clear that the decline in the occupational mix growth rate was far more severe for technical jobs than for professional positions, with a particularly massive fall in the growth rate for technical jobs, from 6.88 per cent in the pre-1996 period, to 3.19 per cent in the post-1996 period. The decline in the growth rate of clerical jobs was also significant, from 5.29 per cent to 2.62 per cent, over the pre- and post-1996 periods, with the available figures again showing that the rate of growth in good jobs has slowed down significantly in the post-1996 period.

Decline in Improvements in Employment Status

The overall quality of jobs can be measured by the employment status of workers, with the productivity of paid employees generally being higher than that of either unpaid family workers or the self-employed, since these latter groups invariably work for small business units which lack economies of scale; for the same reason, pay and working conditions are also better for paid employees.

Thus, all other things being equal, in the category of paid employment, an increase in the share of employment represents an indicator of improvements in both the overall working conditions and the welfare of such employees. During the 1980s, the rate of increase in paid employment was 3.04 per cent, but this subsequently fell to just 1.74 per cent in the post-1996 period (Table 1.4).

Slowdown in Wage Increases

One of the most important indicators of the welfare of workers is the wage rate, since rises in the average wage rate also indicate similar improvements in the overall welfare of workers. During the 1980s and early 1990s, the annual increase in the average wage rate was 9.18 per cent; however, this indicator also fell, to just 2.50 per cent between 1996 and 2000, with a further decline to 0.96 per cent between 2001 and 2004.

Table 1.4   Employment status, 1981-2004

Unit: %

Indicators	1981-1985	1986-1990	1991-1995	1996-2000	2001-2004	1981-1995	1996-2004
Employers	1.57	4.58	3.79	1.35	-0.11	3.44	0.70
Self-employed	2.72	-0.01	-0.07	-0.18	-1.08	0.75	-0.58
Unpaid Family Workers	3.76	-1.49	0.64	-1.52	-0.83	0.77	-1.21
Subtotal	2.65	3.32	2.27	1.51	1.41	2.75	1.46
Paid Employees (Private Sector)	3.00	3.60	2.53	1.96	1.48	3.04	1.74
Paid Employees (Government Sector)	1.20	2.04	0.99	-0.95	1.03	1.43	-0.07
Total	2.72	2.21	1.78	0.97	0.78	2.20	0.88

Source: DGBAS (various years), *Manpower Utilization Surveys.*

Taking the manufacturing sector as an example, the average annual wage increase was 9.18 per cent in the pre-1996 period, as compared to just 2.50 per cent in the post-1996 period. Although the decline in the rate of increase in wages was far less severe within many of the other sectors, it still represented a significant and worrying trend, from a high of about 8.0 per cent to less than 2.0 per cent between the pre- and post-1996 periods. Furthermore, prior to 1996, the rise in overall wage rates had remained evenly distributed throughout all sectors (see Chapter 2 of this volume), indicating that, by and large, all workers across the island were benefiting from the economic growth in much the same way; however, the rate of increase in wages has varied significantly since then. For example, between 1996 and 2004, the average increase in wages was only 0.88 per cent for workers within the construction sector, as compared to the 2.50 per cent (noted above) within the manufacturing sector (DGBAS, 2005).

Worsening Income Distribution

The worsening household income distribution is revealed by changes in the Gini coefficient. In 1980, the Gini coefficient for Taiwan stood at 0.27; although it did rise slightly to 0.30 in 1989, it was still much lower than the 0.42 for Singapore and 0.51 for Malaysia and South Korea (Fields, 1992: 398). From 2000 onwards, however, income distribution, as indicated by the Gini coefficient, was clearly worsening; indeed, by 2003, Taiwan's Gini coefficient had risen to 0.34 (Table 1.5).

Table 1.5   Gini coefficient of household income in Taiwan, 1980-2003

Year	Gini coefficient	Year	Gini coefficient
1980	0.277	1992	0.312
1981	0.281	1993	0.316
1982	0.283	1994	0.318
1983	0.287	1995	0.317
1984	0.287	1996	0.317
1985	0.290	1997	0.320
1986	0.296	1998	0.324
1987	0.299	1999	0.325
1988	0.303	2000	0.326
1989	0.303	2001	0.350
1990	0.312	2002	0.345
1991	0.308	2003	0.343

Source: DGBAS (2005).

If we compare all families in Taiwan in terms of a 'league table' of average income, the ratio of those in the top fifth to those in the bottom fifth was 4.17 in 1980; however, by 2002, this had risen to 6.16. Although there was a slight fall to 6.03 by 2004, the trend in income distribution is still quite alarming (DGBAS, 2005, Table 4).

THE REASONS BEHIND TAIWAN'S DETERIORATING LABOUR MARKET PERFORMANCE

As will be explained in greater detail (by Gary Fields in Chapter 4 of this volume) the exceptional performance of the Taiwanese labour market prior to 1996 was essentially due to the high degree of integration, which basically stemmed from the laissez-faire attitude adopted by the government at that time towards labour market policy. This then begs the question as to whether (and if so, why) the Taiwanese labour market has become so much less integrated in the post-1996 period; however, the simple answer is that it is actually only slightly less integrated now than it was prior to 1996.

If we use the same indicator of labour market integration as that used by Fields, i.e., the coefficient of variation of income amongst workers in different industries, we find that this was 0.22 in 2000 and 0.25 in 2004; but clearly, this is not that much higher than the findings of 0.17 in 1980 and 0.20 in 1993 (see Appendix, Table A1.1). Thus, we can hardly point the finger of blame at lower market integration as a major cause, or even any cause for that matter, for the deteriorating performance of the Taiwanese labour market in recent years. Nevertheless, if lower integration was not the cause, then we clearly need to identify exactly what it was that led to such deterioration. Some scholars in Taiwan have tended to place the blame on the increasing regulation of the labour market, along with the importation of foreign workers, describing these as the two major factors contributing to the deterioration in labour market performance during the post-1996 period. Let us therefore examine this claim.

Increasing Labour Market Regulation

Prior to 1984, the Taiwanese government had continued to adopt a labour market policy approach which was very much 'hands off', because it found that most of the labour laws within the statute books had been enacted in the 1920s and 1930s when the government was still in the mainland; thus, these laws had a socialist orientation, and were therefore not at all compatible with Taiwan's modern-day market-oriented economic environment.

Given the absence of both legal and trade union interference, the labour market was able to operate with considerable efficiency, which enabled Taiwan to achieve, and maintain, essentially full employment from the late 1960s until the 1990s. Since this was also accompanied by high economic growth rates, employers in Taiwan were frequently able to raise employee wage levels, and indeed, by considerable amounts. The resultant rapid rise in wages provided adequate compensation for any discontent that the workers may have encountered within the workplace. In other words, the 'hands-off' labour market policy adopted by the government prior to 1984 made it possible for Taiwan to maintain a virtuous circle of full utilization of all available human resources, high economic growth rates, rapid increases in wages and harmonious workforce and management relations, as well as the unfettered operation of the labour market. However, as Taiwanese workers become more affluent, the simple application of further wage increases was no longer sufficient to compensate for their growing discontent with the problems they were encountering in the workplace; thus there was a rapid rise in incidences of labour unrest in the 1980s.

There was some realization within the government that if it was to successfully cope with increasing labour disputes, it needed to replace its earlier 'hands-off' policy with a more active policy of labour legislation, involving the enactment of comprehensive labour laws, as well as the setting up of minimum legal standards on pay, benefits and working conditions. This shift in policy was aimed at protecting employees' interests whilst enhancing their overall welfare levels, and thereby restoring the harmonious workforce and management relations that had previously been enjoyed on the island. It was felt that by creating a favourable economic climate in this way, Taiwan would ultimately become more attractive to the inflow of foreign direct investment (FDI).

In order to accomplish this, the government enacted several pieces of legislation, starting with the most comprehensive Act in 1984, the Fair Labour Standards Law (FLSL). The government also established the cabinet level Council of Labour Affairs (CLA) in 1987, whose mandate was the enforcement of the FLSL and the overall administration of other labour affairs. At the time of the enactment of the FLSL, its jurisdiction covered only workers in the agricultural, manufacturing, construction and public utilities sectors, whilst excluding all workers in the commerce, finance and service sectors; indeed, it was not until 1995 that the government amended the FLSL to extend its coverage to all sectors including finance, insurance, wholesale, retail and other service sectors. This expanded coverage was implemented in three stages, the last of which was completed in December 1998. In 2000, the government further amended the FLSL, shortening the maximum number of working hours to 84 hours in any two-week period.

A new pension law was enacted in 2004, subsequently coming into force in 2005. This law replaced the pension provisions under the FLSL, thereby ensuring that pension benefits were more portable (most private sector employees had previously been unable to receive pension benefits because the provisions of the FLSL stipulated that employees must work for the same company for 25 years in order to be eligible for pension payments; however, in reality, the average lifespan of small and medium enterprises (SMEs) was a mere 15 years). The government also enacted other labour laws, including the 1992 Employment Services Act and the Equal Gender in Employment and Massive Lay-offs Acts of 2002. In addition to these employment laws, the government also attempted to amend the Trade Unions Law, the Collective Bargaining Law and the Labour Disputes Law; however, the final versions of these laws still await approval in the Legislative Yuan.

A Comparative Analysis of Taiwan's Labour Legislation

Whilst there is no doubt that such labour laws are necessary within a modern, industrialized economy, the major problems lie in the high standards set by such laws, which can ultimately become a barrier to the efficient operation of the labour market. The excessively high standards inherent within Taiwan's labour laws are demonstrated quite appropriately by a set of indices constructed by Botero et al. (2004), which can be used to compare the labour standard levels of 85 countries around the world. These indices were divided into three groups: (i) employment laws governing individual employment contracts; (ii) industrial and collective relations laws regulating collective bargaining, collective agreements, the organization of trade unions and industrial action taken by workers and employers; and (iii) social security laws governing retirement pensions, as well as disability, unemployment and maternity benefits.

Here we select only those economies whose comparison with the case of Taiwan has some relevance, i.e., the Asian NIEs, including Hong Kong, South Korea and Singapore, and the second tier of the Asian NIEs, such as Malaysia, as well as some of the major Western industrialized economies, with the US and the UK being representative of low labour standards countries, whilst France and Germany are representative of countries with high labour standards. The higher the level of each index, the higher the degree of employment regulation and overall level of labour protection. The indices for the Asian economies are presented in Table 1.6, whilst the indices for the Western economies are presented in Table 1.7.

As the figures in Table 1.6 show, the employment laws index for Taiwan, which stood at 1.75 in 2004, was the highest of any of the Asian economies at a similar stage of development. Furthermore, a comparison with Table 1.7 reveals that Taiwan's index is even higher than those of France and Germany, countries renowned for particularly high labour protection standards. According to Botero et al. (2004) the employment laws index can be further divided into three sub-indices: (i) an 'alternative employment contracts' index; (ii) a 'conditions of employment' index; and (iii) a 'job security' index. The alternative employment contracts index measures the freedom of employers to ask their employees to agree to alternative employment contracts aside from their regular employment contracts (including part-time, fixed-term and family member contracts), with workers hired under such individual employment contracts usually receiving lower pay and benefits, whilst also being subject to termination rules that are less onerous for employers.

Employment Laws Index

Alternative employment contracts sub-index
The 'alternative employment contracts' sub-index for Taiwan in 2004 was 0.87, which was not only considerably higher than the indices of any of the other Asian NIEs, but also higher than those of the major Western industrialized economies, including France and Germany, indicating that employers in Taiwan have far less freedom to enter into individual contracts with either part-time or fixed-term workers. It also explains why, amongst all employed persons in Taiwan, the share of part-time employment has remained at just 6.0 per cent for the past 30 years. It is clear, therefore, that as a source of labour market flexibility, an atypical pattern of employment is emerging rapidly across many countries, although this pattern is not discernible in Taiwan.

Table 1.6 Indices of employment, industrial relations and social security laws in Asian economies, 2004

	Hong Kong	South Korea	Malaysia	Singapore	Taiwan
Employment Laws Index	0.76	1.36	0.87	0.85	1.75
Alternative Employment Contracts	0.56	0.35	0.56	0.56	0.87
Conditions of Employment	0.19	0.75	0.22	0.19	0.54
Job Security	0.01	0.26	0.09	0.11	0.34
Industrial Relations Laws Index	1.04	1.69	0.42	0.64	1.10
Collective Bargaining	0.44	0.89	0.00	0.11	0.33
Worker Participation in Management	0.00	0.25	0.00	0.00	0.42
Industrial Disputes	0.60	0.55	0.42	0.53	0.35
Social Security Laws Index	2.44	2.03	0.57	1.36	2.09

Source: Botero et al. (2004).

Table 1.7. Indices of employment, industrial relations and social security laws in Western economies, 2004

	Australia	France	Germany	UK	US
Employment Laws Index	0.92	1.59	1.57	1.02	0.92
Alternative Employment Contracts	0.22	0.74	0.72	0.56	0.56
Conditions of Employment	0.55	0.54	0.35	0.26	0.29
Job Security	0.14	0.31	0.50	0.20	0.08
Industrial Relations Laws Index	0.25	2.13	1.76	0.25	0.36
Collective Bargaining	0.00	0.78	0.78	0.00	0.11
Worker Participation in Management	0.00	0.75	0.50	0.00	0.00
Industrial Disputes	0.25	0.60	0.48	0.25	0.25
Social Security Laws Index	2.25	2.29	2.00	2.06	1.90

Source: Botero et al. (2004).

20

Conditions of employment sub-index

The 'conditions of employment' sub-index measures the flexibility of employers in terms of scheduling the maximum number of hours in any working week, premiums for overtime work, assigning overnight and weekend work, mandatory payments for non-working days (including paid annual leave, public holidays and maternity leave) and minimum wage regulations. This index was 0.54 for Taiwan in 2004, much higher than that of the other Asian NIEs, with the notable exception of South Korea. As compared to the Western industrialized countries, Taiwan's index was lower than that of only Australia, the same as in France, but higher than those of the US, the UK and Germany. The particularly high index for Taiwan was due to the various provisions within the FLSL restricting the rights of employers to allocate overtime or holiday work and requiring employers to pay an overtime premium of an additional one-third of the regular wage rate for the first two hours of overtime worked in any 24-hour period, and an additional two-thirds of the regular wage rate for any overtime work beyond two hours in any 24-hour period; in contrast, labour legislation in most countries provides a flat rate overtime premium equivalent to half of the regular wage rate.

The FLSL also restricts the total number of hours of overtime that employers may require their employees to work each month; this originally stood at 46 hours for male workers and 32 hours for female workers; however, the difference in the maximum total hours for male and female workers caused considerable difficulties for employers, in terms of dealing with the actual allocation of overtime work (Lee and Wu, 1996). Although the total number of hours of overtime remains at a maximum of 46 hours per month, the government recently eliminated the different maximum overtime hours for male and female workers.

Job security sub-index

The 'job security' sub-index measures the legal protection afforded to employees against unfair dismissal, such as the necessary grounds and procedures for dismissal, notice periods and severance payments. For Taiwan, this index was 0.34 in 2004; again, this was higher than any of the other Asian NIEs and higher than virtually all of the western industrialized economies, with the one exception of Germany.

Industrial Relations Laws Index

In the category of industrial relations laws, the overall index for Taiwan was 0.33, lower than those of South Korea, Hong Kong, France and Germany, but higher than all of the other Asian NIEs and the Western industrialized economies. This is not really surprising, however, given that the Trade Unions Law and the Collective Bargaining Law in Taiwan have not been updated for a considerable period of time.

The industrial relations laws index can also be divided into three sub-indices: (i) 'collective bargaining'; (ii) 'workers participation in management'; and (iii) 'industrial disputes'. Although, at 0.33, the 'collective bargaining' sub-index was not particularly high for Taiwan, the 'workers participation' sub-index, at 0.42, was very high, and indeed, higher than all of the Asian NIEs and most of the Western industrialized economies, with the exceptions of France and Germany. This is because a provision exists within the FLSL requiring companies to set up labour-management conferences, similar to the 'works councils' in certain Western European countries, in which employees and employers' representatives periodically meet to discuss matters relating to the allocation of overtime work and other employment-related issues.

Social Security Laws Index

The social security laws index measures the availability and flexibility of retirement pensions, unemployment insurance, and sickness and healthcare coverage. This index was only 2.09 for Taiwan in 2004, which was lower than those of Hong Kong, Australia and France, but higher than the other Asian NIEs, the US, the UK and Germany; however, if the index for Taiwan were to include some of the more recently enacted laws, such as the Employment Insurance Law 2004 and the new Pension Law 2005, it would undoubtedly be much higher than the current level.

By comparing labour standards in Taiwan with those of both the other Asian NIEs and the major Western industrialized economies, one can quickly come to a very clear understanding that labour standards in Taiwan are particularly high, even where such a comparison includes France and Germany, countries renowned for having some of the highest labour standards in the world. However, as was pointed out by Block and Roberts (1998), when engaging in international comparisons, we should not merely look at what is stipulated within the legislation, since this can be quite misleading. The coverage, even in the same types of laws, may be wider in some countries than others, whilst the enforcement of the various laws may also be much stricter in certain countries. Clearly, therefore, before we can accurately assess either the standards or the impact of the labour laws in different countries, they must be compared on the basis of the coverage of the law as well as the enforcement mechanisms in place (Block and Roberts, 1998).

Using the same methodology as that proposed by Block and Roberts (1998), Lee (2000) constructed a similar set of indices for Taiwan for subsequent comparison with those of the US and Canada. The results of these indicators are presented in Table 1.8, which shows that in many areas, although lower than the standards in Canada, labour standards in Taiwan were generally higher than those in the US in 2000; however, in terms of paid holidays, the index for Taiwan (10.00) was higher than both the US and Canada. In 2000, there were a total of 18 national holidays per year in Taiwan (as compared to the ten national holidays per year in the US) and since Article 37 of the FLSL specifies that all national holidays must be paid holidays, this clearly had an effect on this index at that time. Over recent years, however, the number of paid holidays in Taiwan has been reduced to 12 days; thus the index is now closer to that of Canada, although still higher than that of the US.

Table 1.8   Indices of labour standards in the US, Canada and Taiwan, 2000

Labour Standards Indices	US	Canada	Taiwan
Requiring Payment by Employers			
Overtime Premium	10.00	10.00	8.14
Minimum Wage	8.28	0.60	0.30
Paid Holidays	2.21	8.55	10.00
Unemployment Insurance	6.17	7.51	6.79
Restricting Management Behaviour			
Collective Bargaining	1.50	7.85	4.50
Equal Employment Opportunities	8.50	9.00	7.10
Unfair Dismissal	0.00	7.00	7.00
Occupational Health and Safety	3.13	4.33	1.06
Total	39.79	52.99	45.39

Source: Lee (2000).

The index for unemployment insurance in Taiwan was higher than in the US in 2000, largely because, according to the Labour Insurance Law in Taiwan, the maximum taxable income for unemployment premium was US$15,000 per year, as compared to the figure of US$9,050 in the US, whilst the maximum period of entitlement to unemployment benefits was also longer in Taiwan than in the US. 2003 saw the enactment of a new Employment Insurance Law in Taiwan which replaced the unemployment insurance provisions of the Labour Insurance Law; thus, this index would no doubt be somewhat lower today. One may doubt the accuracy of the 4.5 index for collective bargaining, especially when comparing it to the 1.5 index for the US, since this seems to suggest that trade unions are more powerful in Taiwan than in the US. The reason for this is that within the process of establishing legal union representation in Taiwan, certification of unions as being legally representative will be confirmed if an establishment has a minimum of 30 employees and files a petition (the actual size of the establishment is irrelevant). The government will automatically certify the union as being legally representative of all employees within the establishment, including white collar workers; all employees working within the establishment will also be required to join the union. In other words, Taiwan already has in place compulsory legal unionism. In contrast, for a union to be certified as legally representative of the employees within a bargaining unit in the US, it must go through union representative elections and receive a majority of the votes cast.

Furthermore, Taiwan has no legal limitations on bargaining scope; therefore, unions have the right to raise any issue and then seek collective bargaining on that issue with their employers. In the US, there is only limited scope on the areas open to bargaining; thus, unions can only push for bargaining in the areas that are either mandatory or voluntary, with no possibility of entering into the bargaining process in those areas excluded by law. Therefore, employers in the US have greater flexibility than in Taiwan. In reality, however, the power of management has not been greatly curtailed in this particular area because trade unions are not that strong in Taiwan.

It must be noted that this set of indicators was constructed in 2000, and some of these high standards have either been revised or replaced by new laws; thus, if the indices were to be reconstructed to reflect all the laws enacted between 2000 and 2005, the scores on these indices would undoubtedly be even higher. Thus, the picture is very clear; labour standards set by the various labour laws in Taiwan are particular onerous. Indeed, they are not only higher than the other Asian NIEs examined here, all of which are at similar stages of development, but are also higher than many of the Western industrialized economies where standards of living are considerably higher than in Taiwan.

The Rising Costs of Labour Legislation

The high labour standards adopted in Taiwan not only impose greater restrictions on the management flexibility of employers, but also raise employers' overall labour costs, which in turn leads to further reductions in employment. According to a recent report published by the Ministry of Economic Affairs (MOEA), mandatory fringe benefits, such as health insurance, labour insurance, pensions and other benefits are now accounting for up to 18 per cent of employers' total labour costs in Taiwan. This social costs burden is much higher than those faced by employers in many other Asian countries, such as the 5.2 per cent for Thailand, 8.79 per cent for

South Korea, 12.9 per cent for Japan, 13.0 per cent for Singapore and 13.8 per cent for Malaysia (MOEA, 2006).

It has been argued by both Liu (2000) and Jiang (2004) that the higher social costs burden in Taiwan has been the primary cause of the rising unemployment levels over recent years. This is largely because, in the past, SMEs have played a leading role in the generation of new employment opportunities in Taiwan; however, the enactment of the FLSL, which has inadvertently brought about even higher labour costs for SMEs than for the large-sized firms, has therefore had a significant impact on employment as a whole. As a direct result of these higher labour costs, many of the island's SMEs were no longer able to compete within the international markets and therefore had little option but to relocate their production facilities overseas, to places such as mainland China and other Southeast Asian countries, shutting down their facilities in Taiwan and thereby adding to the island's rising unemployment figures. The implementation of the FLSL has also led to rapid deterioration in employee/employer relations. This is because, rather than trying to reach a consensus with their employers, many employees are now adopting a much more legalistic approach (Liu, 2000; Jiang, 2004).

This line of reasoning can be illustrated by dividing Taiwan's labour market into two sectors, the 'covered sector' comprising of the agricultural, manufacturing, construction and public utility industries, and the 'uncovered sector' comprising of the commerce, finance and service industries. These terms indicate that employees within the 'covered sector' are protected by the FLSL, whereas employees in the 'uncovered sector' are not. Prior to the enactment of the FLSL, workers within both sectors had no protection in the areas now dealt with by the FLSL; wage rates in both sectors were determined by market forces within each sector, W^*, with employment in the covered sector being represented by $0E^*$ and employment in the uncovered sector being represented by $0_e{}^*$(Figure 1.1).

Following the enactment of the FLSL, whilst workers in the agricultural, manufacturing, construction and public utility industries came under its jurisdiction, those in the commerce, finance and service industries did not. As a result, the enforcement of the FLSL within the covered sector led to a reduction in management flexibility, thereby raising the labour costs for employers. In response to these changes, employers in the covered sector reduced the number of workers on their payroll, with those workers losing their jobs in the covered sector subsequently moving to the uncovered sector for employment. The net result was a shift in the labour supply curve within the covered sector, from S to S', and a corresponding shift in the labour supply curve within the uncovered sector, from s to s''. Although there was little or no increase in 'open' unemployment, this nevertheless led to higher employment in the uncovered sector, $0e_u$, and lower employment in the covered sector, $0E_c$.

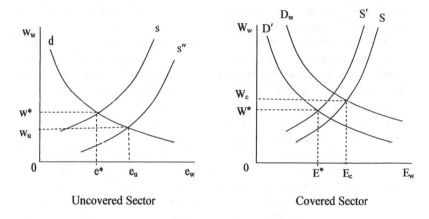

Figure 1.1   The uncovered and covered sectors of the FLSL

This was exactly the situation at the time of the enactment of the FLSL in Taiwan (the late 1980s to the early 1990s). Given that employment was moving rapidly from the manufacturing sector to the commerce and service sectors, the unemployment rate in Taiwan remained relatively low, at less than 2.0 per cent. However, with the expansion of the jurisdiction of the FLSL, in 1995, to the previously 'uncovered' sectors, those workers now losing their jobs in the sectors that were newly covered by the FLSL, as well as those losing their jobs within the sectors that were already covered (as a direct result of the strict enforcement of the FLSL), no longer had the sanctuary of the uncovered sectors to turn to for alternative employment. These workers therefore simply dropped out of the workforce, or became part of the 'open' unemployment statistics.

RESPONSES TO THE INCREASING REGULATION OF THE LABOUR MARKET IN TAIWAN

Whilst excessive labour standards can clearly have direct impacts on employment, if employers can respond to such newly imposed labour standards and higher labour costs by restructuring their enterprises, upgrading their management techniques and introducing efficient wage systems and high-performance human resource management systems, such responses could have very positive impacts on employment, benefits and working conditions for their employees, as well as on the overall competitiveness of their enterprises within the international markets. In recent years, employers in the US have been concentrating on introducing a 'blue ocean' strategy (Kim and Mauborgne, 2005), involving high-performance human resource management systems and the allocation of large sums of money for employee training. They pursue this strategy with one purpose in mind, to recruit and retain the most talented workforce they can find that will ultimately enable them to compete effectively within the international markets. Similar practices have also been adopted by employers in many European countries; indeed, a number of recent studies have warned that where there is excessive deregulation within the labour market, there is a possibility that this can lead to inadequate training of the workforce, thereby creating a low-skills equilibrium, a subsequent productivity lag, and, in the long run, general loss of competitiveness (Soskice, 1990; Snower, 1997).

It would therefore seem prudent to examine whether employers in Taiwan have been responding to the increasing labour market regulation in recent years by upgrading the structure of their enterprises and their general management systems, and by following the lead of employers in the US and many of the European countries to introduce high-performance human resource management systems. Unfortunately, no study of this kind exists for the post-1996 period; there was, however, an earlier study undertaken by Lee and Wu (1992) which examined 8,000 firms in the manufacturing, construction and public utility industries. They found that in response to the higher costs and reduced management flexibility levels brought about by the implementation of the FLSL, most employers had automated their production lines, disposed of unproductive workers, relocated their production facilities abroad to places with lower labour costs and greater levels of management flexibility, subcontracted some elements of their work out for greater flexibility and lower costs, and hired foreign workers.

Anecdotal evidence indicates that whilst there are those employers who are now placing much greater emphasis on the upgrading of their management techniques and hiring experts to manage their workforce, most of these activities are nevertheless limited to employers within the very large-sized firms and high-tech firms; indeed, the evidence suggests that few employers within either the traditional industries or SMEs are paying much attention to the upgrading of their structures and management practices, since their primary focus continues to be on the pursuit of low-cost competitive strategies. The availability of cheap foreign labour has been cited as one of the major reasons for the lack of attention in these areas, since such availability reduces employers' incentives either to upgrade the structure of their organizations (Liu, 2000) or to invest in research and development (Lin and Lo, 2004).

When the government first granted permission for employers to import foreign workers into Taiwan, in 1992, it was made very clear that this was solely for the purpose of relieving the labour shortage that existed at that time and not simply for the purpose of obtaining cheap labour. Clearly, if no foreign workers had been available at that time to many of the island's labour-intensive firms, they may have had to close down their operations completely and relocate their factories abroad, thus adding to domestic unemployment levels. There had also been considerable delays in the completion of many public infrastructure construction projects due to the serious labour shortage, with such delays in these projects having a knock-on effect, in terms of the lack of improvement in investment opportunities. Thus, the importation of foreign workers was put into place as a temporary measure for employers within these firms, essentially to buy them sufficient time to upgrade their production facilities and products and to regain their former competitiveness in the international markets.

The island's foreign worker policy worked well prior to 1996, but since then the government has changed its position so as to promote the major export and high-tech industries, and in some cases this has even become a tool for promoting specific foreign policies (Lee, 2004). Furthermore, in 1997, the CLA announced that although foreign workers were to be covered by the minimum wage law, and were therefore entitled to the same minimum wage rate as native workers, employers would, nevertheless, be allowed to count 'room and board' and certain other expenses as part of this minimum wage. It is, therefore, quite clear that such policies were quite openly seeing foreign workers in a new light, essentially as a source of cheap labour and not as a supplement to the island's labour shortage as had originally been intended (Lee, 2004). By the start of 2006, in addition to maintaining the current quota of foreign workers (in excess of 300,000), an additional 20,000 foreign workers were also being allowed to enter Taiwan in the category of dirty, dangerous and difficult (3D) employment. The impact of such a policy not only enables foreign workers to displace native workers, but also contributes to the slowdown in the upgrading of Taiwan's industrial and economic structure, and hence, the rate of creation of new jobs.

CONCLUSIONS

Economic development in Taiwan was clearly very successful prior to 1996, and indeed was referred to internationally as the 'Taiwanese Miracle', with the efficient operation of Taiwan's labour market having been credited as one of the most important contributors to such success. The rather stagnated economic climate in Taiwan since 1996 has, however, led to a continuing rise in the unemployment rate, which eventually reached a historical high of 5.2 per cent in 2002. The slight decline in the unemployment rate in both 2005 and 2006 should be ignored, since this was essentially due to the implementation of several public employment projects involving mostly temporary, low-skilled and 'dead-end' jobs.

The successful operation of the Taiwanese labour market prior to 1996 has been attributed to the 'hands-off' labour market policy adopted by the government during that period, a policy which succeeded in facilitating a highly integrated labour market within Taiwan, whereas the subsequent poor performance of the labour market in the post-1996 period is generally attributed to increasing labour legislation alongside the importation of low-skilled foreign workers. There have also been suggestions that it was the increasingly arduous labour legislation which caused the greater labour market rigidity and rising labour costs for firms in Taiwan, and which thereby reduced their overall competitiveness in the international markets. However, as this chapter has shown, a rise in labour legislation alone does not necessarily create high unemployment; in fact, there is general agreement amongst scholars in Taiwan that the expansion of labour market legislation is inevitable. As the Taiwanese economy becomes increasingly developed, its labour laws must be updated to meet the needs of the new economic environment and working standards, and also to comply with international standards.

A comparison between Taiwan, other Asian NIEs and Western economies shows that the excessive standards set by many of the newly enacted labour laws are particularly problematic for Taiwan, since its labour standards are not only much higher than those of its neighbouring economies at similar stages of economic development, but in many cases they are also higher than the standards of the advanced economies, such as the US and the UK, and even of those in France and Germany, countries whose labour standards are renowned as the highest and most rigid in the world. Nevertheless, the higher standards adopted by Taiwan do not automatically lead to higher unemployment; the key is the way in which employers respond to these high standards and rising labour costs. If employers respond by raising labour productivity through the introduction of more advanced management techniques, high-performance human resource management systems and performance-based wage systems and benefits, whilst also placing greater emphasis on their efforts in research and development, they can offset the higher labour costs and ultimately turn many of the current disadvantages of inflexibility into advantages.

As the US experience shows, despite the flexibility of its external market, employers have succeeded in adopting high-performance human resource management techniques as a means of training and retaining the most talented employees even though this came at the expense of certain areas of internal flexibility. Having now created significant stability levels for their employees through such an approach, employers in the US are thereby ensuring the continued competitiveness of their enterprises. Unfortunately this is not happening in Taiwan, partly because when enacting the new labour laws the government also sanctioned the importation of low-skilled foreign workers. The availability of low-cost foreign workers clearly provided a source of cheap labour for employers, thereby reducing their incentives to take the 'high road' of competition through the upgrading of their management techniques, the introduction of high-performance human resource management systems and the expansion of their research and development efforts. The ready availability of the alternative, that of relocating production facilities abroad to mainland China and other Southeast Asian countries, and thereby gaining access to cheap labour and greater management flexibility, enables such enterprises to escape the excessively regulated climate of the Taiwanese labour market. This is, however, a further cause of greater labour legislation and subsequent higher unemployment, since this alternative again reduces employers' incentives to engage in upgrading, and instead encourages the continued adoption of low-cost competitive strategies.

Many scholars have noted that when investigating the link between labour legislation and unemployment, we must not ignore the interaction between such legislation and other institutions. Analysis of the Taiwan case also points to the need to take into consideration interactions between labour market policies and other industrial and economic development policies. In implementing such an active labour market policy, it has been the concentration by the government on the promotion of high-tech and manufacturing export industries, as well as its failure to introduce other policies aimed at promoting employment-friendly industries, that are the real causes behind the island's higher unemployment level (see Chapters 5 and 6 of this volume).

Taiwan's experience therefore has a clear message for consideration in the current debate on labour market flexibility and employment. Labour legislation alone does not necessarily cause high unemployment and slower economic growth; the link with higher unemployment lies in the labour legislation standards. If the standards are excessive, then there is the possibility of this leading to higher unemployment and lower economic growth; however, even then, the answer still lies in the way in which employers respond to such high labour standards. If they respond by taking the high road of competition, introducing high-performance management techniques, reengineering their organizational structures and adopting a 'blue ocean' strategy involving the introduction of new and higher value-added products, they can then be in a position to utilize a workforce armed with much higher productive capabilities, which will, in turn, offset the higher costs resulting from such excessive labour legislation. They can then effectively guide their enterprises in a new crusade towards regaining their former competitiveness within the international markets.

REFERENCES

Auer, P. (2005), 'Protected Mobility for Employment and Decent Work: Labour Market Security in a Globalized World', *ILO Employment Strategy Paper No. 2005-1*, Geneva: International Labour Organization.

Baker, D., A. Glyn, D. Howell and J. Schmitt (2004), 'Unemployment and Labour Market Institutions: The Failure of the Empirical Case for Deregulation', *ILO Working Paper No.43*, Geneva: International Labour Organization.

Belot, M. and J.C. van Ours (2000), 'Does the Recent Success of Some OECD Countries in Lowering their Unemployment Rates Lie in the Clever Design of their Labour Market Reforms?', *ILS Discussion Paper No.147*, Geneva: International Labour Organization, Institute for Labour Studies.

Bertola, G. (1990), 'Job Security, Employment and Wages', *European Economic Review*, **34**(4): 851-86.

Bertola, G. and A. Ichino (1995), 'Crossing the River: A Comparative Perspective on Italian Employment Dynamics', *Economic Policy*, **21**: 361-420.

Bertola, G. and R. Rogerson (1995), *Institutions and Labour Relations*, Naples: University of Boccioni.

Bertola, G., T. Boeri and S. Cazes (1999), 'Employment Protection and Labour Market Adjustment in OECD Countries: Evolving Institutions and Variable Enforcement', *ILO Employment and Training Paper No.48*, Geneva: International Labour Organization.

Bierhanzl, E. (2005), 'Lessons from America', *Economic Affairs*, **25**(3): 17-23.

Blanchard, O. (2004), 'The Economic Future of Europe', *NBER Working Paper No. 10310*, National Bureau for Economic Research.

Block, R.N. and K. Roberts (1998), 'An Overview of the Labour Standards in the United States and Canada', paper presented at the *Meeting of the Industrial Relations Research Association* held in Chicago, 9-12 January 1998.

Block, R.N., P. Berg and K. Roberts (2003), 'Comparing and Quantifying Labour Standards in the United States and the European Union', paper presented at the *13th World Congress of the International Industrial Relations Association* held in Berlin, 8-12 September 2003.

Booth A. and D. Snower (eds.) (1997), *Acquiring Skills, Market Failures, Their Symptoms and Policy Responses*, Cambridge, MA: Cambridge University Press.

Botero, J., S. Djankov, R. La Porta, F. Lopez-de-Silanes and A. Shleifer (2004), 'The Regulation of Labour', *Quarterly Journal of Economics* (November): 1329-82.

CEPD (2005), *The Second Manpower Development Plan: 2005-2008*, Taipei: Council for Economic Planning and Development.

Chen, T.J. and J.S. Lee (2004), *The New Knowledge Economy of Taiwan*, Cheltenham, UK and Northampton, MA, USA: Edward Elgar.

Daniel, K. and W.S. Siebert (2004), 'Does Employment Protection Reduce the Demand for Unskilled Labour?', *ILS Discussion Paper No.1290*, Geneva: International Labour Organization, Institute for Labour Studies.

DGBAS (2005), *Survey Report on Personal Income Distribution, Taiwan Area*, Taipei: Directorate-General of Budget Accounting and Statistics.

DGBAS (various years), *Manpower Utilization Surveys, Taiwan Area*, Taipei: Directorate-General of Budget Accounting and Statistics.

Eichhorst, W. and R. Konle-Seidl (2005), 'The Interaction of Labour Market Regulation and Labour Market Policies in Welfare State Reform', *ILS Discussion Paper No. 1718*, Geneva: International Labour Organization, Institute for Labour Studies.

Esping-Andersen, G. and M. Regini (2002), *Why Regulate Labour Markets?*, Oxford, NY: Oxford University Press.

Fei, J.C.H., G. Ranis and S.W.Y. Kuo (1979), *Growth with Equity: The Taiwan Case*, Oxford, NY: Oxford University Press.

Fields, G. (1992), 'Living Standards, Labour Markets and Human Resources in Taiwan', in G. Ranis (ed.), *Taiwan: From Developing to Mature Economy*, Boulder, CO: Westview Press, pp.395-434.

Fields G. (2004), 'Dualism in the Labour Market: A Perspective on the Lewis Model after Half a Century', *The Manchester School* (December), **72**(6): 724-35.

Freeman, R. (1994), *Working Under Different Rules*, New York: Russell Sage.

Galenson, W. (ed.) (1979a), *Economic Growth and Structural Change in Taiwan: The Post-war Experience of the Republic of China*, Ithaca, NY: Cornell University Press.

Galenson, W. (1979b), 'The Labour Force, Wages and Living Standards', in W. Galenson (ed.), *Economic Growth and Structural Change in Taiwan: The Post-war Experience of the Republic of China*, Ithaca, NY: Cornell University Press, pp.39-77.

Heckman, J.J. and C. Page (2000), 'The Costs of Job Security Regulation: Evidence from Latin American Labour Markets', *NBER Working Paper, No.7773*, National Bureau for Economic Research.

Houseman, S.N. and K.G. Abraham (1993), 'Labour Adjustment under Different Institutional Structures: A Case Study of Germany and the United States', *NBER Working Paper No.4548*, National Bureau for Economic Research.

Jiang, F.F. (2004), 'The Impact of Foreign Workers on the Occupational Choice and Wages of Native Workers', paper presented at the *Conference on Foreign Worker Policy* held at the Institute of Economics, Academia Sinica, Taipei, Taiwan, September 2004.

Kim, W.C. and R. Mauborgne (2005), *Blue Ocean Strategy*, Cambridge, MA: Harvard Business School Press.

Kugler, A. (2004), 'The Effects of Job Security Regulations on Labour Market Flexibility: Evidence from Columbian Labour Market Reforms', *NBER Working Paper No.10125*, National Bureau for Economic Research.

Kuznets, P. (1988), 'An East Asian Model of Economic Development: Japan, Taiwan and South Korea', *Economic Development and Culture Change*, **36**(3): S11-43.

Lee, J.S. (1980), 'An Empirical Study of the Functioning of the Labour Market in Taiwan', *Academia Economic Papers* (March): 171-244.

Lee, J.S. (2000), *Labour Standards, Trade, Employment and Economic Development*, Taipei: National Science Foundation.

Lee, J.S. and H.L. Wu (1992), 'Overtime Work: The Fair Labour Standards Law and Taiwan's Labour Market', in J.J. Shih (ed.), *Technological Interactions between Industrial Structures and Patterns of Trade*, Taipei: Academia Sinica, pp.111-46.

Lee, J.S. and H.L. Wu (1996), 'The Fair Labour Standards Act and Its Impacts on Industrial Development in the Republic of China', in J.S. Lee (ed.), *Labour Standards and Economic Development*, Taipei: Chung-Hua Institution for Economic Research, pp.147-72.

Lee, L.S. (2004), 'The Role of Foreign Workers in Taiwan's Process of Economic Development', paper presented at the *Conference on Foreign Worker Policy* held at the Institute of Economics, Academia Sinica, Taipei, Taiwan, September 2004, pp.1- 20.

Lin, C.F. and J. Lo (2004), 'The Impact of Foreign Workers on the Technology and Productivity of Taiwan's Manufacturing Industries', paper presented at the *Conference on Foreign Worker Policy* held at the Institute of Economics, Academia Sinica, Taipei, Taiwan, September 2004, pp.39-65.

Liu, K.C. (2000), 'The Transformation of Taiwan's Labour Market and Its Unemployment', in J.S. Lee (ed.), *Taiwan's Unemployment Problems*, Taipei: National Central University, Research Centre for Economic Development in Taiwan, pp.7-34.

Mai, C.C. and C.S. Shih (eds.) (2000), *Taiwan's Economic Success Since 1980*, Cheltenham, UK and Northampton, MA, USA: Edward Elgar.

MOEA (2006), *A Review of the Costs of Mandatory Fringe Benefits for Employers in Taiwan*, Taipei: Ministry of Economic Affairs.

Nickell, S. (1997), Unemployment and Labour Market Rigidities: Europe Versus America', *Journal of Economic Perspectives*, **11**(3): 55-74.

Nickell, S. and R. Layard (1998), 'Labour Market Institutions and Economic Performance', *Discussion Paper No.407*, London School of Economics, Centre for Economic Performance.

Osterman, P. (2001), 'Flexibility and Commitment in the US Labour Market', *ILO Employment and Training Paper No.18*, Geneva: International Labour Organization.

Ranis, G. (ed.) (1992), *Taiwan: From Developing to Mature Economy*, Boulder, CO: Westview Press.

Saint-Paul, G. (2002), 'The Political Economy of Employment Protection', *Journal of Political Economy*, **110**(3): 672-704.

Saint-Paul, G. (2004a), 'Why are European Countries Diverging in Their Unemployment Experience?', *ILS Discussion Paper No.1066*, Geneva: International Labour Organization, Institute for Labour Studies.

Saint-Paul, G. (2004b), 'Did European Labour Markets Become More Competitive in the 1990s: Evidence from Estimated Worker Rents', *ILS Discussion Paper No.1067*, Geneva: International Labour Organization, Institute for Labour Studies.

Scarpetta, S. (1996), 'Assessing the Role of Labour Market Policies and Institutional Settings on Unemployment: A Cross-country Study', *OECD Economic Study Papers No.6*, Paris: Organization for Economic Cooperation and Development.

Shackleton, J.R. (2005), 'The Labour Market Under New Labour: The First Two Terms', *Economic Affairs*, **25**(3): 31-38.

Shih J.J. (ed.) (1992), *Technological Interactions between Industrial Structures and Patterns of Trade*, Taipei: Academia Sinica.

Siebert, W.S. (1997), 'Labour Market Rigidities and Unemployment in Europe', *Working Paper No.787*, Kiel, Germany: Weltwirtschaft Institute, Kiel University.

Siebert, W.S. (2005), 'Labour Market Regulation: Some Comparative Lessons', *Economic Affairs*, **25**(3): 3-10.

Snower, D. (1997), 'The Low Skills, Bad Job Trap', in A. Booth and D. Snower (eds.), *Acquiring Skills, Market Failures, Their Symptoms and Policy Responses*, Cambridge MA: Cambridge University Press, pp.109-26.

Soskice, D. (1990), 'Wage Determination: The Changing Role of Institutions in Advanced Industrialized Countries', *Oxford Review of Economic Policy*, **6**(4): 36-61.

Yoo, K.S. (2005), 'Financial Crisis and Unemployment Measures: The Experience of Korea', paper presented at the International Conference on *Globalization and National Development: Towards Greater Coherence between Economic and Labour Policies* held in Buenos Aires, 8-9 August 2005.

Appendix

Table A1.1 Variations in income for workers in different industries, 1980-2004

	1980	1993	1996	2000	2004
Agriculture	9,133	18,487	18,752	20,609	17,546
Mining	11,872	30,794	35,878	39,559	39,406
Manufacturing	9,542	21,885	31,361	32,961	32,937
Electricity, Gas and Water	15,131	36,160	45,583	51,287	51,867
Construction	11,830	28,239	34,657	34,416	33,179
Commerce	10,791	22,408	33,489	34,621	32,071
Transportation	14,351	31,103	38,322	40,472	39,248
Finance and Business Service	14,034	28,108	37,578	41,386	40,797
Public Administration and Personal Services	11,456	26,776	34,340	38,401	37,976
Mean	12,015.55	27,106.66	34,440	37,079.11	36,114.11
Std. Dev.	2,107.42	5,449.38	7,138.86	8,224.81	9,179.04
Covariance	0.17	0.20	0.21	0.22	0.25

2 Taiwan's Changing Employment and Earnings Structure

Gary S. Fields

INTRODUCTION

In its determined pursuit of economic development throughout the latter part of the twentieth century, Taiwan consistently succeeded in achieving growth rates that were amongst the highest in the world; however, in tandem with such growth, a number of significant changes also took place in the island's labour market. This chapter begins by highlighting some of the most important of these aggregate changes, as follows: (i) the achievement, and subsequent maintenance of, essentially full employment; (ii) improvements in the overall mix of jobs, in particular, a steady reduction in the share of agricultural employment to total employment, a very important shift given that agriculture remains one of the lowest-paying sectors in the Taiwanese economy; (iii) a rise in the share of wage employees, and, in consequence, a fall in the share of own-account work and unpaid family work; this represents another important shift, since wage employees in Taiwan enjoy much higher standards of living than own-account workers and unpaid family workers; (iv) an increase in the share of professional positions and other high-level jobs; a further significant and valuable development, because these are quite clearly the best-paying jobs; (v) real improvements in the educational level of the labour force as a whole; and (vi) a rise in real earnings throughout every sector of the economy, with both male and female earnings having risen at the same pace, in both farm and non-farm households.

In addition to all of these changes, real earnings across the entire Taiwanese economy have doubled every ten years, absolute poverty has fallen sharply and the Gini coefficient of individual earnings has remained essentially constant, indicating that income inequality remains strong (further details on all of the above developments are provided in the Appendix, Tables A2.1-A2.7). This chapter sets out to present brief analyses of the changes that have taken place in Taiwan between 1976 and 1993.

PSEUDO-COHORT ANALYSIS OF TAIWAN'S CHANGING INDUSTRIAL STRUCTURE

We begin with a brief analysis of the changes that have taken place in Taiwan, to both the industrial structure and the domestic labour market, since 1976; this was a time which heralded the start of the island's spectacular period of economic growth.[1] In terms of the overall share of employment, Taiwan was experiencing a steady and continuous decline in the agricultural sector, alongside continued growth in the commerce and financial services sector. The manufacturing sector as a whole experienced a steady rise, followed by a gradual decline, in its overall level of importance to the Taiwanese economy.[2]

There are two potential alternative adjustment mechanisms to which these changes may be attributable. The first of these was the gradual shift of workers from the declining sectors (for example, agriculture) into the growth sectors (such as manufacturing). If we assume that all workers had exactly the same probability of changing sectors, any increase or decrease in employment within any given sector would have been observed more or less proportionately across all age groups. However, the second potential adjustment mechanism which may have brought about these changes arises from the fact that the process of sectoral reallocation may have been quite age-specific, with older agricultural workers, in particular, not being replaced as they moved into retirement. In such a case, young workers, the new entrants into the labour force, would no doubt have entered directly into the growth sectors, such as manufacturing.

Clearly, when looking into the changes in the sectoral structure of employment over time, an ideal method would be to use panel data which could effectively follow the same individuals, tracing their employment patterns alongside the growth of the economy. Unfortunately, since Taiwan does not possess such panel data, we are limited to other methods; thus, the method proposed for adoption in this chapter is a pseudo-cohort analysis. The Family Income and Expenditure Survey, which measured a variety of labour force characteristics, was carried out in 1976, with the survey subsequently being repeated in 1977 on a new sample of families. In our pseudo-cohort approach, repeated cross-sections are used on a synthetic cohort of workers born during a predetermined time interval to trace these workers as they age. Those people who were born between 1936 and 1940, for example, would have reached the age of 36-40 years by 1976. By looking at those people who were 37-41 years of age in 1977, we can approximate the changing labour market patterns of people born between 1936 and 1940 as they became one year older. Repeating this process, year after year, produces an approximation of the impact that the labour market changes had upon particular groups.

Figures 2.1 to 2.6 present the pseudo-cohort data on separate male and female cohorts for the three sectors within which significant and systematic changes took place, namely, the agriculture, forestry and fisheries sector, the manufacturing sector and the commerce sector. The figures identify workers according to their birth year at five-year intervals. The line labelled 43, for example, which runs through the middle of each of the figures, comprises of workers born between 1941 and 1945. We can see that between 1976 and 1992, there was barely any change in the percentage of men in this cohort working in manufacturing; the same is true of women, although this is not so easily discernible (Figure 2.4). Conversely, the line labelled 63 in the same graphs shows that there was a steady decline within the manufacturing sector in the proportion of both young men and young women (those born between 1961 and 1965). Thus, in net terms, about a quarter of the young men and women who had previously been working in agriculture in 1986 had left for other sectors of the economy within six years, whilst little inter-sectoral mobility was indicated for workers in the older age groups.

Looking at these figures as a whole, we can discern the following. In any given year, the older the worker cohort, the smaller the proportion of the cohort employed in agriculture and the greater the proportion working in the manufacturing sector. This holds for both men and women. Over time, the changes in the proportion of workers employed in agriculture in any given demographic group were quite different for each of the different age-gender groups: (i) there was a rise in the proportion of older men and older women (those born in 1928 or before); and (ii) there was a fall in the proportion of younger men (those born after 1948) and younger women (those born in 1943 or later). The differences in the importance of agricultural employment between the various groups are much greater than the changes over time within the groups. For any given year, the younger the cohort (of both men and women) the greater the proportion of those working in the manufacturing sector. Over time, the proportion of female workers in the manufacturing sector follows an inverted-U pattern for most age groups. The participation of female workers in manufacturing reached its peak around 1986, whereas, with the exception of the very youngest cohorts, the proportion of male workers in the manufacturing sector remained constant for all age groups; however, across different age groups, it became successively higher for the newer cohorts.

Since 1988, women have been moving into the commerce and services sector in large numbers; however, there is no discernible trend in this direction for men. On the whole, the changes over time in the sectoral composition of employment within any of the male age groups were much smaller than the differences across all age groups; however, for those women in the 1943 (or later) cohort, the changes over time within any given age group were substantial, as compared to the differences between groups.

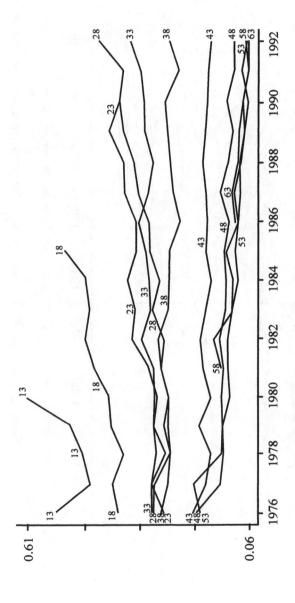

Figure 2.1   The proportion of the economically active male population in agriculture and related industries, by year

Source: Calculations by Dr. Philippe de Vreyer using micro data archives from DGBAS (various years), *Manpower Utilization Surveys.*

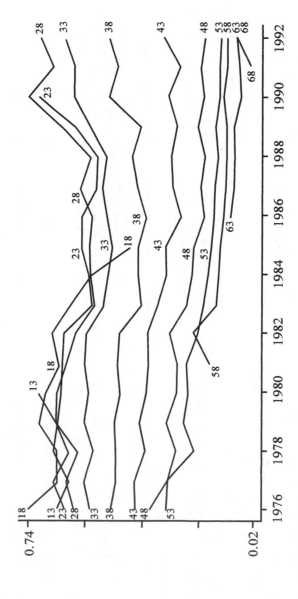

Figure 2.2   The proportion of the economically active female population in agriculture and related industries, by year

Source: Calculations by Dr. Philippe de Vreyer using micro data archives from DGBAS (various years), *Manpower Utilization Surveys.*

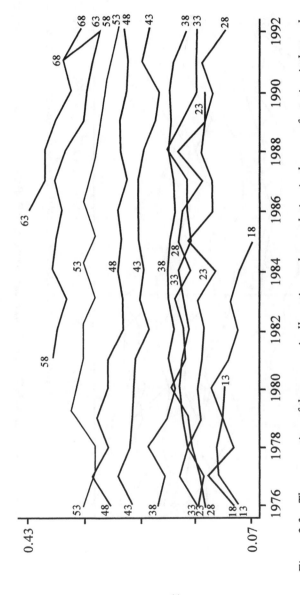

Figure 2.3   The proportion of the economically active male population in the manufacturing industry, by year

Source: Calculations by Dr. Philippe de Vreyer using micro data archives from DGBAS (various years), *Manpower Utilization Surveys.*

41

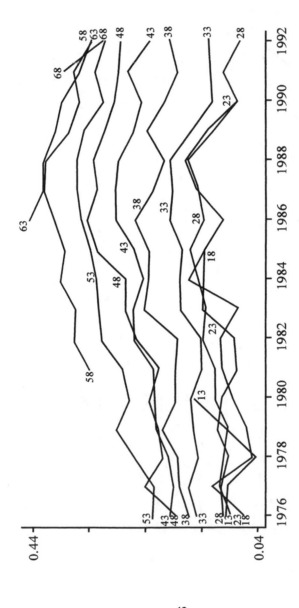

Figure 2.4 *The proportion of the economically active female population in the manufacturing industry, by year*

Source: Calculations by Dr. Philippe de Vreyer using micro data archives from DGBAS (various years), *Manpower Utilization Surveys.*

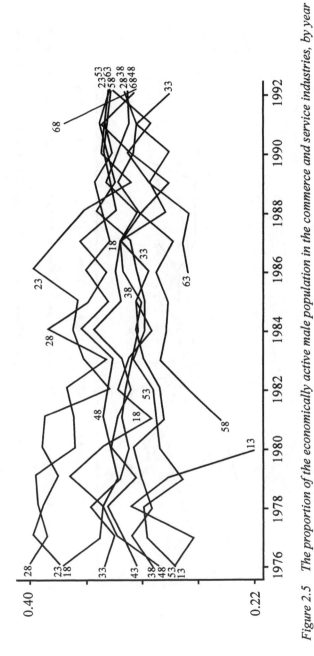

Figure 2.5   The proportion of the economically active male population in the commerce and service industries, by year

Source: Calculations by Dr. Philippe de Vreyer using micro data archives from DGBAS (various years), *Manpower Utilization Surveys.*

43

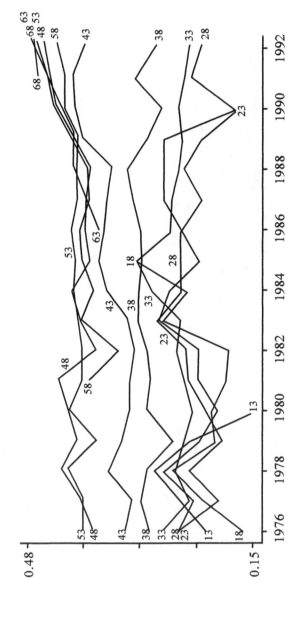

Figure 2.6   The proportion of the economically active female population in the commerce and service industries, by year

Source: Calculations by Dr. Philippe de Vreyer using micro data archives from DGBAS (various years), *Manpower Utilization Surveys.*

The data reveals much greater overall stability for men than for women within the various labour market sectors. Agricultural employment shrank in importance for men, not because individuals moved out of the agricultural sector, but largely because, as older agricultural workers retired, younger people who were newly entering the labour market bypassed agriculture entirely, entering other sectors, particularly manufacturing. There were, however, considerable inter-sectoral shifts for women; it is clear that large numbers of women were leaving agriculture and moving into the manufacturing sector up to the late 1980s, after which there was a further shift out of manufacturing and into the commerce and services sector. One of the implications of these findings is that any subsequent discussion on inter-sectoral shifts in Taiwan should focus more on the new younger cohorts moving into different sectors of the economy, rather than an assumption of large numbers of individuals changing sectors as they became older.

INTER-INDUSTRY EARNINGS DIFFERENTIALS

The data presented above clearly demonstrates a rise in real earnings throughout the Taiwanese economy, with wages doubling about every ten years. Here, we present further details on inter-industry earnings differentials in Taiwan, along with the growth in earnings, essentially establishing the empirical basis for the labour market model that follows in Chapter 4, where it will be argued that the integrated labour market model fits the facts of Taiwan better than any of the other model candidates.

A fundamental aspect of the integrated labour market model is that the changes in earnings for workers in a particular economic sector are not solely dependent upon the demand and supply of labour within that sector alone, but also within the economy as a whole. In an integrated labour market, labour earnings for workers with particular skills levels should be roughly equal across major economic sectors, with earnings increasing at more or less the same rate throughout the economy for similar types of workers. Empirical evidence on these propositions is offered in this section for the case of Taiwan. The data is taken from the micro data archives of the Manpower Utilization Surveys, for the years 1980 to 1993, undertaken by the Directorate-General of Budget, Accounting and Statistics (DGBAS) in Taiwan. All male and female workers in gainful employment within the private or the public sector during the week of the survey, either as waged employees or self-employed, were included in the analysis.

Table 2.1 provides details of the mean incomes for Taiwanese workers, by economic sector, for 1980 and 1993. What stands out immediately is that agricultural workers earned only about half as much as workers in other industries; however, sizeable differences are also apparent outside of the agricultural sector. Furthermore, those industries that were high-income industries in 1993 were the same ones that had previously been high-income industries in 1980.

Table 2.1   Mean wage income levels in Taiwan, by one-digit industries, 1980 and 1993

One-digit Industries	Mean Income	
	1980	1993
Agriculture	9,133	18,487
Mining	11,872	30,794
Manufacturing	9,542	21,885
Electricity, Gas and Water	15,131	36,160
Construction	11,830	28,239
Commerce	10,791	22,408
Transportation	14,351	31,103
Finance and Business Services	14,034	28,108
Public Admin. and Personal Services	11,456	26,776
Std. Dev.	2,107	5,449
Coefficient of Variation	0.1754	0.2010

Source: Author's calculations based on micro data archives from DGBAS (various years), *Manpower Utilization Surveys*.

A breakdown of earnings within the manufacturing sector by two-digit industries (food, beverages and tobacco, textiles, apparel, and so on) is provided in Table 2.2. This breakdown further demonstrates the sizeable differences across sectors along with the persistence of the industry's position in most cases. The question therefore arises as to whether these findings of substantial and persistent earnings differentials invalidate the concept of an integrated labour market in Taiwan. In order to answer this question, a number of tests need to be carried out, with the first of these tests involving an international comparison of inter-industry wage differentials; and, indeed, such data is available for comparison with earnings in the manufacturing sector in the US in 1992, by two-digit industry.

As Table 2.2 shows, the coefficient of variation for earnings was found to be 0.2226 for the two-digit manufacturing industries in Taiwan in 1993, whilst Tables 2.3 reveals that the analogous figure for the US was 0.2523. We may conclude from this that the inter-sectoral inequality in Taiwan is approximately 12 per cent less than that of the manufacturing sector in the

US and that the labour market in Taiwan is therefore more integrated than the labour market in the US. This is especially interesting because the US exhibits much more job mobility than most other countries, which is what generally makes the US labour market more integrated.

Table 2.2   Mean wage income levels in Taiwan, by two-digit industries, 1980 and 1993

Two-digit Industries	Mean Income	
	1980	1993
Food	10,557	23,135
Beverages and Tobacco	11,733	35,829
Textiles	8,848	22,150
Apparel	7,704	16,075
Leather	8,041	19,192
Wood	9,159	20,467
Paper	10,017	22,584
Chemicals	12,840	29,438
Chemical Products	11,499	23,903
Petroleum	15,668	35,462
Rubber Products	9,594	20,630
Plastic Products	9,015	19,805
Non-metallic Minerals	9,906	24,596
Primary Metals	12,705	27,500
Fabricated Metal Products	9,525	22,656
Machinery	10,947	24,906
Electrical Equipment	9,026	21,360
Transportation Equipment	11,187	24,205
Precision Equipment	8,993	18,329
Miscellaneous Manufacturing	8,047	17,959
Std. Dev.	1,946	5,234
Coefficient of Variation	0.1903	0.2226

Source: Author's calculations based on micro data archives from DGBAS (various years), *Manpower Utilization Surveys.*

Care must be taken when determining the requirements for an integrated labour market model since the model will indicate that workers within different sectors of the economy with similar skill levels should earn roughly the same amount; however, since the figures presented so far are non-standardized, they do not reflect the differences in education or other relevant characteristics of workers within any given sector.

Table 2.3   US inter-industry wage differences, by two-digit industries, 1992

Industry Code	Industry	Average Wage
311-3	Food and Beverages	10.19
314	Tobacco	16.69
321	Textiles	8.60
322	Apparel	6.95
323-4	Leather and Leather Products	7.40
331	Wood Products	9.43
332	Furniture	9.00
341	Paper	13.09
342	Paper Products	11.75
351-2	Chemicals and Chemical Products	14.45
353-4	Petroleum	17.87
355-6	Rubber and Plastic	10.37
36	Mineral Products	11.64
37	Basic Metals	13.67
381	Metal Fabrication	11.41
382	Machinery, Non-electrical	12.43
383	Machinery, Electrical	11.01
384	Transport equipment	15.16
385	Medical and Photographic Equipment	11.93
390	Other Manufacturing Industries	9.14
Std. Dev.		2.9291
Coefficient of Variation		0.2523

Source: Author's calculations based upon current population survey data.

Of course, it could well be the case that different wage levels are paid by different industries, perhaps because they have workers who possess varying levels of skills and abilities; if this is the case, then after controlling for these differences, it could also be the case that earnings would once again achieve parity, or very close to it.

Therefore, in order to determine whether different industries in Taiwan pay different wage levels, a number of regressions were run to establish whether or not, after controlling for human capital and other worker characteristics, the industry effects were statistically significant. The controls included measures of education, experience, job tenure, hours worked, gender and marital status. The respective 1993 results for the one- and two-digit industries are presented in Tables 2.4 and 2.5.

Table 2.4 *Determinants of logarithm of income for wage employees in Taiwan, with one-digit industry dummies, 1993*

Variables	Coefficient	t-statistics
Experience	0.027	36.043
Experience squared	0.000	–34.023
Tenure	0.020	18.425
Tenure squared	0.000	-9.425
Hours	0.006	19.885
Female	–0.319	–63.607
Married	0.047	7.916
Changed Job	–0.085	–12.897
Years of Education	0.055	58.376
Mining	0.406	10.034
Manufacturing	0.168	10.212
Electricity	0.338	11.412
Construction	0.400	23.469
Commerce	0.221	12.658
Transportation	0.356	18.978
Finance	0.336	17.847
Public Services	0.257	15.120
Constant	8.688	347.704
Total No. of Observations		22,133
R^2		0.485

Source: Author's calculations based on micro data archives from DGBAS (various years), *Manpower Utilization Surveys*.

We find from these tables that all of the industry effects are statistically significant at the one-digit level, and indeed that most of them are also significant at the two-digit level; the same was also true for 1980.[3] This provides strong evidence to suggest that the differences in measured worker characteristics are not the sole reason for the differences in wage levels offered by the various industries in Taiwan; thus, given that there are such significant inter-industry differences, the next task is to quantify how much of the inter-industry earnings differential can be explained by worker characteristics. Using the regression results from Tables 2.4 and 2.5, along with their 1980 analogues, we first of all set the other variables at values equal to their mean values, with the predicted log earnings subsequently being obtained for representative workers in each sector. The figures are presented in Table 2.6.

*Table 2.5   Determinants of logarithm of income for wage employees in
Taiwanese manufacturing, with two-digit industry dummies,
1993*

Variables	Coefficient	t-statistics
Experience	0.021	18.095
Experience squared	0.000	−19.874
Tenure	0.023	11.302
Tenure squared	0.000	−3.867
Hours	0.007	12.157
Female	−0.392	−47.900
Married	0.034	3.636
Changed Job	−0.071	−6.587
Years of Education	0.043	26.925
Food	0.140	6.013
Beverages and Tobacco	0.344	3.735
Textiles	0.141	6.283
Apparel	0.025	1.117
Leather Goods	0.072	2.455
Wood Products	0.059	2.457
Paper Products	0.104	4.252
Chemicals and Chemical Materials	0.218	7.107
Chemical Products	0.141	4.695
Petroleum	0.262	5.921
Rubber	0.089	3.030
Plastic	0.071	3.150
Non-metallic Products	0.176	7.001
Primary Metals	0.224	7.630
Fabricated Materials	0.113	5.363
Machine Products	0.152	6.165
Electrical Equipment	0.114	5.753
Transportation Equipment	0.130	5.366
Precision Equipment	0.041	1.126
Constant	8.929	226.113
Total No. of Observations	8,021	
R^2	0.509	

Source: Author's calculations based on micro data archives from DGBAS (various
years), *Manpower Utilization Surveys*.

Table 2.6 Non-standardized and standardized wage incomes in Taiwan, by one-digit industries, 1980 and 1993

Industry	Mean ln(Income) 1980	Mean ln(Income) 1993	Change in Mean ln(Income)	% Change in Mean ln(Income)
Non-standardized				
Agriculture	9.02	9.68	0.654	0.072
Mining	9.27	10.28	1.007	0.109
Manufacturing	9.07	9.89	0.822	0.091
Electricity, Gas and Water	9.56	10.45	0.894	0.094
Construction	9.30	10.18	0.882	0.095
Commerce	9.19	9.93	0.740	0.081
Transportation	9.49	10.28	0.794	0.084
Finance and Business Services	9.41	10.13	0.715	0.076
Public Administration and Personal Services	9.22	10.07	0.853	0.093
Std. Dev.	0.1805	0.2367	0.1068	–
Coefficient of Variation	0.0194	0.0234	0.1305	–
Standardized				
Agriculture	9.02	9.77	0.750	0.083
Mining	9.22	10.17	0.957	0.104
Manufacturing	9.16	9.94	0.774	0.084
Electricity, Gas and Water	9.26	10.11	0.844	0.091
Construction	9.27	10.17	0.893	0.096
Commerce	9.20	9.99	0.792	0.086
Transportation	9.34	10.12	0.786	0.084
Business and Financial Services	9.29	10.10	0.813	0.087
Public Administration and Personal Services	9.09	10.02	0.931	0.102
Std. Dev.	0.1015	0.1309	0.0736	–
Coefficient of Variation	0.0110	0.0130	0.0879	–

Source: Author's calculations based on micro data archives from DGBAS (various years), *Manpower Utilization Surveys*.

Measuring the inequality of these 'standardized log earnings' by the coefficient of variation, we obtain a figure of 0.0130. Thereafter, in order to gauge whether these standardized industry effects are large or small, we can compare them with the coefficient of variation for the non-standardized sectoral earnings, which is found to be 0.0234. Thus, the standardized inter-sectoral inequality is –0.0130/0.0234 (55.5 per cent) of the gross inter-sectoral inequality. By this measure, we find that 44.5 per cent of the difference in earnings across one-digit sectors in Taiwan was due to inter-sectoral differences in worker characteristics. A parallel analysis was subsequently carried out at the two-digit industry level within the manufacturing sector (textiles, apparel, and so on), the results of which are presented in Table 2.7.

Table 2.7   Non-standardized and standardized wage incomes in Taiwan, by two-digit industries, 1980 and 1993

Industry	Mean ln(Income) 1980	Mean ln(Income) 1993	Change in Mean ln(Income)	% Change in Mean ln(Income)
Non-standardized				
Food	9.15	9.95	0.800	0.088
Beverages and Tobacco	9.31	10.45	1.135	0.122
Textiles	9.02	9.91	0.893	0.099
Apparel	8.89	9.59	0.707	0.080
Leather	8.93	9.79	0.860	0.096
Wood	9.00	9.84	0.842	0.094
Paper	9.12	9.92	0.797	0.087
Chemicals	9.39	10.22	0.833	0.089
Chemical Products	9.26	9.99	0.735	0.079
Petroleum	9.61	10.44	0.829	0.086
Rubber Products	9.08	9.86	0.780	0.086
Plastic Products	9.04	9.81	0.770	0.085
Non-metallic Minerals	9.14	10.00	0.866	0.095
Primary Metals	9.37	10.14	0.771	0.082
Fabricated Metal Products	9.08	9.95	0.866	0.095
Machinery	9.17	10.06	0.892	0.097
Electrical Equipment	9.01	9.86	0.846	0.094
Transportation Equipment	9.24	10.02	0.785	0.085
Precision Equipment	9.00	9.74	0.742	0.082
Miscellaneous Manufacturing	8.90	9.66	0.758	0.085
Std. Dev.	0.18	0.22	0.090	–
Coefficient of Variation	0.02	0.02	0.109	–

Table 2.7 (Contd.)

Industry	Mean ln(Income) 1980	Mean ln(Income) 1993	Change in Mean ln(Income)	% Change in Mean ln(Income)
Standardized				
Food	9.05	9.92	0.875	0.097
Beverages and Tobacco	9.02	10.13	1.102	0.122
Textiles	9.11	9.92	0.811	0.089
Apparel	9.09	9.81	0.716	0.079
Leather	9.04	9.85	0.813	0.090
Wood	8.99	9.84	0.849	0.094
Paper	9.0I	9.89	0.876	0.097
Chemicals	9.13	10.00	0.869	0.095
Chemical Products	9.12	9.92	0.806	0.088
Petroleum	9.11	10.04	0.934	0.103
Rubber Products	9.09	9.87	0.776	0.085
Plastic Products	9.09	9.85	0.759	0.083
Non-metallic Minerals	9.07	9.96	0.889	0.098
Primary Metals	9.21	10.01	0.797	0.087
Fabricated Metal Products	9.05	9.89	0.846	0.093
Machinery	9.07	9.93	0.862	0.095
Electrical Equipment	9.06	9.90	0.835	0.092
Transportation Equipment	9.10	9.91	0.807	0.089
Precision Equipment	9.04	9.82	0.782	0.087
Miscellaneous Manufacturing	8.99	9.78	0.794	0.088
Std. Dev.	0.05	0.08	0.080	–
Coefficient of Variation	0.01	0.01	0.095	–

Source: Author's calculations based on micro data archives from DGBAS (various years), *Manpower Utilization Surveys.*

The coefficient of variation of 'standardized log earnings' was found to be 0.0085, as compared with a coefficient of variation of 'non-standardized log earnings' of 0.0224. Thus, by this measure, 1−0.0085/0.0224 (62.1 per cent) of the earnings differential across the two-digit manufacturing sectors is accounted for by differences in the personal characteristics of the workers in the different sectors. These findings show that with finer disaggregation of labour market sectors, an even greater share of the inter-sectoral earnings differential is accounted for by differences in worker characteristics.

Finally, it is apparent from Tables 2.6 and 2.7 that earnings increased at very similar rates within different sectors of the Taiwanese economy. This is true both of gross earnings (Table 2.6) and standardized earnings (Table 2.7), and thus provides one additional piece of evidence to support the integrated labour market model.

So, what are we to make of these findings? Clearly, much of the evidence does provide support for the integrated labour market model; and indeed, it is also clear that the gross earnings differentials across different sectors which are apparent from the simple statistical tables substantially overstate the differences in the earnings of comparable workers in different parts of the Taiwanese economy. Furthermore, we have also demonstrated that the inter-sectoral wage differentials in Taiwan are smaller than those of the US, whilst there were also increases at very similar rates in standardized earnings throughout the Taiwanese economy.

Nevertheless, it still cannot be said that Taiwan's labour market is fully integrated in the sense that observationally equivalent workers in different sectors earn the same amount (where the term 'same' refers to no statistically significant differences across sectors). These findings are mostly, but not completely, consistent with the integrated labour market model (which is further formulated in Chapter 4).

CONCLUSIONS

Throughout the course of Taiwan's exceptional performance in economic growth, there have been steady improvements in the island's labour market conditions. Two aspects of the labour market adjustment taking place in Taiwan have been explored in some detail in this chapter.

Firstly, a pseudo-cohort analysis of the changing employment structure has shown that most of the reallocation of workers across sectors took place as a result of young people entering the labour market in sectors that differed from those of their predecessors. By contrast, there were only minor shifts across sectors by prime-age workers.

Secondly, our analysis of inter-industry earnings differentials has demonstrated that although workers in Taiwan do earn different amounts, largely dependent upon the sector in which they are employed, and that the standardized earnings differentials are considerably smaller than the non-standardized differentials, inter-industry earnings differentials are, nevertheless, generally smaller in Taiwan than in the US. Furthermore, both standardized and non-standardized earnings grew at very similar rates across all sectors of the Taiwanese economy. Taken together, most of this data is consistent with an integrated labour market interpretation.

NOTES

[1]   Our analysis starts from 1976, essentially because that was the start of the household income and expenditure survey used here.

[2]   This section extends research carried out by Dr. Philippe de Vreyer, which began at doctoral dissertation research level at Delta in Paris. The author is grateful to Dr. de Vreyer for his work in carrying out the calculations reported in this section.

[3]   The omitted category in the one-digit analysis was agriculture, whilst the omitted category in the two-digit analysis was miscellaneous manufacturing.

REFERENCES

CEPD (1994, 1995), *Statistical Yearbook of the Republic of China*, Taipei: Council for Economic Planning and Development.

DGBAS (1976-1993), *Personal Income Distribution Surveys*, Taipei: Directorate-General of Budget, Accounting and Statistics.

DGBAS (various years), *Manpower Utilization Surveys, Taiwan Area*, Taipei: Directorate-General of Budget, Accounting and Statistics.

Fields, G. (1992), 'Living Standards, Labour Markets and Human Resources in Taiwan', in G. Ranis (ed.) (1992), *Taiwan: From Developing to Mature Economy*, Boulder, CO: Westview Press, pp.395-434

Galenson, W. (ed.) (1979), *Economic Growth and Structural Change in Taiwan: The Post-war Experience of the Republic of China*, Ithaca, NY: Cornell University Press.

Ranis, G. (ed.) (1992), *Taiwan: From Developing to Mature Economy*, Boulder, CO: Westview Press.

Appendix

Table A2.1   Unemployment rates in Taiwan, 1980-1994

Year	%	Year	%	Year	%
1980	1.2	1985	2.9	1990	1.7
1981	1.4	1986	2.7	1991	1.5
1982	2.1	1987	2.0	1992	1.5
1983	2.7	1988	1.7	1993	1.5
1984	2.4	1989	1.6	1994	1.6

Source: CEPD (1995), Table 27.

Table A2.2   Share of total employment, by education and employment type

Unit: %

Year	Share of Total Employment			Employed Persons with Primary Education or Below
	Agricultural Employment	Wage-employed Workers	Professional, Managerial, Technical and Clerical Personnel	
1980	19.5	64.4	21.55	51.31
1981	18.8	64.3	22.12	49.57
1982	18.9	64.1	22.39	48.01
1983	18.6	63.8	22.55	46.74
1984	17.6	64.4	22.92	45.06
1985	17.5	64.1	23.35	43.46
1986	17.0	64.7	23.80	41.67
1987	15.3	66.7	24.87	39.75
1988	13.7	67.1	26.38	37.58
1989	12.9	67.4	27.60	35.79
1990	12.8	67.6	29.48	33.90
1991	13.0	67.1	30.34	32.63
1992	12.3	67.8	31.43	30.75
1993	11.5	68.7	33.88	28.76
1994	11.0	68.9	–	27.50

Source: CEPD (1995), Tables 30-33.

Table A2.3   Real earnings growth, by one-digit industries, 1978-1993

Industry	Real Earnings*		Real Growth
	1978	1993	(%)
Mining	7,683	16,916	+ 120.2
Manufacturing	5,420	14,664	+ 170.6
Electricity, Gas and Water	9,426	31,661	+ 235.9
Construction	6,228	17,113	+ 174.8
Commerce	5,113	14,866	+ 190.8
Transport	7,910	19,325	+ 144.3
Finance	10,877	24,876	+ 128.7
Business Services	11,143	21,422	+ 92.2
Public and Community Services	7,269	14,777	+ 103.3

Note: * Real earnings are in 1978 New Taiwan dollars.

Source: CEPD (1994), Table 35.

Table A2.4   Nominal farm and non-farm household income, selected years

Year	Farm (NT$)	Non-farm (NT$)	Farm/Non-Farm (%)
1964	3,682	5,212	70.6
1980	35,199	52,682	66.8
1991	105,097	148,535	70.8

Source: DGBAS (1976-1993), Table 6.

Table A2.5   Average annual rise in earnings of manufacturing employees *

Year	%	Year	%	Year	%
1980	100.0	1985	130.3	1990	203.0
1981	102.2	1986	142.5	1991	217.4
1982	108.7	1987	155.7	1992	229.4
1983	114.0	1988	170.2	1993	238.2
1984	124.7	1989	186.5		

Note: * 1980 = 100 per cent.

Source: CEPD (1995), Tables 35 and 170.

Table A2.6   Estimated proportion of households with disposable income of less than NT$200,000 *

Year	%	Year	%	Year	%
1980	47.4	1985	38.0	1990	18.1
1981	49.5	1986	34.2	1991	14.4
1982	49.4	1987	29.5	1992	14.5
1983	44.7	1988	23.5	1993	12.5
1984	39.0	1989	19.9	1994	11.7

Note: * Estimations are at 1980 prices.

Sources: DGBAS (1976-1993), Table 7; CEPD (1994), Table 170.

Table A2.7   Gini coefficient of individual earnings for all waged employees

Year	Gini Coefficient	Year	Gini Coefficient
1980	0.249	1987	0.259
1981	0.247	1988	0.251
1982	0.254	1989	0.247
1983	0.261	1990	0.248
1984	0.253	1991	0.244
1985	0.250	1992	0.240
1986	0.261	1993	0.246

Source: Author's calculations based upon DGBAS (1993), *Report on the Survey of Personal Income Distribution.*

3 Education and Taiwan's Changing Employment and Earnings Structure

Gary S. Fields and Amanda Newton Kraus

INTRODUCTION

Between 1980 and 1992, the enormous changes in economic development in Taiwan had significant impacts on the island's labour market. Examples of these changes include the island's almost legendary and meteoric economic growth, the maintenance of essentially full employment, an increase of around 116 per cent in real labour earnings, considerable upgrading of the educational qualifications of the labour force as a whole, a sustained and systematic shift in the composition of the labour force from agriculture into manufacturing and services and occupational upgrading (defined as the expansion of the share of the labour force in the better occupations, at the expense of the lesser occupations).[1]

The main purpose of this chapter is to provide in-depth analysis of these and other underlying changes in the Taiwanese labour market, with the main focal point being, on the one hand, the linkages between the employment and earnings structures, whilst on the other, the changes in the education and qualification levels and the new occupational structure of the island's labour force. Our econometric analysis is based upon a dataset taken from the Manpower Utilization Surveys (MUS) produced by the Directorate-General of Budget, Accounting and Statistics (DGBAS) in Taiwan, covering the years 1980 to 1992. The data for 1993 is not used in this chapter, despite being available to us, essentially because the occupation codes adopted after 1992 were incompatible with those of the earlier years.

The MUS sub-sample used here includes all full-time and part-time workers employed in paid jobs during the week of the manpower survey, as well as other workers also employed in paid jobs who were not working during that week either as a result of illness or absence on holiday. Based upon these criteria, the overall sample includes workers who were either self-employed or who were themselves employers, but does not include unpaid family workers.

The MUS designates individual workers under one of eight educational levels: (i) illiterate; (ii) self-educated; (iii) primary school; (iv) junior high school; (v) academic high school; (vi) vocational high school; (vii) junior college; and (viii) university or higher. The survey also designates occupations according to two-digit occupational codes aggregated into seven broad occupational categories: (i) agriculture and related occupations; (ii) production workers, artisans and labourers; (iii) service workers; (iv) clerical workers; (v) sales staff; (vi) professional and technical staff; and (vii) administrative and managerial staff.

For the purposes of analysis in this chapter, the data is aggregated into three educational levels and three occupational groups, since such aggregation makes it easier to determine any underlying patterns within the data. The three educational levels used here are: (i) primary education, comprising of the illiterate, the self-educated and those with primary school education or below; (ii) secondary education, comprising of those educated to junior high, academic high or vocational high school level; and (iii) higher education, comprising of those educated to junior college level or above.

The three aggregated occupational groups used in this chapter are: (i) unskilled occupations, including agriculture and related occupations, plus production workers, artisans and labourers; (ii) semi-skilled occupations, including service, clerical and sales occupations; and (iii) skilled occupations, including professional, technical, administrative and managerial occupations.

The Employment Structure in Taiwan

Our analysis begins with an examination of the structure of employment and the ways in which this changed over the 1980-1992 period. As Table 3.1 shows, there was an increase in the share of the labour force with both higher and secondary education, alongside a corresponding reduction in the share of workers with only primary education. Table 3.2, which presents details on the share of employment, by occupation, also indicates a substantial increase in the proportion of workers employed in semi-skilled and skilled jobs over the same period, alongside a corresponding decline in the proportion of workers in unskilled jobs.

As the figures in Tables 3.1 and 3.2 indicate, there were significant improvements in the educational and occupational attainments for both men and women throughout the period under examination. Tables 3.3 and 3.4 go on to provide details of the changes in the employment structure, by both educational level and occupation. Evidence of falling occupational attainments for those with higher education is provided in Table 3.3, along with evidence of rising occupational attainments for those educated to secondary level.

Table 3.1 Share of employment, by gender and education, 1980 and 1992

Unit: %

Level of Education	1980	1992	% Change
Primary Education			
Male	53.2	32.2	-21.1
Female	47.8	30.6	-17.3
Totals	51.6	31.6	-20.0
Secondary Education			
Male	36.5	50.9	14.4
Female	42.6	51.0	8.5
Totals	38.3	51.0	12.7
Higher Education			
Male	10.3	16.9	6.7
Female	9.6	18.4	8.8
Totals	10.1	17.4	7.3

Table 3.2 Share of employment, by occupation, 1980 and 1992

Unit: %

Occupation	1980	1992	% Change
Unskilled			
Male	64.6	56.5	-8.1
Female	56.7	36.8	-19.9
Totals	62.2	49.9	-12.3
Semi-skilled			
Male	17.9	20.1	2.2
Female	31.8	43.2	11.4
Totals	22.1	27.9	5.8
Skilled			
Male	17.5	23.3	5.8
Female	11.5	20.0	8.5
Totals	15.7	22.2	6.5

If we divide the whole period into two sub-periods and then undertake a comparison, we can soon determine the causes of the observed changes in occupational attainment; thus, in addition to data on 1980 and 1992, Tables 3.3 and 3.4 also include data on 1986. When we compare the 1980 and 1986 data we can see that from their position in 1980, workers educated to secondary and higher levels achieved lower occupational categories in 1986; however, the same groups of workers succeeded in moving into the higher occupational categories between 1986 and 1992. Such differences in occupational attainment during the two sub-periods can be attributed to the rapid increase in the pace of occupational upgrading during the latter half of the 1980s and the early 1990s.

Table 3.3 *Occupational attainment, 1980-1992**

Occupational Level	Occupational Attainment			% Change		
	1980	1986	1992	1980-1986	1986-1992	1980-1992
Unskilled						
Primary education	77.7	74.3	73.2	-1.5	-2.1	-3.5
Secondary education	55.2	56.3	49.6	1.2	-4.1	-2.9
Higher education	9.5	9.2	8.4	-0.9	-0.8	-1.7
Semi-skilled						
Primary education	14.7	15.7	16.2	0.5	2.3	2.7
Secondary education	30.1	29.5	33.1	-1.0	1.4	0.4
Higher education	29.8	33.2	34.0	2.5	-0.4	2.2
Skilled						
Primary education	7.6	10.0	10.6	1.0	-0.2	0.8
Secondary education	14.7	14.2	17.3	-0.2	2.7	2.5
Higher education	60.7	57.6	57.6	-1.7	1.2	-0.5

Note: * Occupational attainment = percentage of workers in each educational level employed within each occupational group.

Table 3.4 *Education and employment mix, by occupation, 1980-1992**

Occupational Level	Education/Employment Mix			% Change		
	1980	1986	1992	1980-1986	1986-1992	1980-1992
Unskilled						
Primary education	64.5	54.1	46.4	-10.4	-7.7	-18.0
Secondary education	34.0	43.9	50.6	9.9	6.7	16.6
Higher education	1.5	2.0	3.0	0.4	1.0	1.4
Semi-skilled						
Primary education	34.3	27.5	18.4	-6.8	-9.1	-15.9
Secondary education	52.2	55.4	60.4	3.2	5.0	8.2
Higher education	13.5	17.1	21.2	3.6	4.1	7.7
Skilled						
Primary education	25.1	23.7	15.1	-1.4	-8.6	-10.0
Secondary education	36.0	36.1	39.8	0.1	3.7	3.8
Higher education	38.9	40.2	45.1	1.3	4.9	6.2

Note: * Education and employment mix, by occupation = the employment share of each educational level within each occupation group.

The rate of reduction in the share of unskilled jobs to total employment during the second period was twice that of the first period, along with corresponding increases in the share of semi-skilled jobs to total employment (1.8 times faster than in the first period) and the share of skilled jobs (2.1 times faster). Thus, workers with secondary and higher education were able to attain higher occupational levels in the second period, despite the substantial overall increase in the supply of these higher-educated workers within the labour market.

The Earnings Structure in Taiwan

This section presents data on Taiwan's earnings structure, with the simple tabulations of the earnings data for 1980 and 1992 indicating clear patterns for both years (Table 3.5).[2]

Table 3.5   Earnings structure in Taiwan, 1980 and 1992 *

Categories of Workers	1980 (NT$)	1992 (NT$)	% Change
Educational Category			
Primary education	10,350	20,695	100.0
Secondary education	11,140	23,758	113.0
Higher education	16,947	33,128	96.0
Occupational Level			
Unskilled	9,467	20,833	120.0
Semi-skilled	10,901	21,817	100.0
Skilled	19,226	35,758	86.0
Gender			
Male	12,745	27,553	116.0
Female	7,975	18,268	129.0
Experience			
0-8 years	8,842	19,596	122.0
9-16 years	12,534	25,996	107.0
≥17 years	12,204	25,611	110.0
All Employed Persons	11,315	24,421	116.0

Note: * Earnings are quoted in 1991 New Taiwan dollars (NT$).

First of all, we find from Table 3.5 that with a rise in education there was a corresponding rise in earnings, with the secondary to primary earnings ratio standing at 1.1 to 1 in 1980 and 1.2 to 1 in 1992, whilst the higher to secondary ratio was 1.5 to 1 in 1980 and 1.4 to 1 in 1992.

Secondly, workers in skilled occupations earned more than workers in semi-skilled occupations, who in turn earned more than workers in unskilled occupations. Thirdly, men earned substantially more than women, with the male/female earnings ratio standing at 1.6 to 1 in 1980 and 1.5 to 1 in 1992. Finally, the effect of experience on earnings was a rise, followed by a fall, with average earnings being highest for those workers with between 9 and 16 years experience.

We now go on to describe the major changes which took place between 1980 and 1992, beginning with the rise in real earnings for every group of workers in Taiwan. The overall rise in real earnings was 116 per cent, with the highest rises being found amongst women, as well as those workers with the lowest experience, those in the middle education category and those in the lowest occupational category. When breaking down the data, we first consider the fact that the greatest increase in earnings was found amongst workers with secondary education; thereafter, when the data is disaggregated into the eight original educational groups, we can see that the largest increase in earnings was, by far, amongst the group of workers educated to junior high school level, at 125 per cent. The next largest increase, at 108 per cent, was experienced amongst the professional high school group.

If we then go on to add in even more detail, we find that for all workers educated to junior high school level, those in the unskilled occupations enjoyed the greatest increases in earnings, with the rate of increase for this particular education/occupation group being 142 per cent, significantly higher than the overall average increase of 116 per cent. One possible explanation for such disparity in the rise in earnings is that the significant reduction in the supply of workers educated to primary school level may have led to an overall increase in the relative wage of these workers, particularly those in unskilled occupations, where this group was mainly employed.

This increase in the unskilled primary wage may then have led to an increase in demand for the group of workers which could be considered the closest and cheapest substitute, workers with the next highest education level, that is, workers with junior high school education. Such an increase in demand would of course lead to an increase in the relative wages of the unskilled junior high school group. At the same time, workers educated to junior high school level shifted to semi-skilled and skilled jobs, resulting in a reduction in the supply of these workers available to fill unskilled jobs, which thereby led to a further increase in the relative wages of the unskilled junior high school group. These two effects, combined with the rising demand coming as a result of economic growth, may have been sufficient to cause the extraordinary growth in overall earnings for workers educated to junior high school and secondary high school levels.

Next, we consider the fact that earnings increased most in unskilled occupations, which, at first glance, was probably the straightforward result of a significant reduction in the supply of uneducated, cheap labour into the unskilled occupational sectors. As shown in Table 3.3, in 1980, 65 per cent of workers in unskilled occupations were educated to primary level or below; however, by 1992, educational expansion had reduced this share to 46 per cent, indicating that employers who had unskilled jobs which they needed to fill were finding that they needed to hire better-educated and more expensive workers. In specific terms, in 1992, the average earnings of those working in unskilled occupations and educated to secondary level were 13 per cent higher than those with primary level education, whilst the average earnings of those with higher education were 35 per cent higher.

A more detailed look at additional data supports this finding, showing that there was an increase of eight years in the average age of workers in unskilled occupations between 1980 and 1992. By contrast, the average age of workers in semi-skilled occupations increased by only five years, whilst the average age of workers in skilled occupations increased by less than one year. These figures suggest that earnings in unskilled jobs may also have been rising relative to those in the other occupation groups, because unskilled workers were climbing much more quickly up their age/earnings profiles. However, when the earnings data for each occupation is disaggregated by age cohort, we find that earnings in unskilled occupations increased more rapidly for every cohort. This result indicates that the decrease in the supply of workers to fill unskilled occupations, regardless of age, was the main driving force behind the change in the occupational earnings structure. In the next section, we go on to explore the effects on the changing educational earnings structure stemming from the interaction between educational expansion and the changes in occupational attainment.

THE DETERMINATION OF EARNINGS, BY OCCUPATION AND EDUCATIONAL LEVEL

The hypothetical relationships that exist between education, earnings and occupation are illustrated in Figure 3.1, where the arrow marked '1' indicates that education has a direct effect on earnings; that is, in any given occupation, workers with better education are expected to have higher earnings, on average, than workers with lower education. This result may be due to the human capital effects of education, to a correlation between education level and innate ability or to a mixture of both. The arrow marked '2' indicates that there is also some likelihood of the existence of a direct relationship between occupation and earnings which is independent of education; indeed, some occupations pay better than others, regardless of the education level of the employee, and there are in fact many reasons why wages might vary according to occupation.

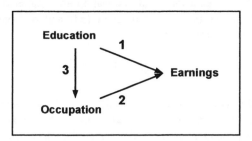

Figure 3.1 The hypothetical relationships between education, occupation and earnings

On the one hand, different occupations are likely to employ different types of workers; indeed, it is much more likely that a higher proportion of highly productive and capable workers will be employed in higher-skilled jobs than in lower-skilled jobs. Thus, it is also expected that the higher-skilled jobs will pay more, on average, than the lower-skilled jobs.[3] On the other hand, it may well be that there is some association between occupational wage differentials and actual job characteristics, such as compensatory differentials and the practice of offsetting training costs, or with labour market institutions such as unions or labour legislation which have greater coverage of certain occupations than others. It is only in the case of offsetting training costs that higher occupational wages will necessarily have any association with greater skills.

The arrow marked '3' indicates that education affects earnings by altering the probability that a given worker will be employed in a given occupation; that is, that there is a greater likelihood of a higher-educated worker having a highly skilled job. This expectation is based upon two factors, each of which may hold simultaneously. The first is that education imparts skills which increase the likelihood of the educated worker being more productive in a highly skilled job, and thus more competitive in the market for such jobs. The second is that education acts as a signal to employers helping them to identify the most capable workers.

Taken together, these three hypothetical relationships constitute an implicit fourth hypothesis. In addition to its direct effect on earnings, education as a determinant of occupation also has an indirect effect, with the acquisition of education being a means of securing the higher wages associated with more highly skilled jobs.

Analysis of the Effects of Education and Occupation on Earnings

Reduced form and structural estimates [4]
The direct effects of education and occupation are estimated here using an earnings function within which education (ed) and occupation (occ) are explicitly entered as explanatory variables:

$$\ln E = h(ed, occ, X), \tag{1}$$

where lnE is the natural log of real earnings and X is a vector of personal characteristics. The direct effects of education and occupation (DIR_e and DIR_o) are simply the estimated coefficients on the education and occupation variables in Equation (1), with these variables being respectively formulated as dummy variables representing secondary and higher education, as well as semi-skilled and skilled occupations.

Thus, the direct effects of education and occupation are measured in terms of the amounts by which higher education and employment in a more skilled job increase the earnings of a worker, relative to the appropriate base categories of primary education and unskilled occupations. The indirect effect of having received higher education is defined as the amount by which the likelihood of workers gaining employment in higher-skilled jobs will effectively raise the expected earnings of those workers with higher education, relative to the expected earnings of those with lower education, thus reflecting the relationships represented by the arrows marked '2' and '3' in Figure 3.1.

To be more specific, the indirect effect of education level e is defined here as: (i) the weighted sum of the direct effects of all occupations on earnings, where these weights are equal to the probability levels of being employed in these occupations conditional on achieving education level e; minus (ii) the weighted sum of the direct effects of all occupations on earnings, where these weights are equal to the probability levels of being employed in these occupations conditional on having some base education level. The indirect effect of education level e is therefore defined in algebraic terms, as:

$$IND_e = \sum_o DIR_o P_{o|e} - \sum_o DIR_o P_{o|b}, \tag{2}$$

where IND_e is the indirect effect of education level e, DIR_o is the direct effect of occupation o, $P_{o|e}$ is the probability of employment in occupation o conditional on having education level e and $P_{o|b}$ is the probability of being employed in occupation o conditional on having the base education level.

The probabilities of being employed in a given occupation conditional on education level are generated by estimating occupational attainment functions of the form:

$$Occ = g(ed, Z), \tag{3}$$

where Occ is a three-way dependent variable (skilled occupation, semi-skilled occupation or unskilled occupation) and Z is a vector of personal characteristics not necessarily equal to X.

Equations (1) and (3) make up a structural model of earnings determination; when occ is dropped, we have the reduced form earnings function:

$$lnE = h'(ed, X), \tag{4}$$

which, although providing the total effect of education on earnings, does not separate out the direct effects from the indirect effects.

We subsequently undertake estimation of both the reduced form and the structural model in order to compare the direct and indirect effects of education on earnings using the total effect, as estimated by the reduced form model. The arguments of the reduced form earnings function (Equation 4) used to measure the total effects of education are:

$$lnE = a + b(exp) + c(exp)2 + d(sex) + e(tenure) + f(tenure)2$$
$$+ g(lnhours) + \Sigma_e \, h_i \, (ed_e) + j(employer) + k(self\text{-}employed) + u, \tag{5}$$

where lnE is the natural log of monthly earnings; sex is a dummy variable with male being equal to 1; tenure is the number of years in the current job; and lnhours is the natural log of hours per week.[5] Since we do not have any actual data on experience or years of schooling, in this analysis, experience (exp) refers to potential experience and is calculated as age, minus six years, minus the estimated years of schooling.[6] The education (ed) variables are entered in three categories, with the omitted variable being primary level education.

The terms 'employer' and 'self-employed' are dummy variables, with the former being equal to 1 if the worker is an employer and the latter being equal to 1 if the worker is self-employed. These variables are included within the equation as a means of separating out the potential returns to capital from the effects of education; such returns may be accrued by those who are self-employed or who own businesses employing others. The estimation results, using the 'ordinary least squares' (OLS) method, are presented in Table 3.6.

Table 3.6 Earnings functions, without occupation variables, 1980-1992*

Variables	1980		1986		1992	
	Coefficient	S.D.	Coefficient	S.D.	Coefficient	S.D.
Secondary Education	0.2086	0.0078	0.2530	0.0080	0.2145	0.0092
Higher Education	0.6195	0.0113	0.6737	0.0105	0.5729	0.0112
Potential Experience	0.0362	0.0009	0.0331	0.0008	0.0309	0.0009
Potential Experience squared	-0.0006	0.0000	-0.0006	0.0000	-0.0006	0.0000
Sex, male = 1	0.3194	0.0070	0.3397	0.0063	0.3363	0.0067
Tenure	0.0114	0.0011	0.0232	0.0001	0.0252	0.0011
Tenure squared	-0.0004	0.0000	-0.0006	0.0000	-0.0008	0.0000
Log of Hours per Week	0.6252	0.0156	0.6067	0.0120	0.7105	0.0150
Semi-skilled	–	–	–	–	–	–
Skilled	–	–	–	–	–	–
Employer	0.5395	0.0145	0.4638	0.0140	0.3424	0.0138
Self-employed	-0.1489	0.0082	-0.1529	0.0076	-0.1711	0.0084
Constant	5.6554	0.0617	6.1655	0.0474	6.4456	0.0589
No. of Obs.	24,403		27,759		27,740	
Adj. R^2	0.3810		0.4106		0.3683	

Note: * All coefficients are significant at better than the 1 per cent level.

From the reduced form analyses for 1980, 1986 and 1992, we can first of all determine that education raises earnings. Specifically, relative to primary education, the effects of such raised earnings are greater for those with higher education than for those with secondary education. We also find that earnings rise with potential experience at a decreasing rate, peaking at about 28-years experience, and that earnings rise with tenure at a decreasing rate, peaking at about 17-years tenure. Men earn more than women, ceteris paribus, and although employers earn significantly more than wage employees, the self-employed earn significantly less. Finally, as expected, earnings increase with hours worked.

Next, we turn to the estimations of the structural earnings model. The parameters of the equation for this model are obtained in the same way as those for the reduced form model, except that the parameters in the structural earnings model also include occupation dummies. These are included first of all to facilitate the estimation of the effect of occupation on earnings, and secondly, to separate out the effect of occupation from the effect of education:

$$
\begin{aligned}
\ln E = a' + b'\,(\exp) + c'\,(\exp)\,2 + d'\,(\text{sex}) + e'\,(\text{tenure}) \\
+ f'\,(\text{tenure})2 + g'\,(\ln\text{hours}) + \Sigma_e\,h'_i\,(ed_e) + \Sigma o\,i'\,o(\text{occ}) \qquad (6) \\
+ j'\,(\text{employer}) + k'\,(\text{self-employed}) + u'.
\end{aligned}
$$

Although the occupation variable is regarded as being endogenous in Equation (6), we have made no attempt at instrumenting this variable. This is essentially because there are no available instruments which have a sufficiently high correlation with occupation; and indeed, it is already well recognized that when there is only a weak correlation between potential instruments and an endogenous variable, the estimation of instrumental variables can produce some serious problems (Bound et al., 1995; Staiger and Stock, 1997). In our view, the prospect of a 'cure' by the use of instrumental variables is worse than the 'disease' of endogeneity bias itself; therefore, the OLS estimation method is used. The estimation results are presented in Table 3.7.

From our standardized earnings function estimates, we find that, in general, all of the previous results provided by the simple earnings functions are confirmed for all three years; however, the inclusion of the occupation dummies substantially reduces the coefficients on all of the education variables. When controlling for occupation, the estimated effects of both secondary and higher education are reduced by about a half for 1980, whilst the education coefficients are reduced by about 40 per cent for 1986 and 1992.

Table 3.7 *Earnings functions, with occupation variables, 1980–1992* *

Variables	1980		1986		1992	
	Coefficient	S.D.	Coefficient	S.D.	Coefficient	S.D.
Secondary Education	0.1037	0.0080	0.1583	0.0080	0.1285	0.0092
Higher Education	0.3281	0.0130	0.4050	0.0118	0.3360	0.0125
Potential Experience	0.0310	0.0009	0.0294	0.0008	0.0288	0.0009
Potential Experience squared	-0.0006	0.0000	-0.0006	0.0000	-0.0005	0.0000
Sex, male = 1	0.3526	0.0069	0.3814	0.0062	0.3798	0.0068
Tenure	0.0094	0.0011	0.0208	0.0010	0.0233	0.0011
Tenure squared	-0.0004	0.0000	-0.0005	0.0000	-0.0008	0.0000
Log of Hours per Week	0.5754	0.0151	0.5478	0.0117	0.6594	0.0147
Semi-skilled	0.1757	0.0077	0.1780	0.0070	0.1388	0.0076
Skilled	0.4120	0.0103	0.3822	0.0090	0.3537	0.0092
Employer	0.3552	0.0148	0.2981	0.0142	0.1906	0.0141
Self-employed	-0.1892	0.0080	-0.2091	0.0075	-0.2246	0.0083
Constant	5.8857	0.0599	6.4158	0.0462	6.6450	0.0576
No. of Obs.	24,403		27,759		27,740	
Adj. R^2	0.4215		0.4490		0.4007	

Note: * All coefficients are significant at better than the 1 per cent level.

We find that earnings are higher in the more skilled occupations, ceteris paribus; however, a further striking finding is that despite the enormous educational expansion which took place in Taiwan after 1980, there was no marked reduction in educational wage differentials. This phenomenon appears not only in the estimates reported above, but also in a number of other studies on Taiwan using data from both the Manpower Utilization Surveys and the Survey of Household Income and Expenditure (Fields and O'Hara, 1999; Bourguignon et al., 1999; Sun and Gindling, 2001; Gindling and Sun, 2002).

We now go on to further discuss the ways in which adjustments occurred within the Taiwanese labour market to bring about this particular phenomenon.

Occupational attainment functions

In this sub-section, we turn our attention to the estimation of the occupational attainment functions. These estimates are generated using a multinomial logit model which provides, as a function of various personal characteristics, the probability of being employed in one occupation, relative to the probability of being employed in another.[7]

In the three-outcome case, the multinomial logit model simultaneously estimates two equations of the following form:

$$\ln(P_o/P_b) = a + b(\text{experience}) + c(\text{sex}) + d(\text{age}) + \Sigma_e \, e_e \, (\text{ed}_e) \qquad (7)$$

where P_o is the probability of being employed in occupation o and P_b is the probability of being in the base category (the unskilled occupation group), Education level is entered as a set of dummy variables, with primary education establishing the base, Sex is a dummy variable, with male being equal to 1, and the Age variable is entered continuously. The estimation results are provided in Table 3.8.[8]

The models perform reasonably well, with the chi-squared statistic being significant at better than the 1 per cent level, as are all of the estimated coefficients. The positive coefficients on secondary and higher education, which are consistent with our expectations, are interpreted to mean that relative to primary education, secondary and higher education increase the probability of being employed in a semi-skilled or skilled job, rather than in an unskilled job.

Similarly, the positive coefficient on the age variable indicates that being older increases the probability of achieving higher occupational categories as opposed to lower ones. The negative coefficient on the sex variable is, however, unexpected, as it indicates that given both education and age, men are less likely than women to work in semi-skilled or skilled occupations.

We can interpret this particular finding as showing that women are not typically employed in unskilled jobs where there is a requirement for physical strength, as opposed to any indication of discrimination against men in the higher-skilled occupations.

Table 3.8   Multinomial logit models of occupational attainment, 1980-1992 [a]

Variables [b]	1980		1986		1992	
	Coefficient	S.D.	Coefficient	S.D.	Coefficient	S.D.
Semi-skilled						
Secondary	1.4700	0.0407	1.3489	0.0407	1.3064	0.0442
Higher	3.1380	0.0816	3.2502	0.0720	3.1181	0.0681
Age	0.0353	0.0015	0.0313	0.0015	0.0095	0.0016
Sex, male = 1	−0.9324	0.0368	−1.0146	0.0331	−1.3150	0.0329
Constant	−2.4763	0.0652	−2.2789	0.0695	−1.1700	0.0789
Skilled						
Secondary	1.8642	0.0533	1.6439	0.0501	1.8178	0.0518
Higher	4.8912	0.0839	4.7536	0.0750	4.7584	0.0717
Age	0.0690	0.0018	0.0694	0.0018	0.0597	0.0018
Sex, male = 1	−0.2341	0.0512	−0.4739	0.0426	−0.6917	0.0399
Constant	−5.1576	0.0913	−4.8788	0.0880	−4.3910	0.0941

Notes:
[a]   For the 1980 equations, $\chi^2(8) = 7646.77$, pseudo $R^2 = 0.1687$ and N = 24,655; for the 1986 equations, $\chi^2(8) = 8439.33$, pseudo $R^2 = 0.1551$ and N = 28,167; and for the 1992 equations, $\chi^2(8) = 9846.39$, pseudo $R^2 = 0.1694$ and N = 28,019.
[b]   All variables are significant at better than the 1 per cent level.

The occupational attainment functions are used to estimate the conditional probabilities of employment in each of the three occupation groups, for each education level, whilst holding both age and sex constant. Details on the estimated probabilities are presented in Panel A of Table 3.9, whilst Panel B of Table 3.9 provides the actual occupation attainment, as reported in Table 3.3.[9] The predicted and actual occupational attainment data demonstrate the same general pattern; in all three years, the employment of workers with primary education is concentrated in unskilled jobs, the employment of workers with secondary education is concentrated in unskilled and semi-skilled jobs, and the employment of workers with higher education is concentrated in skilled jobs. Standardizing for the effects of age and gender changes the average occupational attainment only slightly for all three education groups.

Table 3.9   Predicted and actual occupational attainment, 1980-1992

Unit: %

Variables [a]	1980	1986	1992
Panel A: Predicted Occupational Attainment			
Primary Education			
Unskilled	80.7	79.2	77.1
Semi-skilled	13.2	13.7	16.0
Skilled	6.1	7.1	6.9
Secondary Education			
Unskilled	48.8	50.0	45.9
Semi-skilled	31.5	30.5	31.9
Skilled	19.7	19.5	22.2
Higher Education			
Unskilled	9.8	8.9	8.1
Semi-skilled	29.7	32.3	31.9
Skilled	60.5	58.8	60.0
Panel B: Actual Occupational Attainment [b]			
Primary Education			
Unskilled	77.7	74.3	73.2
Semi-skilled	14.7	15.7	16.2
Skilled	7.6	10.0	10.6
Secondary Education			
Unskilled	55.2	56.3	49.6
Semi-skilled	30.1	29.5	33.1
Skilled	14.7	14.2	17.3
Higher Education			
Unskilled	9.5	9.2	8.4
Semi-skilled	29.8	33.2	34.0
Skilled	60.7	57.6	57.6

Notes:

[a]   Predicted occupational attainment = the level of attainment predicted by the occupational attainment functions minus the predicted probability of being employed in occupation o, conditional on having education level e, whilst holding age and sex constant.

[b]   Actual occupational attainment = the percentage of workers within each education level employed in each occupation group.

THE DIRECT, INDIRECT AND TOTAL EFFECTS OF EDUCATION ON EARNINGS

We now have all the information required to calculate the direct, indirect and total effects of education on earnings. The direct effects are obtained from the estimates of Equation (6), presented earlier in Table 3.7, and are reported in the first rows of Table 3.10.

Table 3.10   The effects of education on earnings, 1980–1992

Unit: %

Educational Effects	Increase in Earnings *		
	1980	1986	1992
Direct Effect			
Secondary Education	10.4	15.8	12.8
Higher Education	32.8	40.5	33.6
Indirect Effect			
Secondary Education	8.8	7.7	7.6
Higher Education	25.3	23.1	21.0
Sum of Direct plus Indirect Effects			
Secondary Education	19.2	23.6	20.5
Higher Education	58.1	63.6	54.6
Total Effects			
Secondary Education	20.9	25.3	21.5
Higher Education	62.0	67.4	57.3

Note: * This uses the standard linear approximation of the effect on the natural log of earnings to the percentage changes in earnings, relative to primary education.

We can see from Table 3.10 that relative to primary education and depending on the year, secondary education raises earnings by 10 to 13 per cent, whilst higher education raises earnings by 33 to 41 per cent. The estimates of the direct effects of occupation can then be combined with the estimates of conditional occupational attainment (Equation (7) and Table 3.8) to calculate the indirect effects of education on earnings according to Equation (2).

For example, the indirect effect of higher education is given by:

$$\text{IND}_{higher} = \sum_o \hat{d}_o \hat{P}_{o \mid higher} - \sum_o \hat{d}_o \hat{P}_{o \mid primary} \qquad (8)$$

where $\hat{d}_o$ is the estimated coefficient on occupation o from Equation (6); $\hat{P}_{o|\,higher}$ is the estimated probability of being employed in occupation o conditional on having higher education; and $\hat{P}_{o|\,primary}$ is the estimated probability of being employed in occupation o conditional on having primary education (i.e., the base-level education). As regards the indirect effects, which are reported in the second group of rows of Table 3.10, all of these are sizeable and in some cases are almost as large as the direct effects. Thus, in Taiwan, a substantial proportion of the returns to education occurs through improved occupational attainment.

The total effect of education on earnings comprises of the effect of the increase in education, in terms of raising earnings within occupations and the improved occupational position of workers. An estimate of this total effect is obtained by means of the reduced form regression (Equation (5) and Table 3.6). In all three years, and for both educational levels, the total effects are quite close to the sum of the direct and indirect effects, which indicates that although there is potential bias in the OLS estimates of the coefficients in the earnings functions (with occupation variables), in practice, the magnitude of this problem actually proves to be quite small.

Analysis of the Effects of Education on Changes in Earnings

The causes of the fairly constant relative wage differentials in Taiwan can be analysed by examining changes over time in the direct, indirect and total effects of education on earnings. These changes are reported in Table 3.11 for two sub-periods, 1980 to 1986 (period 1) and 1986 to 1992 (period 2), as well as for the entire period under examination.

Table 3.11   Changes in the effects of education on earnings, 1980-1992

Unit: %

Educational Effects	% Change		
	1980-1986	1986-1992	1980-1992
Direct Effect			
Secondary Education	5.5	–3.0	2.5
Higher Education	7.7	–6.9	0.8
Indirect Effect			
Secondary Education	–1.1	–0.1	–1.2
Higher Education	–2.3	–2.1	–4.3
Total Effects			
Secondary Education	4.4	–3.8	0.6
Higher Education	5.4	–10.1	–4.7

The changes in the direct and indirect effects in the first period, for both secondary and higher education, generally worked in offsetting directions. For secondary education, although the direct effect increased by 5.5 per cent, the reduction in the indirect effect resulted in the change in the total effect amounting to an increase of only 4.4 per cent. Similarly, for higher education, an increase of 7.7 per cent for the direct effect was reduced to a 5.4 per cent increase in the total effect as a result of the 2.3 per cent negative indirect effect. It should be noted that changes in the direct and total effects were positive for both education levels, despite the substantial increases in the supply of workers with these educational attainments. For both secondary and higher education, all changes in the direct and indirect effects in the second period were negative, as were the total effects. Once again, however, it should be noted that the changes in the direct effects were greater than the changes in the indirect effects for both education levels. For secondary education, there was a 3 per cent reduction in the direct effect, as compared to a mere 0.1 per cent reduction in the indirect effect. For higher education the substantial 6.9 per cent reduction in the direct effect was accompanied by a much smaller reduction, of only 2.1 per cent, in the indirect effect.

For the entire period under examination (1980 to 1992), there was an overall increase in the direct effects of both secondary and higher education on earnings, largely as a result of the substantial increases in the direct effects in the first period. In contrast, reductions in the indirect effects, in both the first and second periods, led to an overall reduction in the indirect effects. For secondary education, the increase in the direct effect over the whole period was large enough to offset the reduction in the indirect effect, resulting in an overall 0.6 per cent increase in the total effect. For higher education, the magnitude of the increase in the direct effect was not sufficient to offset the decrease in the indirect effect, such that there was an overall reduction of 4.7 per cent in the total effect. Thus, relative to primary education, secondary education had a greater effect in 1992 than in 1980, in terms of increasing earnings, whilst in contrast, again relative to primary education, higher education had a greater effect in terms of increasing earnings in 1980 than in 1992.

In order to further analyse the reasons behind the changes in the indirect effect of education on earnings, we disaggregate the indirect effect into changes in occupational attainment conditional on education (i.e., changes in the conditional probabilities) and changes in the direct effect of education on earnings (i.e., changes in the coefficients). Simulated indirect effects of each educational level are calculated by applying the end-of-period probabilities to the initial-period coefficients, so as to isolate the effects of the changes in occupational attainment from those of the changes in the occupational earnings structure. The results are presented in the left-hand side of Tables 3.12 and 3.13. Thereafter, the actual indirect effects at the beginning of the period are subtracted from the simulated indirect effects at the end of the period in order to generate the simulated changes in the indirect effects. These results are presented in the right-hand side of Tables 3.12 and 3.13.

For the first period, the simulated effect of the changes in occupational attainment on the indirect effect of higher education is calculated in accordance with the following formula:

$$\Delta IND_{higher}^{P} = \left(\sum_{o} \hat{d}_{o}^{80} \hat{P}_{o|higher}^{86} - \sum_{o} \hat{d}_{o}^{80} \hat{P}_{o|primary}^{86} \right) - \left(\sum_{o} \hat{d}_{o}^{80} \hat{P}_{o|higher}^{80} - \sum_{o} \hat{d}_{o}^{80} \hat{P}_{o|primary}^{80} \right)$$

(9)

where ΔIND^{P}_{higher} is the simulated change in the indirect effect of higher education on earnings, and the P superscript indicates that this simulation is based upon changes in the conditional probabilities of employment, whilst holding constant the effect of occupation-specific earnings. Similarly, the effects of changes in the occupational earnings structure are also isolated from the effects of the changes in occupational attainment by calculating the simulated changes in the indirect effect in accordance with the following equation:

$$\Delta IND_{higher}^{C} = \left(\sum_{o} \hat{d}_{o}^{86} \hat{P}_{o|higher}^{80} - \sum_{o} \hat{d}_{o}^{86} \hat{P}_{o|primary}^{80} \right) - \left(\sum_{o} \hat{d}_{o}^{80} \hat{P}_{o|higher}^{80} - \sum_{o} \hat{d}_{o}^{80} \hat{P}_{o|primary}^{80} \right)$$

(10)

The C superscript in Equation (10) indicates that this simulation is based upon changes in the occupation coefficients from the earnings functions, whilst holding constant the effect of occupational attainment. Table 3.12 presents the results produced by isolating the effects of the changes in occupational attainment, whilst the results produced by isolating the effects of the changes in the occupational earnings structure are presented in Table 3.13.

Table 3.12   The indirect effects of simulated changes in occupational attainment, 1980-1992

Unit: %

Educational Level	Simulated Indirect Effects		Simulated Change ΔIND^{C}_{e}	
	1986	1992	1980 to 86	1986 to 92
Secondary Education	8.1	8.7	−0.7	1.0
Higher Education	24.6	23.2	−0.7	0.1

Table 3.13   The indirect effects of simulated changes in the occupational earnings structure, 1980-1992

Unit: %

Educational Level	Simulated Indirect Effects		Simulated Change ΔIND^C_e	
	1986	1992	1980-86	1986-92
Secondary Education	8.4	6.7	−0.4	−1.0
Higher Education	23.7	20.9	−1.6	−2.2

In conjunction with the changes in the direct effect of occupation on earnings, the changes in occupational attainment in the first period contributed to the overall reduction in the indirect effects of both secondary and higher education. This is reflected in the negative values for ΔIND^P_{higher} and $\Delta IND^P_{secondary}$. These negative contributions reflect the fact that between 1980 and 1986 there were net shifts of workers with secondary and higher education out of the higher-skilled and higher-paying occupations into the lower-skilled and lower-paying occupations. Similarly, the negative values for ΔIND^C_{higher} and $\Delta IND^C_{secondary}$ reflect the fact that the direct effect on earnings from being employed fell by about 7 per cent over the same period. It should be noted that the reduction in ΔIND^C_{higher} is greater than the reduction in $\Delta IND^C_{secondary}$, which means that the impact of the reduction in the skilled wage premium was greater on the indirect effect of higher education than on the indirect effect of secondary education, because workers with higher education tend to be concentrated more in the higher-skilled jobs.

In the second period, however, changes in the direct effect of occupation on earnings (the coefficient effect 'c') worked in the opposite direction from changes in occupational attainment (the probabilities of employment 'p'). During this period, the direct effect of being employed in a semi-skilled job fell by 22 per cent, whilst the direct effect of being employed in a skilled job fell by 7 per cent. Thus, ΔIND^C_{higher} and $\Delta IND^C_{secondary}$ were both negative for this period; however, the impacts of these reductions were offset by shifts in the employment of workers in both education groups into more skilled jobs; ΔIND^P_{higher} and $\Delta IND^P_{secondary}$ were both positive for this period.

For secondary education, the offsetting effects of the changes in both occupational attainment and the occupational earnings structure are of the same magnitude; indeed, they almost cancel each other out, resulting in the 0.1 per cent reduction in the indirect effect reported in Table 3.12. For higher education, the increase in ΔIND^C_{higher} swamps the decrease in ΔIND^P_{higher}, such that there was a substantial reduction over the period in the indirect effect. Thus, as in the first period, the role played by changes in occupational attainment, with regard to the outcomes of higher education, was relatively minor.

EDUCATIONAL EXPANSION AND THE LABOUR MARKET: TOWARDS AN ANALYTICAL FRAMEWORK

In this section, we begin by taking stock of what has been empirically determined so far in this chapter, and find that the two major economy-wide changes that occurred during the period under examination were rapid economic growth and the high rate of educational expansion. The labour market remained tight, thereby allowing essentially full employment to be maintained and causing real labour earnings to more than double in a period of just 12 years. The labour market improvements were broad-based, insofar as large real wage increases were registered for all labour market groups, including men and women, better-educated and lower-educated workers, highly skilled and lower-skilled workers, experienced workers and recent labour force entrants.

Whilst all of this was happening, two major changes occurred in the occupational structure within Taiwan. Firstly, there were rapid improvements in the occupational mix of jobs, which we refer to as 'occupational upgrading', such that a much larger proportion of workers in Taiwan were able to work in skilled occupations than had previously been the case. Secondly, although better-educated, Taiwanese workers faced declining occupational attainments; that is, given their education, they did not enter the best occupations at the same rate as which they had previously entered, but nor did they remain unemployed; instead, they took up employment in semi-skilled jobs. Overall, then, the educational attainments of workers were higher in each occupational category, although a smaller proportion of workers with higher education was able to enter skilled occupations than before.

What these facts suggest is a standard supply and demand framework with a twist, since the standard framework regards the wages of workers with a given educational attainment as being determined by the demand and supply for that type of worker alone. Suppose, for simplicity, that the labour market can be divided into two segments, skilled and unskilled, with separate labour demand and labour supply curves in each. Workers in this simple model are assumed to be of two types, educated and less-educated, with educated workers supplying their labour only to the skilled market and less-educated workers supplying their labour only to the unskilled market.

Let there be a downward-sloping labour demand curve and an upward-sloping labour supply curve in each segment, with the wage in each being determined by the demand and supply in that segment alone. Skilled jobs pay more than unskilled jobs, which means that demand and supply in the skilled market would have to intersect at a higher wage than in the unskilled market. This is shown in Figure 3.2.

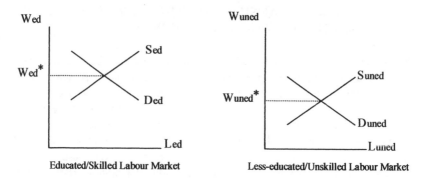

Figure 3.2   Supply and demand in educated and uneducated labour markets

If we now suppose that educational expansion occurs, with this being the only change taking place in the labour market, the labour supply curve of the skilled labour market would shift to the right, whilst the supply curve of unskilled labour would shift to the left. As illustrated in Figure 3.3, the wages for skilled jobs would fall, whilst the wages for unskilled jobs would rise, producing a narrowing of the educated/less-educated wage differential.

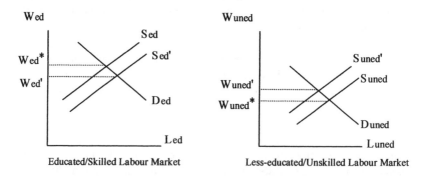

Figure 3.3   Shift in labour supply curves, demand held constant

However, this is not the way that things happened in Taiwan. In the studies mentioned earlier, as well as in our own empirical work, it has been demonstrated that the relative earnings of highly educated workers changed remarkably little, despite the huge increase in their absolute and relative numbers. Furthermore, these same studies have demonstrated that when controls are added, there has in fact been no appreciable fall in the adjusted wage differentials, and indeed, they may even have risen. The theory must therefore be amended to fit these facts. The obvious inference to be drawn from this is that there must also have been a shift in labour demand. If the demand curve for skilled labour shifts sufficiently rightward, the wages for educated labour will remain constant. Shift the demand curve even more rightward and the wages for educated labour will rise. Similarly, a rightward shift of the demand curve for unskilled labour will generate a larger wage increase for less-educated labour than that which is brought about by a leftward shift in the labour supply curve alone.

Figure 3.4 illustrates the way in which these shifts, taken together, could produce identical percentage wage increases in both the skilled and unskilled markets, thereby leaving the educated/less-educated wage differential essentially constant. It should be noted that the shift in the demand curve for educated labour must be greater than that for less-educated labour in order to obtain this result.

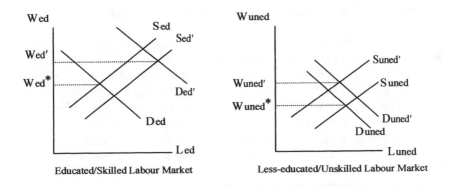

Figure 3.4   Shift in labour supply and labour demand curves

A convenient way of summarizing the argument is to adapt the analysis developed by Bound and Johnson (1992) as a means of explaining rising educated/less-educated wage differentials in the US; our adaptation of their basic diagram is illustrated in Figure 3.5. Initially, the supply of highly educated workers, relative to less-educated workers, is given by S, which is assumed to be invariant with respect to the relative wage W. The initial relative demand curve D depicts the demand by employers for highly educated workers, relative to less-educated workers. This demand is a decreasing function of W.

Equilibrium within the labour market is achieved when the relative demand is equal to the relative supply, producing relative employment E* and relative wage W*. In Taiwan, as in the US, rapid educational expansion shifted the relative labour supply curve to the right from S to S'. This, by itself, would have lowered the relative wage ratio to W^0; however, in Taiwan, the relative wage did not fall.[10]

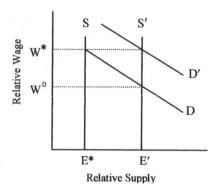

Figure 3.5   Relative supply and demand for educated labour

We can infer from the model that relative wages were maintained by a rightward shift of the relative labour demand curve from D to D'. This shift could have been produced by shifts in product demand in favour of the goods produced by skilled labour, exogenous shifts in the industrial wage structure, or changes in unmeasured labour quality.[11] If the rightward shift of the relative demand curve was of the same magnitude as the rightward shift of the relative supply curve, D' and S' would intersect at the same relative wage as before. This is an alternative way of demonstrating how educational wage differentials in Taiwan could have remained constant even though the labour force became much better educated.

Now, the twist on the theory! The two segments of the labour market have so far been treated as being entirely separate; that is, educated workers have been regarded as belonging to the skilled segment, and less-educated workers to the unskilled segment. However, as we have seen, a large and growing proportion of educated workers came to be employed in the lower-skilled occupations in Taiwan, and even after controlling for education, workers in Taiwan earn different amounts depending on the occupation in which they are employed. Clearly, therefore, both demand-side and supply-side factors come into play in explaining this particular phenomenon. On the demand side, workers with different educational attainments are substitutes for each other, albeit imperfect ones. If the relative wage for workers of a given educational category changes sufficiently, employers will have some incentive to substitute the relatively cheaper labour for labour which has now become relatively expensive. The demand for workers of a certain type would shift as a result of the changes in relative wages, with the amount of this shift being dependent on the elasticity of substitution between different types of labour in different occupations. This theory is developed in the models of Freeman (1980), Katz and Murphy (1992) and Bound and Johnson (1992), amongst others.

At the same time, there is also a supply-side effect. Workers do not invariably supply their labour to a given industry or occupation; rather, if employment and earning opportunities improve sufficiently in one part of the labour market, relative to another, there will be a resultant shift in relative supply. Thus, in Taiwan, many of the highly educated workers found that it was in their best interests to shift to semi-skilled occupations. Although they did not necessarily earn as much in these occupations as they might otherwise have done had they been able to secure employment in skilled occupations, it is precisely because not all of them could find employment in the skilled occupations that they took up employment in the less-skilled ones. In this way, jobs that might previously have been filled by high-school graduates came to be filled instead by college graduates. It may of course be quite feasible that workers in these middle-level occupations would continue to engage in job-search activities whilst in such employment; whether or not it would be in their best interests to do so would depend largely on the monetary and psychic costs of such job searching relative to the perceived benefits (Burdett, 1978).

CONCLUSIONS

In our examination of the Taiwanese labour market, putting the two sides of the market together, we find that it is quite plausible, and indeed perfectly consistent with the models, that the demand for labour increased for every labour category, thereby explaining why wages rose throughout the whole of the economy. Using data from the Manpower Utilization Survey to perform Katz and Murphy's inner-product test, in their attempt to explain Taiwan's changing wage structure, Gindling and Sun (2002) demonstrated that it was clear that changes in relative supply dominated changes in relative demand. These considerations point the way towards the development of an even more comprehensive analytical framework, with a more complete model involving the adaptation of the supply and demand analysis into a cross-classification of educational and occupational groups.

If we were to stick to just two educational groups and two occupational groups, the model would need four segments (skilled/educated, skilled/less-educated, unskilled/educated and unskilled/less-educated) as opposed to two. With three education groups and three occupational groups, as in the empirical work in this chapter, nine segments would be required, since the analysis would involve substitution across categories on the labour demand side, and mobility across occupations on the labour supply side. Adding industries to the analysis would, however, complicate the analysis exponentially. There is no such model at present for Taiwan, or for any other country for that matter; thus, the development of such a model lies at the frontiers of the research profession.

NOTES

1   Comprehensive details of these changes are provided elsewhere in this volume.

2   All figures are in constant (1991) New Taiwan dollars (NT$).

3   Although related, educational level is equivalent to neither ability nor productivity; earnings in the higher-skilled jobs will necessarily be higher in order to attract more capable workers, irrespective of their educational levels.

4   This approach was developed in DeBeyer and Knight (1989).

5   The 'Hours' variable is also included, since the dependent variable is monthly earnings rather than hourly wage.

6   Education is reported in the Manpower Utilization Survey in a small number of categories. Using these categories, we estimate the years of schooling for the potential experience variable as follows: (i) individuals with no education are estimated as having zero years of schooling; (ii) individuals educated to primary school level, or those who were self-taught, are estimated as having six years of schooling; (iii) those educated to junior high school level are estimated as having nine years of schooling; (iv) those educated to high school level (vocational or academic) are estimated as having 12 years of schooling; (v) those educated to junior college are estimated as having 14 years of schooling; and (vi) those educated to university level (or higher) are estimated as having 16(+) years of schooling.

7   It is important to note that occupational attainment functions do not constitute a model of occupational choice. An implicit assumption in this chapter is that workers may not succeed in gaining employment in their preferred occupations. Thus, occupational attainment functions are a means by which we can isolate the effects of education on occupational attainment from the effects of other included variables.

8   Occupational attainment functions were also estimated using potential experience instead of age, with similar results; however, the experience variable was insignificant in the semi-skilled equation.

9   The predicted probabilities are calculated as follows. For each educational level, the data is modified so that all observations are coded as having that particular educational level. Using this modified data, the probabilities of each occupational outcome are then predicted for every observation, with these probabilities then being averaged across the modified dataset in order to generate the predicted probabilities (reported in the table). This process is preferred to that of simply inserting the average values for the age and sex variables into the model, since it avoids the use of fractions, a number form that is never actually observed, in the sex variable.

10 There was a rise in the wage ratio between higher-educated and lower-educated workers in the US, which explains why our diagram differs slightly from that of Bound and Johnson (1992).

11 Any change in the demand for highly educated labour relative to less-educated labour brought about by changes in relative wages is a movement along the relative demand curve, not a shift of this curve.

REFERENCES

Bound, J., D.A. Jaeger and R.M. Baker (1995), 'Problems with Instrumental Variable Estimation when the Correlation between the Instruments and the Endogenous Explanatory Variable is Weak', *Journal of the American Statistical Association*, **90**(420): 443-50.

Bound, J. and G. Johnson (1992), 'Changes in the Structure of Wages in the 1980s: An Evaluation of Alternative Explanations', *American Economic Review*, **82**(3): 371-92.

Bourguignon, F., M. Fournier and M. Gurgand (1999), 'Distribution, Development and Education: Taiwan, 1979-1994', *Revue d'économie du développement*, **3**: 1-13.

Burdett, K. (1978), 'A Theory of Employee Job Search and Quit Rates', *American Economic Review*, **68**(1): 212-20.

DeBeyer, J. and J.B. Knight (1989), 'The Role of Occupation in the Determination of Wages', *Oxford Economic Papers*, **41**(3): 595-618.

DGBAS (various years), *Manpower Utilization Surveys, 1980-1992*, Taipei: Directorate-General, Budget, Accounting and Statistics.

Fields, G.S. and J.C. O'Hara (1999), 'Changing Income Inequality in Taiwan: A Decomposition Analysis', in T.N. Srinivasan and G. Saxonhouse (eds.) (1999), *Development, Duality and the International Regime: Essays in Honor of Gustav Ranis*, Detroit: University of Michigan Press.

Freeman, R. (1980), 'An Empirical Analysis of the Fixed Coefficient Manpower Requirements Model', *Journal of Human Resources*, **15**(2): 176-99.

Gindling, T.H. and W. Sun (2002), 'Higher Education Planning and the Wages of Workers with Higher Education in Taiwan', *Economics of Education Review*, **21**(April): 153-69

Katz, L. and K.M. Murphy (1992), 'Changing Relative Wages, 1963-1987: Supply and Demand Factors', *Quarterly Journal of Economics*, **107**(1): 35-78.

Staiger, D. and J.H. Stock (1997), 'Instrumental Variables Regression with Weak Instruments', *Econometrica*, **65**(3): 557-86.

Sun, W. and T.H. Gindling (2001), 'Educational Expansion and Earnings Inequality in Taiwan: 1978-1995', *Journal of Social Science and Philosophy*, **8**(12): 597-629.

4 Taiwan's Private Sector Labour Market Prior to 1996

Gary S. Fields

INTRODUCTION

The preceding chapters have already reached some important empirical conclusions with regard to the labour market in Taiwan, and indeed, one of the most noteworthy of these is that virtually full employment was successfully maintained in Taiwan for more than a quarter of a century. It is also very clear that during the course of the island's economic development, considerable improvements have been made in the types of employment available to workers. As a result, real earnings have risen dramatically throughout the entire economy, poverty has fallen sharply and inequality in Taiwan remains the lowest of any country in the world for which current data exists.

The pseudo-cohort analysis (presented in Chapter 2 of this volume) demonstrated that rather than being caused by the mobility of prime-age workers, the inter-sectoral shifts which had occurred in Taiwan were actually brought about more by young workers coming into the labour force and entering into sectors that differed from those that were being vacated by older workers. Some potentially important labour market institutions were also examined in Chapter 2, with one particularly important finding (with regard to institutional factors) being that wages, benefits and working conditions were, on average, much better in the public sector than in the private sector (Chang, 2000). However, many other institutional factors which have been found to be very important in other countries (such as unions, the minimum wage, and so on) are seen as having only a minor role to play in Taiwan (Lee, 1988; Chang, 2000; Chuang and Jiang, 2003).

Analysis of the inter-industry earnings differentials revealed that these differentials were quite small by international standards, and indeed, that earnings were rising at roughly the same rate in every sector of the labour market in Taiwan. Wage differentials in Taiwan's private sector are generally in line with the economy as a whole; quite small by international standards, with real wages rising at very similar rates throughout all of the major private sector industries, whilst also demonstrating similar growth and decline patterns. For example, the agricultural sector in Taiwan is a declining sector of the economy, relative to non-agriculture, whilst within the manufacturing industry, textiles is a declining sector relative to electronics; and yet, the incomes of farm and non-farm households grew at essentially the same rate, as did earnings in both the electronics and textiles sectors. This chapter therefore proposes a labour-market model which provides a good fit with these aspects of the private sector.

We consider three kinds of models: (i) a segmented labour-market model in which the wages in each sector are set by the demand and supply for labour in that sector alone; (ii) a Harris–Todaro-type model with wage dualism/segmentation (Harris and Todaro, 1970); and (iii) an integrated multi-sector labour-market model. This chapter aims to demonstrate why the integrated labour-market model is better suited to the Taiwan case than any of the other models and that this model can help us to gain a better understanding of some of the important aspects of Taiwan's economic development.

What all of these models have in common is that they are judged against specific facts underpinning Taiwan's economic development, some of which are well-known, including the growth of the manufacturing sector vis-à-vis the contraction of the agricultural sector, the transfer of employment from agriculture to manufacturing and the equitable rise in wages throughout the economy. The share of national output accounted for by agriculture fell from 23.6 per cent in 1965 to just 3.7 per cent in 1993, alongside a corresponding fall in the share of total employment accounted for by agriculture, from 46.5 per cent to 11.5 per cent over the same period.[1]

In real terms, labour earnings have been doubling every ten years; however, what has not been explored thus far is the labour earnings growth structure. We therefore proceed with a breakdown of the labour earnings growth structure by economic sector, although, given the available data, the closest that anyone can get to a comparison between labour earnings in the manufacturing and agricultural sectors is a comparison of the per capita disposable incomes of farm and non-farm households. Such a comparison reveals that the incomes of farm households were 70.6 per cent of those of non-farm households in 1964 and 70.8 per cent in 1991, demonstrating that the earnings structure had remained virtually unchanged for over a quarter of a century. However, by 1995, the relative earnings of farm households had increased to 76.2 per cent, and yet, the share of total employment accounted for by the agricultural sector had been in continuous decline. Such a comparison of farm/non-farm households clearly indicates that the employment growth which was going on in the manufacturing sector did not lead to any higher earnings growth within that sector, relative to the agricultural sector.

A parallel conclusion can be reached if we focus instead on the various industries within the manufacturing sector. Figure 4.1 illustrates the growth in earnings vis-à-vis the growth in employment for various manufacturing sectors between 1980 and 1990, the last year for which such information was available at the time when the study upon which this chapter is based was carried out.

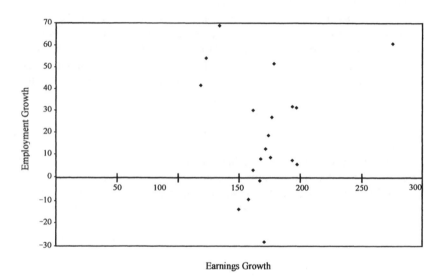

Figure 4.1   Employment growth vs. earnings growth

The lack of correlation is apparent, with the correlation coefficient being statistically insignificant, at +0.1. What is also striking about Figure 4.1 is the way in which the indicators of growth in earnings are closely bunched (with the exception of the petroleum sector which is a publicly regulated monopoly industry) and the way in which those on growth in employment are scattered.

An issue which is of particular interest is a comparison between the electronics sector (a rapidly growing sector) and the textiles sector (a correspondingly rapidly declining sector); we can see that throughout the 1980-1990 period, nominal earnings grew by 89 per cent in the former and 85 per cent in the latter. It is therefore clear that the construction of any labour-market model must be able to fit these data. After considering a number of simple models in this chapter that do not fit the data, a model is subsequently presented that does.

SEGMENTED LABOUR-MARKET MODELS

This section proposes a number of labour-market models, all of which have one feature in common, that employment and wages within any given sector are determined by the labour market conditions within that sector alone. The purpose of this section is to demonstrate that when attempting to explain the Taiwan situation, such models do not work. We begin with the following simple model.

Let each of two sectors (agriculture and manufacturing) have its own labour force, with the inelastic supply of labour being readily available to each sector. Each sector has its own labour demand curve which is derived from the demand for a product. Wages are set in the usual way, by the point of intersection of demand and supply. Now let the manufacturing sector experience an economic boom.

As Figure 4.2 demonstrates, the boom leads to a shift in the labour demand curve for the manufacturing sector, from D_M to D_M', which causes wages in the manufacturing sector to rise from W_M^* to W_M', although manufacturing employment is unaffected. Since the demand and supply curves in the agricultural sector remain unchanged, both employment and wages in that sector are also unaffected.

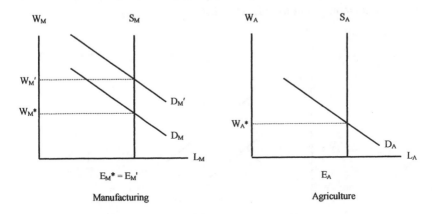

Figure 4.2   A simple segmented labour-market model with inelastic supply of labour

The model predicts that there will be no change in employment for the two sectors, which is clearly at odds with the growth in manufacturing employment and the decline in agricultural employment; for this reason, the model outlined in Figure 4.2 must be rejected. The problem with this model is the assumption that each sector has its own labour supply curve and that such labour supply curves are vertical. This assumption may be relaxed by positing instead a labour supply curve which slopes upwards; that is, a situation in which higher wages in a given sector will induce more workers to offer their labour to that sector. Some of this additional labour will come from outside of the labour force and some from other sectors of the economy.

Let us now consider a simple lagging sector model, which is illustrated with the aid of Figure 4.3. If we assume that the labour supply curve is upward-sloping, we can link the labour market to a standard development economics account of changing agricultural conditions, in an otherwise segmented labour market, armed with the knowledge that agricultural employment in Taiwan has fallen. A story which is commonly recited in Taiwan in an effort to explain this issue is that labour-saving technological changes have occurred within the agricultural sector. Such technological changes induced both a substitution effect (with less labour being required to produce a given level of output) and a scale effect (production is now cheaper, so more labour and more capital will be used to produce greater output). When the technology is labour-saving, the reduction in labour demand as a result of the substitution effect may be assumed to outweigh the increase in labour demand arising as a result of the scale effect. The net effect is therefore a leftward shift in the curve of the derived demand for labour in agriculture from D_A to D_A', along with a resultant fall in agricultural employment from E_A to E_A'.

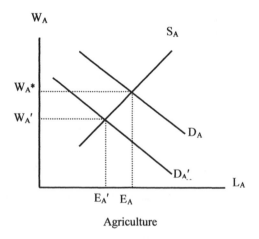

Agriculture

Figure 4.3   A simple lagging sector model

According to this model, some of those workers who are no longer employed in agriculture will, as a result, start crowding into the manufacturing sector, driving manufacturing wages down. Furthermore, since it is very likely that some of those who are no longer employed in agriculture will, as a result, leave the labour force, there will be a consequent fall in the labour force participation rate within the economy as a whole. The problem with this model is that it is inconsistent with a number of known facts about the Taiwanese economy. The model predicts that wages in the agricultural sector, as well as other sectors of the economy, will fall, but as we know, they have risen. The model also predicts that there will be a fall in the labour force participation rate for the economy as a whole, but again, this has risen. Clearly, therefore, this model will not do.

A segmented labour-market model is an alternative model in which the leading sector, manufacturing, also faces an upward-sloping labour supply curve. As shown in Figure 4.4 (left-hand diagram), when a manufacturing boom takes place, the demand curve for labour shifts rightward from D_M to D_M'. Manufacturing wages rise from W_M^* to W_M' and manufacturing employment rises from E_M^* to E_M'.

Some of this increase in manufacturing employment is accounted for by those who are drawn into manufacturing from outside of the labour force, thereby raising the labour force participation rate, whilst others who are drawn in from the agricultural sector account for the remainder of the increase in manufacturing employment. As shown in Figure 4.4 (right-hand diagram), the effect of the move of the latter group is to shift the supply curve for agricultural labour leftward from S_A to S_A'; in consequence, agricultural employment falls from E_A^* to E_A', with a resultant rise in agriculture wages from W_A^* to W_A'.

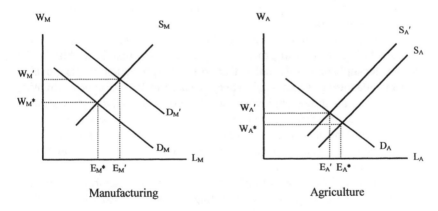

Figure 4.4   A segmented labour-market model with manufacturing as the leading sector and agriculture as the lagging sector

Several of the predictions of this model are actually consistent with the facts; the shift in employment from agriculture to manufacturing, rising wages in both manufacturing and agriculture, and rising labour force participation rates in the economy as a whole. There are, however, some problems. Indeed, what drives the model is that economic growth in manufacturing leads to a rightward shift in the labour demand curve of that sector. Consider now the effects of accelerated economic growth (Figure 4.5).

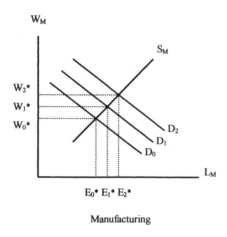

Figure 4.5   Accelerated economic growth in manufacturing in a segmented labour-market model

When there is a shift in the derived labour demand curve from D_0 to D_1, we have a corresponding rise in manufacturing wages from W_0^* to W_1^*, and an increase in manufacturing employment from E_0^* to E_1^*. If the manufacturing sector had grown more rapidly, resulting in a shift in the labour demand curve to D_2 rather than to D_1, the prediction of this model is that manufacturing wages would have increased to W_2^* as opposed to W_1^*, and that manufacturing employment would have increased to E_2^* as opposed to E_1^*. The model therefore predicts that, within any given sector, the growth rate in employment will have a positive correlation with the growth rate in wages within that sector. So what does the data on Taiwan reveal with regard to this issue?

Figure 4.6 plots the growth of employment in manufacturing against the growth rate of real wages in manufacturing for each year from 1980 to 1993. It is clear that there is no statistically significant correlation between the two. This poses a puzzle to which there is an easy, yet profound, answer, since all of the preceding models share a common problem; they assume that the wages in a sector are determined by the supply and demand for labour in that sector alone. This, however, ignores inter-market equilibrium, a feature which this author argues is an essential element of a complete understanding of the labour market conditions in Taiwan.

Inter-market equilibrium refers to the general tendency for wages to equalize across sectors. If the wages for labour of a certain type are not equal across sectors, those workers in the lower-paying sectors will clearly have an incentive to migrate to the higher-paying sectors. In Taiwan, such migration is extremely easy, since information is good, transportation is ubiquitous and manufacturing employment is highly decentralized. Therefore, in such circumstances, any earnings differentials across sectors are likely to be only temporary in nature.

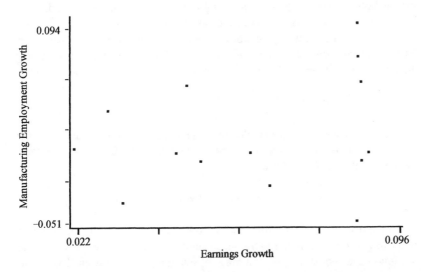

Figure 4.6   Annual unemployment growth rate in manufacturing vs. wage growth rate, 1980-1993

Note: * Correlation coefficient = +0.22; *p* = 0.44.

Inter-market equilibrium therefore brings into play a wage determination process which differs fundamentally from what we have so far examined here. We now find that wages are determined, not by supply and demand within a single sector, as in the preceding models, but rather, by the aggregate supply and demand in all sectors taken together. The models presented thus far have no such inter-market features; let us now consider models that do.

LABOUR MARKET EFFECTS ON ECONOMIC GROWTH

The Effects in a Harris–Todaro-type Model with Wage Dualism

A well-known multi-sector model of labour markets within the developing economies is the model devised by Harris and Todaro (1970), a model which posits an economy with a dualistic labour market. Within this model, manufacturing sector wages are set rigidly above the market-clearing level for institutional reasons; meanwhile, in agriculture, where such wage-setting institutions are absent, wages are determined by supply and demand. Manufacturing is thus the high-wage sector and agriculture the low-wage sector. Unemployment arises in the Harris–Todaro model because the high manufacturing wage encourages migration of job seekers into the locations (presumably urban) where these high-wage jobs can be found. The Harris–Todaro model may be summed up algebraically as follows.

Let W^* denote the wage that would have cleared the labour market; however, for some institutional reason, a wage floor is established in manufacturing, raising the wage there by γ per cent, as compared to what it would otherwise have been:

$$W_M = W^*(1+\gamma). \tag{1}$$

The higher wage reduces employment in the manufacturing sector by γe per cent, where e is the (arc) wage elasticity of manufacturing labour demand, evaluated between W^* and W_M:

$$E_M = E_M (1+\gamma e). \tag{2}$$

In the original variant of the Harris–Todaro model, it was assumed that in order to get jobs within the high-wage sector, workers must physically leave the low-wage sector; i.e., no 'on the job' searching was allowed. Under this assumption, whilst also assuming the probability of all hiring, the wages expected by those seeking manufacturing jobs are:

$$E(W_M) = W_M (E_M / L_M). \tag{3}$$

Those workers who settle for agricultural sector jobs will receive the lower wage W_A. In the Harris–Todaro equilibrium, these two expected wages are equal:

$$W_M (E_M / L_M) = W_A. \tag{4}$$

It is easy to see from Equation (4) that the wage floor in manufacturing causes unemployment; this is for two reasons: (i) because the higher wages in manufacturing lead employers in this sector to demand less labour than they would actually have hired at lower wages; and (ii) because it is in the interest of some workers to risk unemployment whilst trying to secure one of these relatively attractive jobs. It is also easy to see from Equation (4) that the higher the W_M/W_A ratio, the higher the equilibrium rate of unemployment.

So, what would happen in this model if the manufacturing sector were to achieve economic growth? The derived demand for manufacturing labour would increase, thereby raising E_M; however, there would be no need for employers within the manufacturing sector to raise wages, since they could simply hire from the pool of unemployed labour. Hence, W_M would remain unchanged.

If agricultural wages are largely invariant with regard to the movements of workers into and out of that sector (an assumption that has been made in quite a few studies using the Harris–Todaro model), then, in order for the left-hand and right-hand sides of Equation (4) to remain equal, each single unit increase in E_M must lead to an increase in L_M by $W_M/W_A>1$ units. This is the famous conclusion reached by Harris and Todaro; that an increase in manufacturing employment actually increases unemployment as a whole because of the induced migration into those locations where the manufacturing jobs are to be found.

The preceding conclusion is logically correct, but doubts remain with regard to its relevance for Taiwan; firstly, because Taiwan had no significant unemployment problem during the period under examination, whereas the Harris–Todaro model does incorporate unemployment, and secondly, because the model predicts that manufacturing wages will not change in response to economic growth, essentially because they are set institutionally in the first place. As for the agricultural sector, if wages do change at all, it will be largely due to the migration of labour from agriculture into manufacturing leading to an increase in the wages of those left behind in the agricultural sector. The model therefore predicts that if there is any correlation between the growth rate in employment within a given sector and the wage growth rate within that sector, then the correlation will be negative. However, empirically, no such negative correlation is found in Taiwan, since, as already reported, the correlation is positive and statistically insignificant. This is one empirical strike against the Harris–Todaro model; however, other empirical evidence also runs contrary to the model in the Taiwan context.

As demonstrated earlier, the institutional forces that might set wages above market-clearing levels are either absent or ineffectual in Taiwan; indeed, wage dualism is not an important feature of the Taiwanese economy, as is assumed in the Harris–Todaro model. The model states that workers must migrate from the low-paying rural areas in order to seek work in the higher-paying sectors of the economy, but as a result of Taiwan's exceptionally decentralized development profile, this has not proved necessary.

In 1964, about 65 per cent of the income of farm households came from agriculture; however, by 1994, this had fallen to just 20 per cent.[2] This indicates that rural households have been able to diversify into non-farm activities to such an extent that they are able to derive four times as much of their income off the farm as they do on the farm. The model predicts a high rate of unemployment in those areas where manufacturing jobs are found, and indeed, even in an economy with a manufacturing sector as geographically dispersed as it is in Taiwan, manufacturing remains disproportionately urban. Yet, urban unemployment rates were no higher than rural unemployment rates in Taiwan; employment was essentially full in both urban and rural areas.

In sum, then, the empirical evidence also leads to a rejection of the Harris–Todaro model for Taiwan. The question therefore arises as to whether there exists a multi-sector labour-market model capable of fitting these and other facts better, and indeed, there is. Such a model follows.

The Effects on Economic Growth in an Integrated Multi-sector Labour-market Model

Consider an economy in which the standard neoclassical labour market assumptions are fulfilled, and within which the equilibrium forces posited by such models are free to operate. What then are the predicted effects of economic growth on the labour market? The single most important effect is that if the derived demand for labour increases in one sector of the economy it will result in an increase in wages, not only in that sector, but in all sectors of the economy. The analysis is aided by considering Figure 4.7.

Two sectors are assumed so that the effects of greatest interest can be easily plotted. As before, these sectors are referred to as manufacturing (M) and agriculture (A). Within the manufacturing sector, the initial labour demand curve, D_M, is downward-sloping relative to origin 0_M. Similarly, the initial labour demand curve for agriculture, D_A, is downward-sloping relative to origin 0_A. The labour market clears when the same wage is paid in the two sectors and the combined demand for labour by employers in the two sectors is exactly equal to the available labour supply which, for ease of graphical analysis, is assumed for now to be fixed and equal in amount to $O_M O_A$. At the market-clearing wage, denoted in the figure by $W_M{}^* = W_A{}^*$, $O_M E^*$ workers will be employed in manufacturing and the remaining $O_A E^*$ workers will be employed in agriculture. The total demand for labour in the economy, $O_M E^* + O_A E^*$, is equal to the total supply of labour, $O_M O_A$.

Suppose now that economic growth occurs in the manufacturing sector as a result of improved product market conditions. More labour will be demanded in manufacturing, thereby producing a rightward shift in the demand curve for manufacturing labour, from D_M to $D_M{}'$.

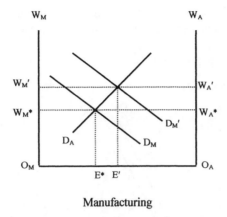

Manufacturing

Figure 4.7   An integrated labour-market model with fixed labour supply and full wage equalization

Following the same logic as in the preceding paragraphs, the model predicts that the labour market will equilibrate at a new, higher wage level in both sectors of the economy ($W_M' = W_A'$) along with some reallocation of the labour force towards the growing manufacturing sector ($E*E'$ workers shifting out of agriculture into manufacturing). This provides us with a key prediction which distinguishes the integrated labour-market model from all other models; i.e., that wages in both manufacturing and agriculture are predicted to grow at the same rate as each other, irrespective of the rate of growth or decline in employment within the different sectors.

The empirical evidence for Taiwan provides strong support for this prediction. As we have seen, the incomes of both farm households and non-farm households have moved in tandem, whilst the earnings of workers in the different sub-sectors of manufacturing have also maintained a similar pace. The way in which the preceding labour-market model explains this is that the wage growth rate within a given sector is determined not by output and employment growth within that sector, but rather by the growth in output and employment within the economy as a whole. These and other implications of the integrated multi-sector labour-market model are detailed further in what follows; although first, we should consider two refinements to the model.

Integrated labour-market model refinements

One criticism of the integrated labour-market model, as formulated above, is that it assumes that the total labour force is fixed in amount at level O_MO_A. This was merely a simplifying assumption which can now be relaxed. Suppose that the aggregate supply of labour to the labour market is an upward-sloping function of wages which, in the integrated labour-market model, is the same across all sectors. Figure 4.8 depicts this aggregate labour supply as curve S.

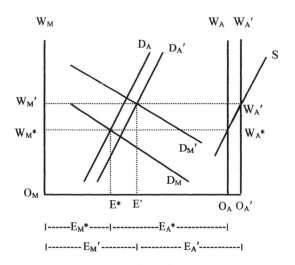

Figure 4.8   An integrated labour-market model with variable labour supply and full wage equalization

As wages rise, so too does the aggregate labour supply, which leads to the origins, O_M and O_A, moving further apart. Sector-specific growth within the manufacturing sector shifts the labour demand curve of that sector from D_M to D_A'. As origin O_A moves, the labour demand curve for agriculture (D_A) moves along with it in order to maintain the same distance as before from the origin.

When the labour market is in equilibrium, the new wage level in the two sectors is W', the total labour force is $O_M O_A'$, and employment levels within the two sectors are $O_M E'$ for manufacturing and $O_A' E'$ for agriculture. As a result, the wages in the two sectors have increased by $W' - W^*$, the labour force has increased by $O_A' - O_A$, manufacturing employment has increased by $E_M' - E_M^*$ and agricultural employment has decreased by $E_A^* - E_A'$. This approach allows for changing labour force participation rates.

An objection which differs somewhat from those of the integrated labour-market model is that wages are not really equal across sectors. It will be demonstrated later in this volume that a large firm/small firm wage differential does exist in Taiwan, and indeed, that it has done so for quite some time. The model can, however, easily be amended to allow for this.

Suppose that the large firm/small firm wage differential is fixed in amount and equal to Δ; if there was no wage differential, then the market would clear at wage W*, as shown in Figure 4.9.

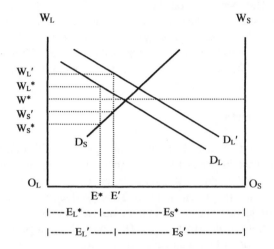

Figure 4.9   An integrated labour-market model with fixed wage differential Δ

Note: * The fixed wage differential $\Delta = W_L^* - W_S^* = W_L' - W_S'$

However, because of the large-firm/small-firm wage differential, wages in the large firms are W_L^*, whilst wages in the small firms are W_S^*. Assuming that everyone is employed at these wages, either in the large-firm sector or the small-firm sector, O_LE^* workers are employed in the large-firm sector and O_SE^* workers are employed in the small-firm sector.

Now, assume that sector-specific economic growth takes place within the large-firm sector. The labour demand curve in that sector shifts rightward from D_L to D_L'. Wages in the two sectors must increase by equal amounts in order to maintain the fixed wage differential Δ. The wage rate increase will be such as to once again equalize the total amount of labour demanded to the total amount of labour supplied. This is depicted in the figure as an increase to W_L' in the large-firm sector and to W_S' in the small-firm sector, with corresponding employment levels, O_LE' and O_SE'.

An important implication of both of these refined models should be noted; economic growth in one sector leads to parallel wage increases in all sectors. This is the essential feature of integrated labour-market models, a feature which accords closely with the empirical facts of the private sector in Taiwan, and which is precisely why such models are proposed here.

INTERPRETATION

The integrated labour-market model presented above is useful in terms of providing an understanding of many of the features of Taiwan's economic development. Here we focus on three of these features; (i) how to interpret Taiwan's remarkable 'productivity growth' (measured in the usual way as growth in real value added per worker); (ii) how to understand the growth and decline of the various economic sectors in the context of overall economic growth; and (iii) how to explain Taiwan's extraordinary improvements in the standard of living for all households.

Productivity Growth

It is already well documented that economic growth in Taiwan was marked by a rapid increase in productivity;[3] however, the integrated labour-market model offers a rather different interpretation of this productivity increase from the usual one. It is often said that rising productivity comes as a result of the push of labour out of agriculture due to the emergence of labour-saving innovations within that sector. However, it is suggested here that a better interpretation of this is that agricultural workers in Taiwan were pulled out of that sector as a result of the growth in employment opportunities elsewhere within the economy, which, in turn, led to a rise in agricultural productivity. The mechanism is as follows.

When the manufacturing sector and other sectors of the Taiwanese economy began to grow, there was a requirement for more labour in the textile mills, electronics factories, and the like. Once the Lewis/Fei-Ranis turning point had been passed and no surplus labour remained, the only way for employers within these growth sectors to obtain additional workers was to pay higher wages in order to attract workers away from the agricultural sector and other relatively stagnant sectors of the economy, as well as from outside of the labour force (Lewis, 1954; Fei and Ranis, 1964). This posed a difficult choice for employers in the stagnating sectors; they either had to pay the higher wages or watch their workers being lured away (in the case of self-employment, they themselves could leave).

For those choosing to pay higher wages, what enabled them to do so was that they were able to complement the remaining workers with additional productivity-augmenting machinery and equipment. There was indeed an increase in productivity, but this was not what caused labour to be released from agriculture. Causality ran in precisely the opposite direction, with the pull of labour out of agriculture leading to a rise in productivity amongst those who remained. Thus, the role of productivity growth in Taiwan's economic development needs to be rethought.

Sectoral Growth and Decline

In planning Taiwan's future development strategy, there are those who contend that steps must be taken to increase the productivity of workers in textiles and agriculture. In the case of textiles, this call is motivated by the desire to keep the sector internationally competitive; in the case of agriculture, the desire is to maintain food security and self-sufficiency in staple products. The integrated labour-market model offers insights into the first of these (but not the second, since it is essentially a national security issue, not an economic one).

Although the decline of Taiwan's textiles sector is sometimes lamented, it should be viewed otherwise. From the point of view of production, the decline of the textiles sector was better than the alternative, because labour was redeployed to those sectors that were willing to pay workers the most, apparently because they could utilize these workers more productively and were willing to pay to do so. Although the textiles sector declined as a result, this was better than the alternative, both for workers in Taiwan and for Taiwan's economy as a whole; it was better for the former textile workers who earned more because their labour was sought elsewhere, and it was better for the economy, because economic growth would have been stifled had textiles not declined, releasing labour and other resources for use elsewhere. A country's development strategies must change in the same way as its comparative advantage does. The faster an economy grows, the faster its comparative advantage changes. This is to be welcomed not spurned.

Improvements in Household Standard of Living

The integrated multi-sector labour-market model helps us to understand how it was that Taiwan's labour market transmitted its extraordinary economic growth to households. Essentially, there were three mechanisms; (i) the economic growth in certain manufacturing and service industries raised the demand for labour and the real labour earnings of the workers who were already in those sectors; (ii) the economic growth in certain manufacturing and service industries enabled more jobs to be created at higher rates of pay for workers who moved into these sectors from the declining sectors of the economy; and (iii) employers in agriculture and other declining sectors raised the wages of the workers who remained in these declining sectors of the economy in order to prevent all of their workers from leaving.

The only important group to be left out was those who, for one reason or another, could not, or would not, move into the growth sectors. The parallel rates of growth in labour earnings across the major economic sectors therefore come as no surprise, since they are exactly what the integrated labour-market model would predict.

NOTES

[1] See CEPD (1994), *Statistical Data Book for the Republic of China*, pp.20 and 42.
[2] Refer to DGBAS (1994), *Report on the Survey of Family Income and Expenditure in the Taiwan Area of the Republic of China*, p.20.
[3] See, for example, the figures presented in CEPD (1994), *Statistical Data Book for the Republic of China*, Tables 2-13, 4-3 and 4-4.

REFERENCES

CEPD (1994, 1995), *Statistical Data Book for the Republic of China, 1994*, Taipei: Council for Economic Planning and Development.

Chang, C.H. (2000), 'A Study of the Labour Market in Taiwan', paper presented at the *Joint Conference on Industrial Policies of the ROC and ROK* sponsored by the Chung-Hua Institution for Economic Research and the Korea Development Institute, Taipei, Taiwan.

Chuang, Y.C. and P.F. Hsu (2004), 'The Employer Size-Wage Differentials in Taiwan', *Small Business Economics*, **23**(4): 285-97.

Chuang, Y.C. and W.C. Jiang (2003), 'The Effects of the Minimum Wage on Youth Employment and Unemployment in Taiwan', paper presented at the *Pacific Rim Conference*, Western Economic Association International held at Academia Sinica, Taipei.

DGBAS (1994), *Report on the Survey of Family Income and Expenditure in the Taiwan Area of the Republic of China, 1994*, Taipei: Directorate-General of Budget, Accounting and Statistics.

Fei, J.C.H. and G. Ranis (1964), *Development of the Labour Surplus Economy*, Homewood, IL: Irwin & Co.

Fei, J.C.H., G. Ranis and S.W.Y. Kuo (1978), 'Growth and Family Distribution of Income by Factor Components', *Quarterly Journal of Economics*, **92**: 17-53.

Fei, J.C.H., G. Ranis and S.W.Y. Kuo (1979), *Growth with Equity: The Taiwan Case*, New York: Oxford University Press.

Fields, G.S. and J.O. Mitchell (1999), 'Changing Income Inequality in Taiwan: A Decomposition Analysis', in G. Saxonhouse and T.N. Srinivasan (eds.), *Development, Duality and the International Economic Regime: Essays in Honor of Gustav Ranis*, Michigan: University of Michigan Press, pp.130-55..

Harris, J. and M. Todaro (1970), 'Migration, Unemployment and Development: A Two-sector Analysis', *American Economic Review*, **40**: 126-42.

Lee, J.S. (1988), 'Stages of Economic Development and Labour Relations: The Case of the ROC', paper presented at the *Conference on Labour and Economic Development* held at the Chung-Hua Institution for Economic Research, Taipei, Taiwan.

Lewis, W.A. (1954), 'Economic Development with Unlimited Supplies of Labour', *The Manchester School*, **22**: 139-91.

PART II

Employment Development in a Regulated and Globalized Labour Market

5 Cyclical Employment Changes in Taiwanese Industry

Christina Y. Liu, Wei-Chiao Huang and Chia-Wei Wang

INTRODUCTION

In any developing country, there are a variety of factors that can lead to changes in the overall employment and unemployment situation within the economy that are, essentially, unavoidable. Unfortunately, such changes will invariably have major impacts on certain industries, often resulting in the total transformation of the employment structure within those industries. The two main factors responsible for such changes in the overall employment structure within an economy are the cyclical fluctuations occurring as a result of the economic business cycle and the resultant transformation of both the structure and composition of certain industries and sectors.

The aim of this chapter is to determine the nature of the changes to the employment structure within the various industries during the business cycles that have occurred in Taiwan over the past three decades. As compared to the job losses induced by the inevitable business cycle, the decline in employment caused by changes to the industrial structure are of a more permanent nature and cannot be effectively addressed by any attempts at temporary stimulation of the economy through fiscal policy adjustments. Therefore, if we hope to deal effectively with this particular problem of structural unemployment, a more appropriate approach would perhaps be to develop fundamental long-term industrial policies incorporating supply-side measures for manpower adjustment, such as job training and 'retrofitting' skills programmes. Clearly, therefore, an extremely important mission for any government is to determine the nature of the changes in employment and unemployment within the economy as a whole, so that appropriate policy action can be quickly taken to deal with any structural unemployment problems that may arise in any particular industry.

A puzzling phenomenon has engulfed the Taiwanese economy over recent years. Following the recent regional slump, in terms of output growth, the Taiwanese economy appears to be well on the way towards full recovery, which is supposed to lead to growth in jobs; however, despite such signs of recovery, the actual employment statistics show no discernible signs of improvement, particularly in the private sector. This 'jobless recovery' was also apparent in the most recent recession and recovery phase of the US economy, prompting analysts to seek explanations and formulate appropriate policy prescriptions. Amongst these, Groshen and Potter (2003) hypothesized that structural change, the permanent shifts occurring in the distribution of workers throughout the economy, was responsible for such a phenomenon. They explained that permanent job losses (gains), resulting from industries going through periods of structural contraction (expansion), were now overlapping and dominating the course of cyclical adjustments, which would normally involve temporary layoffs and recalls. Those workers displaced from the declining industries have found that there is no hope of them returning to their former jobs, since these jobs no longer exist; therefore, there is no possibility of this form of structural unemployment being alleviated by economic recovery.

Groshen and Potter provided convincing evidence to support their 'jobless recovery' hypothesis, using a four-quadrant bubble approach which tracked the direction of job flows, during and after recession, in 70 industries in the category of SIC-2. We adopt a similar approach here, extending the Groshen and Potter (2003) model to our analysis, not only of the most recent episode of recession and recovery (2001-2002), but also of the five earlier business cycles, starting in 1974-1975. Although simple and straightforward, this approach is quite innovative and, as it turns out, is capable of generating an impressive amount of information and insight. Furthermore, to the best of our knowledge (based upon an extensive literature review), no prior study has ever attempted to explore the linkages between changes in the domestic industrial structure and the dynamics of labour utilization within these industries, in similar fashion.[1]

Following Groshen and Potter (2003), our analysis is based upon a graph displaying job changes over a business cycle for industries of different size (as measured by their employment share in the economy); the graph is illustrated in Figure 5.1. As a general rule, the horizontal axis of the graph represents the average job change rates in each industry during the period of recession, whilst the vertical axis measures the corresponding job change rates within the industry during the period of recovery. The position of each industry group in the grid is determined by its respective job growth rates during the recession phase (the value of the x coordinate) and recovery phase (the value of the y coordinate), with the value (x,y), in turn, forming the centre of a circle representing that industry. The size of the circle reflects that industry's share of all jobs in the economy during the recovery period.

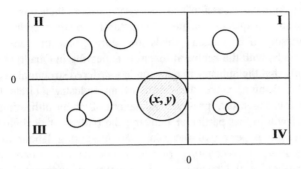

Figure 5.1   A simple illustration of job adjustment over a business cycle, by industry

The algorithm used to calculate the respective job growth rates and employment shares is as follows. Taking year t as the recession year, the job growth rate, $ER_{i,t}$ (which is more likely to be negative growth), is computed as:

$$ER_{i,t} = \frac{E_{i,t} - E_{i,t-1}}{E_{i,t-1}} \quad (= x),$$

whilst the job growth rate during recovery $(ER_{i,\,t+1})$ is:

$$ER_{i,t+1} = \frac{E_{i,t+1} - E_{i,t}}{E_{i,t}} \quad (= y),$$

and the employment share ratio for industry i (S_i) is:

$$S_i = \frac{E_{i,t+1}}{\sum\limits_{i=1}^{83} E_{i,t+1}}$$

where $E_{i,t} \equiv$ the average employment level of industry i at year t, and $i \equiv$ one of the 83 industry groupings in Taiwan.

Based on the benchmark horizontal and vertical axes formed by zero job growth rates in the two periods, the grid illustrated in Figure 5.1 can be partitioned into four quadrants representing the four possible combinations of positive or negative job growth rates at one of two cyclical points. The quadrant in which the centre of the industry circle falls reveals the nature of the different job changes over the business cycle. If the centre of the industry circle falls into Quadrant I, indicating that this industry had positive job gains during both the recession and recovery periods, then this will imply that the industry in question achieved structural growth over the business cycle. Conversely, if an industry sheds jobs during both the recession and recovery periods, with the centre of its circle appearing in Quadrant III, then this will imply that the industry in question has suffered structural decline.

In similar fashion, when the centre of an industry's circle lands in Quadrant II, this suggests a 'pro-cyclical' pattern of labour utilization for that industry, i.e., within that particular industry, the pattern of declining labour utilization during a period of recession and increasing labour utilization during the subsequent recovery period is in line with the contraction and expansion phases of the business cycle. Finally, an industry falling into Quadrant IV is classified as a 'counter-cyclical' industry, since jobs are gained during the period of recession and lost during the recovery period, running against the job flows associated with the phases of the business cycle. The classifications and characteristics of each type of industry are summarized in Figure 5.2, along with the economic meaning of each of the quadrants.

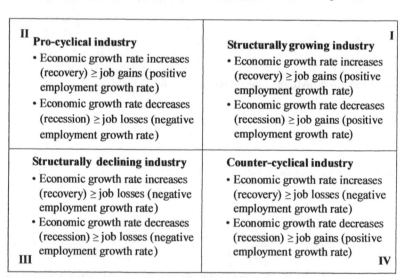

Figure 5.2   Industry classifications and the meaning of each quadrant

A critical factor affecting the resultant shape of the graphical display of job changes over a business cycle is the identification and selection of the cyclical turning points separating the recession and recovery phases of the cycle. Before proceeding further, we need to determine the appropriate time point, t, for the above formulae; that is, we must identify the specific period of time where the economy was in recession, prior to its subsequent recovery. A historical overview of Taiwan's annual economic growth rates since 1967 is therefore provided in Figure 5.3.

From a close examination of this figure, we can identify and select six cyclical phases for the construction and subsequent analysis of the job-change graph, with the three most prominent periods of economic downturn (1974, 1978 to 1982, and 2001) being easily detectable, since they show substantial declines in the growth rates of the economy. The first two phases were of course associated with the two oil crises, whilst the third marked the unprecedented negative growth of the Taiwanese economy. The years 1985, and 1987 to 1990, are selected as the fourth and fifth phases, since they also show relatively clear signs of economic downturn, whilst the sixth phase is the discernible dip in the island's growth rate in 1998. Despite the fact that Taiwan was enjoying steady economic growth throughout the golden era of the 1990s, it was not entirely immune to, although not particularly hard hit by, the negative effects of the Asian financial crisis of 1997. Taken together, these six phases, selected as the main periods of recession in Taiwan's recent history, form the basis of our construction of the horizontal axis of the graph.

As in Groshen and Potter (2003), the recovery period corresponding to each of the six recessions is set as the subsequent year. In other words, if year *t* is the recession year, then year *t*+1 represents the recovery year. Setting a one-year lag may imply, and uniformly impose, an assumption that industries typically rebound about one year after the economy has reached the trough of a business cycle; this is of course a debatable assumption, since it does not take into account the special characteristics or idiosyncrasies of each industry. However, we deliberately adhere to the research design of Groshen and Potter, since our intention is also to observe whether, given only one year, a particular industry can make the necessary adjustments to its labour utilization rate. Thus, by standardizing the recovery time lag to only one year, we can also observe the variations in the pace of recovery across different industries.[2]

This chapter uses Manpower Utilization Survey data compiled by the Directorate-General of Budget, Accounting and Statistics (DGBAS) containing the annual time series of workers employed in each industry.[3] The employment data on the earlier years is incomplete, since it lacks detailed information and classification of the service sector; our analysis does not, therefore, cover the changes in employment within the service sector during the earliest of the cyclical phases (1974-1975). However, our analysis of the employment changes, for both the earlier and later years, naturally focuses on the manufacturing sector, given that this sector represented the predominant component of Taiwan's industrial structure throughout all six phases. Thus, we do not expect the omission of the service sector from our analysis of the first phase to impose any bias on the overall conclusions drawn in this chapter.

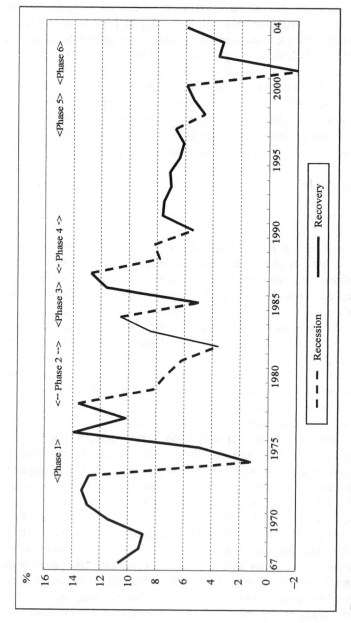

Figure 5.3 Economic growth rates and the six cyclical phases of recession and recovery in Taiwan, 1967–2004

Source: DGBAS (2004a).

112

SIX CYCLICAL PHASES OF CROSS-INDUSTRY EMPLOYMENT CHANGES [4]

There have been many factors involved in the overall transformation of Taiwan's employment structure over the past few decades, one of the most prominent of these being the increasing integration of the island into the global economy, largely as a result of the inexorable march of globalization and the 'magnetic pull' resulting from the rapid emergence of the mainland China economy. In addition to these factors, Taiwan's enviable position was also being undermined by the general rise in labour costs and the various restrictions arising from increasing environmental awareness, both of which were major contributory factors to the gradual disappearance of the comparative advantage previously enjoyed by Taiwanese manufacturing firms engaging in domestic production in Taiwan. It was not long, therefore, before many of the island's labour- and capital-intensive industries turned, one after the other, to investment in lower-cost countries throughout the region (with the notable and major exceptions of the consumer electronics and electronic components industries). As a result, there was a steady decline in the overall employment share of these industries within Taiwan, starting with the textiles and clothing industries in the early stages, and moving on to the metallic and plastics industries later on.

From 1970 to the mid-1980s (Phases 1 and 2), there were no major changes in the labour utilization rates for both the manufacturing and service sectors, and despite the gradual increase in the demand for labour in the service sector from the mid-1970s onwards, within the economy as a whole, even up to 1986, the overall share of employment accounted for by this sector remained relatively small (at about 33 per cent). At that time, the manufacturing sector continued to be the main contributor to the livelihoods of most of the island's citizens, comprising largely of the capital-intensive and energy-intensive industries, such as textiles, plastics and metals. However, following the two oil crises of the 1970s, there was a growing recognition, within many of Taiwan's industries, of the need to make structural adjustments, which in turn led to changes in the island's employment structure, as evidenced by the declining importance of the textiles industry within the labour market at the expense of the growing importance of the electronics industry. The rise in the importance of the latter was largely attributable to the Taiwanese government, which had recognized that the island's high-tech and high value-added industries were the key to the island's long-term sustainable development. As a result, the government introduced a series of policy measures aimed at supporting the development of these industries, including the establishment of the Hsinchu Science-based Industrial Park for agglomeration in the integrated circuit (IC), information technology (IT) and automation equipment industries.

The mid-1980s heralded the start of the major structural changes in the overall employment situation in Taiwan, and within many specific industries, with such changes being evidenced by the gradual decline in the share of employment accounted for by the manufacturing sector and the steady rise in the share of employment accounted for by the service sector. By the late 1990s, the service sector had caught up with the manufacturing sector, in terms of its overall share of employment, and subsequently overtook manufacturing to become the primary employment generator within the economy in 2000.

In 2001, Taiwan was deeply entrenched in the global recession which had initially been caused by the bursting of the economic bubble within the information technology (IT) and 'dotcom' industries throughout the world; however, this situation had also been exacerbated, again on a global scale, by the political upheaval triggered in the US by the devastating '911' terrorist attacks on 11 September 2001. Whilst being dragged down by these global recessionary effects, the Taiwanese economy was further devastated by a number of internal natural disasters, dampening the prospects of any solid turnaround. Thus, the island's economy sank to an unprecedented –2.2 per cent growth rate, the first negative growth rate ever experienced in the island's recorded history of economic development. Thereafter, despite all the indicators suggesting that the economy was moving towards a recovery, there was no sign of relief within the labour market, with the unemployment rate reaching a historical high of 5.17 per cent in 2002.

Figure 5.4 reveals that the 2001 recession had brought about significant structural changes to the labour market in Taiwan, with those industries that proved to be resilient to the recession (in terms of hiring), being predominantly the service-oriented industries, such as the retail and wholesale trade, passenger, freight and storage services, banking services and the healthcare and medical insurance industries, whilst in the labour-intensive manufacturing sector, including industries such as textiles and clothing, many companies were shedding large numbers of jobs within their domestic labour force and relocating to mainland China to take advantage of the availability of cheap labour there. In the absence of these industries, the island was left with the electronics-related industries as the sole remaining element of the manufacturing sector that still maintained a healthy employment share in Taiwan.

Despite the steady rise in the employment share of the service sector as a whole, there were actually ups and downs, over time, in the various service industries, largely dependent on the different time periods, circumstances and policy measures adopted by the government. The slump in the housing market, for example, a market which had previously been extremely vibrant during the period of the housing boom of the mid-1980s, had enormous impacts, not only directly upon the construction and real estate and leasing industries, but also on employment levels within many other housing-related industries, whereas the telecommunications industries had experienced outstanding employment growth in the 1990s as a direct result of the dramatic rise of these industries following the deregulation of the telecommunications laws and the opening up of the telecommunications market.

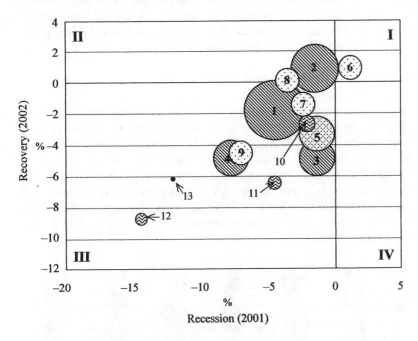

Figure 5.4   Job adjustments during the periods of recession and recovery in the early 2000s, by industry

Note: * The numbers refer to the following industries: 1: manufacturing; 2: wholesale and retail trade; 3: banking and insurance; 4: construction; 5: transportation, storage and communications; 6: medical treatment; 7: professional, scientific and technological services; 8: other services; 9: hotels and restaurants; 10: power industry; 11: culture, sports and leisure; 12: real estate; and 13: mining.

Finally, the employment structure in the finance and insurance industry in Taiwan was being shaped not only by economic conditions, but also by government policies following the opening up of the financial markets in the 1990s, which explains why the employment shares of the credit unions, credit cooperatives and credit departments of the Farmers' and Fishermen's Associations continued to shrink, as a direct consequence of the financial reform measures introduced by the government.

SIX CYCLICAL PHASES OF INDUSTRY-SPECIFIC EMPLOYMENT CHANGES

In the preceding section, we analysed, from a cross-sectional perspective, the employment structure across all industries during the six cyclical turning points. This section complements that analysis by examining, from a time-series perspective, the changes in employment structure for specific industries over the same six cyclical phases (for the purpose of brevity, not all industries are illustrated within the figures shown).

Overview of the Employment Trends in All Industries

In order to observe the overall trend in Taiwan's industrial employment structure, we begin by grouping those industries which experienced structural employment changes into the first and third quadrants, and those industries which experienced cyclical employment changes into the second and fourth quadrants.[5] We then use the results from the preceding section to calculate the employment ratios of these two categories of industries during each cyclical phase. As can be seen from Figure 5.5, there is a clear downward trend in cyclical employment, from 40 per cent of the changes in labour market employment in the early 1970s to only about 15 per cent in 2002.

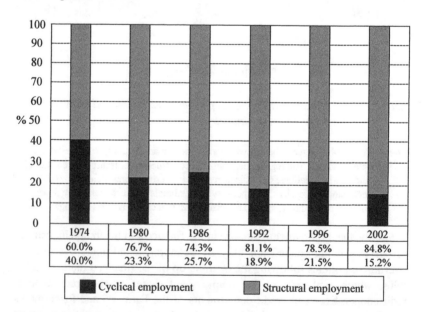

	1974	1980	1986	1992	1996	2002
Structural employment	60.0%	76.7%	74.3%	81.1%	78.5%	84.8%
Cyclical employment	40.0%	23.3%	25.7%	18.9%	21.5%	15.2%

■ Cyclical employment   ▦ Structural employment

Figure 5.5   Changes in structural and cyclical employment ratios in Taiwan, 1974-2002

In contrast, changes in structural employment were now demonstrating a clear rising trend, with the overall employment changes in the labour market in Taiwan at that time coming mainly as a result of structural adjustments; indeed, by 2002, such structural adjustments were accounting for about 85 per cent of all changes in the overall make up of employment on the island. Nevertheless, the inexorable rise in the importance of structural changes in the labour market was not a phenomenon which could be described as being unique to Taiwan. As far back as the mid-1970s, even in the US labour market, only about 50 per cent of all employment could be considered to be structural employment, whereas, it is now well documented that almost 80 per cent of all adjustments in employment in the US labour market are structural in nature (Figura, 2003; Groshen and Potter, 2003).

In the following subsections, we undertake a comprehensive examination of the changes in the structure of employment over the six cyclical phases within the traditional manufacturing, high-tech manufacturing and service sectors. Whilst we continue to use the same four-quadrant bubble approach in this section, with these quadrants relating to the overall job gains and job losses during the recession and recovery phases, in contrast to the figures illustrated in the previous section the circles in the diagrams in this section now represent labour adjustments for a particular industry during the different cyclical phases. In order to simplify the observation of the ways in which labour utilization rates have changed within a particular industry (changes which can be observed by the way in which the industry has moved around the four quadrants), as well as the observation of the ways in which the labour absorption capacities of the various industries have evolved during the different phases, a number is contained within each circle, with this number (between 1 and 6) representing the appropriate cyclical phase, as identified in the previous section, whilst a percentage figure alongside each of the circles represents the employment share of that industry within the economy during that particular phase.

Employment Changes in the Manufacturing Sector

As Figure 5.6 shows, Taiwan's manufacturing sector, as a whole, had continued to thrive throughout the 1970s and 1980s (Phases 2 and 3 located in the first quadrant); however, as a result of the decline in the late 1980s and the early 1990s (Phase 4), this sector subsequently moved into Quadrant III. Although there was something of a recovery during the late 1990s (Phase 5), this sector was, nevertheless, destined to become deeply entrenched in the structurally declining quadrant. The declining size of the circles over time also indicates the gradual shrinkage of the labour market share accounted for by the manufacturing sector.[6]

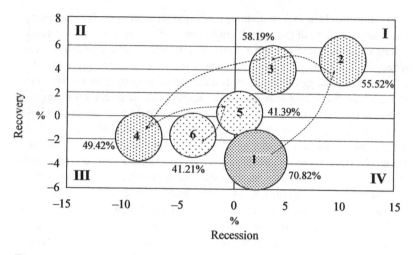

Figure 5.6   Employment changes in the manufacturing sector, 1974-2002

Employment Changes in the Traditional Manufacturing Industries

The food and beverages industry and the textiles and clothing industry were selected to represent the traditional manufacturing industries that were largely responsible for the livelihoods of the island's citizens.[7] Figure 5.7 shows that these industries were mainly located in the structurally declining (third) quadrant throughout most of the six phases.

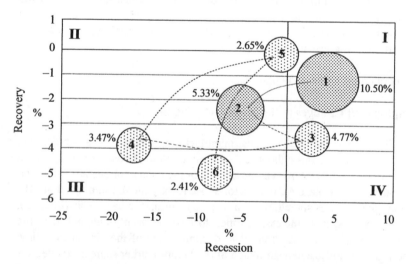

Figure 5.7   Employment changes in the textiles and clothing industry, 1974-2002

Figure 5.7 also shows that the employment share of the textiles and clothing industry was shrinking continuously, thereby revealing the gradual reduction in the labour absorption capacity of this industry. The food and beverages industry (not shown here) also exhibited a similar trend to that of the textiles and clothing industry.

We further analyse four industries, referred to as the capital-intensive industries, which represent an additional category within the traditional manufacturing industries. As Figure 5.8 shows, prior to 2001, the employment situation within the chemical materials industry had a rather optimistic outlook, maintaining positive job growth rates and providing a positive contribution to the labour market through continual provision of new jobs, even during periods of severe economic downturn. It was only in the final recessionary period that employment adjustment in this particular industry departed from the earlier patterns, with the circle eventually falling into the third quadrant and showing no signs of any rebound. However, it remains to be seen whether this is any indication that the chemical materials industry has become a structurally declining industry.[8]

The chronological pattern for the job adjustment circles in other capital-intensive industries within the traditional manufacturing sector, including the plastic products, metals and transport equipment industries (none of which are shown here) were similar to the pattern revealed by the chemical materials industry, with only slight variations during the last period, when the latter industry fell into the third quadrant.

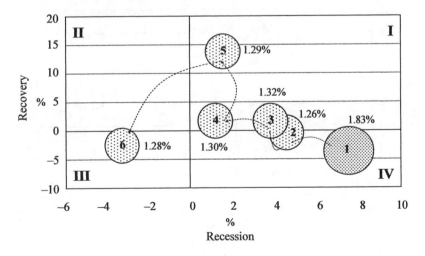

Figure 5.8   Employment changes in the chemical materials industry, 1974-2002

Within the traditional manufacturing sector, the food and beverages and textiles and clothing industries, those industries which had previously been regarded as the main providers of the livelihoods of many of the island's citizens, had quickly begun to lose their overall level of importance within the labour market in the 1970s, moving fairly early into the structurally declining quadrant. Although many of the capital-intensive, traditional manufacturing industries were able to maintain more or less steady employment shares for much of the time, some of these industries (such as the plastic products industry) also began to experience structural changes in the 1980s, whilst the decline in certain others (such as the chemical materials industry) began in the late 1990s. By the last of the recessionary phases (Phase 6), all of the traditional manufacturing industries had become deeply entrenched in the third quadrant and were therefore characterized as structurally declining industries.

Employment Changes in the High-tech Manufacturing Industries

Figure 5.9 illustrates the pattern of employment changes over time for the mechanical equipment and maintenance industry, which became a structurally growing industry in the early 1980s and was to be found in the first quadrant for the next two decades. It was not until the 2001 recession that this industry was pushed, for the first time, into the structurally declining quadrant.

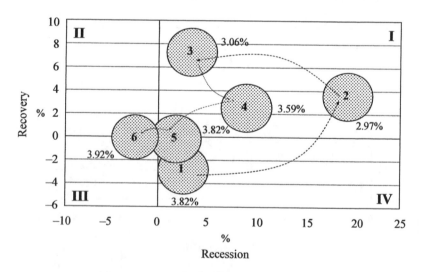

Figure 5.9   Employment changes in the mechanical equipment and maintenance industry, 1974-2002

Although the circle corresponding to Phase 6 in Figure 5.9 shows that the hiring rate within this industry was still slightly negative in 2002 (which is typical of the phenomenon of a 'jobless recovery'), the job growth rate had nevertheless rebounded to about 4.0 per cent by 2003. Thus, unlike the chemical materials industry, in which there was no improvement in jobs (despite having a longer period of time to recover from the recession), the high-tech industries, such as the mechanical equipment and maintenance industry, have demonstrated the ability to resume growth in jobs if given a longer recovery period.

Figure 5.10 provides an illustration of the pattern of employment changes within the electronic components industry, demonstrating steady growth in this industry over time, through the expanding size of the circles; indeed, this industry now accounts for more than 5.0 per cent of the overall share of employment within the economy, thereby clearly signalling its growing importance as a net contributor to employment within the Taiwanese labour market. Furthermore, with the exception of the late 1980s (Phase 4), a period when this industry moved fairly close to entry into the third quadrant, for most of the time the hiring levels within this industry were not dampened by recession; and indeed, thanks partly to the government's supportive industrial policy, labour usage continued to expand within the electronic components industry, even during periods of dramatic economic downturn.

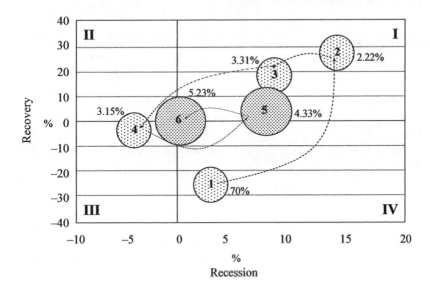

Figure 5.10   Employment changes in the electronic components industry, 1974-2002

A profile of employment changes in another high-tech manufacturing industry, the consumer electronics industry, was also constructed (although not shown here).[9] This industry encompasses a wide variety of consumer products such as personal computers, liquid crystal display (LCD) units, digital video discs (DVDs), mobile phones, and so on, and was thought to be a mainstream manufacturing industry within the labour market; indeed, its employment share has hovered around 2.0 to 4.0 per cent. Although the circle did move around the cyclical quadrants, it nevertheless remained within the third (pro-cyclical) quadrant for most of the time. This type of employment adjustment pattern is consistent with the notion that the demand for consumer-oriented products, and hence the derived demand for labour to produce such products, is highly cyclical.

Employment Changes in the Service Sector

For the service sector as a whole, as illustrated in Figure 5.11, almost all the job adjustment circles (with the exception of 6, which represents the latest recessionary phase) are found in the structurally growing first quadrant. The increasing size of the circles, representing the increase in overall employment share, also corroborates our findings in the previous section of a shift, over time, from the manufacturing sector to the service sector as the major contributor to employment in Taiwan.

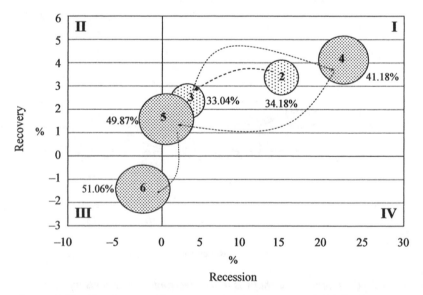

Figure 5.11   Employment changes in the service sector, 1979-2002

Although the service sector hiring rate declined to –1.5 per cent in 2002 (as shown in Figure 5.11), if we use 2003 employment data, the circle does rebound into positive territory; thus, despite being hard hit by the recession of 2001, the service sector as a whole demonstrates that it is capable of regaining its labour absorption capacity if given a longer period of recovery.

If we examine the pattern of employment changes in certain representative service industries over time, as Figure 5.12 shows, the wholesale and retail trade industry, which has the highest employment ratio within the service sector, continually gained employment shares, demonstrating its ability to withstand economic downturns and maintain positive job growth rates. Indeed, it only fell into the structurally declining third quadrant during the last recessionary period when the hiring rate dipped to an unprecedented low of –1.6 per cent, but soon rebounded to positive job growth in the following year.

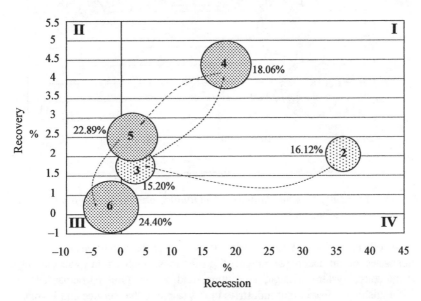

Figure 5.12 Employment changes in the wholesale and retail trade industry, 1979-2005

As Figure 5.13 shows, the circle representing the finance and insurance industry has grown steadily since 1979, signifying its growing importance in the labour market. Despite falling into the third quadrant in the most recent recession, this does not necessarily imply that it is becoming a structurally declining industry. As discussed in the preceding section on labour adjustments across industries in Phase 6, the domestic banks, which account for the largest employment share in this industry, were able to withstand the negative impacts of the last recession, maintaining their position in the structurally growing first quadrant. As also noted earlier, there has been a decline in the employment share of the credit departments of the Farmers' and Fishermen's Associations as a result of government action to resolve their non-performing loan problems; thus, the movement of this industry into the third quadrant during Phase 6 may simply reflect the impact of the financial reform policies, as opposed to any intrinsic structural change within this industry.

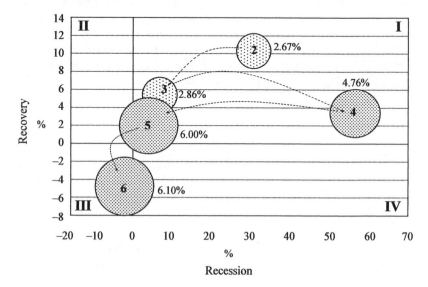

Figure 5.13   Employment changes in the finance and insurance industry,
            1979-2002

Another service industry worthy of note is professional services, which comprises of an extensive range of professions, such as law, accounting, architecture, systems design, consulting, and so on. One particular aspect distinguishing it from other industries in this sector is that service employment usually requires higher qualifications, such as those required by a CPA or an architect, special skills for computer system consultants or engineers, or a legal practice licence. As Figure 5.14 shows, there was a substantial increase in hiring in this industry in the 1980s (from Phase 3 to 4), which reached its climax in the late 1990s. Although falling into the third quadrant in the latest cyclical phase, which seemed to indicate that it had reached a bottleneck and that hiring had stalled, the circle is, nevertheless, not too far away from its origin. In fact, if allowed a slightly longer recovery period, this industry can substantially improve its hiring record, since its employment growth rate rebounded to a robust 3.57 per cent in 2003. Clearly, as an economy advances further, there will be a rise in the demand for professional service personnel; therefore, the outlook for jobs in this industry should remain promising in the long run, and could be a suitable target for employment promotion policies.

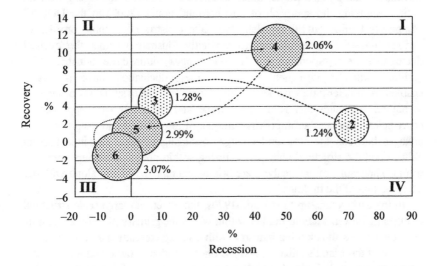

Figure 5.14   Employment changes in the professional services industry, 1979-2002

Summary of Industry-specific Employment Changes in Taiwan

In general, the findings of this section are consistent with those of the preceding section, in that the service sector has gained importance within the labour market (in terms of employment share) whilst the manufacturing sector (in particular, the traditional manufacturing industries) has continued to decline. In addition, whilst most industries in the manufacturing sector gradually moved into the structurally declining third quadrant from the 1980s onwards (and subsequently became locked into that quadrant), most industries within the service sector have shown no such tendency, with the economic downturns having no real adverse impacts on their hiring levels. Despite the fact that some service industries experienced unprecedented negative job growth rates during the last recession, if given a longer recovery period (usually two years) they are able to resume their hiring growth; this is also the case for the high-tech manufacturing industries. Thus, if the formulation of industrial policy in the future is to incorporate employment-generation (or unemployment-reduction) objectives, these two industries could be considered as job promotion targets.

CONCLUSIONS

The overall aim of this chapter has been to determine, from a perspective of changing industrial structure, the nature of the job gains and losses within Taiwanese industry as a whole, which occurred as a result of the recent business cycles. Applying the approach of Groshen and Potter (2003) to the DGBAS Manpower Utilization Survey data, we have constructed graphic profiles of various industries in an attempt to explicitly illustrate whether the cyclical fluctuations were responsible for the job changes within these industries. The findings from our subsequent analysis of these fluctuations have essentially enabled us to determine whether the job flows were either structural or cyclical in nature. Although this is a very simple and straightforward approach, it nevertheless generates an impressive amount of information and insight into the linkages between the structural changes occurring in particular industries in Taiwan and the structural changes occurring within domestic employment as a whole. The results of our analysis are briefly summarized below, along with our interpretation of the findings.

In the early years, up to the mid-1970s, there were no large-scale structural changes in Taiwan's labour market within which the primary players at that time were the textiles and clothing industry (with a strong correlation to the livelihood of many of the island's citizens) and the plastics industry (an extremely energy-intensive industry), both of which were the mainstays of the manufacturing sector. Nevertheless, after being hit by the two oil crises, these industries began to lose their firm hold on the job market. Meanwhile, the support and promotion of government policies led to the emergence of the electronics-related industries within the manufacturing sector, which quickly began to gain a position of growing importance within the labour market as a whole.

The effects of the structural changes which subsequently occurred in both the manufacturing and service sectors, from the mid-1980s onwards, were soon reflected in the changes in their relative positions, with regard to their overall share of employment within the economy. Indeed, Taiwan is now generally characterized as a largely service-oriented economy, since those industries making up the service sector have essentially managed to surpass those industries making up the manufacturing sector (in terms of overall employment shares). Nevertheless, there have also been shifts in the relative positions of the employment shares of different types of industries within the service sector.

One of the reasons behind this overall change in the employment structure was the changes taking place in the macroeconomic conditions; featuring prominently amongst these was the rise of the construction and real estate and leasing industries in response to the housing boom of the mid-1980s. A further reason, however, was the effects of government policies, some of which gave rise to the telecommunications and finance industries in the mid-1990s.

The structural changes occurring within the labour market, which have been described throughout this chapter, were brought about by a variety of factors including Taiwan's increasing integration into the world economy and the 'magnetic pull' effect arising from the huge market and investment opportunities that have emerged in mainland China. In terms of the impact upon their domestically produced products, the inevitable result was that many of the industries within the manufacturing sector lost the comparative advantage that they had previously enjoyed. In response to such a major change, they had no alternative but to relocate elsewhere, which in turn led to the continuous and steady decline in labour utilization rates in Taiwan within many of these industries. What's more, there were no discernible signs, or expectations, of any real turnaround in their hiring levels, even during those periods when the economy was already in a recovery or expansion phase.[10]

In the past, when formulating its industrial policies, the government in Taiwan tended to consider only the effects of, and the relationships between, industrial development and macroeconomic competitiveness, whilst often overlooking any possible policy implications on other corresponding segments of the labour market. Consequently, the targeted industries did turn out to be quite successful, in terms of both revenue and profit-making, but paradoxically, such successes have been of no help whatsoever in bringing down the unemployment rate in the economy as a whole. Taking one recent industrial development policy as an example, the government placed considerable effort into the promotion of the high-tech electronics industry, an industry which, by its very nature, demands highly educated scientists and engineers, but is nevertheless limited in its capacity to absorb general labour. As a result, the policy was very effective in boosting economic growth (output), but appears to have been totally ineffective with regard to alleviating the growing problem of unemployment within the Taiwanese economy.

There is, therefore, a clear need to reassess the adequacy and merits of such lopsided and uncoordinated policies, particularly those that favour employment generation in certain industries, at the cost of job losses in other industries. Despite the concentration of effort on the high-tech industries in Taiwan, according to the findings from the graphs presented in this chapter, there are a number of structurally growing industries, most of which are located in the service sector, and these may well be worthy of promotion and subsequent support by the government. In particular, the government may wish to consider promoting the finance and insurance, retail and wholesale trade, healthcare and professional service industries, since all of these industries clearly have further growth potential, carry a promise of greater labour absorption, and, unsurprisingly, are all to be found in the first quadrant of our graphs.

NOTES

[1] Refer to Chapter 2 of Huang et al. (2005), pp.6-32, for a detailed literature review.

[2] A sensitivity analysis was also undertaken, which involved alternating the recovery time lag immediately following the trough of the recession, from one to two years. The results using the two-year time lag were essentially the same as those obtained under the one-year time lag specification, with the exception that some industries, such as the communications and electronics industries, demonstrated a stronger rebound, in terms of hiring levels, when allowing for the extra one-year period of recovery. For details, see Chapter 2 of Huang et al. (2005); pp.6-32.

[3] The Manpower Utilization Surveys (for various years) carried out by the Directorate-General of Budget, Accounting and Statistics, Executive Yuan are available at website: http://www.dgbas.gov.tw/earning/ht456.asp.

[4] Many of our original graphs, with complete contents, are not included in this chapter so as avoid taking up excessive space; however, all of the graphs, and complete details, are available either upon request or can examined by referring to Chapter 2 of Huang et al. (2005); pp.6-32.

[5] Refer to Figure 5.2 and the discussion in the second section of this chapter, 'Six Cyclical Phases of Cross-industry Employment Changes', for the reasoning behind our method of industrial classification.

[6] From further examination of Phase 6, in which a two-year time lag recovery period was allowed, there was some slight improvement (to 0.12 per cent) in the job growth rate within the manufacturing industry (from the –1.76 per cent negative growth rate when allowing only a one-year time lag).

[7] A total of 83 industries were studied; see Huang et al. (2005) for a discussion on the selection criteria for the representative industries within the analysis, as well as the industrial classification groupings.

[8] When extending the recovery period for Phase 6, from one to two years, that is, when using the 2003 employment data as opposed to the 2002 data, there is still no sign of improvement in hiring levels for this industry, with virtually identical job loss rates being found for both the one-year and two-year post-recessionary periods.

[9] Those figures referred to within the text, but not shown here (for the purpose of space-saving), are available either upon request or can be examined by referring to Chapter 2 of Huang et al. (2005); pp.6-32.

[10] A direct survey of over 1,000 randomly elected firms provides corroborating evidence on the findings of structural changes within the respective industries. See Huang et al. (2005) for the detailed survey results.

REFERENCES

Aghion, P. and P. Howitt (1994), 'Growth and Unemployment', *Review of Economic Studies*, **61**: 477-94.

Audretsch, D.B. and R. Thurik (eds.) (1999), *Innovation, Industry Evolution and Employment*, Cambridge MA: Cambridge University Press.

Balakrishnan, R. and C. Michelacci (2001), 'Unemployment Dynamics across OECD Countries', *European Economic Review*, **45**: 135-65.

DGBAS (various years), *Manpower Utilization Surveys*, Taipei: Directorate-General of Budget, Accounting and Statistics.

DGBAS (2004a), *Statistical Abstract of National Income*, Taipei: Directorate-General of Budget, Accounting and Statistics.

DGBAS (2004b), *Earnings and Productivity Statistical Tables: Timetables*, Taipei: Directorate-General of Budget, Accounting and Statistics.

European Parliament (2002), *Impact of Technological and Structural Change on Employment: Prospective Analysis 2020*, project report submitted to the Committee on Employment and Social Affairs of the European Parliament.

Figura, A. (2003), 'Is Reallocation Related to the Cycle? – A Look at Permanent and Temporary Job Flows', *Finance and Economics Discussion Series*, Federal Reserve Bank of New York: Board of Governors of the Federal Reserve System.

Groshen, E. and S. Potter, (2003), 'Has Structural Change Contributed to a Jobless Recovery?', *Current Issues in Economics and Finance*, **9**(8): 124-36.

Huang, W.C., C.Y. Liu and C.W. Wang (2005), *A Study of Taiwan's Structural Unemployment Problem from the Perspective of Industrial Changes*, final report submitted to the Council for Economic Planning and Development, Executive Yuan, Taiwan.

Huang, W.C. and I. Mazare (2004), 'Labour Market Dynamics in a Transition Economy: Evidence from Rumania', *Working Paper*, Michigan: Western Michigan University, Department of Economics.

Liu, C.Y., W.C. Huang and C.W. Wang (2004), 'Examining Employment Changes in Taiwan's Industries over Business Cycles', *Working Paper*, Michigan: Western Michigan University.

Loungani, P. and B. Trehan (1997), 'Explaining Unemployment: Sectoral vs. Aggregate Shocks', *Federal Reserve Bank of San Francisco Economic Review*, San Francisco, CA: Federal Reserve Bank, pp.3-15.

Mortensen, D.T. and C.A. Pissarides (1998), 'Technological Progress, Job Creation and Job Destruction', *Review of Economic Dynamics*, **1**: 733-53.

Pianta, M. and M. Vivarelli (2000), *Unemployment, Structural Change and Globalization*, Geneva: International Labour Organization.

6 Industrial Change and Structural Unemployment in Taiwan

Chung-Chi Wu

INTRODUCTION

Taiwan is recognized for the achievement of many successes during the early stages of its protracted period of industrialization; indeed, prominent amongst these was the steady fall in overall unemployment across the entire island. Although the unemployment rate did gradually begin to rise as a result of the second oil crisis in 1979, climbing from 1.25 per cent in 1980 to 2.91 per cent in 1985, it nevertheless once again resumed its steady fall in the aftermath of the crisis, eventually reaching a low of 1.45 per cent in 1993. Clearly, therefore, in its heyday, Taiwan was very close to achieving full employment; nevertheless, following those early years of development, the island was never again destined to see such a low unemployment rate. Although the rise in unemployment on the island began quite slowly, rising to just 1.79 by 1995, it subsequently shot up to 2.60 per cent in 1996, then rose again to 2.72 per cent in 1997 before falling back slightly to 2.69 per cent in 1981 and then once again resuming its upward climb to 2.92 per cent in 1999 and 2.99 per cent in 2000. The island's unemployment rate saw a dramatic rise in 2001, to 4.57 per cent, with the rate eventually reaching an all-time high of 5.17 per cent in 2002. The years 1996, 2001 and 2002 are thus characterized by marked increases in unemployment in Taiwan; hence, the purpose of this chapter is to investigate the major causes of the rapid rise in unemployment in Taiwan over that particular period.

The Transformation of the Taiwanese Economy

By the 1980s, with a falling birth rate, wider availability of education and the withdrawal from the workforce of large numbers of older manual workers, Taiwan was gradually transforming itself from an economy in which labour was plentiful, although capital was in short supply, into an economy in which a surplus of capital was accompanied by a shortage of labour. The excess capital led to a fall in the share of GDP held by fixed assets, thereby contributing to the emergence of a significant trade surplus and the accumulation of huge foreign exchange reserves. Since mainland China and many of the Southeast Asian countries were going through rapid industrialization at that time, they were consequently beginning to compete in the international markets. As a result, since Taiwan had relied on importing production equipment and raw materials from Japan, followed by export of the finished products to the US, it soon found that it was losing its comparative advantage. In terms of trading with Japan and the US, Taiwanese labour was less competitive than that of China or Southeast Asia, whilst in terms of trading with China or Southeast Asia, Taiwan could not compete with the technology and marketing capabilities of the US or Japan. With this weakening of its comparative advantage on two fronts, Taiwan's traditional industries soon began to experience a rapid decline in their export performance; thus, by 1988, the annul production of Taiwan's manufacturing sector had begun to shrink.

The rapid economic growth which the island had experienced had led to steadily rising income levels which thus enabled households to accumulate high levels of savings; as a result, the consumer spending rate increased from 47.65 per cent in 1988 to 63.56 per cent by 2001, with the share of total consumer spending on services rising steadily from 37.34 per cent in 1988 to 50.38 per cent by 2001. There was also an increase in spending on healthcare over the same period, from 5.21 per cent to 9.03 per cent, whilst spending on cultural activities, education and entertainment rose from 15.23 per cent to 19.50 per cent. At the same time, there was also a steady increase in the demand for financial planning and money management services. All of this helped to stimulate the growth of those service industries oriented towards the domestic market. Thus, the 1990s heralded the gradual transformation of Taiwan's industrial structure, with services replacing manufacturing as the heart of the economy.

The Bubble Economy and the Construction Industry

As Taiwan continued to build up its significant trade surplus, foreign exchange holdings rose by US$55.8 billion over the period from 1980 to 1987. The money supply, which had stood at NT$751.5 billion in 1985, had risen by 108.7 per cent by 1987; however, rather than pushing prices up, the excess money flowed into real estate investment, with nominal real estate values rising rapidly at that time. This real estate bubble pushed up the net worth of business enterprises, leading to the stock market mania of 1987 and 1988. Figure 6.1 illustrates the stock price and consumer price trends between 1984 and 2002, whilst Figure 6.2 provides an illustration of the real fixed capital formation in Taiwan between 1980 and 2001.

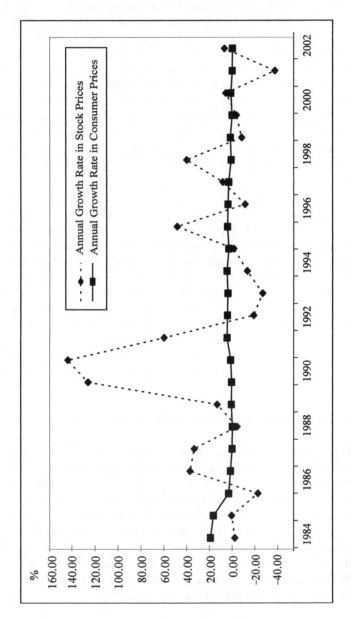

%

Figure 6.1   Stock price and consumer price trends in Taiwan, 1984-2002

Source: Taiwan Economic Forum (2003).

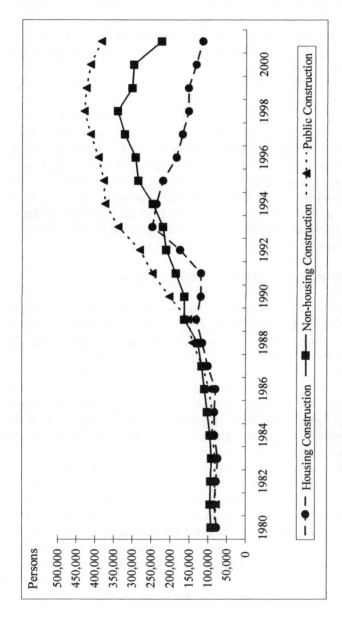

Figure 6.2   Real fixed capital formation in Taiwan, 1980-2001

Source: DGBAS (2002).

133

As rising real estate prices fuelled a construction industry boom, it was not until 1993 – when high vacancy rates began to force house prices down leading to a reduction in personal wealth – that the era of the bubble economy ended. The number of housing construction projects began to fall from 1996 onwards, as did the number of people employed within the construction industry. By 1998, non-residential building projects were also in decline; as a result, in the following year, the availability of work within public construction projects also began to wither, largely as a result of delays in the implementation of existing projects.

The downturn in the construction industry affected both the quarrying industry and the building materials industry. With property values falling, financial institutions found that the value of the collateral they held was far lower than the value of the loans, and with borrowers having become increasingly unwilling, or unable, to repay their debts, the banks saw their non-performing loan ratios soaring. This problem was particularly severe within Taiwan's many 'grassroots' financial institutions. At the same time, households which had seen their wealth declining became more reluctant to spend. As a result, the impact of the downturn in the real estate market was not limited to higher unemployment in the construction industry, since it had also led to reduced growth within the economy as a whole.

The Transformation of Taiwan's Manufacturing Sector

By 1985, faced with the growing competition from mainland China and Southeast Asia (both of which were able to offer low labour costs), the annual production volume of Taiwan's traditional industries, which had always accounted for the lion's share of Taiwanese exports, had begun to fall. With the considerable acceleration of this decline in 1988, the knock-on effects were soon felt by the petrochemicals industry. Throughout the 1990s, only the electronics and precision machinery industries continued to grow. As a result, these two industries replaced Taiwan's traditional industries as the backbone of the industrial structure and Taiwan's manufacturing sector was metamorphosing into a 'high-tech' sector.

The number of people employed within the manufacturing sector had begun to fall in the late 1980s, from 2,821,000 in 1987 to 2,422,000 in 1996. Although this sector did start to rise again in 1997, climbing to 2,655,000 by 2000, it nevertheless fell back again to 2,587,000 in 2001. Analysis of the total number of people employed within the manufacturing sector vis-à-vis the unemployment rate for the country as a whole reveals a tendency for a rise in the number of workers within the manufacturing sector when unemployment was rising, and a decline in employment in that sector when unemployment was falling (Figures 6.3 and 6.4).

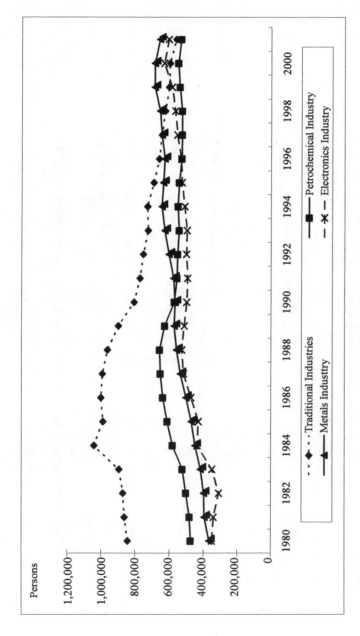

Figure 6.3   Total employment in the manufacturing sector, by industry, 1980-2001

Source: DGBAS (various years).

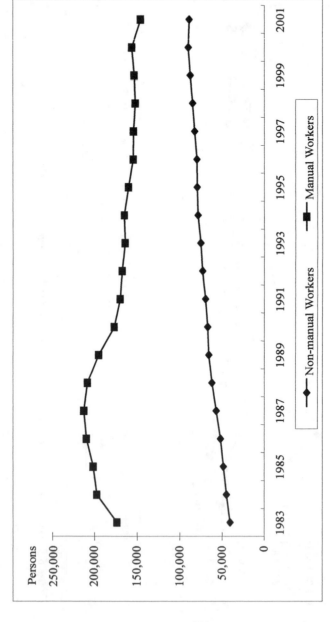

Figure 6.4   Total employment in the manufacturing sector, by type of workers, 1983-2001

Source: DGBAS (various years).

It is worth noting that between 1988 and 1996, the fall in the total number of manufacturing sector employees had been largely confined to production line workers, with the total number of higher-level employees continuing to rise throughout this period. However, from 2001 onwards, the fall in the total number of employees began to affect both groups of workers. The data seems to indicate that, with the changes in the international business environment and Taiwanese industry investing overseas and reorienting itself towards a focus on hi-tech manufacturing, the demand for unskilled and semi-skilled labour fell, whilst the demand for 'high-end' labour increased. This did not, however, lead to any significant increase in unemployment, since the reduction in the number of (mainly female) unskilled and semi-skilled employees within the traditional industries was offset by the growth of the service sector. The risk of unemployment was nevertheless greater for male workers, since they found it more difficult to change careers.

Between 1988 and 1995, there was an overall decline of 353,000 in the total number of persons employed within the manufacturing sector, from 2,802,000 to 2,449,000; however, the number of people working within the construction industry rose from 577,000 to 1,003,000 during the same period, an increase of 426,000. It would therefore appear that the construction industry was able to absorb many of the excess workers who had previously been employed within the manufacturing industries. Alongside the absorption of unemployed male workers by the construction industry, since the service sector was also absorbing many of the surplus unskilled and semi-skilled female workers from the manufacturing sector, as opposed to a rise in unemployment, there was actually a fall in the total number of unemployed workers.

Whilst the total number of persons employed within the construction industry fell from 1,003,000 in 1995 to 746,000 in 2001, the total number of unskilled and semi-skilled workers employed within the manufacturing industry remained roughly the same. It would therefore appear that the transfer of production to overseas bases by Taiwanese manufacturing firms was not the main cause of the rise in unemployment which Taiwan was experiencing at that time. A more significant factor seems to have been the decline in the total number of people working within the construction industry, as noted above.

Service Sector Growth

Whilst both agriculture and manufacturing declined, the service sector mushroomed. In 1988, 47.13 per cent of all employed persons in the service sector (excluding government employees) were employed in commerce, 31.14 per cent were working in the social services and personal services industry, 13.04 per cent were in the transportation, warehousing and communications industry, 4.94 per cent were working in the finance, insurance and real estate industry, and 3.75 per cent were employed in industrial and commercial services. The figures for all paid employees were 50.16 per cent in commerce, 17.30 per cent in social and personal services, 16.46 per cent in transportation, warehousing and communications, 10.87 per cent in finance, insurance and real estate, and 5.21 per cent in industrial and commercial services. The social and personal services industry thus had a particularly high proportion of self-employed persons at that time.

By 2001, the distribution of employed persons within the service sector was 43.55 per cent in commerce, 31.58 per cent in social and personal services, 9.78 per cent in transportation, warehousing and communications, 8.25 per cent in finance, insurance and real estate, and 6.83 per cent in industrial and commercial services. The distribution of all paid employees was 49.64 per cent in commerce, 14.85 per cent in social and personal services, 11.65 per cent in transportation, warehousing and communications, 15.88 per cent in finance, insurance and real estate, and 7.98 per cent in industrial and commercial services (Figure 6.5).

During the period from 1988, when shrinkage in the manufacturing sector had first begun to occur, to 1995, at which time unemployment had yet to become a serious problem, the number of persons employed within the manufacturing sector fell by an average of 0.81 per cent per annum, whilst the number of persons employed within the service sector rose by an average of 7.18 per cent per annum. New jobs were therefore being created within the service sector at quite a rapid pace (Table 6.1). However, having grown steadily since 1983, by 1996 the number of persons gaining employment within the service sector was beginning to level off; clearly, therefore, the service sector was becoming less able to absorb the surplus labour created by the decline in agricultural and manufacturing employment. Between 1996 and 2001, the total number of paid employees within the manufacturing sector was falling at an average rate of 0.74 per cent per annum, whereas the total number of paid employees within the service sector was increasing at an annual rate of just 0.06 per cent; employment opportunities were therefore becoming much scarcer.

As unemployment had become quite severe over this period, of the three service industries which came under the category of 'commerce' (i.e., wholesaling, retailing and restaurant operations), only the retailing industry saw some slight growth in the number of paid employees, whilst the two other industries saw a fall in the total number of paid employees. Of the eleven individual service industries making up the transportation, warehousing and communications sector, only the rail transport, tour bus operations, post and telecommunications industries experienced some growth in the total number of paid employees.

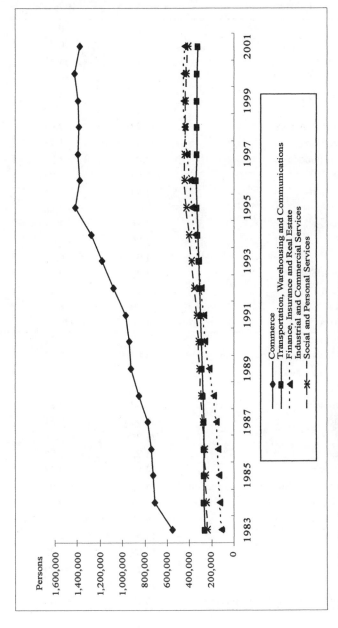

Figure 6.5 Total employment in the service sector, 1983-2001

Source: DGBAS (various years).

139

Table 6.1   Average increase in total employment, by different industries, 1988-2001

Unit: %

Industry	1988-1995	1996-2001
Wholesaling	10.32	−0.10
Retailing	6.93	0.76
Department Stores	6.28	−1.57
International Trade	6.21	−0.53
Restaurant Industry	5.89	−1.74
Rail Transport	−2.29	1.79
Road Passenger Transport	−5.23	−2.92
Tour Bus Operations	5.42	1.43
Road Transport (Goods)	4.87	−1.29
Marine Transport	−0.82	−1.82
Harbour Operations	−1.44	−2.54
Air Transport	7.65	−0.88
Logistics Services	5.56	−3.14
Warehousing	3.79	−1.64
Postal	1.58	0.12
Telecommunications	1.46	4.91
Domestic Banks	7.51	5.39
Foreign Banks	9.39	6.14
Investment Trusts	−1.20	−10.40
Credit Cooperatives	5.75	−14.17
Farmers' and Fishermen's Associations	3.84	−0.02
Other Financial Institutions	13.72	5.04
Life Insurance	13.21	4.61
Property Insurance	10.37	−0.37
Other Insurance	−39.96	7.54
Real Estate	21.24	−3.16
Legal Services	1.72	−1.06
Accounting Services	14.68	5.73
Civil Engineering and Building Construction	24.42	0.04
Product Distribution	1.13	0.14
Consulting Services	4.55	−0.66
Information Services	17.51	7.85
Advertising	12.52	0.25
Design	9.20	−1.99
Leasing	13.25	−4.31
Other Industrial and Commercial Services	15.98	−1.81

Table 6.1   (Contd.)

Unit: %

Industry	1988-1995	1996-2001
Environmental Services	9.85	−2.31
Medical and Healthcare	6.14	2.44
Publishing	6.79	−3.16
Entertainment	8.88	−7.72
Broadcasting	5.39	−0.55
Hotel Operations	3.27	−2.21
Car and Motorcycle Repair	6.25	−3.71
Dyeing	3.49	−0.48
Hairdressing and Skin Care	1.89	−5.92
Other Services	1.60	−2.44
Mining and Quarrying	−7.37	−8.38
Manufacturing	−1.64	−0.08
Water, Electricity and Gas	0.21	0.20
Construction	3.98	−3.98
Commerce	7.53	−0.06
Transport, Warehousing and Communication	2.59	−0.80
Finance and Insurance	10.89	2.23
Industrial and Commercial Services	12.47	0.80
Social and Personal Services	5.48	−1.35
Industrial Sector	−0.81	−0.74
Service Sector	7.18	0.06
Private Employment	2.25	1.86
All Employed Persons	2.04	1.36

Source: DGBAS (various years).

Although the number of paid employees within the finance, insurance and real estate sector grew by an average of 2.23 per cent per annum, declines were experienced in the number of paid employees in the investment trust, credit cooperative and farmers' and fishermen's associations, along with the casualty insurance and real estate industries. Within the industrial and commercial services industry, of the ten individual industries, only the accounting services industry and information services industry saw any significant growth in employment. The situation within the social and personal services industry was much the same; of the ten individual industries, the medical and healthcare industry was the only one to achieve positive growth in the total number of paid employees, with an average growth rate of 2.44 per cent per annum.

From 1997 onwards, the situation in Taiwan was no longer merely one of economic transformation; it was in fact a serious downturn which would ultimately have major impacts upon almost every industry. The only industries which have demonstrated any significant vitality over the last few years are the financial management, information services, healthcare and beauty industries; every other industry has seen some gradual weakening. Within the financial sector, the bursting of the bubble economy had a particularly severe impact on the 'grassroots' financial institutions (i.e., the financial arms of the farmers' and fishermen's associations).

THE PATTERN OF UNEMPLOYMENT IN TAIWAN

Unemployment Trends

The ratio of male employees to female employees has remained very high within the agricultural and manufacturing sectors, both of which have experienced an overall decline in employment. By contrast, the service sector, which has a relatively high proportion of female employees, has seen some expansion in employment. A comparison between Taiwan's employment structure and the previous occupations of the unemployed shows that whilst the number of persons employed within the agricultural sector fell by 22.88 per cent, from 918,000 to 708,000; as regards those who had previously worked in agriculture, the unemployment density was 0.21 for men and 0.09 for women (with an overall average of 0.19). What this shows is that whilst large numbers of workers are no longer employed within agriculture, a rather high proportion of these workers have withdrawn from the workforce altogether, with only a relatively small proportion of these former agricultural workers going on to look for work in other sectors. The reduction in the total number of employees within the agricultural sector has thus had only a limited impact on the overall unemployment situation in Taiwan.

Of the total number of unemployed workers within the population, 48.40 per cent had previously worked within the manufacturing sector and 49.93 per cent had previously been employed within the service sector. The manufacturing sector accounted for 37.33 per cent of all employed persons, as compared to the 53.99 per cent of all employed persons accounted for by the service sector. There was, therefore, a discernibly greater propensity for unemployment within the manufacturing sector than within the service sector. The unemployment density within the manufacturing sector was 1.30 (48.40 per cent/37.33 per cent), whereas it was only 0.92 (49.93 per cent/53.99 per cent) within the service sector. In terms of the unemployment density, within the manufacturing sector this was 1.33 for men, as compared to 1.04 for women, whilst within the service sector, the figures were 0.88 for men and 1.07 for women. It is therefore clear that within the manufacturing sector, the risk of unemployment was higher for men, whereas within the service sector, the risk of unemployment was higher for women.

Within the manufacturing sector as a whole, although the mining and quarrying industry and the water, electricity and gas industry accounted for a high proportion of male employees, these industries also accounted for very small shares of the total number of employed persons in Taiwan. Within the mining and quarrying industry in particular, the share of the unemployed was actually higher than its share of employed persons, with an unemployment density of 1.78 for men, 1.80 for women and 1.92 for a combination of both men and women; this industry therefore represents a very high unemployment industry, as compared to the water, electricity and gas industry, which, with an unemployment density of just 0.32, is a very low unemployment industry.

The overall unemployment density within the manufacturing industry was 1.01, with the density for each gender being more or less the same at 1.01 for men and 0.99 for women. Manufacturing industry employees were mostly male and the industry was about average in terms of its propensity for unemployment. The construction industry was also a largely male-dominated industry, with an overall unemployment density of 2.19 (2.02 for men and 1.62 for women), making this a high unemployment industry. Overall, the risk of unemployment was highest within the mining and quarrying industry and the construction industry. There was a moderate risk of unemployment within the manufacturing industry and a low risk of unemployment within the water, electricity and gas industry.

Within the service sector, the social and personal services industry and the commerce, finance, insurance, real estate and industrial and commercial services industries had higher proportions of female employees than male employees, whilst the transportation, warehousing and communications industry had a higher proportion of male employees. The unemployment densities for these industries were 1.06 for the commerce industry, 0.97 for the finance, insurance, real estate industry and the industrial and commercial services industry, 0.84 for the transportation, warehousing and communications industry and 0.77 for the social and personal services industry. All of these industries demonstrate a moderate propensity for unemployment. Overall, the risk of unemployment in the service sector was higher for women than for men.

The agricultural sector and the water, electricity and gas industry can thus be regarded as having a low risk of unemployment, whilst the mining and quarrying and construction industries are both industries with a high risk of unemployment. The manufacturing industry, the commerce industry, the transportation, warehousing and communications industry, the finance, insurance, real estate and industrial and commercial services industry, and the social and personal services industry each display a moderate risk of unemployment. Irrespective of the overall level of unemployment risk within the industry in question, men have a higher risk of unemployment than women within the manufacturing and agricultural sectors, and women have a higher risk of unemployment than men within the service sector.

Table 6.2   Employed, unemployed and laid-off workers, by industry, 1996-2001

Unit: %

Industry	Male	Female	Total
Employed Workers			
Industrial sector	42.43	29.66	37.33
Service sector	47.24	64.15	53.99
Agriculture, forestry and fisheries	10.33	6.19	8.68
Mining and quarrying	0.18	0.05	0.13
Manufacturing	28.20	26.92	27.69
Water, electricity and gas	0.54	0.14	0.38
Construction	13.51	2.55	9.14
Commerce	19.36	26.88	22.37
Transportation, warehousing and communications	6.83	2.54	5.12
Finance, insurance, real estate and industrial and commercial services	5.89	8.93	7.11
Social and personal services	15.15	25.80	19.40
Unemployed Workers			
Industrial sector	56.40	30.89	48.40
Service sector	41.43	68.54	49.93
Agriculture, forestry and fisheries	2.17	0.57	1.67
Mining and quarrying	0.32	0.09	0.25
Manufacturing	28.63	26.59	27.99
Water, electricity and gas	0.15	0.06	0.12
Construction	27.30	4.15	20.04
Commerce	19.53	32.88	23.72
Transportation, warehousing and communications	5.30	2.06	4.28
Finance, insurance, real estate and industrial and commercial services	5.84	9.26	6.91
Social and personal services	10.76	24.34	15.02

Table 6.2   (Contd.)

Unit: %

Industry	Male	Female	Total
Laid-off Workers			
Industrial sector	66.35	41.93	60.68
Service sector	31.37	57.11	37.34
Agriculture, forestry and fisheries	2.28	0.96	1.98
Mining and quarrying	0.44	0.15	0.37
Manufacturing	26.96	33.80	28.55
Water, electricity and gas	0.10	0.12	0.10
Construction	38.85	7.85	31.66
Commerce	16.03	28.51	18.93
Transportation, warehousing and communications	4.10	2.13	3.64
Finance, insurance, real estate and industrial and commercial services	3.78	7.04	4.54
Social and personal services	7.45	19.43	10.23

Source: DGBAS (1995-2002).

From 1996 onwards, not only was there a continual rise in the overall unemployment rate, but there was also an alarming and steady rise in the average length of time that people were remaining unemployed following the loss of their previous jobs. The overall period of unemployment grew from an average of 20.45 weeks in 1996 to 30.26 weeks in 2002, and although higher levels of education were associated with shorter periods of unemployment, generally, the older the worker, the longer the period of unemployment.

Between 1996 and 2002, the overall unemployment density in Taiwan was 0.39 for professionals, 0.58 for elected representatives and managers, 0.93 for technical and specialist personnel, 0.97 for clerical workers, 0.96 for service and sales personnel, 0.19 for persons employed within agriculture, forestry and fisheries, and 1.39 for production workers. Although the propensity for unemployment amongst those employed within the agriculture, forestry and fisheries industry was relatively low, broadly speaking, the higher unemployment rates were invariably seen in the lower-skilled occupations; in contrast, the higher-skilled occupations tended to have lower unemployment rates.

With the exceptions of production workers, elected representatives and managers, where unemployment tended to be higher amongst men than amongst women, for all other occupational types (professionals, technical and specialist personnel, clerical workers and sales and service personnel) unemployment was higher for women than for men (Table 6.3). Within the categories of technical and specialist personnel, clerical workers and sales and service personnel, unemployment was higher amongst female workers than the average for the workforce as a whole.

Table 6.3   Employed, unemployed and laid-off workers, by occupations, 1996-2001

Occupations	Male	Female	Total
Employed Workers			
Professionals	5.15	8.00	6.29
Elected representatives and managers	6.42	1.59	4.49
Technical and specialist personnel	16.22	16.35	16.27
Clerical workers	4.13	20.12	10.51
Sales and service personnel	13.53	23.65	17.57
Agriculture, forestry and fisheries	10.18	6.08	8.54
Production workers	44.38	24.23	36.34
Unemployed Workers			
Professionals	1.51	4.62	2.48
Elected representatives and managers	3.50	0.62	2.60
Technical and specialist personnel	14.33	16.91	15.14
Clerical workers	3.49	24.90	10.20
Sales and service personnel	11.84	28.07	16.93
Agriculture, forestry and fisheries	2.11	0.52	1.61
Production workers	62.60	24.31	50.59
Laid-off Workers			
Professionals	1.01	4.26	1.77
Elected representatives and managers	4.38	0.80	3.54
Technical and specialist personnel	10.74	13.39	11.36
Clerical workers	2.43	18.65	6.20
Sales and service personnel	10.03	24.34	13.35
Agriculture, forestry and fisheries	2.19	0.93	1.90
Production workers	69.21	37.64	61.88

Source: DGBAS (1995-2002).

Involuntary Unemployment

If we examine closely the underlying causes of unemployment in Taiwan over recent years, as the figures in Table 6.4 indicate, there has been a steady rise in the share of unemployment resulting from factory closures, business contraction and the termination of seasonal or temporary work. Thus, a major unemployment trend in Taiwan over the past few years has been the increase in involuntary unemployment.

Between the years 1996 and 2001, amongst all unemployed people in Taiwan, the share of those who were involuntarily unemployed – excluding those who were looking for their first job – stood at 54.44 per cent (60.92 per cent for men and 40.28 per cent for women). The share of involuntary unemployment within the manufacturing sector was 68.26 per cent (71.66 per cent for men and 54.66 per cent for women), whilst within the service sector, the figure was 40.72 per cent (46.12 per cent for men and 23.57 per cent for women). It is clear, therefore, that the involuntary unemployment rate was higher within the manufacturing sector than within the service sector, and also that involuntary unemployment was far higher amongst men than amongst women.

As regards the involuntary unemployment situation within the different industries, those industries with the highest rates of unemployment due to termination of temporary or seasonal work were the construction industry and the mining and quarrying industry. Although the overall rate of unemployment within the agricultural sector was low, a rather high proportion of this unemployment was due to business contraction or the termination of temporary or seasonal work. In contrast, the rate of involuntary unemployment within the service sector was quite low; the proportion of all workers within the service sector leaving their jobs voluntarily was high, reflecting a much higher level of labour mobility within this sector as a whole (Figure 6.6).

In terms of occupational categories, the one with the highest rate of involuntary unemployment was elected representatives and managers, followed by production workers, those who had previously worked in the agriculture, forestry and fisheries industry, sales and service personnel, technical and specialist personnel, clerical workers and professionals, in that order (Figure 6.7). Factory closure was the main cause of unemployment amongst managers, which suggests that those managers who are used to traditional ways of doing business may well find it difficult to adjust after being laid off. Since it was less likely for higher-skilled workers to become unemployed as a result of business contraction, this suggests that higher skills either translate into a lower risk of unemployment or greater ability to more rapidly obtain a new job after becoming unemployed.

Table 6.4 Causes of unemployment, 1995-2002

Year	Causes of Unemployment (%)					Unemployment Total (persons)
	New Labour Force Entrants	Business Contraction	Dissatisfaction with Employer	End of Temporary or Seasonal Work	Other	
1995	28.48	17.58	40.00	6.06	8.48	165,000
1996	23.14	28.10	32.64	7.85	8.68	242,000
1997	22.27	27.73	32.81	8.59	8.59	256,000
1998	22.96	28.02	31.91	9.73	7.78	257,000
1999	21.20	32.16	30.39	9.19	7.42	283,000
2000	19.80	30.72	32.42	9.90	6.83	293,000
2001	16.67	45.78	19.56	11.56	6.22	450,000
2002	15.73	48.16	21.36	9.13	5.83	515,000

Sources: DGBAS (1995-2002).

148

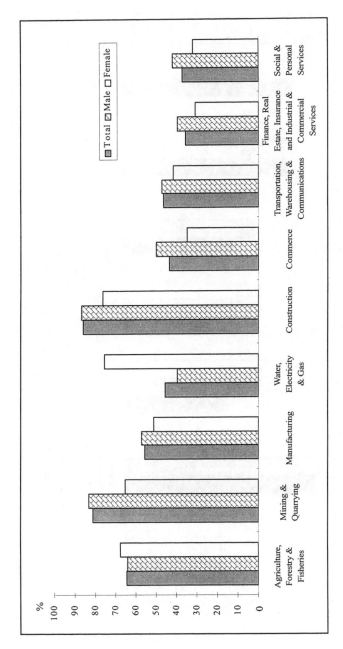

Figure 6.6 Comparison of involuntary unemployment rates, by industry, 2001

Source: DGBAS (1995-2002).

149

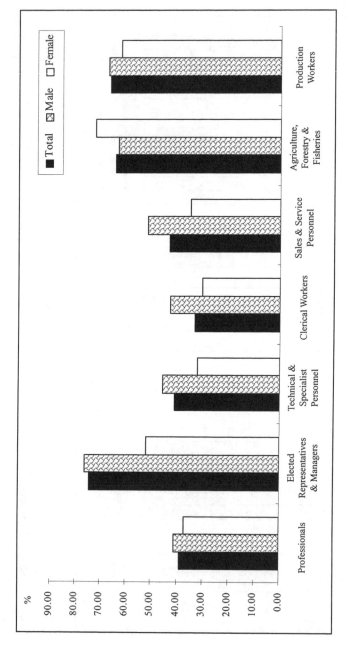

Figure 6.7   Comparison of involuntary unemployment rates, by occupation, 2001

Source: DGBAS (1995-2002).

150

INDUSTRY CHARACTERISTICS

The manufacturing and agricultural sectors in Taiwan have been steadily shrinking since 1988, whilst the service sector has experienced significant expansion. Any particular industry within which the share of female workers divided by the share of all female workers throughout industry as a whole is greater than 1 may be classified as an industry with a high density of female workers; conversely, any industry within which the figure is less than 1 may be classified as an industry with a high density of male workers. As Table 6.5 shows, most of the industries in Taiwan's declining agricultural and manufacturing sectors have a high density of male workers; this is particularly so in the mining and quarrying industry and the construction industry. Within the continually expanding service sector, industries tend to have a high density of female workers, with the one exception of the male-dominated transportation, warehousing and communications industry.

Table 6.5 Density of female workers, by industry, 1995-2001

Industry	Density of Female Workers
Agriculture	0.7228
Mining and Quarrying	0.4345
Manufacturing	0.9912
Water, Electricity and Gas	0.3531
Construction	0.2904
Commerce	1.2031
Transport, Warehousing and Communications	0.4991
Finance, Insurance and Real Estate	1.3261
Industrial and Commercial Services	1.1449
Service Sector	1.4039
Public Administration	0.9114
Manufacturing Sector	0.8073
Service Sector	1.1824

Source: DGBAS (1995-2002).

Any industry where the share of all workers educated to senior high school (or senior vocational school) level, or above, divided by the share of all workers within all industries educated to senior high school (or senior vocational school) level, or above, is greater than 1, may be classified as an industry with a high density of high-level labour; any industry where the figure is less than 1 may be classified as an industry with a high density of low-level labour.

As Table 6.6 shows, within the shrinking agricultural and industrial sectors, most industries have a high density of low-level labour (with the exception of the water, electricity and gas industry, which is largely state-owned). The agriculture, forestry and fisheries industry and the construction industry also have particularly high densities of low-level labour. By contrast, all of the industries in the expanding service sector have a high density of high-level labour.

Table 6.6   Density of higher-educated workers, by industry, 1995-2001

Industry	Density of Workers with High School Education or Above
Agriculture	0.2794
Mining and Quarrying	0.8026
Manufacturing	0.9595
Water, Electricity and Gas	1.4354
Construction	0.6694
Commerce	1.0438
Transport, Warehousing and Communications	1.0870
Finance, Insurance and Real Estate	1.5870
Industrial and Commercial Services	1.5095
Social and Personal Services	1.2194
Public Administration	1.5628
Industrial Sector	0.8912
Service Sector	1.1992

Source: DGBAS (1995-2002).

Taiwan's agricultural and manufacturing sectors have experienced declining production value and worsening employment structures since 1988; by contrast, the employment structure of the service sector has improved. Most of the industries in the declining sectors are industries with a high density of male workers and low-level labour, whereas the majority of the industries within the expanding service sector generally display a high density of female workers and high-level labour. Since the demand within the service sector is mainly for high-level, female labour, very little of the low-level (largely male) surplus labour released as a result of the decline of the agricultural and industrial sectors has been absorbed by the service sector.

Disadvantaged by gender and low-level education and skills, unemployed males have therefore found it difficult to find new jobs. However, as shown in Table 6.7, although women are less likely than men to change jobs, they do withdraw from their current jobs more frequently than men (due largely to the pressures of marriage, child-rearing, and so on).

Table 6.7 Labour turnover rates, 1980-2002

Unit: %

Year	Male			Female		
	Workers Leaving their Current Jobs	Workers Changing Jobs	Workers Leaving Current Jobs and Finding New Jobs	Workers Leaving their Current Jobs	Workers Changing Jobs	Workers Leaving Current Jobs and Finding New Jobs
1980-1994	10.27	8.48	96.69	18.32	9.11	97.17
1995	7.67	5.96	96.08	13.15	6.86	96.28
1996	9.37	7.18	92.44	14.45	7.83	94.76
1997	8.63	6.84	91.12	12.86	7.10	95.79
1998	8.68	6.81	89.90	13.19	7.49	96.79
1999	8.91	6.79	86.20	13.18	7.25	93.53
2000	9.37	7.07	86.24	12.49	7.26	92.86
2001	9.98	7.24	80.73	13.41	7.73	89.37
2002	10.44	7.75	76.64	12.62	7.05	86.88

Source: DGBAS (1995-2002).

153

Between 1980 and 1994, an average of 96.69 per cent of male workers wanting to change their job succeeded in doing so; the average figure for women was even higher, at 97.17 per cent. However, from 1996 onwards, this extremely high success rate fell for both men and women. By 2002, of all women leaving their job to find new work, only 86.88 per cent succeeded in finding a new job; the success rate for men was even lower, at 76.64 per cent. The inability to find work was thus more problematic for men than for women; and indeed, it was this difficulty in finding new jobs after leaving previous employment that was the main cause of the dramatic rise in the unemployment rate in Taiwan.

CONCLUSIONS

The decline in the production value of the manufacturing and agricultural sectors in Taiwan from 1988 onwards was accompanied by deterioration in the employment structure within these sectors. At the same time, the rise in the share of household income that was being spent, rather than being saved, the increase in the share of consumer spending on services, and the growing demand for financial services, all helped to stimulate the development of the service sector in Taiwan.

Within the manufacturing sector as a whole, the traditional industries had begun to give way to the electronics and precision machinery industries. Although this had led to an overall reduction in employment opportunities for low-skilled workers, the growth of the construction industry nevertheless helped to absorb much of the surplus male manpower coming out of the manufacturing industry; in the meantime, low-skilled female workers from the manufacturing industry were also migrating to the service sector. As a result, by 1993, the overall unemployment rate had actually fallen, to just 1.45 per cent.

However, as a result of the rapidly rising vacancy rates, the rapid growth in the construction of new buildings which had accompanied the bubble economy eventually came to an end, and by 1994, property prices were also beginning to fall. The financial institutions found that they had insufficient collateral to cover their non-performing loans (NPLs), and business enterprises saw their net values shrinking. With the rise in the NPL ratio, the cash flow problems in many enterprises and falling consumer confidence, the downturn soon began to affect every sector of the economy. Furthermore, it was not just the agricultural and manufacturing sectors that were depressed, since the creation of new jobs also began to level off in the service sector. Business contraction then led to a rise in unemployment, which, by 2002, had reached a historical high of 5.17 per cent.

Within the industrial sector, men were at a greater risk of unemployment than women, whilst in the service sector, the reverse was true. Those with superior education and skills were less likely to become unemployed, and, for the most part, those who were unemployed had previously been working in low-level occupations. The older the worker, the longer the period of time they could expect to spend unemployed, although this was less true for those educated to higher levels. As the transformation of the industrial structure continued, unemployed men who had previously been working in low-level occupations increasingly found that their gender, age and low skills made it very difficult for them to find new jobs. From 1996 onwards, the unemployment rate rose steadily, and whilst this is often blamed on Taiwanese companies relocating their production bases to mainland China where they could benefit from cheap labour – which, it is argued, is what subsequently led to major changes in Taiwan's industrial structure – it would be more accurate to say that the responsibility lay squarely with the bubble economy that had developed in the 1980s.

The excess money supply, which at that time was ubiquitous, led to dramatic increases in the book value of various companies, despite there being no real increase in their underlying value. As real estate prices soared, fuelling a headlong rush to build more houses and office buildings, the vacancy rates ultimately started to rise; thus, by 1994, real estate prices were starting to fall again. The decline in property values led to a reduction in household wealth, subsequently leading to a drop in the net value of business enterprises, and thereby pushing up the NPLs of the financial enterprises. The bursting of the bubble economy inevitably brought about a downturn which would ultimately go on to affect every part of the economy. For example, the effects of the reduction in the number of new housing projects were felt not only by the construction industry itself, but also by many related industries, such as the quarrying and building materials industries, which were also badly hit; indeed, the impact even spilled over into the service sector. The general slump within the building industry was ultimately the spark which set off a steady increase in unemployment, and indeed, the after-effects of the bubble economy and the potential for a major financial crisis ensured that unemployment remained high.

Thus, the rise in unemployment in Taiwan actually had its origins in several areas, including the decline in the construction industry and the mining and quarrying industry (both of which had a high density of male employees), in the transformation of the manufacturing sector and its reorientation towards hi-tech industries, as well as in the growing demand for high-skilled labour (and the corresponding fall in the demand for low-skilled labour) within the service sector. The growth of the service sector nevertheless meant improved employment opportunities for women.

Overall, however, the restructuring of the labour force lagged behind the changes in Taiwan's overall industrial structure. Unemployed low-skilled labour was not being successfully absorbed into other sectors; at the same time, the high-level labour that Taiwan needed was not being cultivated rapidly enough. Following the bursting of the bubble economy which had ultimately prevented the service sector from creating the new jobs needed to absorb the unemployed from other sectors, it was the slowdown in the development of this sector, combined with the imbalance between the industrial structure and the labour structure, that were the main factors behind the increase in the unemployment rate in Taiwan since 1996, and indeed, the main reasons why unemployment has remained stubbornly high ever since.

REFERENCES

CEPD (2003), *Taiwan Economic Forum*, Taipei: Council for Economic Planning and Development.

Chang, C.H. (1988), 'A Review of Labour Market Studies in Taiwan', *Review of Economics*, 16(2): 125-30.

DGBAS (1995-2002), *Yearbook of Manpower Survey Statistics*, Taipei: Directorate-General of Budget, Accounting and Statistics.

DGBAS (2002), *National Income of the Republic of China*, Taipei: Directorate- General of Budget, Accounting and Statistics.

DGBAS (various years), *Yearbook on Earnings and Productivity Statistics*, Taipei: Directorate-General of Budget, Accounting and Statistics.

Hsin, P.L. (2001), 'Unemployment Policies in OECD Countries', *Weekly Report of National Economic Development*, 1380: 6-15.

Lee, J.S. (1998), *Unemployment in Taiwan*, Taipei: National Science Council.

Liu, Y.C. (1998), *A Study of Unemployment Among College-educated Workers*, Taipei: National Science Council.

Liu, Y.L., J.S. Lee and H.L. Wu (2001), 'Is Rising Unemployment in Taiwan Inevitable?' *Economic Outlook*, 74(March): 20-32.

Tsai, C.L., W.L. Chung and F.M. Hwang (1994), 'A Dynamic Approach to Studying Manpower Problems: The Experiences of Taiwan and Abroad', *Economic Forecasting and Policies*, 25(1): 39-92.

Wu, C.C. and S.F. Lee (2001), *Policies for Tackling Current Unemployment*, Taipei: Council for Economic Planning and Development.

7 The Deterioration in Employment: Regional Unemployment Dynamics

Feng-Fuh Jiang and Paul K.C. Liu

INTRODUCTION

The aim of this chapter is to provide some in-depth analysis of the rapid and alarming deterioration in employment in Taiwan over recent years. We believe that it is important, and certainly relevant, to attempt to provide a very firm understanding of the employment situation in Taiwan from an international perspective, given that up until the late 1980s the island's economy had enjoyed a protracted period of low unemployment for a considerable number of years. Since then, however, Taiwan has experienced unemployment levels more akin to those of the European economies.

As the Taiwan Statistical Data Book[1] reveals, between 1978 and 1993, the average unemployment rate in Taiwan stood at approximately 1.86 per cent, a level much lower than those of both the US (at 6.8 per cent) and the UK (at 9.6 per cent). However, this stands in stark contrast to the subsequent 1994-2001 period, a period in which the unemployment rate in Taiwan rose continuously, whilst the US and many of the major European economies were watching their unemployment figures declining steadily. Most noticeably, the unemployment rate in Taiwan saw a dramatic leap from 2.99 per cent in 2000, to 4.57 per cent in 2001, representing a 50-year high for the island, and indeed, a level comparable to the much improved unemployment rates of 4.8 per cent in the US and 5.0 per cent in the UK.

The recent increase in the unemployment rate in Taiwan is already well documented, with Jiang having noted that the dramatic rise in unemployment was characterized by a number of demographic features that were quite distinct from those exhibited during the earlier years of Taiwan's economic development (Jiang 2001a, 2001b). The first of these features was that from 1993 onwards, unemployment amongst males in Taiwan rose at a much more rapid pace than amongst females, consequently exceeding the female unemployment rate, for the first time ever, in 1996.

Secondly, less-experienced workers, and those with an educational level of junior high school or below, experienced a rise in unemployment towards the end of 2000, whilst those with higher education levels experienced a decline in the unemployment rate. Thirdly, although the unemployment rates had always been highest for those workers in the 15 to 24 age group, the rates for those in the prime working-age group, as well as in the middle-age and higher-age groups, began to exhibit dramatic increases, along with a steady increase in the duration of unemployment.

One aspect which has thus far evaded adequate consideration is the pronounced unemployment differentials across the 23 different geographical regions of Taiwan, these regions comprising of two municipalities, five cities and 16 counties. Details of the distribution of unemployment rates for these 23 regions are provided in Table 7.1, where the letters 'L', 'M' and 'H' are respectively used to signify 'low-unemployment' regions (those with unemployment rates between the minimum levels and the first quartile of the overall unemployment rate), 'medium-unemployment' regions (those with unemployment rates between the first quartile and the average of the second and third quartiles of the overall unemployment rate) and 'high-unemployment' regions (those with unemployment rates between the average of the second and third quartiles and the highest levels of the overall unemployment rate).

Table 7.1   Average unemployment rates and regional distribution, 1987-2000

Unit: %

	Regional Distribution of Unemployment Rates [a]		Average Unemployment Rate [b]
	1987	2000	
Taipei Municipality	M	H	2.25
Kaohsiung Municipality	H	H	2.48
Keelung City	H	H	3.61
Hsinchu City	M	M	2.08
Hsinchu County	L	L	1.32
Taichung City	M	H	2.43
Yunlin County	L	L	1.45
Chiayi City	M	H	2.51
Tainan City	H	H	2.87
Hualian County	H	H	2.52

Notes:
[a]   'L', 'M' and 'H' respectively refer to low-, medium- and high-unemployment regions.
[b]   The overall average unemployment rate between 1987 and 2000 was 2.05 per cent.

Source: DGBAS (various years).

There are two points which stand out from Table 7.1. Firstly, it is clear that Taiwan's cities suffer higher unemployment rates than most of its counties; and secondly, many of the regional differentials are somewhat persistent. For example, between 1987 and 2000, Kaohsiung Municipality, Keelung City and Tainan City remained within the regional 'high-unemployment' category, whereas the unemployment rates for Taipei Municipality, Taichung City and Chiayi City saw significant changes, resulting in their shift away from the 'high-unemployment' category to the 'medium-unemployment' category. By contrast, throughout the same period, both Hsinchu County and Yunlin County remained within the 'low-unemployment' category. Again, over the same period, there were no significant changes in the unemployment rates for Hsinchu City and Hualien County, which respectively remained in the 'medium- and 'high-unemployment' categories.

The persistence of the regional variations in unemployment levels implies that it will be necessary to use regional panel data for any analysis of the causes of Taiwan's unemployment rates. In this chapter, therefore, we estimate a model using a longitudinal dataset comprising of 322 observations on the 23 regions, with these observations covering a period of 14 years for each of 12 distinct age-gender groups. The results indicate that the regional effects are significant and that there are substantial differences across the various demographic groups. Consequently, we find that both the direction and the degree of the impacts of certain macro variables differ significantly from those reported in a number of studies in Taiwan, each of which failed to take into consideration regional or demographic variables. One novelty that we therefore introduce into this chapter is the inclusion of a comparison of the appropriateness of the model specifications by performing an F-test, an LM test and a Hausman-type test.

MODELLING UNEMPLOYMENT

The Basic Model

We examine the unemployment function for each age-gender group of region i in year t, under the following basic model:

$$U_{it} = \alpha + \beta \cdot M_t + \gamma \cdot R_{it} + \varepsilon_{it} \tag{1}$$

$$E(\varepsilon_{it}) = 0,$$

$$Var(\varepsilon_{it}) = \sigma_\varepsilon^2, \quad \forall \ i = i' \text{ and } t = t',$$

$$= 0, \text{ otherwise}$$

where M_t is a vector of region-invariant variables and R_{it} is a vector of region-specific variables. The region-invariant variables include macro and policy variables, whilst the region-specific variables relate to the important characteristics of the regional labour market. In order to effectively take into account the distinct unemployment trends discernible amongst the different demographic groups, it is necessary to estimate all of the groups separately, using the same model, but allowing for variations in the coefficients.

The basic relationship can be extended into a two-factor effects model which includes both region and time effects. There are two possible approaches to be taken within the model in order to account for these two effects; namely, the 'fixed-effects' approach and the 'random-effects' approach. The former model specifies the region- or time-specific constant terms, whilst the latter specifies the region- or time-specific disturbances.[2]

Fixed-effects Approach

In a two-factor fixed-effects model, the basic model (presented above) is modified by adding two sets of fixed-effects terms:

$$U_{it} = \alpha + \psi_i + \varphi_t + \beta \cdot M_t + \gamma \cdot R_{it} + \varepsilon_{it} \tag{2}$$

where ψ_i is the 'region-specific fixed effect' for each region i, and φ_t is the 'time-specific fixed effect' for time t. Both ψ_i and φ_t are constant terms, with the region-specific fixed effect ψ_i representing the time-invariant impact of a region which cannot be predicted by considering time or other independent variables, whilst φ_t measures the time-specific fixed effect resulting solely from a particular year.

Random-effects Approach

In the fixed-effects model, the effects are specified as constants; however, a competing approach would be to treat the effects as disturbances, as follows:

$$U_{it} = \alpha + \beta \cdot M_t + \gamma \cdot R_{it} + u_i + v_t + \varepsilon_{it} \tag{3}$$

$$E(u_i) = 0,$$

$$Var(u_i) = \sigma_u^2, \ \forall \ i = i'$$

$$= 0, \text{ otherwise,}$$

$$\text{Cov}(\varepsilon_{it}, u_i) = 0, \quad \forall \; i \text{ and } t;$$

$$E(v_t) = 0,$$

$$\text{Var}(v_t) = \sigma_v^2, \quad \forall \; t = t'$$

$$= 0, \text{ otherwise,}$$

$$\text{Cov}(\varepsilon_{it}, v_t) = 0, \quad \forall \; i \text{ and } t;$$

$$\text{Var}(\varepsilon_{it} + u_i + v_t) = \sigma_\varepsilon + \sigma_u + \sigma_v$$

where u_i and v_t are region-specific and time-specific disturbance terms, which are similar to ε_{it}, except that for each region or time, there is only one single draw which has an identical entry into the regression.

Choice of Specification

Testing the significance of fixed effects
In order to effectively test the significance of fixed effects, we must first of all determine whether there is any significant improvement in the fit when the fixed-effects model is substituted for the basic regression model with only a single overall constant term. To achieve this, the hypothesis that all constant terms are equal can be examined by carrying out an F-test, as follows:

$$H_0: \quad \psi_1 = \psi_2 = \psi_3 = \dots = \psi_{23}; \quad \varphi_1 = \varphi_2 = \varphi_3 = \dots = \varphi_{14}$$

Under the null hypothesis, all of the fixed effects converge into a single constant term; therefore, the most efficient estimation method would be the 'pooled least-squares' method. If the F-statistic is small, such that the null hypothesis cannot be rejected, this would imply that the basic regression model with only a single constant term is more appropriate for the regional unemployment data. Conversely, if the F-statistic exceeds the critical value, such that the null hypothesis is rejected, then this would imply that the fixed-effects model provides the data with a better fit than the basic model.

Testing the significance of random effects
A test which has been widely used for examining the significance of random effects is the Breusch–Pagan test (Breusch and Pagan, 1980). The null hypothesis is formulated as follows:

$$H_0: \quad \sigma_u^2 = 0 \text{ and } \sigma_v^2 = 0$$

The *LM*-test statistic is obtained based upon the least-square residuals. Under the null hypothesis, the *LM*-statistic is distributed as being chi-squared; if the *LM*-statistic is small, then the null hypothesis cannot be rejected and the basic model is the more appropriate choice. Conversely, if the *LM*-statistic exceeds the critical value from the chi-squared table, then the null hypothesis is rejected and the random-effects model is more appropriate for the regional data. However, since the fixed-effects model may well produce the same result, it would clearly be inappropriate to conclude that the specifications of the random-effects model would be any better than those of the fixed-effects model if the *LM*-statistic was large. Further tests are therefore necessary.

The Hausman test for fixed or random effects
Whilst the random-effects approach assumes that there is no correlation between the individual effects and other regressors, the fixed-effects model makes no such assumption. Therefore, as a result of potential correlation between the random effects and the regressors included in the model, the random-effects approach may be prone to inconsistencies. The specification test devised by Hausman (1978) can be adopted to test for the orthogonality of both the regressed variables and the random effects; the null hypothesis can therefore be formulated as follows:

$$H_0: \ Cov(u_i, [M_t\, R_{it}]) = 0, \quad \text{and} \quad Cov(v_t\, [M_t\, R_{it}]) = 0, \quad \forall\ i \text{ and } t$$

As in the Wald test, this test statistic is based upon a quadratic form with a limiting chi-squared distribution under the null hypothesis. Specifically, the quadratic form can be expressed as the product of three components, namely, the transpose of the difference in coefficient vectors between the fixed-effects and random-effects models with exclusion of the constant term, the inverse covariance matrix of this difference in coefficient vectors, and the difference in the coefficient vectors themselves.

Under the null hypothesis, although both the 'ordinary least-squares' (OLS) estimations in the fixed-effects model and the 'generalized least-squares' (GLS) estimations in the random-effects model are consistent, the OLS is, nevertheless, inefficient. Conversely, under the alternative hypothesis, the OLS method is consistent whilst the GLS method is not. Hence, if the Hausman test statistic is smaller than the critical chi-squared value, then the null hypothesis cannot be rejected, which implies that the random-effects model is more appropriate than the fixed-effects model. Conversely, if the Hausman statistic is larger than the critical chi-squared value, then this implies that the fixed-effects model is the more appropriate choice.

DATA SOURCES AND CONSTRUCTION OF THE VARIABLES

Data Sources

The data for this examination of the deterioration in employment in Taiwan is drawn mainly from the Manpower Survey Statistics, prepared by the Directorate-General of Budget, Accounting and Statistics (DGBAS, various years). This dataset provides details of all of the regional unemployment rates for the various demographic groups, comprising of all four of the region-specific explanatory variables (COLL, EMPL, PROF and OLD), along with two of the five region-invariant explanatory variables (FWK and CONS). Of the remaining three region-invariant explanatory variables, LLAW and MINI are obtained from the Monthly Bulletin of Labour Statistics, published by the Council of Labour Affairs at the Executive Yuan, and FAC is obtained from the Economic Statistics Monthly, published by the Ministry of Economic Affairs. All of these variables are described fully in the following sub-sections using annual time-series data for the years 1987 to 2000. The first year of the study sample period was chosen simply on the basis that regional unemployment data was not available prior to 1987.

Dependent Variables

The annual unemployment rate in Taiwan is assessed, in the normal way, as the percentage of the labour force not in gainful employment, and is calculated for each demographic group within each region from 1987 to 2000. A panel of 322 observations (23 regions over the 14 years of the study) is constructed for each of the 12 age-gender groups (three gender groups x four age groups). The three gender groups are 'male', 'female' and 'male and female', whilst the four age groups are 'youths' (aged 15-24 years), 'prime' (aged 25-44), 'middle-aged and older-aged' (i.e., higher-aged workers) and 'total' (all workers aged 15 years or over). The same model is estimated for each demographic group, although different coefficients are adopted.

Macro and Policy Variables

We must now be more specific with regard to the various arguments surrounding the unemployment equation. Five of the variables, the index of firms inspected under the Labour Standards Law (LLAW), the minimum wage index (MINI), the index of foreign industrial workers (FWK), the proportion of total employment in the construction industry (CONS) and the index of newly registered firms (FAC), are national in scope and are region-invariant;

164 Employment Development in a Regulated and Globalized Labour Market

these variables are either macroeconomic or policy variables, either of which have direct impacts on the economy as a whole.

Index of firms inspected under the Labour Standards Law (LLAW)

The variable LLAW refers to the index of the number of cases of firms inspected under the Fair Labour Standards Law 1984 (FLSL), with the number of inspections indicating both the extent and the intensity of the FLSL. Earlier studies have suggested that Taiwan's labour standards are, in general, more stringent than those of the US, and also that they are more likely to have unfavourable effects on the Taiwanese labour market (Lee and Wu, 1992; Jiang, 2000; Lee, 2000; and Jiang et al., 2002). Thus, LLAW is expected to be positively correlated with the unemployment rate.

Minimum wage index (MINI)

Although the minimum wage in Taiwan was established in 1955, it failed to keep pace with the strong growth of the Taiwanese economy until the late-1970s.[3] Over the 1979-2001 period, the ratio of the minimum wage vis-à-vis the average manufacturing wage, rose markedly, to 43.98 per cent, a figure considerably higher than those recorded in the US, at 35.6 per cent for 1990 and 38.3 per cent for 1991 (Filer et al., 1996). Jiang and San (1987) also found that the minimum wage level had a weak, but nevertheless positive, effect on youth unemployment. It is therefore likely that a rise in the minimum wage rate will have a positive association with the unemployment rate.

Index of foreign industrial workers (FWK)

One candidate touted as having an unfavourable effect on employment levels for domestic workers is the total number of foreign labourers employed within the industrial sector. The general increase in the number of alien workers within this sector was exponential, with as much as a 70-fold increase between 1991 and 2001, and although the introduction of foreign workers into the economy was originally designed to supplement the efforts of domestic workers, some studies have concluded that they may have turned out to be substitutes for local workers, thereby having an unfavourable effect on overall unemployment levels (Jiang, 2001a; 2001b). We therefore expect to see the index of the number of foreign workers being positively correlated with overall unemployment levels.

Proportion of total employment in the construction industry (CONS)

The expansion of the construction sector is usually taken as a leading indicator of the upturn of the entire economy; thus, a retrenchment of this industry also indicates the shift of an economy into a period of recession. We therefore expect to see the percentage share of total employment accounted for by the construction industry having a negative association with unemployment.

Index of newly registered firms (FAC)

The number of newly registered firms is yet another indicator of the current status of the business cycle. If the economy is booming, it is likely that more firms will emerge within the various industries, thereby creating more job opportunities. Thus, the number of new firms registering with the Ministry of Economic Affairs is expected to have a negative correlation with unemployment.

Region-specific Labour Market Characteristics

We have selected four variables as characterizing the regional labour market in Taiwan. These include the quality of human capital (COLL), the employment status (EMPL), the class of occupation (PROF) and the age structure of the non-labour force (OLD). These region-specific variables will, in theory, affect unemployment for each demographic group in differing degrees, as follows.

Highly educated proportion of the civil population (COLL)

There has been a continual rise in the proportion of the civil population in Taiwan completing college, university or post-graduate studies, with the total number of new graduates having more than tripled between 1980 and 1999. Whilst the process of industrial upgrading has also continued in Taiwan, there has been a corresponding rise in the demand for highly educated human resources. Thus, despite the apparent positive relationship between years of schooling and unemployment prior to 1995 (Jiang, 1997), there was a decline in the unemployment rate amongst the highly educated, from 3.13 per cent in 1996 to 2.67 per cent in 2000. The disaggregated study in this chapter should shed some light on the ways in which the educational composition affects regional unemployment for each of the demographic groups.

Proportion of paid employees within the total workforce (EMPL)

A second influence on the regional labour market is the percentage share of paid employees within the total working population. There has been a general increase in the overall number of paid employees over time, as compared to employers, owner-operators and unpaid working family members. This indicates a gradual shift in industrial organization, from small family businesses to large modern enterprises (Liu and Tung, 2001). Since employment within such large modern enterprises is presumably more stable than self-employment or employment in small enterprises, it is therefore likely that the increase in paid employees has a negative correlation with the unemployment rate.

Proportion of professionals within the total workforce (PROF)
The percentage share of highly skilled workers within the total workforce is
a third potential influence on the regional labour market. Given that, during
periods of recession, it is more likely that blue-collar workers will become
unemployed than professional and technical workers, the share of the latter
group within the total workforce is expected to have a negative association
with the unemployment rate.

Proportion of elderly and disabled people in the non-labour force (OLD)
The fourth labour market influence considered here is the percentage share
of elderly and disabled people within the non-labour force. Although not part
of the labour force, these people may actually become potential competitors
for jobs; thus, any increase in the proportion of elderly and disabled people
may result in higher unemployment, particularly for the middle- and
older-aged groups. The estimations provided by this examination should help
to clarify whether there is in fact any truth in such conjecture.

EMPIRICAL RESULTS

Testing the Hypotheses

Table 7.2 summarizes the results of the *F*-test, the *LM*-test and the Hausman
test, as described earlier in this chapter. The *F*-test statistics are found to be
substantially greater than the critical values across all age-gender groups.
Such evidence is strongly in favour of a model with both regional and time-
fixed effects, as opposed to the basic model. Furthermore, the *LM*-test
statistic for the female middle-aged and older-aged group is smaller than
the critical value. Therefore, based upon the results of the *F*-test, we reject
the random-effects model and conclude that the fixed-effects model is
more appropriate for this particular group. Since the *LM*-test statistics are
greater than the critical values for the remaining 11 groups, further tests are
required in order to determine whether the fixed-effects model or the
random-effects model provides a better fit.

Next, we carry out the Hausman tests, from which we find that although
the test statistics are greater than the critical values for eight of the groups, this
is not so for the male youth, female youth and female prime-aged groups. For
these three groups, the hypothesis of no existence of any correlation between
the individual effects and the other regressors in this model cannot be rejected;
therefore, the random-effects model provides a better alternative in these three
cases. However, for the remaining eight groups, the fixed-effects model
remains more appropriate.

Table 7.2   Model specification tests

Tests	Total Unemployment	Age 15-24	Age 25-44	Age 45-64
Male				
F-test	17.53 ***	6.64 ***	6.12 ***	4.07 ***
LM-test	806.16 ***	369.28 ***	211.04 ***	70.62 ***
Hausman test	38.33 ***	4.79	21.22 **	25.3 **
Best model fit	Fixed-effects	Random-effects	Fixed-effects	Fixed-effects
Female				
F-test	14.91 ***	6.45 ***	3.49 ***	1.60 **
LM-test	606.06 ***	291.29 ***	74.29 ***	0.68
Hausman test	55.73 ***	13.80	8.49	11.97
Best model fit	Fixed-effects	Random-effects	Random-effects	Fixed-effects
Male and Female				
F-test	20.52 ***	8.74 ***	13.98 ***	3.69 ***
LM-test	839.46 ***	407.43 ***	593.36 ***	75.67 ***
Hausman test	49.79 ***	23.08 ***	33.27 **	20.34 **
Best model fit	Fixed-effects	Fixed-effects	Fixed-effects	Fixed-effects

Note: *** denotes significance at the 1 per cent level; and ** denotes significance at the 5 per cent level.

Determination of Unemployment Rates

The regression results for the best model fit are presented in Table 7.3, the first part of which shows the impacts of the region-invariant macro variables. Most of the estimated coefficients have the correct signs and are statistically significant, the exceptions being the coefficients of MINI for male youths, LLAW for males aged 45-64, FWK for female youths and LLAW, MINI, CONS and FAC for females aged 45-64.

It is interesting to note that, relative to the entire labour force, MINI contributes to unemployment positively and significantly to all male and female workers, prime-aged males and females (both separately and combined) and female youths. This contradicts earlier findings where it was suggested that basic wages have no significant unfavourable impacts on employment (see, for example, Card and Kreuger, 1995; and Huang, 2001). In addition, the macro variables seem to exert the highest impact on the youth groups and the lowest impact on the middle- and older-aged groups. The estimates for the regional variables are reported in the lower portion of Table 7.3.

Table 7.3   *Estimation results* [a]

	Age 15-24 [b]		Age 25-44 [d]		Age 45-64 [d]		Totals [d]	
Panel A: Male cohort								
LLAW	0.0124	(1.524)	0.0039	(1.623)	-0.0002	(-0.082)	0.0034**	(2.287)
MINI	-0.0309	(-0.573)	0.0369**	(2.270)	0.0020	(0.126)	0.0172*	(1.694)
FWK	0.0509**	(2.429)	0.0221***	(3.522)	0.0142**	(2.358)	0.0155***	(3.946)
CONS	-60.6660*	(-1.906)	-55.3530***	(-5.508)	-27.2570***	(-2.825)	-40.4560***	(-6.428)
FAC	-0.0448***	(-2.643)	-0.0116**	(-2.372)	-0.0022	(-0.463)	-0.0081***	(-2.644)
COLL	0.3710***	(4.491)	-0.0343	(-0.870)	0.0390	(1.032)	-0.0122	(-0.495)
EMPL	0.0915**	(2.380)	-0.0518**	(-2.292)	-0.0376*	(-1.736)	-0.0188	(-1.329)
PROF	-0.3097***	(-5.333)	-0.0202	(-1.053)	-0.0092	(-0.499)	-0.0261**	(-2.171)
OLD	0.0646	(0.896)	-0.0073	(-0.244)	0.0656**	(2.296)	0.0333*	(1.786)
Constant	6.9919	(1.625)	8.116***	(4.530)	3.0737*	(1.787)	5.4545***	(4.862)
$\bar{R}^2$	0.304		0.760		0.579		0.811	
F-test	–		23.640***		10.820***		31.510***	
Explanatory Variable Effects	0.302		0.630		0.447		0.466	
Regional Effects (%)	0.311	(49.73)	0.155	(19.55)	0.140	(21.97)	0.361	(43.17)
Time Effect (%)	0.012	(1.99)	0.009	(1.08)	0.051	(8.03)	0.009	(1.12)
Total Effects	0.625		0.794		0.638		0.837	

Table 7.3   (Contd.) [a]

	Age 15-24 [c]		Age 25-44 [c]		Age 45-64 [d]		Totals [d]	
Panel B: Female cohort								
LLAW	0.0255***	(3.701)	0.0087***	(4.005)	-0.0008	(-1.077)	0.0037**	(2.303)
MINI	0.1299***	(2.842)	0.0385***	(2.654)	-0.0087*	(-1.738)	0.0197*	(1.775)
FWK	-0.0032	(-0.180)	0.0014	(0.255)	0.0050**	(2.575)	0.0077*	(1.790)
CONS	-96.5420***	(-3.580)	-36.1540***	(-4.193)	-1.0306	(-0.334)	-24.0440***	(-3.505)
FAC	-0.0371***	(-2.584)	-0.0207***	(-4.570)	0.0006	(0.416)	-0.0100***	(-2.992)
COLL	0.1309*	(1.855)	0.0428*	(1.755)	0.0241**	(1.993)	-0.0688**	(-2.559)
EMPL	0.0227	(0.691)	-0.0040	(-0.339)	-0.0061	(-0.882)	-0.0191	(-1.236)
PROF	-0.1196**	(-2.430)	-0.0314**	(-1.994)	-0.0080	(-1.360)	-0.0058	(-0.446)
OLD	-0.1409**	(-2.295)	-0.0181	(-0.885)	0.0153*	(1.669)	-0.0475**	(-2.336)
Constant	6.2152*	(1.700)	2.9728*	(2.430)	0.4678	(0.850)	6.5973***	(5.395)
R^2	0.303		0.505		0.275		0.648	
F-test	–		–		3.710***		14.130***	
Explanatory Variable Effects	0.289		0.503		0.248		0.110	
Regional Effects (%)	0.287	(46.88)	0.134	(20.29)	0.053	(14.00)	0.542	(77.70)
Time Effect (%)	0.037	(5.97)	0.022	(3.27)	0.076	(20.25)	0.045	(6.45)
Total Effects	0.613		0.658		0.377		0.697	

169

Table 7.3 (Contd.) [a]

	Age 15-24[d]		Age 25-44[d]		Age 45-64[d]		Total[d]	
Panel C: Male and Female cohort								
LLAW	0.0101*	(1.863)	0.0017	(1.028)	0.0001	(0.049)	0.0036***	(2.641)
MINI	0.0495	(1.332)	0.0257**	(2.250)	0.0043	(0.365)	0.0189**	(2.037)
FWK	0.0256*	(1.783)	0.0190***	(4.316)	0.0110**	(2.438)	0.0123***	(3.434)
CONS	-59.7090***	(-2.598)	-36.7540***	(-5.201)	-22.9560***	(-3.163)	-34.4270***	(-5.983)
FAC	-0.0187*	(-1.662)	-0.0065*	(-1.873)	-0.0023	(-0.644)	-0.0090***	(-3.189)
COLL	-0.0481	(-0.534)	-0.0466*	(-1.684)	0.0270	(0.948)	-0.0374*	(-1.660)
EMPL	-0.0504	(-0.976)	-0.0396**	(-2.498)	-0.0254	(-1.560)	-0.0184	(-1.422)
PROF	-0.0825*	(-1.878)	-0.0159	(-1.181)	-0.0079	(-0.572)	-0.0183*	(-1.663)
OLD	0.0129	(0.189)	-0.0249	(-1.190)	0.0395*	(1.838)	0.0026	(0.150)
Constant	12.3460***	(3.013)	6.753***	(5.361)	2.4631*	(1.903)	5.8749***	(5.727)
R^2	0.590		0.783		0.600		0.789	
F-test	11.250***		26.760***		11.680***		27.660***	
Explanatory Variable Effects	0.246		0.475		0.491		0.335	
Regional Effects (%)	0.375	(58.02)	0.333	(40.93)	0.128	(19.51)	0.469	(57.27)
Time Effects (%)	0.025	(3.93)	0.006	(0.72)	0.037	(5.67)	0.016	(1.92)
Total Effects	0.647		0.814		0.656		0.819	

Notes:
[a]   *** denotes significance at the 1 per cent level; ** denotes significance at the 5 per cent level; and * denotes significance at the 10 per cent level.
[b]   In the male cohort, figures in parentheses in the 15-24 age group refer to the coefficients divided by the standard error.
[c]   In the female cohort, figures in parentheses in the 15-24 and 25-44 age groups refer to the coefficients divided by the standard error.
[d]   Figures in parentheses refer to *t*-values.

170

We can see from Table 7.3 that the signs of the estimated coefficients for EMPL and PROF are largely as anticipated (the exceptions being the cases of the coefficients of the male and female youth groups) whilst the signs for COLL are somewhat mixed. In particular, the percentage shares of the highly educated show a positive association with unemployment for female youths, prime-aged, middle-aged and older-aged females, male youths and middle-aged and older-aged males, but a negative association with both the male and female labour force as a whole. This may result from the fact that these groups have, on average, fewer years of schooling as compared to the prime-aged male group, and are therefore less competitive in the regional job market amongst their more highly educated counterparts. The signs for OLD are also mixed, with positive effects on the unemployment rates of the middle-aged, older-aged and male groups. It is likely that those featured in OLD are potential competitors of the middle-aged and older-aged groups, and indeed, of male workers as a whole, but not so unfavourable to the other groups.

The effects of the explanatory variables, calculated as the marginal contributions of each variable to the unadjusted R^2, are reported in the lower panel of Table 7.3. The regional effects are quite large in most, although not all, cases. As reported in the final column of Table 7.3, for the labour force as a whole, the regional effect is 57.27 per cent of the total effect, which exceeds both the effects of the explanatory variables (40.81 per cent) and the effects of time (1.92 per cent); that is, the regional effect is most powerful in accounting for unemployment amongst most of the demographic groups.

Comparing the Regional Effects

The regional fixed effects for each demographic group are summarized in Table 7.4. After controlling for other variables, a number of points become obvious from the table.[4] Firstly, with the exceptions of the middle-aged and older-aged female groups, the regional effects are significant. For the labour force as a whole, as the 'Totals' column of Table 7.4 shows, 16 of the 23 regional coefficients were significant at the 1 per cent level, four at the 5 per cent level and one at the 10 per cent level, whilst only two of the regional coefficients were insignificant. The regional effects are clearly quite high, accounting for 57.27 per cent of the total effects.

Secondly, there are obvious variations between the different demographic groups; for example, in the case of Keelung City, the regional effect is positive for all demographic groups, whereas, in the case of Taipei Municipality, the regional effect is much higher for the female 15-24 year group (3.280) than for the male 15-24 year group (0.458). Furthermore, only the middle-aged and older-aged female groups seem to benefit from living in Taipei, since the fixed-effect coefficient is negative (-0.103), although insignificant.

Table 7.4 Regional fixed effects [a]

	Age 15-24 [b]		Age 25-44 [d]		Age 45-64 [d]		Total [d]	
Panel A: Male cohort								
Taipei Municipality	0.458	(0.224)	1.978 ***	(3.344)	0.492	(0.828)	0.956 **	(2.558)
Keelung City	5.628 ***	(4.865)	1.403 ***	(4.191)	0.249	(0.739)	1.720 ***	(8.130)
Hsinchu City	-2.954 ***	(-3.044)	0.084	(0.299))	-0.109	(-0.385)	0.468 ***	(2.635)
Taipei County	-0.402	(-0.382)	0.789 ***	(2.587)	1.356 ***	(4.425)	0.415 **	(2.153)
Ilan County	0.248	(0.330)	0.285	(1.311)	0.601 ***	(2.750)	0.294 **	(2.143)
Taoyuan County	-1.055	(-1.178)	0.026	(0.100)	0.329	(1.262)	-0.229	(-1.397)
Hsinchu County	-3.720 ***	(-3.935)	-0.385	(-1.406)	-0.280	(-1.017)	-0.727 ***	(-4.203)
Taichung City	1.952	(1.532)	0.938 **	(2.545)	0.163	(0.439)	0.844 ***	(3.624)
Miaoli City	-0.479	(-0.593)	-0.375	(-1.604)	-0.293	(-1.247)	-0.536 ***	(-3.633)
Taichung County	-0.192	(-0.250)	-0.272	(-1.221)	0.465 **	(2.078)	-0.270 *	(-1.916)
Changhua County	-0.371	(-0.391)	-1.090 ***	(-3.971)	-0.308	(-1.117)	-1.020 ***	(-5.879)
Nantou County	2.108 **	(1.977)	-0.908 ***	(-2.943)	-0.697 **	(-2.248)	-0.629 ***	(-3.227)
Yunlin County	0.735	(0.479)	-1.451 ***	(-3.265)	-1.190 ***	(-2.664)	-1.348 ***	(-4.799)

Table 7.4   (Contd.)

	Age 15-24 [b]		Age 25-44 [d]		Age 45-64 [d]		Total [d]	
Chiayi City	-1.846 *	(-1.817)	0.369	(1.254)	-0.182	(-0.616)	0.924 ***	(4.971)
Tainan City	1.232	(1.403)	1.468 ***	(5.777)	0.706 ***	(2.765)	1.227 ***	(7.640)
Kaoshiung Municipality	1.076	(0.881)	1.353 ***	(3.829)	0.934 ***	(2.628)	0.924 ***	(4.136)
Chiayi County	-0.050	(-0.034)	-1.161 ***	(-2.740)	-0.888 ***	(-2.085)	-1.068 ***	(-3.988)
Tainan County	1.144	(1.452)	-0.200	(-0.876)	-0.042 *	(-0.182)	-0.345 **	(-2.396)
Kaohsiung County	0.898	(1.215)	0.430 **	(2.008)	0.728 ***	(3.382)	-0.295 **	(2.177)
Pingtung County	0.015	(0.016)	-0.827 ***	(-3.092)	-0.150	(-0.558)	-0.755 ***	(-4.471)
Penghu County	-3.945 ***	(-4.186)	-1.438 ***	(-5.273)	-0.563 **	(-2.053)	-0.938 ***	(-5.442)
Hualian County	0.645	(0.818)	0.108	(0.472)	-0.583 **	(-2.541)	0.194	(1.342)
Taitung County	-1.124	(-0.905)	-1.125 ***	(-3.132)	-0.738 **	(-2.045)	-0.396 *	(-1.744)
Explanatory Variable Effects	0.302		0.630		0.447		0.466	
Regional Effects (%)	0.311 (49.73)		0.155 (19.55)		0.140 (21.97)		0.361 (43.17)	
Time Effects	0.012		0.009		0.051		0.009	
Total Effects	0.625		0.794		0.638		0.837	

173

Table 7.4 (Contd.)

	Age 15-24[c]		Age 25-44[c]		Age 45-64[d]		Total[d]	
Panel B: Female cohort								
Taipei Municipality	3.280*	(1.842)	1.001*	(1.807)	-0.103	(-0.547)	1.529***	(3.608)
Keelung City	4.279***	(4.247)	1.173***	(3.741)	0.118	(1.101)	1.932***	(8.055)
Hsinchu City	-2.301***	(-2.722)	0.178	(0.675)	-0.034	(-0.380)	0.260	(1.293)
Taipei County	0.248	(0.271)	0.629**	(2.203)	0.239**	(2.454)	-0.082	(-0.373)
Ilan County	0.704	(1.077)	0.250	(1.229)	0.083	(1.204)	0.276*	(1.771)
Taoyuan County	-0.762	(-0.977)	0.082	(0.337)	0.057	(0.693)	-0.496***	(-2.671)
Hsinchu County	-2.885***	(-3.503)	-0.338	(-1.320)	-0.025	(-0.291)	-0.597***	(-3.044)
Taichung City	2.375**	(2.140)	0.386	(1.118)	-0.120	(-1.025)	0.765***	(2.893)
Miaoli City	-0.347	(-0.494)	0.035	(0.158)	0.054	(0.721)	-0.278*	(-1.659)
Taichung County	-0.657	(-0.980)	-0.043	(-0.207)	0.088	(1.241)	-0.614***	(-3.849)
Changhua County	-1.338	(-1.620)	-0.684***	(-2.659)	-0.019	(-0.221)	-1.161***	(-5.903)
Nantou County	0.496	(0.534)	-0.329	(-1.137)	-0.064	(-0.651)	-0.305	(-1.381)
Yunlin County	-1.188	(-0.888)	-0.882**	(-2.118)	-0.130	(-0.915)	-1.092***	(-3.430)

Table 7.4 (Contd.)

	Age 15-24[c]		Age 25-44[c]		Age 45-64[d]		Total[d]	
Chiayi City	0.385	(0.435)	-0.345	(-1.254)	-0.090	(-0.958)	0.574***	(2.723)
Tainan City	2.142***	(2.800)	0.608**	(2.554)	0.004	(0.054)	0.753***	(4.134)
Kaoshiung Municipality	2.140**	(2.011)	0.911***	(2.751)	0.057	(0.507)	0.708***	(2.796)
Chiayi County	-2.110*	(-1.655)	-0.846**	(-2.131)	-0.100	(-0.742)	-1.085***	(-3.575)
Tainan County	0.034	(0.050)	-0.405*	(-1.898)	-0.024	(-0.331)	-0.551***	(-3.374)
Kaohsiung County	0.333	(0.517)	0.345*	(1.719)	0.189***	(2.763)	-0.156	(-1.018)
Pingtung County	0.257	(0.319)	-0.436*	(-1.739)	-0.061	(-0.711)	-0.678***	(-3.537)
Penghu County	-3.378***	(-4.115)	-0.712***	(-2.789)	-0.030	(-0.348)	0.199	(1.020)
Hualian County	0.467	(0.680)	0.119*	(0.556)	-0.059	(-0.813)	0.406**	(2.485)
Taitung County	-2.177**	(-2.013)	-0.697**	(-2.069)	-0.028	(-0.247)	-0.308	(-1.194)
Explanatory Variable Effects	0.289		0.503		0.248		0.110	
Regional Effects (%)	0.287	(46.88)	0.134	(20.29)	0.053	(14.00)	0.542	(77.70)
Time Effects	0.037		0.022		0.076		0.045	
Total Effects	0.613		0.658		0.377		0.697	

175

Table 7.4 (Contd.)

	Age 15-24 [d]		Age 25-44 [d]		Age 45-64 [d]		Total [d]	
Panel C: Male and Female cohort								
Taipei Municipality	3.814***	(2.779)	1.756***	(4.243)	0.450	(1.022)	1.228***	(3.555)
Keelung City	5.537***	(7.131)	1.474***	(6.295)	0.321	(1.288)	1.797***	(9.198)
Hsinchu City	0.429	(0.659)	0.372*	(1.893)	-0.136	(-0.650)	0.382**	(2.329)
Taipei County	0.273	(0.387)	0.350	(1.638)	0.943***	(4.153)	0.228	(1.282)
Ilan County	0.310	(0.615)	0.396***	(2.607)	0.409**	(2.531)	0.279**	(2.202)
Taoyuan County	-0.864	(-1.437)	-0.108	(-0.595)	0.221	(1.147)	-0.331**	(-2.192)
Hsinchu County	-1.610**	(-2.537)	-0.399**	(-2.085)	-0.241	(-1.183)	-0.685***	(-4.289)
Taichung City	2.250***	(2.630)	0.839***	(3.254)	0.116	(0.422)	0.844***	(3.922)
Miaoli City	-0.747	(-1.378)	-0.370**	(-2.263)	-0.229	(-1.317)	-0.445***	(-3.261)
Taichung County	-1.109**	(-2.147)	-0.521***	(-3.343)	0.254	(1.534)	-0.404***	(-3.107)
Changhua County	-2.757***	(-4.330)	-1.093***	(-5.691)	-0.277	(-1.356)	-1.076***	(-6.713)
Nantou County	-0.475	(-0.663)	-0.673***	(-3.115)	-0.406*	(-1.766)	-0.515***	(-2.861)
Yunlin County	-2.701***	(-2.620)	-1.248***	(-4.013)	-0.849**	(-2.564)	-1.259***	(-4.852)

Table 7.4 (Contd.)

	Age 15-24 [d]		Age 25-44 [d]		Age 45-64 [d]		Total [d]	
Chiayi City	2.354***	(3.451)	0.735***	(3.572)	-0.208	(-0.947)	0.814***	(4.739)
Tainan City	2.355***	(3.995)	1.204***	(6.773)	0.495***	(2.613)	1.048***	(7.061)
Kaoshiung Municipality	2.164***	(2.638)	0.866***	(3.499)	0.719***	(2.729)	0.853***	(4.133)
Chiayi County	-2.881***	(-2.932)	-1.113***	(-3.754)	-0.562*	(-1.781)	-1.081***	(-4.372)
Tainan County	-0.689	(-1.304)	-0.176	(-1.103)	-0.031	(-0.181)	-0.430***	(-3.233)
Kaohsiung County	-0.245	(-0.493)	0.256*	(1.712)	0.557***	(3.492)	0.106	(0.852)
Pingtung County	-1.472**	(-2.373)	-0.793***	(-4.237)	-0.155	(-0.781)	-0.727***	(-4.656)
Penghu County	-2.890***	(-4.568)	-1.406***	(-7.369)	-0.425**	(-2.093)	-0.528***	(-3.318)
Hualian County	0.171	(0.323)	0.210	(1.318)	-0.431**	(-2.535)	0.276**	(2.069)
Taitung County	-1.217	(-1.460)	-0.561**	(-2.231)	-0.536**	(-2.005)	-0.374*	(-1.781)
Explanatory Variable Effects	0.246		0.475		0.491		0.335	
Regional Effects (%)	0.375	(58.02)	0.333	(40.93)	0.128	(19.51)	0.469	(57.27)
Time Effects	0.025		0.006		0.037		0.016	
Total Effects	0.647		0.814		0.656		0.819	

Notes:
[a] *** denotes significance at the 1 per cent level; ** denotes significance at the 5 per cent level; and * denotes significance at the 10 per cent level.
[b] In the male cohort, figures in parentheses in the 15-24 age group refer to the coefficients divided by the standard error.
[c] In the female cohort, figures in parentheses in the 15-24 and 25-44 age groups refer to the coefficients divided by the standard error.
[d] Figures in parentheses refer to t-values.

177

Thirdly, we can see that, in general, cities have higher coefficients than counties. As Table 7.4 shows, the fixed effects of the five cities and two municipalities are shown to be higher than those of the counties. We can also see that Keelung City has the highest fixed effects of the seven regional demographic groups. One of the main reasons for this is because this port city is locked in by mountains to the north and east, and the ocean to the west and south, geographical factors which place considerable limitations on the city's growth potential. By contrast, Hsinchu City has smaller fixed effects than the other six cities in nine of the demographic groups, with the fixed effect being negative in five other demographic groups.

The success of the Hsinchu Science-based Industrial Park, which was established in Hsinchu City in the early 1980s, has not only contributed to the industrial upgrading of Taiwan as a whole, but has also ensured that the regional unemployment rates, including those of neighbouring areas such as Hsinchu county, have been maintained at relatively low levels. In summary, these findings suggest that after controlling for macro and policy variables, as well as other local labour market characteristics, the specific regional advantages or disadvantages have significant impacts on the employment of residents within that region.

CONCLUSIONS

In this chapter, we have carried out some in-depth analysis of regional panel data for different demographic groups as a means of exploring the main sources of the rapidly rising unemployment rates in Taiwan between 1987 and 2000. We have also undertaken a series of tests in an effort to determine which of the various models would provide the best fit for the unemployment rates in each of the demographic groups. The major findings from this analysis are as follows.

Firstly, after controlling for a variety of labour market conditions including macro variables, policy variables, local labour market features and demographic characteristics, we find that wide regional unemployment differentials are discernible in Taiwan. Admittedly, this finding indicates that those residing in the regions with less favourable labour markets (e.g., the cities and neighbouring areas) face higher unemployment levels than would otherwise be the case.

Secondly, and on a much more specific level, we have determined that these regional effects come in the form of fixed effects for nine of the 12 demographic groups, although this is not the case for the male youth, female youth and prime-aged female groups, for whom the regional effects are more random in nature.

Thirdly, by using region-specific demographic data, obtained by disaggregating the macro data and simultaneously controlling for the regional and time effects, we are able to obtain a more accurate measure of the impact of the macro and policy variables on the unemployment rates. Specifically, the unemployment rates are found to be highly correlated to the level of the minimum wage in a positive direction for almost all demographic groups, with the exceptions of young males, and both males and females in the middle-aged and older-aged groups. By contrast, the prior studies, which usually employed aggregated national-level data, found only a negligible association between the level of unemployment and the variations in the minimum wage.

Finally, the coefficient estimates of the local labour market variables vary significantly across the different demographic groups. For example, within a given region, the percentage share of highly educated workers in the total labour force has a positive and significant impact on the unemployment rates of male and female youths, as well as on those in the prime-aged female group, whereas it exerts a negative effect on the unemployment of those in the prime-aged male group. This may be due to the fact that in Taiwan, male and female youths, as well as females as a whole, have a relatively lower educational level, and hence are less competitive within the labour market, as compared to the prime-aged male group.

These results clearly indicate a need for the adoption of a set of regionally diversified policies, along with nationwide macroeconomic and demographic-specific policies, in order to achieve regional economic growth and labour market flexibility. Given that the unemployment rate is worsening over time, it is all the more important to gain an understanding of the sources of unemployment at a disaggregated level, and to determine ways in which these problems can either be overcome, or compensated for, by appropriate public policies.

NOTES

[1]   The Taiwan Statistical Data Book has been published annually since 1964 by the Council for Economic Planning and Development, a department of the Executive Yuan in Taiwan.

[2]   Refer to Greene (2000, pp.560-77) for a comparison of the 'fixed-effects' and 'random-effects' approaches.

[3]   In 1986, the Minimum Wage Law was replaced by the Basic Wage Act; with the basic wage, in principle, being indexed to the consumer price index (CPI) and labour productivity growth.

[4]   It should be noted that the fixed effects are reported for all demographic groups, even though the random-effects model is considered more appropriate for the male youth, female youth and prime-aged female groups.

REFERENCES

Breusch T. and A. Pagan (1980), 'The Lagrange Multiplier Test and its Application to Model Specification in Econometrics', *Review of Economic Studies*, **47**(1): 239-53.

Card, D. and A.O. Kreuger (1995), *Myth and Measurement: The New Economics of the Minimum Wage*, New Jersey, NY: Princeton University Press.

CEPD (various years), *The Taiwan Statistical Data Book*, Taipei: Council for Economic Planning and Development.

CLA (various years), *Monthly Bulletin of Labour Statistics*, Taipei: Council of Labour Affairs.

DGBAS (various years), *Yearbook of Manpower Survey Statistics*, Taipei: Directorate-General of Budget, Accounting and Statistics.

Filer, R.K., D.S. Hamermesh and A.E. Rees (1996), *The Economics of Work and Pay* (6th edn.), Hong Kong: Harper Collins College Publishers.

Greene, W.H. (2000), *Economic Analysis* (4th edn.), New Jersey, NY: Prentice Hall.

Hausman, J. (1978), 'Specification Tests in Econometrics', *Econometrica*, **46**(6): 1251-71.

Huang, J.D. (2001), *Estimation of the Economic Effects of Basic Wages in 2001*, Taipei: Council of Labour Affairs (in Chinese).

Jiang, F.F. (1997), 'The Current Problem of Unemployment in Taiwan and its Possible Resolution', *Taiwan Economic Forecast and Policy*, **27**(2): 41-73 (in Chinese).

Jiang, F.F. (2000), 'The Impacts of Demographic, Economic and Political Trends on the Social Security Net in Taiwan: The Evolution of the National Pension Insurance and Unemployment Insurance Programs', paper presented at the Network Meeting on *Building a Safety Network for the Asian Societies in Transition*, organized by the Institut de Recherches Economiques et Sociales and the Louvain Euroasia Center for Asian Studies, Universite Catholique de Louvain, Belgium, sponsored by the European Science Foundation, Asia Committee and held in Louvain-le-Neuve, Belgium, 27-30 April 2000, pp.1-63.

Jiang, F.F. (2001a), 'On the Unemployment of Middle- and Older-aged Primary Labourers', proceedings of the *Symposium on Current Unemployment*, Taipei: the Committee for the Promotion of Research into Social Problems, Institute of Sociology and Institute of Economics, Academia Sinica, pp.48-88 (in Chinese).

Jiang, F.F. (2001b), 'Problems and Policies Regarding the Unemployment of Middle- and Older-aged Primary Workers', *Industry of Free China*, **91**(7): 41-82 (in Chinese).

Jiang, F.F., A. Tung and P.K. Liu (2002), 'Impacts of Demographic, Economic and Political Trends on Taiwan's Social Security Net: The Evolution of the National Health Insurance, Pension Insurance and Unemployment Insurance Programs', *Industry of Free China*, **92**(3): 37-84.

Jiang, M. and G. San (1987), 'Impacts of Basic Wages on the Labour Market', Proceedings of the Chinese Economic Association Annual Meeting, Taipei: Chinese Economic Association, pp.61-98 (in Chinese).

Layard, R., S. Nickell and R. Jackman (1991), *Unemployment, Macroeconomic Performance and the Labour Market*, Oxford, NY: Oxford University Press.

Lee, J.C. (2000), 'An Enquiry into the Impacts of Labour Standards on Trade, Employment and Economic Development', proceedings of the *Symposium on Current Economic Problems*, Taipei: Chinese Economic Association (in Chinese).

Lee, J.C. and H. Wu (1992), *Survey Report on the Dynamic Impacts of the Labour Standards Law on Industrial Development and Firms' Employment Behaviour*, Taipei: Chung-Hua Institution for Economic Research and the Industrial Development Bureau (in Chinese).

Liu, P.K. and A. Tung (2001), 'Taiwan's Labour Market and Unemployment', *Industry of Free China*, **91**(4): 1-40 (in Chinese).

MOEA (various years), *Economic Statistics Monthly*, Taipei: Ministry of Economic Affairs.

San, G. (1987), 'Study and Survey of the Contribution Rate for Pension Funds in the Labour Standards Law of Taiwan', *CIER Economic Monograph, No.110*, Taipei: Chung-Hua Institution for Economic Research (in Chinese).

8 The Role of Foreign Workers in Taiwan's Economic Development

Joseph S. Lee

INTRODUCTION

As a direct result of the serious shortage of low-skilled labour which Taiwan was encountering in the late 1980s, the government introduced a 'temporary foreign workers programme' (TFWP) which would allow foreign workers to work under contracts of employment in Taiwan for specific periods, on completion of which they would be required to return to their home countries. The intention thereafter was that if the need for such foreign workers continued, a different group of workers could be admitted to take over the positions of those who had been required to leave. In accordance with the provisions of the TFWP, the period of stay in Taiwan for any of these foreign workers was to remain temporary; furthermore, they would not be permitted to bring their family members with them into Taiwan.

Temporary foreign workers programmes of this type are by no means a modern concept; indeed, a very similar programme was in place in the US as far back as 1942 (the 'Bracero' programme) involving the introduction of Mexicans workers into the US on temporary work contracts, with a subsequent US administration also introducing a similar high-skilled (H1-B) workers programme in 1952. West Germany, as it was then, also had a similar 'Gastarbeiter' (guest worker) programme in place from 1955 onwards. Furthermore, Kuwait has been running its Kafala-Visa 18 programme since 1973, whilst Singapore, Hong Kong and Korea also went on to introduce similar programmes in the late 1980s or early 1990s.

On the introduction of temporary foreign workers programmes, the intention is that such programmes will benefit all of the parties involved; for labour-receiving countries, there is the expected increase in labour supply and resultant resolution of labour shortage problems, whilst for labour-sending countries there is an expected reduction in the unemployment rate and a resultant inflow of remittances. For foreign workers themselves, there are important increases in family income as well as human capital, because, apart from their wages, these workers will invariably receive on-the-job training in the host countries, thereby accumulating valuable work experience. The inflow of remittances is also an important source of foreign exchange for labour-sending countries; in 2001, for example, Indian workers abroad remitted an estimated US$10 billion, whilst Mexican workers sent home about US$9.9 billion and Filipino workers remitted about US$6.4 billion (Martin, 2004).

However, many of the empirical studies on TFWPs have shown that they do not actually produce the positive effects that are expected of them; indeed, it has been argued that such programmes demonstrate adverse effects for both the host country and home country alike. Such criticism of these types of programmes was given a considerable boost following the termination of the Bracero programme in the US in 1964, when it was found that there was no decline in productivity whatsoever within the agricultural sector, as the advocators of such programmes had constantly proclaimed, but that it actually rose (Wise, 1974; Morgan and Gardner, 1982; Levine, 2004). Some years later, in 1973, West Germany also ended its Gastarbeiter programme.

Nevertheless, in 2004, President George W. Bush announced that he intended to introduce a similar foreign workers programme in an effort to resolve the problem of the large numbers of illegal immigrants coming into the US. Many economists were, however, strongly opposed to President Bush's proposal, citing the experiences of the 'Bracero' and other similar programmes (Martin, 2001; Ruhs, 2002; Briggs, 2004). These critics generally contended that, firstly, temporary foreign workers programmes produced distorted dependency effects for employers in the host country; secondly, that such programmes brought illegal immigrants into the host country; and thirdly, that these programmes were not temporary at all, and that if such foreign workers were to become permanent, they would not only displace native workers but also hold down native worker wage rates. Indeed, as one critic noted: "there is nothing more permanent than a temporary foreign workers programme" Martin (2001). Finally, it was also argued that the availability of low-cost labour reduced employers' incentives to introduce new technologies and to upgrade their products, citing the notion that scarcity leads to innovation:

It is important to recognize that discoveries of improved methods or substitute products are not just luck. They happen in response to 'scarcity' and increases in costs. Even after a discovery is made, there is a good chance that it will not be put into operation until there is need for it, due to rising costs. This point is important; scarcity and technological advance are not two unrelated competitors in a race, but rather, each influences the other (Simon, 1981).

Since the late 1980s Taiwan, Hong Kong, South Korea and Singapore have all experienced serious labour shortages and have installed similar TFWPs as a means of resolving their problems. However, the experiences of these countries are not all positive; indeed, Singapore is now trying various alternatives to keep the numbers of foreign workers down (Hui and Hashmi, 2004), whilst South Korea is also revising its labour market policy and is now attempting to reduce the adverse effects of its own TFWP (Park, 2005). Nevertheless, despite the reported adverse effects, the governments of a number of Western industrialized countries are currently in the process of revitalizing their own foreign worker programmes, based essentially on the requirement in the new globalized and knowledge-based economy for such countries to recruit the most talented workers from abroad, whether temporary or permanent, so as to increase their domestic competitiveness.

However, within many of the developing countries, there appears to be no shortage of governments interested in getting involved in overseas foreign workers programmes as labour-sending countries. This is largely because they see considerable value in both the reduction in unemployment rates at home arising from the job opportunities in the labour-receiving countries, as well as the inflow of currency from abroad coming as a result of the remittances home by these newly employed workers. Within some countries that are already involved in such programmes, such as India and the Philippines, the inflow of these remittances are seen as an important source of foreign income which can be extremely useful for financing construction and infrastructure projects (Martin, 2004).

Furthermore, many of the foreign workers programmes introduced in Canada, such as the 'seasonal agricultural workers programme' and the 'Quebec and Guatemala agricultural workers programmes', have also been found to have achieved considerable success. It has been pointed out that the keys to the success of these programmes are their seasonality, the lack of alternative sources of labour for employers (i.e., no illegal population) and the vested interests of all the parties involved. This is essentially because the labour-sending countries benefit from the stable source of employment for their workers, whilst employers benefit from the ready availability and stability of workers for their farming operations. Furthermore, the workers entering Canada from the developing countries also benefit from the employers' promises to comply with Canadian labour legislation and wage standards (Ruddick, 2004).

In this chapter, our aim is to analyse the Taiwanese experience of its temporary foreign workers programme, and to determine what effects (whether positive or negative) the programme has had on the Taiwanese labour market as a whole, as well as on individual Taiwanese citizens, in terms of the effects on the employment and wages of native workers.

BASIC PRINCIPLES BEHIND THE IMPORTATION OF LOW-SKILLED FOREIGN WORKERS INTO TAIWAN

The fundamental reason behind the introduction of the low-skilled foreign workers programme in Taiwan was to alleviate the labour shortages within the construction and labour-intensive industries, and in many of the dirty, dangerous and difficult (3D) jobs, those jobs that are invariably shunned by native workers. The enactment of the Employment Service Act (ESA) in 1992 was essentially based upon this rationale, with this legislation establishing a number of official principles and procedures for the admission of foreign workers into Taiwan. Firstly, foreign workers were to be admitted on a strictly temporary basis; it was never intended that they should become permanent immigrants. Under this principle, all foreign workers would be allowed to stay in Taiwan for only three years; if the continued services of individual workers were deemed necessary, their stay could be extended for up to a further three years, thereby providing for a maximum period of six years.

Secondly, such workers were to be admitted solely for the purpose of supplementing native workers and not as a means of replacing them. The government therefore set quotas which restricted the admission of temporary foreign workers into designated industries and occupations. Employers wishing to hire foreign workers were required to clearly show the existence of a serious labour shortage within their industry, or in particular occupations, and that the shortage was hindering their effective operations, their expansion, or the upgrading of their production facilities. The government also excluded the employment of foreign workers in administrative and management positions, since there was no indication of any labour shortage in these particular occupations. Small firms, that is, those with less than ten employees, would also be prohibited from hiring foreign workers on the grounds that they had a minimal impact on the economy, and also because of the difficulties in administering these programmes.

Thirdly, foreign workers could not be admitted if, as a consequence, the upgrading of Taiwan's industrial structure would be delayed. Finally, the admission of foreign workers was to be conducted under a condition of minimum social costs; thus, none of these workers would be allowed to bring any of their family members with them into Taiwan, and any foreign workers who were found guilty of committing a crime, regardless of how small, would be immediately deported.

Essentially, the purpose of admitting foreign workers into Taiwan was strictly to relieve the labour shortages in the construction and labour-intensive industries. It was also the government's original intention that once employers in the labour-intensive industries had completed their adjustment, the demand for foreign workers could be reduced, if not totally eliminated.

THE ROLE OF FOREIGN WORKERS

1992-1995

Resolving labour shortages and supplementing native workers

During the late 1980s, many infrastructure projects had totally failed to get off the ground due to the severe shortage of low-skilled labour. Furthermore, private employers' production operations were also being constantly interrupted in some of the labour-intensive industries. In order to resolve these problems, in 1992 the government enacted the ESA and began to admit foreign workers into Taiwan, on an official basis, for the first time. These workers were allocated to the severe labour shortage areas, such as the public construction projects (40.59 per cent) as well as those labour-intensive industries that were experiencing labour shortages (52.93 per cent); there were also a few foreign workers admitted as household maids and healthcare service workers (4.2 per cent).

Since then the government has been allowing greater numbers of foreign workers to enter Taiwan and has also been allocating a greater share of these workers into the manufacturing sector, as compared to the construction sector, largely because the manufacturing sector had encountered considerable difficulties in recruiting low-skilled workers. Thus, although there was a total of only 15,942 foreign workers in Taiwan in 1992, by 1995 this figure had risen exponentially, to 189,051, with the share of such workers in the manufacturing sector rising from 52.49 per cent in 1992 to 67.83 per cent in 1995 (Table 8.1).

Foreign workers were initially allocated to the 68 industries and 15 occupations within the manufacturing sector which had been identified by the government as those industries and occupations facing the most serious labour shortage problems. An additional 73 manufacturing industries, six ceramics industries and certain 3D jobs were subsequently added to this list of serious labour shortage industries. As the figures in Table 8.2 show, during the period under examination, large numbers of temporary foreign workers were to be found in the textiles, plastics, metal products, wood and bamboo, and electrical and electronic products industries, those industries that were experiencing the most severe labour shortages at that time.

There was some reduction in the labour shortage problem during the mid-1990s, largely as a result of the shift in the structure of the manufacturing sector, from predominately labour-intensive industries towards more capital- and skills-intensive industries. With greater numbers of workers being released from the labour-intensive industries, these workers became available for use in other industries. In 1992, the vacancy rate in the manufacturing sector, for example, was 7.32 per cent, a figure which rose to 9.83 per cent in 1993, but subsequently fell to 3.82 per cent by 1999. Within the construction sector, the vacancy rate fell from a high of 7.29 per cent in 1992, to 3.21 per cent in 1999 (Tu, 2000: 2).

Table 8.1 Number of foreign workers in Taiwan, by admission categories, 1992-2005

Admission Categories	1992		1995		1997		1999	
	Total No.	%	Total No.	%	Total No.	%	Total No.	%
Major Government Construction Projects	6,463	40.59	35,117	18.58	40,138	16.16	41,588	14.10
6 Industries and 15 Occupations	7,886	49.52	6,433	3.40	5,875	2.37	2,259	0.77
Healthcare Workers	306	1.92	8,902	4.71	26,233	10.56	67,063	22.74
Household Maids	363	2.28	8,505	4.50	12,879	5.18	7,730	2.62
Fishing Boat Crewmen	70	0.44	1,454	0.77	1,144	0.46	993	0.34
68 Manufacturing Industries	836	5.25	18,157	9.60	17,636	7.10	12,785	4.33
73 Manufacturing Industries	–	–	20,423	10.80	16,107	6.48	892	0.30
6 Ceramics Industries	–	–	16,597	8.78	19,534	7.86	1,438	0.49
New Plants or Expanding Production Facilities	–	–	34,654	18.33	37,018	14.90	7,251	2.46
Export Processing Zones and Industrial Parks	–	–	4,813	2.55	4,607	1.85	467	0.16
3D Jobs	–	–	20,537	10.86	3,428	1.38	146	0.05
Major Investment Projects: Manufacturing	–	–	11,089	5.87	36,160	14.56	67,128	22.76
Major Investment Projects: Construction	–	–	1,095	0.58	1,405	0.57	2,929	0.99
7 Manufacturing Projects	–	–	1,275	0.67	3,304	1.33	142	0.05
Traditional Manufacturing Replacements *	–	–	–	–	–	–	241	0.08
Non-traditional Manufacturing Replacements *	–	–	–	–	–	–	–	–
Total	15,924	100.00	189,051	100.00	248,396	100.00	294,967	100.00

Table 8.1   (Contd.)

Admission Categories	2001		2003		2005	
	Total No.	%	Total No.	%	Total No.	%
Major Government Construction Projects	29,619	9.72	12,747	4.25	6,193	1.89
6 Industries and 15 Occupations	208	0.07	71	0.02	55	0.02
Healthcare Workers	103,780	34.07	115,724	38.56	141,752	43.30
Household Maids	9,154	3.01	4,874	1.62	2,263	0.69
Fishing Boat Crewmen	1,249	0.41	3,396	1.13	3,147	0.96
68 Manufacturing Industries	2,292	0.75	387	0.13	178	0.05
73 Manufacturing Industries	207	0.07	158	0.05	147	0.04
6 Ceramics Industries	192	0.06	135	0.04	117	0.04
New Plants or Expanding Production Facilities	459	0.15	193	0.06	168	0.05
Export Processing Zones and Industrial Parks	212	0.07	18	0.01	6	–
3D Jobs	51	0.02	50	0.02	45	0.01
Major Investment Projects: Manufacturing	50,520	16.59	47,226	15.73	40,379	12.33
Major Investment Projects: Construction	2,502	0.82	301	0.10	6,087	1.86
7 Manufacturing Projects	17	0.01	14	–	12	–
Traditional Manufacturing Replacements *	10,361	3.40	22,206	7.40	36,163	11.05
Non-traditional Manufacturing Replacements *	377	0.12	922	0.31	3,027	0.92
Total	304,605	100.00	300,150	100.00	327,396	100.00

Note: * The term 'replacements' refers to the replacement of temporary foreign workers whose contracts have expired.

Source: CLA (various years), *Monthly Labour Statistics Report.*

188

1995 to Date

Promoting the high-tech and major exporting industries

With the labour shortage problem in the labour-intensive industries having been alleviated, the government subsequently began to readjust the role of the temporary foreign workers towards the promotion of the high-tech and major exporting industries, providing these industries with this readily available source of low-cost labour.

In 1995, about 21,230 temporary foreign workers (or 12.87 per cent of all foreign workers in Taiwan) were to be found in the electrical and electronics industries; however, alongside the rapid transformation of the previously labour-intensive electrical and electronic industries, into modern high-tech industries, there had also been a rapid increase in the number of foreign workers employed within these industries. By 1997, the high-tech sector had surpassed the textiles sector to become the largest employers of foreign workers in Taiwan, employing a total of 35,825 of these workers (or 14.58 per cent of all foreign workers in Taiwan). By 2005, the total number of temporary foreign workers employed within the high-tech sector had risen still further, to 57,057 employees, or 17.4 per cent of all foreign workers in Taiwan.

Conversely, having formerly been the largest employer of foreign workers in Taiwan in 1995, with about 23,435 foreign workers (or 14.21 per cent of all the foreign workers in Taiwan), and despite the continuing rise in the number of foreign workers employed within the textiles sector (to about 32,956 persons), by 1997, the overall share of foreign workers employed within the textiles sector had fallen to 13.41 per cent of the total (Table 8.2). Thereafter, there were further declines in the total number of foreign workers accounted for by the textiles industries, as well as their overall share of all foreign workers in Taiwan; by 2005, these industries were accounting for 23,995 persons, or just 7.33 per cent of all foreign workers in Taiwan.

The same trend is also discernible from 1997 onwards for other labour-intensive industries such as the food, apparel, leather, lumber and bamboo, paper, rubber and plastics industries, with a steady decline in both the total numbers and the overall shares of foreign workers in these industries. Foreign workers were also used to promote the expansion of the major exporting industries. As the share of all exports accounted for by chemical products rose from 2.2 per cent in 1992, to 4.4 per cent in 2005, alongside other rises in the share of all exports over the same period by basic metals products (7.9 per cent to 10.5 per cent), electronic and electrical products (14.1 per cent to 27.9 per cent) and precision instrument products (2.5 per cent to 6.5 per cent), there was a steady rise in both the number and the share of foreign workers employed within these industries (Table 8.2).

Table 8.2 Distribution of foreign workers by industry, 1992-2005

Industry	1992 Total No.	1992 %	1995 Total No.	1995 %	1997 Total No.	1997 %	1999 Total No.	1999 %
Manufacturing								
Food	287	0.56	3,366	2.04	4,402	1.79	4,305	1.54
Textiles	4,369	8.54	23,435	14.21	32,956	13.41	33,113	11.87
Apparel	635	1.24	3,331	2.02	3,577	1.46	3,023	1.08
Leather and Fur Products	158	0.31	2,639	1.60	2,663	1.08	2,189	0.78
Pulp and Paper	452	0.88	3,587	2.17	3,824	1.56	3,490	1.25
Chemicals and Chemical Products	51	0.10	2,861	1.73	3,571	1.45	3,219	1.16
Rubber Products	30	0.06	4,678	2.84	4,463	1.82	4,763	1.71
Plastic Products	2,184	4.27	11,566	7.01	11,211	4.56	10,582	3.79
Non-metal Products	–		8,042	4.87	9,688	3.94	7,460	2.68
Basic Metal Products	1,704	3.33	15,363	9.31	14,885	6.06	12,128	4.35
Metal Products	3,520	6.88	14,758	8.95	18,994	7.73	17,304	6.20
Machinery and Equipment	1,247	2.44	3,876	2.35	4,195	1.71	6,300	2.26
Electrical and Electronic Products	1,492	2.92	21,230	12.87	35,825	14.58	42,105	15.10
Transportation Equipment	748	1.46	4,616	2.80	6,844	2.79	6,881	2.47
Precision Instruments	14	0.03	536	0.32	624	0.25	704	0.25
Miscellaneous and Others	1,047	2.05	2,519	1.55	2,679	1.10	6,690	2.40
Construction	6,463	64.93	38,570	23.38	48,786	19.86	51,894	18.61
Household Maids and Healthcare Workers	–	–	–	–	35,245	14.34	61,723	22.13
Crewmen	–	–	–	–	1,265	0.51	999	0.36
Total	51,155	100.00	164,973	100.00	245,697	100.00	278,872	100.00

Table 8.2 (*Contd.*)

Industry	2001		2003		2005	
	Total No.	%	Total No.	%	Total No.	%
Manufacturing						
Food	4,511	1.48	4,680	1.56	4,970	1.52
Textiles	28,026	9.20	26,911	8.97	23,995	7.33
Apparel	2,575	0.85	2,318	0.77	1,748	0.53
Leather and Fur Products	1,613	0.53	1,441	0.48	1,320	0.40
Pulp and Paper	3,455	1.13	3,339	1.11	3,316	1.01
Chemicals and Chemical Products	3,499	1.15	3,286	1.12	3,502	1.17
Rubber Products	4,251	1.40	4,475	1.49	4,475	1.37
Plastic Products	10,184	3.34	9,880	3.29	10,052	3.07
Non-metal Products	6,141	2.02	6,177	2.06	6,195	1.89
Basic Metal Products	10,315	3.39	9,717	3.24	9,853	3.01
Metal Products	16,413	5.39	17,175	5.72	17,895	5.47
Machinery and Equipment	6,643	2.18	7,120	2.37	7,455	2.28
Electrical and Electronic Products	44,135	14.19	51,135	17.04	57,057	17.4
Transportation Equipment	6,949	2.28	7,253	2.42	8,260	2.52
Precision Instruments	752	0.25	695	0.23	840	0.26
Miscellaneous and Others *	7,593	2.49	6,437	2.14	5,995	1.84
Construction	33,367	10.95	14,117	4.70	13,306	4.06
Household Maids and Healthcare Workers	112,934	37.08	120,598	40.18	144,015	43.99
Crewmen	1,249	0.41	3,396	1.13	3,147	0.96
Total	304,605	100.00	300,150	100.00	327,396	100.00

Note: * 'Miscellaneous and Others' includes 'wood and bamboo products', 'furniture and fixtures' and 'printing'.

Source: CLA (various years), *Survey on the Management and Utilization of Foreign Workers in Taiwan*.

191

Conversely, textile products, which, in 1992, had accounted for 10.7 per cent of all exports in Taiwan, had fallen to 6.5 per cent by 2005, whilst the share of exports accounted for by garment production had also fallen, from 8.4 per cent in 1992 to just 1.0 per cent in 2005. As the figures in Table 8.2 show, by and large, all industries within which there had been declines in the overall share of exports also saw declines in their share of employment of temporary foreign workers.

The rapid development of the high-tech sector had clearly come at exactly the right time to save Taiwan from the worst ravages of the 1997 Asian financial crisis. It was quite fortunate that at just that time, the declining share of Taiwanese exports to Southeast Asian countries was being largely offset by the rise in exports of high-quality high-tech goods to the US and other industrialized countries. In a comparison undertaken in a recent study between the characteristics of firms employing foreign workers vis-à-vis those with no foreign workers, it was found that the former were invariably in the capital-intensive industries (where the workforce was dominated by males and where a larger proportion of the products were for export), whereas those firms that did not employ foreign workers were invariably found to be in the labour-intensive industries (where there was a greater proportion of females in the workforce and the firms had established overseas subsidiaries). Clearly, the latter group remained in a better position to utilize low-cost labour overseas, and therefore had no requirement to employ foreign workers in Taiwan (Wu, 2004).

Raising the female labour force participation rates

Another role which the government was keen to see foreign workers playing was that of raising the labour force participation rates amongst female workers; this was essentially because, as compared to other neighbouring Asian countries, Taiwan has consistently had the lowest females labour force participation rates. In 2004, for example, the average female labour force participation rate in Taiwan was 47.7 per cent, as compared to 48.3 per cent in Japan, 49.8 per cent in Korea, 51.9 per cent in Hong Kong and 54.2 per cent in Singapore (CLA, 2005).

One of the reasons that the government allowed the introduction of foreign household maids and healthcare workers into Taiwan in 1992 was that it felt that such a policy might help to free up some Taiwanese women (better-educated women in particular) from their household chores, and that these women would then enter the labour market, thereby increasing the overall labour supply in Taiwan. As a direct result of this policy, the demand for foreign household maids and healthcare workers has been rising rapidly, from 16,472 persons in 1995 to 112,934 persons in 2001, and still further to 144,015 persons in 2005 (Table 8.2).

The share of all foreign workers in Taiwan accounted for by these foreign household maids and healthcare workers has also been rising rapidly, from 9.21 per cent in 1995 to 37.08 per cent in 2001, and to 43.99 per cent in 2005 (Table 8.2). Nevertheless, the female labour force participation rates in Taiwan have changed very little; indeed, between 1995 and 2005 the rate actually rose, albeit only by 2.78 per cent (from 45.34 per cent in 1995 to 48.12 per cent in 2005). Such a minimal impact on the female labour force participation rates in Taiwan can be partly attributed to the fact that within those households that had begun employing foreign household maids, a considerable proportion of the housewives had already been participating in the labour market. Although, in many cases, the availability of foreign household maids may well have helped them to reduce their responsibilities within the family home, it nevertheless did nothing to bring about any increase in the labour market participation rates amongst females.

For example, in 1994, 97 per cent of all households in Taiwan employing foreign maids were families within which there was a housewife. It was estimated that within these households, 86.7 per cent of these housewives were already in gainful employment prior to taking on their maids, and indeed, continued in their employment after employing their maids. A further 1.5 per cent of all housewives had not been participating in the labour market prior to employing their foreign household maids, nor did they begin to participate in the labour market after taking them on. A very small proportion of housewives (0.5 per cent) subsequently dropped out of the labour market after hiring their foreign household maids (CLA, 1994: 127).

Thus, it was only in about 11.3 per cent of all households that there were housewives who were not previously employed; clearly, therefore, both prior to and after the introduction of the policy allowing the entry of foreign household maids into Taiwan, there was only a very small proportion of all households that could possibly provide any boost to the female labour market participation rates. A subsequent survey carried out in 1998 by the Council for Labour Affairs (CLA) showed a similar picture, with the only difference being the proportion of housewives who were not participating in the labour market prior to employing a foreign household maid, but who subsequently entered the labour market after taking on the maid; this figure fell slightly, to 7.1 per cent (CLA, 1998: 71).

Furthermore, some of the foreign workers being brought into Taiwan, ostensibly as healthcare workers, are not actually freeing up housewives from their household chores at all, largely because they are being assigned to carry out work other than caring for elderly or disabled family members. Such healthcare workers have often been assigned to factory and other jobs essentially because small businesses in Taiwan are not permitted to hire foreign workers. It is quite clear that, in order to circumvent this regulation, some of the employers within these small businesses (those who have elderly family members at home) have been taking advantage of the programme to apply for foreign healthcare workers, albeit for use for other purposes. Once approval is received and the foreign healthcare workers arrive, they are subsequently assigned to work in family-owned factories, restaurants or shops, as opposed to carrying out their intended role of taking care of the elderly or disabled members of the family.

This practice is evidenced by the registration within the government of a greater number of foreign healthcare workers than the actual number of registered disabled persons who have been certified by the government as being qualified to hire foreign healthcare workers. A 2003 survey clearly showed that there were 26,249 disabled persons in Taipei City, of which only 15,209 were entitled to employ foreign healthcare workers (essentially those who had been certified by the government as being seriously disabled). However, of the total disabled population of Taipei City, 5,188 had been admitted to public or private institutions; this therefore left a maximum of 10,021 disabled persons entitled to hire foreign healthcare workers, and yet there were 26,632 foreign healthcare workers registered within the Taipei City government at that time. Similarly, the records for Taipei County, Taoyuan County, Hsinchu City and Taichung City all revealed greater numbers of foreign healthcare workers than the number of disabled persons actually entitled to employ them (Liu and Hsia, 2004).

Providing management flexibility
As Taiwan becomes more affluent, increasing numbers of native workers are demonstrating their growing reluctance to work on overtime assignments; employers are therefore becoming increasingly reliant upon foreign workers as their main source of labour for performing such overtime work. As the figures in Table 8.3 show, foreign workers consistently worked, on average, 37 to 40 hours overtime work each month, twice as much as the overtime work undertaken by native workers within the manufacturing sector, and four times as much as that for native workers within the construction sector.

The figures in Table 8.3 also indicate that this dependency upon foreign workers as the primary source of overtime work has continued to grow amongst many employers in Taiwan particularly within the manufacturing sector. This is revealed by the increasing number of overtime hours performed by foreign workers in the manufacturing industries, from 38.2 hours per month in 1993 to 46.6 hours per month in 2005. Although the same cannot be said for the construction sector, this can be explained by the nature of the work within the construction industries, since any extension of the long hours of hard physical work would be likely to lead to an increase in the rate of industrial accidents.

Table 8.3   Average monthly working hours for foreign workers in the manufacturing and construction industries, 1993-2005

Year	Monthly Working Hours for Foreign Workers *					
	Regular Work		Overtime		Total	
	Average	FW/NW	Average	FW/NW	Average	FW/NW
Manufacturing Industry						
1993	201.1	1.07	38.2	2.73	239.2	1.18
1995	209.9	1.13	36.7	2.37	246.6	1.22
1997	204.1	1.10	40.7	2.50	244.8	1.21
1999	203.4	1.11	37.6	2.27	241.0	1.21
2001	196.5	1.15	28.3	2.02	224.8	1.22
2002	189.7	1.10	42.4	2.68	232.1	1.24
2004	180.5	1.04	44.8	2.52	225.3	1.18
2005	184.6	1.08	46.6	2.73	231.2	1.22
Construction Industry						
1993	201.7	1.08	40.5	8.44	242.2	1.27
1995	210.2	1.12	34.8	4.52	245.0	1.26
1997	208.3	1.13	49.1	6.06	257.3	1.34
1999	218.6	1.23	42.9	6.04	261.4	1.41
2001	199.8	1.15	34.1	4.67	233.9	1.29
2002	190.7	1.12	41.8	6.33	232.5	1.32
2004	188.1	1.10	37.6	6.48	225.7	1.27
2005	178.5	1.03	41.0	8.20	219.6	1.24

Note: * 'FW/NW' refers to average working hours for foreign workers/average working hours for native workers.

Sources: [1]   DGBAS (various years), *Employees Pay and Working Hours.*
        [2]   CLA (various years), *Survey on the Management and Utilization of Foreign Workers in Taiwan.*

Providing low-cost labour
The provision of low-cost labour was not a role assigned to foreign workers; indeed, it was made clear by the government when it first started admitting foreign workers that the main purpose behind the policy was simply to supplement native workers. However, once the government put into place legislation covering both foreign and native workers by the same minimum wage standards, employers soon began to complain about the high cost of employing foreign workers. Although other regional economies, such as Hong Kong and Singapore, either provided no minimum wage coverage at all, or had separate minimum wage provisions for their foreign workers, the CLA in Taiwan refused to exclude foreign workers from the minimum wage law.

As pressure mounted from various groups of employers, the government eventually came to a compromise by issuing a new policy in 1997 which directed that whilst foreign workers would continue to have the same minimum wage protection as native workers, employers would nevertheless be allowed to count 'room and board' and certain other expenses paid to their foreign workers as part of this minimum wage. It was, however, explicitly stated that such deductions should not exceed NT$4,000 per month (exchange rate US$1.00:NT$33.00). The net result of this additional policy is that foreign workers have essentially become a source of cheap labour in Taiwan. Figures published by the government show that the wages of foreign workers have been kept at a level of about NT$15,000-NT$16,000 since the mid-1990s, which is close to the minimum wage rate, and that the wage gap between inexperienced native workers and foreign workers has consistently been maintained at around 15 to 20 per cent (Table 8.4); nevertheless, the actual income received by foreign workers is now much lower as a result of employers deducting 'room and board' expenses at an average of about NT$3,771 from these workers (CLA, 2004, 2005).

Although government reports show that only about 30 per cent of all employers currently hiring foreign workers are making such deductions from their wages, it does, nevertheless, appear that the number of employers deducting such expenses is on the increase (CLA, 2004, 2005). Furthermore, there are very few native workers who work side-by-side with foreign workers, so the comparison in Table 8.4 may be somewhat misleading. If we compare the wages of foreign workers with the average salary of native workers within the manufacturing sector as a whole, we find that the gap has continued to widen, from 40 per cent in 1993 to 50 per cent in 2004. The gap between the wages received by foreign household maids and healthcare workers and those received by native workers is even wider, since these foreign workers are not covered by the Fair Labour Standards Law (FLSL); thus, they have to negotiate their pay scales and working conditions with their employers. The available data shows that the average wage for a foreign healthcare worker in 2005 was NT$15,000, whereas native healthcare workers were receiving a minimum of NT$35,000; some of the more experienced native healthcare workers were even receiving as much as NT$60,000 per month (Chen and Wang 2006).

In an attempt to encourage families in Taiwan to hire native healthcare workers, in January 2006, the CLA implemented a new policy whereby the government would provide qualified families with a subsidy of NT$10,000 per month for the first year if they chose to hire a native healthcare worker instead of a foreign worker. However, from the estimates of Chen and Wang (2006), it is clear that even after receiving the subsidy, a substantial difference remains between hiring a foreign and a native healthcare worker (i.e., NT$10,000), not to mention the fact that the subsidy is available only for the first year; in subsequent

The Role of Foreign Workers in Taiwan's Economic Development   197

years the cost difference would of course be in excess of NT$20,000. Thus, between January and March 2006, of the total of 3,300 native healthcare workers who had received specific training, and the 9,980 who were subsequently referred by government employment agencies to families applying for foreign healthcare workers, only 34 were employed, revealing a placement rate for native healthcare workers of less than 0.5 per cent (Chen and Wang, 2006).

Table 8.4   Comparison of average monthly foreign worker earnings and native worker earnings, 1993-2005

Year	Regular Wages [a]		Monthly Earnings [a]		Average [a,b]	
	FW	%NW	FW	%NW [c]	FW	%NW
Manufacturing Industry						
1993	14,079	80.70	17,525	88.22	14,100	75.50
1995	15,410	83.30	19,529	90.70	15,487	80.12
1997	16,167	86.90	20,963	96.90	16,059	84.00
1999	16,542	87.40	21,006	95.00	16,507	85.10
2001	16,435	76.00	19,496	80.40	16,353	73.60
2002	16,332	75.80	20,561	83.90	16,353	73.90
2004	16,224	86.40	21,305	–	16,221	85.10
2005	16,506	87.40	21,577	–	16,525	85.90
Construction Industry						
1993	14,268	58.80	19,565	75.50	17,603	84.83
1995	15,736	63.90	19,533	75.00	19,530	88.80
1997	15,710	65.00	20,662	80.80	20,892	96.00
1999	16,395	65.00	20,645	76.90	20,919	95.30
2001	16,315	62.10	19,743	72.00	19,502	79.00
2002	16,478	71.90	20,385	84.10	20,536	82.80
2004	16,154	79.30	20,685	–	21,275	–
2005	16,797	79.30	20,504	–	21,507	–

Notes:
[a]   'FW' refers to foreign worker and '%NW' refers to the percentage of the average earnings of native workers; the comparison of earnings is made with native workers with less than two years' experience working within the same company; it does not refer to the earnings of those working side-by-side with foreign workers.
[b]   Average refers to the average earnings of foreign workers across all industries.
[c]   Data for comparison with the years 2004 and 2005 was unavailable at the time this chapter was concluded.

Sources: [1]   DGBAS (various years), *Yearbook of Manpower Survey Statistics.*
          [2]   CLA (various years), *Survey on the Management and Utilization of Foreign Workers in Taiwan.*

THE EFFECTS OF THE POLICY ON FOREIGN WORKERS IN TAIWAN

The purpose of this section is to examine the impact that the temporary foreign workers programme has had on the labour market in Taiwan, with particular emphasis on the impact on recent developments in unemployment. Empirical studies of the US 'Bracero' programme, the 'Gastarbeiter' programme undertaken in Germany and other temporary foreign workers programmes, indicate that all of these programmes have some serious negative effects for both the host countries and the labour-sending countries. For the host countries, the main problem appears to be that these programmes change from being temporary to permanent; indeed, so do the foreign workers themselves. The consequence of this is that employers' incentives to improve productivity amongst native workers are reduced, since they can easily replace such high-cost native workers with low-cost foreign workers. As Martin pointed out:

> all guest workers programmes fail, in the sense that some of the migrants settle in destination countries and the employment-migration ratio falls over time, leading to the aphorism that there is nothing more permanent than temporary workers (Martin, 2004).

Martin (2001), Ruhs (2002) and Martin (2004), amongst others, have pointed out three adverse effects of such programmes: (i) a temporary foreign workers programme can change from being temporary to permanent; (ii) the temporary foreign workers themselves can change into permanent migrants, thereby not only displacing native workers, but also creating segregated migrant sectors in the host country; and (iii) low-cost foreign workers not only take away the employment opportunities for native workers, but also reduce incentives amongst employers to upgrade the productivity of their workforce and the quality of their products, encouraging them instead to adopt the low road of a 'race to the bottom' competitive strategy, as opposed to choosing the high road of a high-performance competitive strategy.

Thus, there are a number of questions with regard to the overall purpose and current status of the temporary foreign workers programme in Taiwan, the first of which seeks to determine whether the programme has in fact changed in nature, from temporary to permanent. As stated earlier, when the government first set up the programme in Taiwan, it was meant to be a temporary programme, with the sole purpose of resolving the labour shortages in Taiwan's labour-intensive industries. Thus, with a reduction in the labour shortage, the number of foreign workers admitted into Taiwan should also have declined. However as the figures in Table 8.1 have already shown, there was a rapid increase in the number of foreign workers being admitted into Taiwan during the early 1990s, which then stabilized at a total of about 300,000.

This is a situation which has been allowed to prevail, despite the fact that many labour-intensive firms have actually relocated their operations abroad and that employment within these industries has declined. It has also been allowed to prevail despite Taiwanese President Chen Shui-Bian's pledge to the trade unions, in 2000, that the total number of foreign workers in Taiwan would be reduced by 15,000 workers per year until an acceptable level was reached. However, not only has there been no decline in the total number of foreign workers in Taiwan since that pledge was made, but in fact, the quota of foreign workers being allowed into Taiwan was actually increased by a further 20,000 starting from January 2006, with this additional quota being targeted specifically at the category of 3D jobs. It also appears that the U-turn by the government has been largely ignored, since many employers in the rubber, plastics, leather, paper and cement industries, as well as the other 19 traditional industries, have continued to bring pressure to bear on the government to actually increase the quota by a further 10,000 foreign workers (Hsueh, 2005).

Nevertheless, we should not simply regard the extension and apparent open-endedness of the temporary foreign workers programme as a negative development within the Taiwanese labour market, because the functions of foreign workers have been continually changing, from their initial purpose of resolving the labour shortages in the labour-intensive industries to their subsequent promotion of the high-tech and major exporting industries. Furthermore, it cannot be said that foreign workers have been monopolized by a small group of privileged employers; indeed, it would be fair to say that the programme has been used quite successfully by the government to achieve a variety of different objectives during the different stages of Taiwan's continuing economic development.

The second question to be resolved is whether foreign workers in Taiwan have actually become permanent migrants, and if so, whether they have formed separated migrant sectors. The ESA made it clear that foreign workers would be allowed to work for a period of three years in Taiwan, and that after this initial three-year period, if their services were still deemed necessary, their employers could apply for an extension of their employment contracts for a further three years, thus providing for a maximum stay in Taiwan of six years. There are, however, several ways that foreign workers can circumvent the regulations to become permanent migrants in Taiwan.

Firstly, some foreign workers are known to have returned to their home countries and to have changed the name appearing on their passport; they then apply, ostensibly as a totally different person, for a further period of work in Taiwan. The reports suggest that this practice has been more common amongst Filipino workers. Secondly, as their employment contracts are about to expire, some foreign workers will simply run away from their current employers and seek jobs in a different area with an alternative employer. Since it is illegal for any of these foreign workers to switch between employers without the express permission of the government, such runaway foreign workers thereby render themselves illegal workers and fugitives of the law; however, since their whereabouts are unknown to the government, they are able to stay in Taiwan indefinitely, or until such time as they are apprehended. As the figures in Table 8.5 show, in 1998, the total number of missing foreign workers was 4,679 persons (or 1.8 per cent of all foreign workers in Taiwan); this number has subsequently increased year on year, eventually reaching a total of 12,937 workers in 2005 (or 4.16 per cent of all foreign workers). The number of foreign workers who currently remain at large has also risen, from 6,646 in 1998, to a reported 21,679 workers in 2005.

The 'missing rate' varies for different labour-sending countries; it is particularly high for workers from Vietnam, but low for workers from the Philippines and Thailand. Part of the high missing rate amongst Vietnamese workers may be due to the already large, but increasing, number of cross-border marriages of Vietnamese women to Taiwanese men, since these Vietnamese wives, who have permanent status by virtue of their marriage, are able to provide sanctuary for runaway Vietnamese workers and also help them to find new jobs, essentially because they are more familiar with the local situation and can speak the local language. Illegal Vietnamese workers are therefore difficult to trace, particularly as they are very similar in appearance to native Taiwanese people.

Although the number of runaway foreign workers is not particularly large, their impact is becoming increasingly troublesome. Many of these runaway workers have been in Taiwan long enough to gain a very good understanding of the local situation, and those that have managed to evade the law for considerable periods of time are able to provide detailed information and assistance, through telephone and written communications to their friends and relatives in their home country, on effective ways for their fellow countrymen to come into Taiwan to work, either legally or illegally. Anecdotal evidence suggests that these foreign workers advise their friends and relatives to initially apply for a legal work permit and to enter Taiwan on a legal working basis or to apply for a tourist visa, again entering Taiwan legally although with the intention of working illegally. A further, rather extreme method would be to enter Taiwan through various illegal channels and then work illegally in Taiwan. Since these are all illegal workers, their wages and working conditions are usually much lower than those of legal foreign workers and substantially lower than those of native workers.

Table 8.5 Runaway foreign workers, by country of origin, 1998-2005

Country of Origin	Runaway Workers[a]	Year							
		1998	1999	2000	2001	2002	2003	2004	2005
Indonesia	Total No.	493	760	1,680	2,804	3,809	3,411	1,978	1,973
	Runaway Rate (%)	2.8	2.5	2.9	3.2	4.0	4.6	4.9	6.7
Philippines	Total No.	2,450	1,882	1,303	1,048	643	873	1,177	1,543
	Runaway Rate (%)	2.3	1.6	1.2	1.2	0.9	1.2	1.4	1.7
Thailand	Total No.	1,728	1,403	1,234	942	1,042	1,171	1,369	2,040
	Runaway Rate (%)	1.3	1.0	0.9	0.7	0.9	1.1	1.3	2.1
Vietnam	Total No.	–	–	35	293	1,584	4,233	7,536	7,363
	Runaway Rate (%)	–	–	0.7	2.8	7.8	9.6	10.2	8.2
Malaysia	Total No.	6	12	16	2	1	–	–	–
	Runaway Rate (%)	0.9	2.2	12.1	2.5	2.8	–	–	–
Mongolia	Total No.	–	–	–	–	–	–	2	–
	Runaway Rate (%)	–	–	–	–	–	–	3.3	–
Total No. of Runaway Workers/Year		4,677	4,057	4,268	5,089	7,079	9,688	12,062	12,937
Total Runaway Rate (%)		1.8	1.4	1.4	1.6	2.3	3.2	4.0	4.2
Total No. of Foreign Runaway Workers (still at large)		6,646	5,504	5,514	6,220	8,143	11,125	16,593	21,679

Note: * Runaway Rate = Total No. of runaway workers/Total number of foreign workers from that particular country x 100.

Source: CLA (various years), Survey on the Management and Utilization of Foreign Workers in Taiwan.

Details on the overall numbers and types of workers entering Taiwan from the four Southeast Asian labour-sending countries, through the various channels, are provided in Table 8.6. As the figures show, the number of workers in the 'legally admitted but illegally working' category increased from 36,386 in 1992 to 88,375 in 2003, whilst the number of workers in the category of 'illegally admitted and illegally working in Taiwan' increased from 4,550 in 1992 to 16,365 in 2003.

The combined total of all legal and illegal foreign workers in Taiwan is estimated to have risen from 77,857 in 1992 to 600,177 in 2003; however, it is generally agreed that the actual number of illegal foreign workers in Taiwan is significantly greater than 16,365, largely because it is very difficult to estimate the number of illegal workers from mainland China because of the similarity in appearance between mainland Chinese workers and Taiwanese citizens.

Table 8.6   Legal and illegal foreign workers in Taiwan, 1991-2003

Year	Foreign Workers in Taiwan *				
	(1)	(2)	(3)	(4)	(5)
1991	2,999	36,724	4,135	1,926	45,784
1992	15,924	36,386	6,336	4,550	77,857
1993	97,565	47,650	10,164	7,414	181,815
1994	151,989	59,796	16,209	8,963	232,318
1995	189,051	75,883	33,814	10,046	309,538
1996	236,555	34,074	47,129	10,840	319,649
1997	248,396	37,768	60,720	11,407	354,650
1998	270,620	33,777	78,479	12,030	394,679
1999	294,967	51,118	97,842	12,884	453,451
2000	326,515	47,402	128,454	13,620	502,316
2001	304,605	57,939	152,857	14,328	516,541
2002	303,684	78,296	182,314	15,307	569,671
2003	300,150	88,375	202,759	16,365	600,177

Note: * The numbers in parentheses refer to the following categories of foreign workers: (1) workers who were legally admitted into Taiwan; (2) workers who were legally admitted, but who are working illegally in Taiwan; (3) workers from mainland China who are legally admitted, but who are working illegally in Taiwan; (4) workers who have entered Taiwan illegally and are working illegally; and (5) the total number of legal and illegal foreign workers in Taiwan.

Source: Lan (2004).

The current ESA prohibits marriages between any of the temporary foreign workers, or between temporary foreign workers and native workers, with any contravention of this law resulting in immediate deportation. However, for certain groups of men in Taiwan (those who have real difficulty in finding a local woman to marry) the availability of foreign household maids and healthcare workers gave them the idea that they could bring in foreign women from these labour-sending countries and then make them their spouses. They could contact job brokers, whose real purpose was to provide services to employers in terms of finding foreign workers, but who would nevertheless readily serve as matchmakers and bring in their foreign spouses for them.

The available data shows that between 1999 and 2003, there were, on average, 2,111 foreign spouses applying for permits to migrate into Taiwan from Southeast Asia each year, and a further 7,249 from mainland China. The approval rate was 12.3 per cent for spouses from Southeast Asian countries and 27.0 per cent for those from mainland China (CEPD, 2004: 6). As a result, the number of cross-border marriages has been rising steadily, from 15.6 per cent of all newly married couples in 1999, to 32.1 per cent in 2003 (CEPD, 2004: 8). Furthermore, in the majority of cases, the husbands of these foreign spouses have very low educational attainment, whilst some even have physical or mental disabilities. Since these Taiwanese men have difficulty in finding jobs themselves, they become heavily dependent upon their foreign spouses to work outside of the home in order to support both the husband, and very often, the extended family. In reality, these foreign spouses are simply another source of low-cost foreign labour in Taiwan.

Legal foreign workers, runaway foreign workers and illegal foreign workers have come together to form their own communities in Taiwan, with migrant communities of Filipinos, Thais and Vietnamese known to exist in Taipei, Taichung and Taoyuan. They have their own churches and temples, and meet there each week to share all kinds of information, including employment opportunities. They also establish small restaurants and shops to provide foreign workers with their traditional native meals and food ingredients for home use. It is even reported that some runaway female foreign workers who have been unable to find appropriate jobs have taken advantage of the fact that foreign workers are not allowed to bring their family members with them into Taiwan and have gone on to form sex businesses to provide services to these male foreign workers (Wu and Lin 2006).

In accordance with the original purpose of the temporary foreign workers programme, such workers were intended to supplement native workers and not to replace them; thus during the early-1990s, the allocation of foreign workers by the government was targeted strictly at the labour-intensive and construction industries where the labour shortage problems were the most severe. However, the decision by the government, in 1997, to allow the deduction of 'room and board' expenses from foreign workers' wages, has effectively made foreign workers a source of low-cost labour and not a supplement to native workers as originally intended. As the figures in Table 8.4 have already shown, the wage gap between native and foreign workers had previously stood at about 15 per cent, which was not that significant; however, with the CLA's new policy implementation in 1997, whereby 'room and board' expenses could be counted as part of the minimum wage, the wage gap between native and foreign workers has expanded. As a result, employers have new incentives to replace their native workers with inexpensive foreign workers. Liu (2000) and Jiang (2004) found that in those regions where there was a larger share of foreign workers, unemployment rates amongst native workers were higher, as was the share of native workers in white collar occupations.

Lin (2003) found that in those areas with a higher share of foreign workers, it was more difficult for native workers to find production jobs. Hsin also noted that between 1995 and 2002, the employment of foreign workers in the electronic and electrical industries increased by 3,114 annually, which was much higher than the annul rate of increase in foreign worker employment in other industries, yet the annual increase in employment of native workers in these industries was only 33,125 persons, indicating that there is one foreign worker for every 10.64 native workers in these industries. This is much lower than the ratio of 1:36.4 in the plastics industry and 1:34.8 in the clothing industry, with the absolute number of foreign workers having declined in both of these industries (Hsin 2004).

Wu (2004) found a large coefficient of wage elasticity for native workers, at 1.92, thus any wage increases for native workers, or wage decreases for foreign workers, could cause a significant reduction in employment opportunities for native workers. In addition to replacing native workers, Lin and Lo (2004) also found that firms employing greater shares of foreign workers had lower R&D expenses; this is a clear indicator of the employment of foreign workers having adverse effects on the upgrading of Taiwan's industrial structure. The strongest evidence of foreign workers replacing native workers is in the area of foreign healthcare workers, not simply because their wages are much lower than those of native workers, but because they are not protected by the minimum provisions of the FLSA and therefore they have to negotiate their wages and benefits with their employers. Their impact on native workers is also significant because their numbers are large, in fact, 40 per cent of all foreign workers in Taiwan in 2005 were healthcare workers

According to two surveys undertaken by the CLA on families making use of foreign healthcare workers, if the foreign workers were not available today, 52.66 per cent of those employing such workers in 2004, and 46.02 per cent of those employing such workers in 2005, would send their aged or disabled family members to private or publicly operated care-giving institutions (CLA

2004: 24, CLA 2005: 33). In 2004, 19.16 per cent of the families indicated that they would take care of their elderly or disabled family members themselves and 20.06 per cent would employ native healthcare workers to care for their family members. The figures for both of these outcomes in 2005 were identical at 21.88 per cent. In other words, a reduction in the number of foreign healthcare workers in Taiwan could assist in the development of, and improvement in, the quality of care-giving industries in Taiwan. This would clearly be useful in terms of upgrading the structure of the social services in Taiwan and in the creation of more professional and semi-professional jobs for female workers in the care-giving industries, thereby raising the labour force participation rates amongst women in Taiwan.

CONCLUSIONS

In an attempt to solve its labour shortage problems, the Taiwanese government officially introduced a low-skilled foreign workers policy into the island by means of the implementation, in 1992, of a temporary foreign workers programme (TFWP). The TFWP was considered by many to be an excellent programme, largely because it would, theoretically, benefit all parties involved, including the labour-sending countries, the labour-receiving countries and the foreign workers themselves. However, in a number of countries, the actual experience of such programmes reveals that there are serious adverse effects. This explains why the 'Bracero' programme in the US was terminated in 1964, and why West Germany terminated its own 'Gastarbeiter' programme in 1973.

However, not all TFWPs are seen as such failures; for example, the farm workers programmes introduced into Canada are considered by the government to be very successful, whilst Singapore's own TFWP is considered by many as having been successful from a number of aspects. It is quite clear that the keys to the successes of the Canadian and Singaporean programmes are their temporary nature, the foreign workers that are targeted for legal entry into the countries and the lack of any displacement effect on native workers. We must therefore consider the question of whether the TFWP in Taiwan has these characteristics; and indeed, the simple answer, for all three characteristics, would be 'no'! It is clear that the programme has now been established in Taiwan for a period spanning 14 years, and that the number of foreign workers being admitted has risen continuously throughout that period. Furthermore, it is also clear that despite having stabilized at a level of about 300,000 foreign workers over the last few years, in 2006, the figure nevertheless started to rise once again, and indeed, there is no sign of any reduction in the number of foreign workers being allowed into Taiwan in the near future. Therefore, the programme will no doubt remain in place for some time to come.

However, the apparent permanence of the programme should not be seen as a failure, especially as the adverse effects described by Martin (2001) and Ruhs (2002) have not become apparent in Taiwan. This is seen as being largely attributable to the fact that the functions of the TFWP in Taiwan have continued to change over time, according to the needs of the economy at various stages of development. For example, at the time of its introduction, the primary purpose of the programme was to resolve the labour shortage that existed at that time, and essentially to buy time for the labour-intensive industries to adjust to the loss of their competitive edge and raise Taiwan from its position, at that time, as a second-tier newly industrialized economy (NIE). Thereafter, these foreign workers began to play an important role in the promotion of the high-tech and major exporting industries. Thus, there has been no tendency for the temporary foreign workers in Taiwan to be monopolized by any specific groups, and thereby to become a supply of cheap labour to certain sectors of the economy and to certain groups of employers. The current requirement for foreign workers has changed significantly from the initial requirement for low-skilled workers, towards the need to attract high-skilled and professional workers in certain fields; therefore, the government now needs to modify some of the features of this programme so as to ensure that the TFWP is suitable for facilitating its new role.

The study underpinning this chapter has shown that foreign workers in Taiwan have found a number of ways of circumventing the government regulations to become permanent migrants in Taiwan. The first, and simplest, of these methods is simply to run away from their current employers and find 'underground' work with other employers, thereby rendering themselves liable for arrest both as both an illegal alien and illegal worker in Taiwan. Although the number of these missing workers is still small, it is nevertheless increasing rapidly; therefore the government needs to strengthen its enforcement mechanisms and do everything in its power to effectively curtail the expansion of the number of illegal foreign workers in Taiwan. In South Korea, the approach taken was to install an amnesty programme as a means of discovering the size of the illegal migrant problem, and of reducing the number of illegal migrants in the country; this is an approach which the Taiwanese government may also wish to consider.

Secondly, many of the foreign workers who have become illegal runaway workers have now been in Taiwan long enough to gain a firm understanding of the local situation. Having formed their own communities, and thus, having created segregated sectors in Taiwan, they are not only able to provide information to their friends and relatives back home, but also to assist their fellow countrymen to come into Taiwan, either legally or legally, through the various channels. Again, this shows the importance of strengthening the government's enforcement programme, essentially as a means of reducing the number of illegal migrants in Taiwan and thereby ensuring the temporary nature of such foreign workers, such that they do not succeed in becoming permanent migrants into Taiwan.

This chapter has also revealed evidence of foreign workers displacing native workers as a result of the low costs involved in employing foreign workers. Although this is caused partly by the 1997 policy permitting employers to count 'room and board' expenses as part of the minimum wage paid to foreign workers, the most obvious displacement effect arises in the area of foreign healthcare workers, since their wage levels are less than half of those of native healthcare workers. The displacement effect of foreign healthcare workers not only undermines the employment opportunities available to native workers, but also slows down the development and upgrading of the healthcare and care-giving sector. As a result, the island does not have the ability to create large numbers of professional, semi-professional and low-skilled jobs for female workers within this sector.

In order to dispose of this image of foreign workers as a source of cheap labour and deal with the resultant problem of displaced native workers, the government could consider installing a levy system similar to that installed by the Singaporean government which imposes a tax on employers who use foreign workers, thereby equalizing the costs of employing foreign and native workers. Such an approach ensures that employers use foreign workers purely as a result of their inability to find native workers and not based upon their low cost. A variable tax rate could be introduced for different industries and occupations according to the current labour market conditions, as well as the needs of industrial development policy in Taiwan. The tax revenue collected could then be used to train and upgrade those native workers whose jobs are being threatened by the importation of foreign workers or whose skills are becoming obsolete and in need of upgrading. The government could also use such revenue to provide loans or grants to firms for use in the modernization of their management systems or to support their innovative activities in the upgrading of their production processes or products in response to foreign competition and to the rising labour costs caused by the revision and modernization of the labour laws in Taiwan.

In conclusion, the current temporary foreign workers programme in Taiwan has not been a total failure and should not be seen as the major cause of the rising unemployment in Taiwan over recent years; however, it does have some drawbacks, given the fact that some foreign workers have become permanent migrants in Taiwan and that there has been some displacement of native workers. Nevertheless, it cannot be said that there are any large-scale adverse effects. Some corrections to the TFWP are clearly called for, but with proper revision, the government can ensure that the programme is suitable for the needs of the Taiwanese economy in the twenty-first century.

REFERENCES

Boswell, C. and T. Straubhaar (2004), The Backdoor: Temporary Migration and Illegal Employment of Workers, *ILO Discussion Paper*, Geneva: International Labour Organization, International Institute for Labour Studies.

Briggs, V.M. (2004), 'Guest Worker Programmes for Low-skilled Workers: Lessons from the Past and Warnings for the Future', testimony on the *Evaluation of a Temporary Guest Worker Proposal* presented to the US Senate Judiciary Committee on 5 February 2004.

Chen, L.Y and R.L. Wang (2006), 'Cheap Foreign Workers are Taking over Local Healthcare Service Workers' Jobs', *United Daily*, 17 May 2006, p.A12.

Chiswick, B. (ed.) (1982), *The Gateway: US Immigration Issues and Policies*, Washington, DC: American Enterprise Institute.

CLA (1994, 1998, 2004, 2005), *Survey on the Management and Utilization of Foreign Workers in Taiwan*, Taipei: Council of Labour Affairs.

CLA (various years), *Monthly Labour Statistics Report*, Taipei: Council of Labour Affairs.

Cornelius, W.A. and Y. Kuwahara (1998), 'Changing Ways of Utilizing Foreign Labour in the US and Japanese Economies', mimeo.

DGBAS (1998), *Report on Work Experience in Taiwan, 1997*, Taipei: Directorate-General of Budget, Accounting and Statistics.

DGBAS (2000), *Monthly Bulletin of Manpower Statistics*, Taipei: Directorate-General of Budget, Accounting and Statistics.

DGBAS (various years), *Yearbook of Manpower Survey Statistics in the Taiwan Area*, Taipei: Directorate-General of Budget, Accounting and Statistics.

DGBAS (various years), *Employees' Pay and Working Hours*, Taipei: Directorate-General of Budget, Accounting and Statistics; available at website: http://win.dgbas. gov.tw/dgbas04/bc5/earning/ ht456.asp.

DLA (1996), *Survey of Workers' Attitudes on Work and Employment Relations in the Taiwan Area*, Taipei: Provincial Government, Department of Labour Affairs.

Hsin, P.L. (2004), 'The Determination of Quotas and the Allocation of Foreign Workers in Taiwan', paper presented at the *Conference on Foreign Worker Policy*, held at the Institute of Economics, Academia Sinica, Taipei, 3 September 2004, pp.101-28.

Hsueh, M.C. (2005), 'More Quotas of Foreign Workers in 3D Industries', *Commercial Times*, 28 December 2005, p.A2.

Hui, W.T. and A.R. Hashmi (2004), Foreign Labour and Economic Growth Policy Options for Singapore, *Discussion Paper No.04/2*, Crawley, Australia: The University of Western Australia, Centre for Labour Market Research.

Jiang, F.F. (2004), 'The Impact of Foreign Workers on the Occupational Choices of Native Workers' paper presented at the *Conference on Foreign Worker Policy*, held at the Institute of Economics, Academia Sinica, Taipei, 3 September 2004, pp.67-100.

Lan, C.C. (2004), 'An Estimation of the Total Number of Foreign Workers in Taiwan', paper presented at the *Conference on Foreign Worker Policy*, held at the Institute of Economics, Academia Sinica in Taipei, 3 September 2004, pp.173-214.

Lee, J.S. (1992), 'Capital and Labour Mobility in Taiwan', in G. Ranis (ed.) (1992), *Taiwan: From Developing to Mature Economy*, Boulder, CO: Westview Press, pp. 305-56.

Lee, J.S. (1996), 'Recruiting and Managing Foreign Workers in Taiwan', *Asian and Pacific Migration Journal*, **5**(2-3): 281-99.

Lee, J.S. (1998), 'The Impact of the Asian Financial Crisis on Foreign Workers in Taiwan', *Asian and Pacific Migration Journal*, **7**(2-3): 145-69.

Lee, J.S. and H.L. Wu (1992), 'Unskilled Foreign Workers in Taiwan, Causes and Consequences', *Asia Club Papers, Tokyo*, **2**: 107-22.

Levine, L. (2004), 'Immigration: The Labour Market Effects of a Guest Workers' Programme for US Farmers', Washington, DC: CRS Report for Congress No.95-7-12 E (20 February 2004).

Lin, C.F. and J. Lo (2004), 'The Impact of Foreign Workers on the Technology and Productivity of Taiwan's Manufacturing Industries', paper presented at the *Conference on Foreign Worker Policy*, held at the Institute of Economics, Academia Sinica, Taipei, 3 September 2004, pp.39-65.

Lin, G.P. (2003), 'Providing Reemployment Opportunities for the Unemployed: Labour Mobility', in J.S. Lee (ed.) (2003), *Who Stole Our Jobs: Taiwan's Unemployment Problems Since 1996*, Taipei: Commonwealth Publishing Company, pp.339-72.

Liu, P.K.C. (2000), 'The Transformation of Taiwan's Labour Market and Its Unemployment', in J.S. Lee (ed.) (2000), *Taiwan's Unemployment Problems*, Taipei: National Central University, Research Centre for Economic Development in Taiwan, pp.7-34.

Liu, Y.L. and C.Y. Hsia (2004), 'Foreign Healthcare Workers and the Development of a Care-giving System in Taiwan', paper presented at the *Conference on Foreign Worker Policy*, held at the Institute of Economics, Academia Sinica, Taipei, 3 September 2004, pp.151-72.

Martin, P. (1996), 'Labour Contractors: A Conceptual Overview', *Asian and Pacific Migration Journal*, **5**(2-3): 201-18.

Martin, P. (2001), *There is Nothing More Permanent than Temporary Foreign Workers: Backgrounder*, San Diego, CA: University of San Diego, Centre for Immigration Studies.

Martin, P. (2004), Migration and Development: Towards Sustainable Solutions, *ILO Discussion Paper No.DP/153/2004*, Geneva: International Labour Organization, International Institute for Labour Studies.

Martin, P. and M. Teitelbaum (2001), 'The Mirage of Mexican Guest Workers', *Foreign Affairs*, **80**(6): 117-31.

Meissner, D. (2004), *US Temporary Worker Programmes: Lessons Learned*, Washington, DC: Migration Policy Institute.

Morgan, L.C. and B. Gardner (1982), 'Potential for a US Guest Workers' Programme in Agriculture: Lessons from the Braceros', in B. Chiswick (ed.) (1982), *The Gateway: US Immigration Issues and Policies*, Washington, DC: American Enterprise Institute, pp.361-411.

Park, Y.B. (2005), 'Country Report: Korea', proceedings of the *Workshop on International Migration and the Labour Market in Asia*, Tokyo: Japanese Labour Institute.

Ratha, D. (2003), 'Workers' Remittances: An Important and Stable Source of External Development Finance', *Global Development Finance*, World Bank, pp.157-75.

Ruddick, E. (2004), 'Canada's Seasonal Agricultural Worker Programme', paper presented at the IOM-WTO World Bank Seminar, Session III, on *Managing Trade and Migration: Bilateral Approaches to Managing the Movement and Temporary Stay of Workers*, held in Geneva, 4-5 October 2004.

Ruhs, M. (2002), 'Temporary Foreign Workers Programmes: Policies, Adverse Consequences and the Need to Make them Work', *Working Paper No.56*, San Diego, CA: University of California, Centre for Comparative Immigration Studies.

Simon, J. (1981), *The Ultimate Resource*, Princeton, NJ: Princeton University Press.

Tu, W.Y. (2000), '120,000 Unemployed Low-skilled Workers', *Commercial Times*, 15 August 2000, p.2.

Wise, D.E. (1974), 'The Effect of the Bracero on Agricultural Production in California', *Economic Inquiry* (December), **12**(4): 547-58.

Wu, C.C. (2004), 'A Study of the Relationships between the Utilization of Foreign Workers and Overseas Investments', paper presented at the *Conference on Foreign Worker Policy*, held at the Institute of Economics, Academia Sinica, Taipei, 3 September 2004, pp.39-66.

Wu, P.L. and P.K. Lin (2006), 'How Many Taiwanese Depend on Filipinos and Thai Workers for a Living', *United Daily*, 18 May 2006, p.A.12.

9 Involuntary Job Turnover in Taiwan, 1996-2000

Ji-Ping Lin

INTRODUCTION

The primary aim of this chapter is to provide in-depth analysis of involuntary job turnover levels in Taiwan between the years 1996 and 2000. The analysis is based upon the Manpower Utilization Surveys carried out between 1997 and 2001 by the Directorate General of Budget, Accounting and Statistics (DGBAS), a department of the Executive Yuan within the central government of Taiwan. In light of the impacts stemming from the protracted period of industrial restructuring in Taiwan (from the early 1990s onwards) and the short-term economic downturn (throughout the late 1990s), much public attention is now being focused on the issue of job turnover, in particular, turnover which is involuntary in nature. This is an issue which, in recent years, has also become a major concern for employment policymakers.

The labour market in Taiwan experienced dramatic changes during the mid- to late 1990s, with the most prominent characteristics of the transition at that time being the overall decline in job security, soaring unemployment rates (along with the corresponding socioeconomic problems) and the persistent and all-pervasive disturbance to working conditions, all of which have become issues of major concern, since 1996, both at government level, and to ordinary people nationwide (Lee, 2003). Aside from the problem of unemployment itself, a further problem associated with involuntary turnover is the requirement for subsequent adjustment by those involuntarily mobilized within the Taiwanese labour market. Indeed, the dwindling job security of this growing group of workers has now led to the phenomenon of involuntary turnover becoming an issue of major socioeconomic and political concern in this first decade of the new century (Lin, 2005).

Turnover, which obviously refers to job changes, can be split into the two very broad categories of voluntary turnover and involuntary turnover. Voluntary turnover refers to those job changes in which the decision to move

211

is undertaken by the individuals themselves, with such turnover usually resulting in specific benefits to the individual; conversely, involuntary turnover, which, as the term suggests, does not involve a decision by the individual, tends to impose costs upon workers, particularly low-skilled and marginal workers. Turnover is seen as an indicator of the dynamism of an economic system, since it serves to promote the efficiency of the transfer of manpower within the labour market. In the absence of turnover, the reallocation of the labour force cannot be achieved from the less-productive sectors to those sectors in which productivity is demonstrating a growth trend; in such circumstances, we would expect to see a general reduction in overall economic performance.

In terms of socioeconomic status and economic wellbeing, involuntary turnover is generally associated with downward mobility, as opposed to the upward mobility associated with voluntary turnover. As such, the research in this field suggests that corresponding policy measures should aim to prevent further involuntary downward mobility and actively help those who are involuntarily placed in a position of having to change their jobs to reduce the potential difficulties arising from their need for continuous adjustment within the labour market. Indeed, a number of empirical studies have suggested that involuntary turnover is associated not only with the short-term and long-term wage losses of individuals (Rhum, 1991; Jacobson et al., 1993; Stevens, 1997), but also with the downward mobility of their personal careers (Sicherman and Galor, 1990).

Using the British Household Panel Survey (BHPS) to test the long-term effects of involuntary turnover on working careers, Malo and Munoz-Bullon (2003) found that the reduction in the occupational prestige of the working career of an individual as a direct result of involuntary job separation was non-negligible; in particular, they found that when an individual endured further involuntary job separation, the cumulative negative impact tended to be persistent and related directly to the loss of any specific human capital previously possessed by the individual. Furthermore, there was a discernible tendency for those individuals who were involuntarily displaced from their previous job to subsequently take on occupations that might well be described as less prestigious. The importance of this analysis, in the context of Taiwan, lies not only in the fact that involuntary turnover is associated with personal economic losses and social hardship to the individuals concerned, but also in the correlation with aggregate political instability and social unrest.

From official Taiwanese statistics, of the total labour market turnover in Taiwan between 1991 and 1995, involuntary turnover has, on average, accounted for around 13 per cent; however, between 1996 and 2000, the share of involuntary turnover rose sharply, to over 20 per cent (DGBAS,

2001), with the main reasons for such growth in involuntary turnover being business shutdowns, shrinkage and layoffs. Nevertheless, whilst this rise in involuntary turnover can be attributed, in part, to the effects of the business cycle, it is in fact more attributable to the effects of economic restructuring (Tsay and Lin, 1999). It is rather surprising, therefore, that despite having gained increasingly greater public attention, no comprehensive exploration has yet been undertaken of either involuntary job changes, per se, or the resultant potential socioeconomic problems, as noted earlier. In light of these problems, and with Taiwan's economy becoming increasingly open and integrated into the world system, an effective policy remedy is clearly of major importance.

In addition to the above preamble, the significance of the analysis in this chapter also lies, both conceptually and practically, in the following four factors. Firstly, from a classical perspective of economic assumption, the purpose behind the job search activities of individuals within the labour market, whether they are employed or unemployed, is to maximize their career wellbeing and their lifetime expected income. However, this assumption may not hold for those who are involuntarily mobilized, because the theory behind job search activities implicitly assumes that the decision to initiate the search for a new job occurs voluntarily (Barron and McCafferty, 1977; Burdett, 1978).

Secondly, it is already well recognized that due to the dynamic nature of the labour force, disadvantaged employees – essentially those in the more unstable or less successful jobs within the labour market – are at much greater risk of becoming unemployed than their more 'advantaged' counterparts (Clark and Summers, 1979). In other words, it would seem reasonable to argue that if they are unable to adjust to the labour market after their job change, a substantial proportion of those who change their jobs involuntarily have far greater potential for subsequent further unemployment (Hall, 1972; Marston, 1976). Thus, any workers who are involved in involuntary job turnover may well be regarded as a group at potential risk of further unemployment.

Thirdly, in conjunction with economic restructuring, new patterns of manpower demand have emerged within the Taiwan labour market over the past decade, with the infrastructural changes having brought with them the inevitable problem of human capital and occupational skills becoming dated amongst certain groups of employed workers in the face of this new manpower demand. We can therefore assume that, in line with the experiences of a number of other countries, these workers will find that their disadvantaged position within the labour market will lead to them becoming increasingly subject to even higher levels of involuntary job turnover (Gallaway, 1963; Turvey, 1977; Diamond, 1981; Samson, 1985).

Finally, given that those who are forced to change jobs involuntarily are, by their very nature, disadvantaged within the labour market, they are also, in consequence, associated with the greater likelihood of a mismatch with the new manpower demand in the overall labour market; clearly, therefore, there will be a tendency for them to experience greater difficulties in the process of searching for jobs than those who move voluntarily (Marston, 1976). Given the dynamic nature of the labour force as a whole, involuntary job movers have become a new sub-group in Taiwan at much greater risk of filling the ranks of the unemployed, particularly in the fading traditional industries, from within which it seems reasonable to assume that a substantial stock of this disadvantaged workforce has yet to emerge. Indeed, the major problems associated with their inevitable job change, and in many cases, their involuntary moves, are expected to emerge in the not-too-distant future.

RESEARCH DATA

The analysis in this chapter of the trends in voluntary and involuntary job turnover over the latter half of the 1990s relies mainly upon pooled data obtained from the 1997-2001 Manpower Utilization Surveys (MUS) carried out by the DGBAS. The MUS datasets are cross-sectional in nature and have been widely used in Taiwan in research undertaken throughout the academic community in general. It is worth emphasizing that these surveys are supplements of the May round of 'human resource surveys' (HRS), which, in terms of the questionnaire design and sampling framework, are essentially very similar to the 'labour force surveys' (LFS) used in the US and Canada; therefore, our research results are, to a large extent, internationally comparable. Nevertheless, despite the many advantages of using the MUS, some potential disadvantages remain within our research data, the most crucial of which is the potential for selection bias, given that, for any of the surveys, around half of all respondents are resurveyed in the subsequent year.

Since job turnover is measured over a one-year period, we must therefore restrict our study sample to those who were: (i) at least 16 years of age at the time of the survey; and (ii) employed and residing within Taiwan both at the time of the survey, and in the preceding year. Pooling together the 1997-2001 MUS, the total number of respondents qualifying for inclusion in the pooled data amounted to more than 161,000; all military sub-samples were excluded from the study as non-qualified subjects. With the original weight corresponding to each qualified respondent being rescaled by a factor of one-fifth in the pooled data, the overall number of qualified respondents in the study amounted to approximately 9,338,000 employed workers between 1996 and 2000.

Our main area of interest in this chapter lies in the measurement of the labour market, by industry; we therefore follow a method of industry classification which is widely used in Taiwan. This method classifies all industries into the 13 categories of agriculture, mining, light industry, machinery, petrochemicals, electrical and electronics, public utilities, construction, commerce, transportation, finance and insurance, commercial services and social and personal services. For the sake of simplicity, this chapter follows the traditional convention, which is to divide these 13 industries into three main categories, the primary sector (including agriculture and mining), the secondary sector (made up of traditional manufacturing, other manufacturing and construction) and the tertiary sector (comprising of utilities, transportation, communications, commerce, finance, insurance and commercial services, and social and personal services).

In order to determine what constitutes any incidence of job turnover, the pooled data within the study was based upon a single direct question 'how many times did you change your job in the preceding year?' Respondents were categorized as 'movers' if they had made at least one job change in the preceding year of the survey, otherwise they were categorized as 'stayers'. Based on the industrial classification outlined above, the study further classified 'movers' into two sub-groups: 'inter-industry turnover' and 'intra-industry turnover', with the former referring to those who had moved from one industry to another, whilst the latter referred to those who had remained within the same industry in their subsequent job. Based upon the responses to a single question on the reasons for leaving their previous jobs, those engaging in job changes were divided into the two broad categories of 'voluntary' and 'involuntary' job turnover. The reasons for voluntary turnover were grouped into four categories: 'low pay', 'poor working conditions', 'poor job prospects' and all 'other reasons' (including health, disability, a dislike of the working hours or location, interpersonal relationships, family or personal reasons, becoming self-employed and others). The reasons for involuntary turnover were classified as 'plant shutouts', 'business shrinkages and layoffs', 'job transfers' and all 'other reasons' (including end of seasonal or temporary work, female marriage or maternity leave, retirement and others).

The study upon which this chapter is based used three types of industry-specific mobility rates – the 'inward-mobility' rate, the 'outward-mobility' rate and the 'net mobility' rate – demonstrating the different scenarios involving the transfer of human capital throughout the labour market. The inward-mobility rate within a specific industry was defined as the proportion of the total labour force moving from other industries in the preceding year. Conversely, the outward-mobility rate was defined as the proportion of the total labour force moving out of a specific industry into other industries. The net mobility rate was thus defined as the difference between the inward-mobility and outward-mobility rates.

In addition to its attempt to distinguish between the industrial patterns of labour mobility, the study also aimed to explore the differences between voluntary and involuntary turnover workers, in terms of their geographical labour mobility. In processing this particular element of the study, the 23 prefectures and/or cities in Taiwan were initially used as the geographical unit of labour mobility. Similar to the method used to define industrial labour mobility, workers were regarded as having engaged in geographical labour mobility if the location of their current job differed from the location of their previous job. If the location remained the same, then the workers were defined as 'stayers'. The 23 prefectures/cities in Taiwan are grouped into six categories in order to reflect the regional industrial structuring, as follows: Taipei/Taoyuan Metropolitan Area, Hsinchu Metropolitan Area, Taichung Metropolitan Area, Tainan-Chiayi Metropolitan Area, Kaohsiung Metropolitan Area and the agricultural areas (see Figure 9.1).

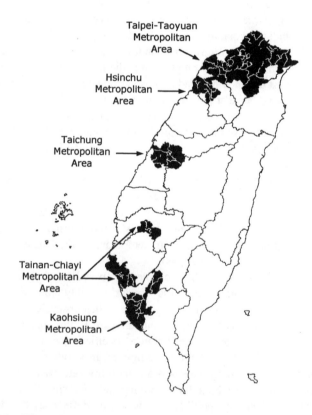

Figure 9.1   The major metropolitan areas of Taiwan

No sophisticated mathematical model is employed in this study, since, as noted in the introductory section, the main aim is to provide a general understanding of involuntary turnover in Taiwan. In terms of research procedure, we begin by demonstrating the trend in involuntary turnover as compared to that of voluntary turnover, and then compare the involuntary and voluntary turnover rates, by industry and by workers' educational attainment and age. Our subsequent focus is on the analysis of the reasons for engaging in job changes, before concluding with the presentation of our final analysis of both voluntary and involuntary labour mobility, from both inter-industry and geographical perspectives.

CHARACTERISTICS OF JOB TURNOVER

The overall aim of this section is to characterize the main differences between voluntary and involuntary job turnover in Taiwan, in terms of industry-specific mobility, labour selectivity and current trends. We begin this characterization by providing a clear picture of the changing trends in voluntary and involuntary job turnover. Detailed information on the total volume of the labour force involved in either voluntary or involuntary job changes, between 1996 and 2000, is provided in Table 9.1.

Table 9.1   Involuntary and voluntary job turnover, by employment volume, 1996-2000

Year	Employment Volume	Type of Turnover			Turnover Ratio (1) / (2)
		Involuntary (1)	Voluntary (2)	(1) + (2)	
1996	9,166,015	93,986	505,356	599,342	0.19
1997	9,296,970	107,332	510,985	618,317	0.21
1998	9,366,482	114,981	476,948	591,929	0.24
1999	9,495,235	120,654	490,236	610,890	0.25
2000	9,366,678	161,742	438,439	600,181	0.37
1996-2000	9,338,276	119,739	484,393	604,132	0.25

Source: Compiled by the author from *Manpower Utilization Surveys*, 1997-2001.

As the table indicates, over the latter half of the 1990s, although there was an increase of around 200,000 in the total number of employed workers within the labour force, the total volume of those who had previously been involved in job changes remained steady, at a level of around 600,000 workers. Whilst there was no significant change in overall job turnover volume, there was, nevertheless, an increase of about 68,000 in the number of workers involved in involuntary job turnover over the period of our study (from 93,986 workers in 1996 to 161,742 workers in 2000).

Conversely, the number of workers involved in voluntary job turnover declined by about 70,000 over the same period (from 505,356 workers in 1996 to 438,439 workers in 2000). There was, therefore, a slight decline in the corresponding job turnover rate, from 6.5 per cent in 1996, to 6.4 per cent in 2000 (Table 9.2), along with an overall declining trend in the voluntary job turnover rate (from 5.5 per cent in 1996 to 4.7 per cent in 2000), whereas there was a significant rise in the involuntary job turnover trend (from 1.0 per cent in 1996 to 1.7 per cent in 2000). Further examination reveals a substantial increase in the ratio between the volumes of involuntary and voluntary job turnover, from 0.19 in 1996 to 0.37 in 2000; thus, throughout the period under examination, the incidences of involuntary job turnover have clearly outweighed those of voluntary turnover.

Table 9.2   Involuntary and voluntary job turnover, by turnover rate, 1996-2000

Year	Type of Turnover			Turnover Ratio
	Involuntary (1)	Voluntary (2)	(1) + (2)	(1) / (2)
1996	1.0	5.5	6.5	0.19
1997	1.2	5.5	6.7	0.21
1998	1.2	5.1	6.3	0.24
1999	1.3	5.2	6.4	0.25
2000	1.7	4.7	6.4	0.37
1996-2000	1.3	5.2	6.5	0.25

Source: Compiled by the author from *Manpower Utilization Surveys*, 1997-2001.

We now turn to an examination of voluntary and involuntary job turnover, by industry. As suggested by Table 9.3, those industries associated with higher job turnover rates generally have a higher proportion of job changes of a voluntary nature. For instance, the job turnover rate for the primary sector was 2.1 per cent, whilst that for the secondary sector was 6.2 per cent, and for the tertiary sector, 7.3 per cent. The ratios of involuntary job turnover over voluntary turnover were 0.47 for the primary sector, 0.31 for the secondary sector and 0.20 for the tertiary sector. This suggests that although the tertiary sector is associated with much higher job turnover rates than other sectors, job turnover within this sector is mainly voluntary in nature, in contrast to the situation observed in both the secondary and primary sectors.

Table 9.3   Involuntary and voluntary job turnover rates, by industry,
1996-2000

Industry	Average Employment Volume	Job Turnover Rate (%) Involuntary (1)	Voluntary (2)	(1)+(2)	Turnover Ratio (1)/(2)	Rank
Primary Sector						
Mining	11,610	3.5	3.7	7.3	0.94	2
Agriculture	781,468	0.6	1.4	2.0	0.45	4
Sub-totals	793,078	0.7	1.4	2.1	0.47	–
Secondary Sector						
Light industry	791,300	1.5	4.7	6.1	0.32	6
Petrochemicals	411,191	1.1	4.4	5.5	0.25	7
Machinery	775,418	1.4	4.3	5.7	0.33	5
Electrical and Electronics	642,217	1.9	7.8	9.6	0.24	8
Utilities	35,347	1.0	0.6	1.6	1.70	1
Construction	845,492	1.5	3.3	4.7	0.46	3
Sub-totals	3,500,965	1.5	4.7	6.2	0.31	–
Tertiary Sector						
Commerce	1,876,425	1.3	6.6	7.9	0.19	12
Transport	466,709	1.2	5.1	6.2	0.23	9
Finance and Insurance	388,466	1.3	6.9	8.3	0.19	11
Commercial Services	499,335	1.4	7.8	9.2	0.18	13
Social/Personal Services	1,813,019	1.2	5.2	6.3	0.23	10
Sub-totals	5,043,954	1.2	6.1	7.3	0.20	–
All Industries	9,337,997*	1.3	5.2	6.5	0.25	–

Note: * Since qualified persons with missing industry data are excluded, the total number of employed persons, over the 1996-2000 period, differs from the corresponding figures in Tables 9.1 and 9.2.

Source: Compiled by the author from *Manpower Utilization Surveys*, 1997-2001.

More specifically, with the exception of mining, those industries associated with higher job turnover rates are generally in the growth sectors (e.g., 7.9 per cent for commerce, 8.3 per cent for finance and insurance, 9.2 per cent for commercial services, and 9.6 per cent for the electrical and electronics industry), within which, the high job turnover rates are largely shaped by the mobility of the highly educated labour force. By contrast, those industries with lower job turnover rates are generally associated with the declining industries (e.g., 2.0 per cent for agriculture, 1.6 per cent for utilities, and 4.7 per cent for the construction industry). These industries are characterized by higher incidences of involuntary job turnover and by a lower-skilled and lower-educated labour force.

Table 9.4 provides details of labour mobility by gender, education and age for both voluntary and involuntary job turnover. In terms of gender, two distinct features are worth highlighting; firstly, the mobility of females (7.0 per cent) is apparently greater than that of males (6.1 per cent); and secondly, as suggested by the ratio between involuntary and voluntary job turnover rate by gender, males are more susceptible to involuntary job turnover (0.27) than females (0.22).

Table 9.4   Involuntary and voluntary job turnover rates, by age, gender and education, 1996-2000

Demographic Characteristics	Average Employment Volume	Job Turnover Rate (%)			Turnover Ratio (1) / (2)
		Involuntary (1)	Voluntary (2)	(1) + (2)	
Age					
15-19	249,554	1.1	10.8	11.8	0.10
20-24	885,651	1.5	11.1	12.5	0.13
25-29	1,368,687	1.7	9.3	11.0	0.18
30-34	1,446,876	1.3	6.1	7.4	0.21
35-44	2,847,527	1.3	3.6	4.9	0.36
45-54	1,697,438	1.1	1.9	3.0	0.61
55-64	695,725	0.7	1.2	1.9	0.60
≥65	146,817	0.4	0.3	0.7	1.43
Gender					
Male	5,578,490	1.3	4.8	6.1	0.27
Female	3,759,786	1.2	5.7	7.0	0.22
Education					
Primary or Below	1,871,540	1.1	2.0	3.1	0.53
Junior High School	1,774,391	1.5	4.6	6.1	0.33
Senior High School	3,267,148	1.3	6.3	7.7	0.21
University	2,262,181	1.2	6.5	7.7	0.19
Postgraduate	163,016	0.8	7.1	7.9	0.11
Overall	9,338,276	1.3	5.2	6.5	0.25

Source: Compiled by the author from *Manpower Utilization Surveys*, 1997-2001.

The selective nature of voluntary and involuntary job turnover, by education, is characterized by the following four distinct features. Firstly, as expected, higher education has a positive association with job turnover; that is, better-educated workers will tend to play a leading role in the process of job turnover. Secondly, as opposed to those turnover incidences which are voluntary in nature, lower educational achievement has an association with involuntary job turnover, that is, lower-educated workers will feature strongly in involuntary job turnover. Thirdly, the positive association discernible between higher education and job turnover is mainly due to the fact that the positive effect on voluntary job turnover far outweighs the corresponding negative effect on involuntary job turnover. Fourthly, with educational attainment, a steady decline is discernible in the ratio between involuntary and voluntary job turnover, which suggests that lower-educated workers are generally more susceptible to involuntary job turnover than better-educated workers (Table 9.4).

An additional important feature of the selective nature of job turnover is that it can also be attributed to age. As Table 9.4 shows, job turnover with regard to age can largely be explained by three distinct features. Firstly, job turnover is selective of the younger elements of the labour force, particularly those aged between 15 and 29 years (11.8 per cent for the 15-19 age group, 12.5 per cent for the 20-24 age group and 11.0 per cent for the 25-29 age group); moreover, beyond the age of 30, there is a substantial decline in the corresponding job turnover rates. Secondly, the selective pattern of job turnover by age is mainly shaped by voluntary job turnover rather than by its involuntary counterpart. Thirdly, the ratio between involuntary job turnover and voluntary job turnover is seen to increase monotonically with age, suggesting that there is an increase, by age, for those elements of the workforce susceptible to incidences of involuntary job turnover.

In summary, although it is clear that there has been a slight decline in the overall incidences of job turnover between 1996 and 2000, as compared to voluntary turnover, there is, nevertheless, a corresponding increase in both the volume and the rate of involuntary job turnover, with time. The industrial pattern of job turnover suggests that job turnover within the tertiary sector is mainly voluntary in nature, as opposed to the situation observed in both the secondary and primary sectors. In terms of the selective nature of job turnover, males are more susceptible to involuntary job turnover than females and, as expected, involuntary job turnover is associated with negative educational achievement, with lower-educated workers being more susceptible to involuntary job turnover than their better-educated counterparts Finally, with the increase in the age of the workforce, involuntary job turnover incidences are becoming increasingly dominant.

REASONS FOR JOB TURNOVER

This section aims to determine the forces driving both voluntary and involuntary job turnover based upon the reasons cited for job changes in the MUS surveys. As stated in the preceding section, the reasons for voluntary job turnover include 'low pay', 'poor working conditions', 'poor job prospects' and 'other reasons', whilst the reasons for involuntary job turnover are essentially 'business shutouts', 'shrinkage and layoffs', 'job transfers' and 'others'. We begin by differentiating between involuntary and voluntary job turnover trends between 1996 and 2000, based upon the reasons for the job changes; thereafter, we attempt to distinguish between the reasons for voluntary and involuntary job turnover in the major industries.

As revealed by Table 9.5 (panel A), the reason most often cited for voluntary job turnover throughout the whole of the 1996-2000 period was 'poor working conditions', accounting, on average, for about 40 per cent of all voluntary job changes each year.

Table 9.5   Reasons for voluntary and involuntary job turnover, 1996-2000

Reasons for Job Turnover	Year					Average Turnover 1996-2000
	1996	1997	1998	1999	2000	
Panel A: Voluntary Job Turnover						
Poor Working Conditions (%)	38.9	41.2	40.5	40.2	39.6	40.1
Low Pay (%)	22.0	22.7	20.9	22.1	22.1	22.0
Poor Job Prospects (%)	13.0	13.6	14.9	15.5	15.0	14.4
Others (%)	26.1	22.4	23.8	22.2	23.3	23.6
Turnover (No. of Persons)	505,356	510,985	476,948	490,236	438,439	484,393
Panel B: Involuntary Job Turnover						
Shutouts (%)	62.8	61.3	67.3	59.2	72.5	65.3
Shrinkage/ Layoffs (%)	19.5	19.4	19.0	16.3	14.8	17.5
Job Transfers (%)	13.0	11.6	11.9	16.3	10.2	12.5
Others (%)	4.7	7.6	1.8	8.2	2.6	4.8
Turnover (No. of Persons)	93,986	107,332	114,981	120,654	161,742	119,739

Source: Compiled by the author from *Manpower Utilization Surveys*, 1997-2001.

'Low pay' was cited as a further important factor contributing to voluntary job turnover, accounting for about 22 per cent of all incidences, with the trend for this response also appearing to remain very stable over time. It is worth stressing that whilst 'poor job prospects' was not a decisive factor for involuntary job turnover, it nevertheless accounted for around 14 per cent of voluntary job turnover, and demonstrated a gradual upward trend throughout the latter half of the 1990s (from 13.0 per cent in 1996 to 15.0 per cent in 2000). In terms of the corresponding patterns for involuntary job turnover, as suggested by Table 9.5 (panel B), the most often cited reason was 'business shutouts' which accounted, on average, for 65 per cent of all annual involuntary job changes. Such high incidences of involuntary job turnover were in fact mainly attributable to the prolonged industrial restructuring which has been taking place in Taiwan since the early 1990s; nevertheless, the citing of this single reason increased by about 10 per cent between 1996 and 2000 (from 62.8 per cent in 1996 to 72.5 per cent in 2000).

Although some way behind, the second most often cited reason for involuntary job turnover was 'business shrinkage and layoffs', which accounted, on average, for about 17.5 per cent of all annual involuntary job turnover between 1996 and 2000. It is, however, worth noting that its importance, in terms of accounting for involuntary job turnover, has been dwindling; in 1996, for example, 19.5 per cent of involuntary job movers cited this reason, whereas, by 2000, the figure had shrunk to just 14.8 per cent. Furthermore, although 'job transfers' accounted for about 12.5 per cent of involuntary job turnover, its changing pattern, over time, is not as distinct as that associated with either 'business shutouts or 'shrinkage and layoffs'. In brief, 'business shutouts' was the most often cited and most crucial factor determining involuntary job turnover, far outweighing 'shrinkage and layoffs'.

As regards the reasons associated with job turnover for each industry, Table 9.6 (panel A) indicates that 'poor working conditions' was the most crucial determinant of job turnover for both the secondary (41.6 per cent) and tertiary (40.5 per cent) sectors, whereas it appeared to have little importance for the primary sector (11.4 per cent). Furthermore, whilst the three major turnover reasons, 'poor working conditions', 'low pay' and 'poor job prospects', accounted for more than 75 per cent of all incidences of job turnover in the secondary and tertiary sectors, again, these were not so crucial for the primary sector. Specifically, 'poor working conditions' accounted for 46 per cent of all turnover in the manufacturing sector and 47 per cent in the social and personal services sector. 'Low pay' was also an important factor associated with manufacturing (29.2 per cent for traditional manufacturing, and 26.7 per cent for other manufacturing), and although 'poor job prospects' did not appear to have any particular impact on voluntary job turnover as a whole, we nevertheless find that it was of particular importance to the construction industry.

Table 9.6 Reasons for voluntary and involuntary job turnover, by industry, 1996-2000

Reasons for Job Turnover	Industrial Sectors*											All Industries
	Primary		Secondary			Tertiary						
	(1)	(2)	(3)	(4)	Total	(5)	(6)	(7)	(8)	Total		
Panel A: Voluntary Job Turnover												
Turnover Volume (No. of Persons)	13,548	38,746	98,072	33,199	170,017	23,081	125,288	60,450	92,009	300,827		484,393
Poor Working Conditions (%)	11.4	39.6	46.2	30.5	41.6	41.3	34.8	42.2	47.0	40.5		40.1
Low Pay (%)	8.0	29.2	26.7	19.8	25.9	21.5	21.8	20.7	17.9	20.4		22.0
Poor Job Prospects (%)	11.4	12.2	10.6	26.8	14.1	13.7	13.5	18.3	14.0	14.6		14.4
Other Reasons (%)	69.2	19.0	16.5	22.9	18.3	23.4	29.9	18.8	21.1	24.5		23.6
Panel B: Involuntary Job Turnover												
Turnover Volume (No. of Persons)	1,956	13,658	28,277	21,905	63,839	4,810	19,427	10,899	18,809	53,944		119,739
Shutouts (%)	49.5	76.3	71.8	69.2	71.8	58.6	76.8	59.5	37.8	58.1		65.3
Shrinkage/Layoffs (%)	40.9	14.2	15.8	25.1	18.7	12.8	13.1	4.3	24.3	15.2		17.5
Job Transfers (%)	2.1	5.4	7.7	3.4	5.7	24.2	7.6	30.7	27.8	20.8		12.5
Other Reasons (%)	7.5	4.1	4.8	2.2	3.8	4.4	2.4	5.6	10.2	5.9		4.8

Note: * Numbers in parentheses indicate industrial sectors, as follows: (1) agriculture and mining; (2) traditional manufacturing industries; (3) other manufacturing industries; (4) construction; (5) utilities, transportation and communications; (6) commerce; (7) finance, insurance and commercial services; and (8) social and personal services.

Source: Compiled by the author from *Manpower Utilization Surveys*, 1997-2001.

As shown earlier in Table 9.5, the three most often cited reasons for involuntary job turnover were 'business shutouts', 'shrinkage and layoffs' and 'job transfers'. Table 9.6 provides further indication, in greater detail, that 'business shutouts' are still the most important factor for all industries, accounting for 49.5 per cent of all turnover in the primary sector, 71.8 per cent in the secondary sector and 58.1 per cent in the tertiary sector. In specific terms, the industries for which this was the most often cited reason were manufacturing, finance, and insurance and commercial services.

As noted earlier, on the whole, 'shrinkage and layoffs' accounted for only 17.5 per cent of involuntary turnover, with the respective figures for the secondary and tertiary sectors being 18.7 per cent and 15.2 per cent; nevertheless, within the primary sector, incidences of involuntary turnover accounted for by 'business shrinkage and layoffs' were as high as 40.9 per cent. The corresponding figure for the construction industry was 25.1 per cent, whilst this reason was cited in 24.3 per cent of all cases within the social and personal services sector.

In terms of the incidences of involuntary job turnover associated with 'job transfers', as panel B of Table 9.6 reveals, only 2.1 per cent of all job turnover within the primary sector, and 5.7 per cent of turnover within the secondary sector, was attributable to such involuntary 'job transfers'. It is, however, quite surprising to find that the figure for the tertiary sector was around 20.8 per cent, far outweighing the corresponding figures for both the primary and secondary sectors. In addition, the incidences of involuntary job transfers which were associated with the finance, insurance and commercial services industry reached an alarmingly high level of 30.7 per cent, whilst the figure for the social and personal services sector also reached a similar high of 27.8 per cent.

In summary, throughout the 1996-2000 period, incidences of voluntary turnover have generally exhibited a declining trend. Overall, the most often cited reasons for voluntary job turnover were 'poor working conditions', followed by 'low pay'. In contrast, over the same period, the trend in involuntary job turnover has shown a marked increase, with 'business shutouts', 'shrinkage and layoffs' and 'job transfers', in that order, being the three most often cited reasons for involuntary job change. Furthermore, in terms of the selective nature of job turnover, by sector, 'business shutouts' appears to be very selective of the secondary sector (71.8 per cent), whilst 'shrinkage and layoffs' appears to be selective of the primary sector (40.9 per cent), and involuntary 'job transfers' is selective of the tertiary sector (20.8 per cent). Finally, it should be stressed once again that the increasingly high incidences of involuntary job turnover would appear to be mainly attributable to the prolonged industrial restructuring which has been occurring in Taiwan since the early 1990s.

VOLUNTARY AND INVOLUNTARY LABOUR MOBILITY

Our main aim in this section is to assess the roles of both voluntary and involuntary job turnover throughout the period under examination (1996-2000), in terms of the effects on the transfer of manpower within the overall labour market. In order to determine the extent to which involuntary labour mobility differs from voluntary labour mobility, we need to ascertain why workers decide to engage in labour mobility, and then how, within any specific industry, the flows of such workers who have taken the decision to move are distributed amongst the remaining industries.

Two highly interrelated approaches are utilized to achieve this goal, the first of which aims to examine the general 'departure' behaviour of workers by examining the inward, outward and net 'inter-industry' labour mobility rates of both voluntary and involuntary job turnover. The subsequent approach involves an examination of the industrial flows of workers engaging in either voluntary or involuntary job turnover. In addition to examining both the departure and the industrial flows of movers, we further examine the geographical redistribution of workers from such voluntary and involuntary turnover.

The 'Departure' Behaviour of Workers

As regards the voluntary and involuntary departure behaviour of workers, as Table 9.7 indicates, on average, the proportion of the employed labour force actively engaged in voluntary inter-industry labour mobility each year between 1996 and 2000 was about 5.2 per cent, whilst the corresponding figure for involuntary inter-industrial labour mobility was only 1.3 per cent. This suggests that workers involved in involuntary turnover are less likely to undertake an inter-industry move than those engaging in voluntary turnover. Indeed, this is in line with our expectations and is not too difficult to explain, since it can be attributed, in part, to the fact that inter-industry mobility does tend to impose much greater barriers on workers than intra-industry mobility, and also in part to the fact that involuntary job turnover is selective of workers with lower human capital and lower skills levels, since they are less capable of overcoming the various mobility constraints.

Based upon the details contained in Table 9.7, we can now characterize the differences in manpower transfer between voluntary and involuntary labour mobility in the major economic sectors. As regards voluntary labour mobility, there are two distinct features worth noting. Firstly, inter-industry labour mobility is much more pervasive in the tertiary sector than in the secondary sector, whilst the labour mobility rate in the primary sector is considerably lower.

Table 9.7 *Voluntary and involuntary inward, outward and net inter-industry labour mobility, 1996-2000* [a]

Industry	Employment Volume	Voluntary Mobility (%)			Involuntary Mobility (%)		
		Inward	Outward	Net	Inward	Outward	Net
Primary Sector	793,078	1.4	1.7	-0.3	0.7	0.2	0.4
Agriculture	781,468	1.4	1.6	-0.3	0.6	0.2	0.4
Mining	11,610	3.7	6.2	-2.5	3.5	2.9	0.6
Secondary Sector	3,500,965	4.7	4.9	-0.1	1.5	1.8	-0.4
Light Industry	791,300	4.7	4.9	-0.2	1.5	1.7	-0.2
Petrochemical	411,191	4.4	4.4	0.1	1.1	1.7	-0.6
Machinery	775,418	4.3	4.5	-0.3	1.4	1.3	0.1
Electrical & Electronics	642,217	7.8	7.0	0.8	1.9	1.8	0.1
Utilities	35,347	0.6	0.6	–	1.0	1.5	-0.5
Construction	845,492	3.3	3.9	-0.7	1.5	2.6	-1.1
Tertiary Sector	5,043954	6.1	6.0	0.1	1.2	1.1	0.2
Commerce	1,876,425	6.6	6.7	–	1.3	1.0	0.2
Transportation	466,709	5.1	4.9	0.2	1.2	0.9	0.2
Finance & Insurance	388,466	6.9	5.3	1.6	1.3	1.3	–
Commercial Services	499,335	7.8	8.0	-0.2	1.4	1.2	0.3
Social & Personal Services	1,813,019	5.2	5.1	0.1	1.2	1.0	0.1
All Industries	9,337,997 [b]	5.2	5.2	–	1.3	1.3	–

Notes:
[a] All figures refer to the average over the 1996-2000 period.
[b] Since qualified persons with missing industry data are excluded, the total number of employed persons in all industries, over the 1996-2000 period, differs from the corresponding figure in Table 9.1.

Source: Compiled by the author from *Manpower Utilization Surveys, 1997-2001.*

Secondly, the tertiary sector has a net labour gain of 0.1 per cent which comes at the expense of net losses in both the primary sector, at -0.3 per cent, and the secondary sector, at -0.1 per cent. In specific terms, the industry with the most substantial net labour loss as a result of voluntary labour mobility is mining, at -2.5 per cent, whilst the industrial sector which appears to be most attractive for those engaging in voluntary inter-industry labour mobility is the finance and insurance sector, with a net labour gain of 1.6 per cent (Table 9.7).

The outcomes for involuntary labour mobility are, however, rather different from those of voluntary labour mobility. Firstly, involuntary labour mobility is much more pervasive within the secondary sector than in either the tertiary or primary sectors, a phenomenon which comes essentially as a result of the prolonged industrial restructuring which has been taking place in Taiwan since the early 1990s. Secondly, the primary and tertiary sectors both have net labour gains (0.4 per cent, and 0.2 per cent, respectively) at the expense of a net labour loss in the secondary sector (-0.4 per cent). Those industries with the highest net gains from involuntary labour turnover include agriculture (0.4 per cent) and mining (0.6 per cent), while the one industry associated with the most substantial labour loss is construction (-1.1 per cent).

The Industrial Flow of Workers

The preceding discussion on the departure behaviour of workers is insufficient to reveal the whole picture of inter-industry manpower transfer, since it is also necessary to examine the industrial flows of workers, that is, the redistribution of those workers who decide to undertake an inter-industry move. Between 1996 and 2000, there were about 253,000 workers each year engaging in voluntary labour mobility, and, as Table 9.8 suggests, the tertiary sector was the major 'winner' from such mobility. About 3.3 per cent of those moving chose to move to the primary sector, whilst 35.1 per cent went to the secondary sector, and as many as 61.6 per cent entered the tertiary sector. However, in stark contrast to voluntary turnover, as Table 9.9 shows, of the total of around 57,000 workers involved each year in involuntary inter-industry mobility, approximately 8.1 per cent go to the primary sector, 35.4 per cent go to the secondary sector and 56.5 per cent go to the tertiary sector.

Some of the more salient aspects of involuntary and voluntary turnover flows, as revealed by Tables 9.8 and 9.9, are worth highlighting. Firstly, for voluntary labour mobility, commerce appears to be a favourite industry of choice for job movers in general. Secondly, although not large in number, workers moving from the agricultural and mining industries, either voluntarily or involuntarily, seem to favour the utilities, transportation and communications industries (22.1 per cent for voluntary mobility, and 40.5 per cent for involuntary mobility).

Table 9.8 *Voluntary inter-industry labour mobility flows, 1996-2000* [a]

Industry of Origin	Inter-industry Worker Outflow (No. of Persons)	Choice of Destination Industry for Outflow Workers (%)									
		Primary Sector (1)	Secondary Sector				Tertiary Sector				
			(2)	(3)	(4)	Total	(5)	(6)	(7)	(8)	Total
Primary Sector											
Agriculture & Mining	10,724	–	13.7	12.2	22.1	47.9	4.6	27.6	6.2	13.7	52.1
Secondary Sector											
Traditional Manufacturing	25,504	4.0	–	34.1	4.8	38.8	5.0	27.9	9.7	14.6	57.2
Other Manufacturing Industries	45,668	3.1	16.9	–	8.7	25.6	6.5	29.8	15.9	19.0	71.2
Construction	23,471	7.8	9.1	23.7	–	32.8	6.4	26.5	11.2	15.3	59.5
Tertiary Sector											
Utilities, Transportation & Communications	15,740	2.4	6.2	18.6	3.7	28.5	–	31.1	18.2	19.8	69.1
Commerce	60,367	3.6	9.9	27.0	7.2	44.1	7.9	–	20.6	23.8	52.3
Finance, Insurance and Commercial Services	30,678	1.9	5.6	19.4	7.5	32.5	9.5	30.8	–	25.4	65.7
Social & Personal Services	41,190	2.4	8.7	19.5	7.3	35.5	6.4	37.2	18.5	–	62.1
All Industries	253,342	3.3	9.3	19.3	7.0	35.6	6.5	23.5	14.2	16.9	61.1

Notes:

[a] All figures refer to the average over the 1996-2000 period.

[b] Numbers in parentheses indicate industrial sectors, as follows: (1) agriculture and mining; (2) traditional manufacturing industries; (3) other manufacturing industries; (4) construction; (5) utilities, transportation and communications; (6) commerce; (7) finance, insurance and commercial services; and (8) social and personal services.

Source: Compiled by the author from *Manpower Utilization Surveys, 1997-2001.*

Table 9.9 *Involuntary inter-industry labour mobility flows, 1996-2000* [a]

Industry of Origin	Inter-industry Worker Outflow (No. of Persons)	Choice of Destination Industry for Outflow Workers (%)									
		Primary Sector (1)	Secondary Sector				Tertiary Sector				
			(2)	(3)	(4)	Total	(5)	(6)	(7)	(8)	Total
Primary Sector											
Agriculture & Mining	1,260	–	7.9	13.6	40.5	61.9	2.9	18.6	–	16.6	38.1
Secondary Sector											
Traditional Manufacturing	8,071	9.4	–	32.1	11.4	43.5	8.4	21.0	4.8	13.0	47.2
Other Manufacturing Industries	11,393	5.4	17.1	–	4.5	21.6	7.2	38.0	6.7	21.1	73.0
Construction	13,014	15.0	10.4	25.2	–	35.7	6.2	24.3	10.7	8.2	49.4
Tertiary Sector											
Utilities, Transportation & Communications	2,624	17.3	9.4	16.4	14.6	40.4	–	12.2	9.4	20.8	42.4
Commerce	9,365	1.6	18.2	18.8	4.4	41.4	6.2	–	17.0	33.8	56.9
Finance, Insurance and Commercial Services	4,235	2.1	1.3	15.8	12.8	29.9	4.9	41.3	–	21.7	68.0
Social & Personal Services	7,036	8.5	10.6	22.4	6.7	39.6	5.8	27.1	19.0	–	51.9
All Industries	56,998	8.1	10.8	18.4	6.6	35.8	6.2	23.5	10.0	16.4	56.1

Notes:
[a] All figures refer to the average over the 1996-2000 period.
[b] Numbers in parentheses indicate industrial sectors, as follows: (1) agriculture and mining; (2) traditional manufacturing industries; (3) other manufacturing industries; (4) construction; (5) utilities, transportation and communications; (6) commerce; (7) finance, insurance and commercial services; and (8) social and personal services.

Source: Compiled by the author from *Manpower Utilization Surveys, 1997-2001.*

Thirdly, as compared to those moving voluntarily, involuntary job movers from the secondary sector do not generally have the capabilities to move into the tertiary sector, and are therefore much more likely to flow into the primary sector. Fourthly, the transfer of the labour force from the tertiary sector to other sectors is rather rigid, in the sense that most of the inter-industry labour mobility from the tertiary sector tends to be concentrated on certain sectors, regardless of whether the move is voluntary or involuntary. However, when taking the decision to make the move, involuntary job movers from the tertiary sector are more likely to leave the tertiary sector than their voluntary counterparts.

Geographical Redistribution of Labour

Since job turnover is often associated with a change in the geographical location of the workplace, it is worth examining the extent to which workers will go to secure their new job. Firstly, as indicated in panel A of Table 9.10, around 45.1 per cent of all job movers will ultimately work within the Taipei-Taoyuan Metropolitan Area. It is, however, a little surprising to find that the share of job movers working in the Kaohsiung Metropolitan Area is only 11.5 per cent, particularly when considering that Kaohsiung serves as the second largest domestic labour market and that it is second only to the Taipei-Taoyuan Metropolitan Area in scale. Its share is even lower than the corresponding figure for the Taichung Metropolitan Area, at 13.8 per cent, despite Taichung being a lesser-populated area.

A comparison between panels B and C of Table 9.10 reveals the marked differences between voluntary and involuntary job movers, with regard to the geographical redistribution of these workers following job turnover. Firstly, as compared with the proportion of voluntary job movers (17.7 per cent), a larger proportion of involuntary job movers (20.2 per cent) will find work in rural areas. Secondly, involuntary job movers tend to be more geographically concentrated than voluntary job movers; taking Hsinchu Metropolitan Area as an example, about 70.5 per cent of voluntary job movers from this area choose to remain working within this same area after changing jobs, whilst around 80.0 per cent of involuntary job movers will tend to remain in the Hsinchu area.

From the scenarios examined here, it seems that involuntary job movers are less likely than voluntary job movers to undertake migration over any significant distance in cases where job turnover triggers the need for geographical migration. However, such a distinction is in fact highly likely, given that, as compared to voluntary job movers, involuntary job movers are likely to be less capable of overcoming the intervening factors with regard to migration between origin and destination.

Table 9.10 *Geographical redistribution of voluntary and involuntary job turnover, 1996-2000* [a]

Unit: % share, unless otherwise stated

Prior Job Location (Metropolitan Area) [b]	Turnover Volume (No. of Persons) [c]	Current Job Location (Metropolitan Area)					
		Taipei-Taoyuan	Hsinchu	Taichung	Tainan	Kaohsiung	Others
Panel A: Voluntary Mobility							
Taipei-Taoyuan	225,239	91.7	0.9	1.8	0.7	1.1	3.9
Hsinchu	15,947	9.0	70.5	1.4	1.0	–	18.2
Taichung	67,391	5.5	0.5	84.5	0.8	0.9	7.8
Tainan	37,580	5.4	1.3	0.9	80.4	7.9	4.2
Kaohsiung	52,775	4.5	0.1	1.1	5.2	84.4	4.7
Others	85,461	10.1	3.8	5.6	2.2	2.5	75.8
Totals	484,393	46.4	3.6	13.8	7.7	10.9	17.7
Panel B: Involuntary Mobility							
Taipei-Taoyuan	48,089	92.9	0.7	1.3	0.7	1.2	3.2
Hsinchu	3,429	9.1	79.7	–	2.2	–	9.1
Taichung	16,629	3.6	0.1	86.6	0.7	1.5	7.5
Tainan	11,027	5.2	–	0.4	86.2	5.8	2.4
Kaohsiung	17,200	4.4	–	1.4	2.8	84.7	6.7
Others	23,365	4.2	2.7	4.6	1.6	2.7	84.3
Totals	119,739	40.0	3.1	13.7	9.1	13.9	20.2

Table 9.10 (Contd.) [a]

Unit: % share, unless otherwise stated

Prior Job Location (Metropolitan Area) [b]	Turnover Volume (No. of Persons) [c]	Current Job Location (Metropolitan Areas)					
		Taipei-Taoyuan	Hsinchu	Taichung	Tainan	Kaohsiung	Others
Panel C: Voluntary and Involuntary Mobility							
Taipei-Taoyuan	273,328	91.9	0.8	1.7	0.7	1.1	3.8
Hsinchu	19,376	9.0	72.1	1.1	1.2	–	16.6
Taichung	84,020	5.1	0.4	84.9	0.7	1.0	7.8
Tainan	48,607	5.3	1.0	0.8	81.7	7.4	3.8
Kaohsiung	69,976	4.5	0.1	1.1	4.6	84.4	5.2
Others	108,826	8.8	3.5	5.4	2.1	2.6	77.6
Totals	604,132	45.1	3.5	13.8	7.9	11.5	18.2

Notes:

[a] All data refers to the average over the 1996-2000 period.

[b] The composition of the metropolitan areas is as follows: Taipei-Taoyuan metropolitan area includes Taipei City, Keelung City, Taipei Prefecture and Taoyuan Prefecture; Hsinchu metropolitan area comprises of Hsinchu City; Taichung metropolitan area includes Taichung City and Taichung Prefecture; Tainan metropolitan area includes Tainan City and Tainan Prefecture; Kaohsiung metropolitan area includes Kaoshiung City and Kaohsiung Prefecture; Others includes all remaining agricultural prefectures.

[c] Turnover volume refers to all job turnover, including those remaining within their original job location and those engaging in prefectural migration as a result of their re-employment.

Source: Compiled by the author from *Manpower Utilization Surveys*, 1997-2001.

234 *Employment Development in a Regulated and Globalized Labour Market*

In summary, as compared to voluntary movers, workers involved in involuntary job turnover are less likely to undertake inter-industry mobility and are less capable of making any long-distance move in cases where there is a need to engage in geographical migration. Such differences are actually a reflection of the differentials between the ability of voluntary and involuntary job movers to overcome labour market constraints; indeed, the inference is that this distinctive differential between voluntary and involuntary job movers is very likely to be due to the inherent differences in their human capital stock and skills levels.

CONCLUSIONS

This chapter has been more descriptive than analytical, since it does not employ any sophisticated econometric models; however, the findings from the examination of turnover in this chapter serve to characterize the central features of voluntary and involuntary job turnover in Taiwan between 1996 and 2000, based upon pooled data from the 1997-2001 Manpower Utilization Surveys. On the whole, the factors affecting job turnover, whether voluntary or involuntary, can be examined under two broad dimensions, the first of which is at individual level, whilst the second is essentially attributable to the prolonged economic restructuring which has been taking place in Taiwan since the early 1990s and short-term economic downturn which took place in the late 1990s.

In terms of turnover trends, we find that between 1996 and 2000, the aggregate incidence of general job turnover has been in decline; nevertheless, whilst voluntary job turnover seems to follow the general trend, involuntary job turnover appears to be on the rise. By examining the situation in the major economic sectors, we find that job turnover in the tertiary sector is mainly voluntary in nature, in stark contrast to the situations observed in both the secondary and primary sectors. As regards the selective nature of turnover by gender, we find that males are more vulnerable than females to involuntary job turnover. As for the educational effect, in contrast to the association with voluntary turnover, incidences of involuntary job turnover are negatively associated with education. In terms of the selective nature of turnover by age, older workers are more likely to be involved in turnover of an involuntary rather than voluntary nature; clearly, there is a greater likelihood of workers being susceptible to involuntary job turnover with advancing age.

By examining the reasons for job turnover, we find that the most often cited reasons for voluntary turnover are poor working conditions and low pay, whereas business shutouts, shrinkage and layoffs, and job transfers are the three most often cited reasons for involuntary job changes. Workers within the primary sector are generally subject to business shrinkage and layoffs, whilst those in the secondary sector seem fairly susceptible to business shutouts, and those in the tertiary sector are more vulnerable to involuntary job transfers. As such, the increasing incidence of involuntary job turnover is largely due to two factors, that is, the prolonged industrial restructuring in Taiwan since the early 1990s and the short-term economic downturn of the late 1990s.

The general pattern of inter-industry labour mobility is characterized by a net transfer of the labour force from the primary and secondary sectors to the tertiary sector, suggesting that job turnover, in general, has a positive effect in raising personal socioeconomic status and economic wellbeing. Indeed, this pattern of voluntary manpower transfer is fairly consistent with the historical patterns of development observed within many of the developed countries. In Taiwan, this pattern of manpower transfer is, however, mainly shaped by voluntary labour mobility as opposed to mobility of an involuntary nature. As compared to voluntary movers, workers involved in involuntary job turnover are less likely to engage in inter-industry mobility, and indeed, are also less capable of making a long-distance move in cases where geographical labour migration is required.

Voluntary and involuntary labour mobility are very distinct in the sense that the direction of inter-industry mobility relating to involuntary turnover runs relatively counter to that of voluntary turnover. In other words, involuntary job turnover is characterized by downward mobility as opposed to the upward mobility associated with voluntary turnover. In conjunction with the findings on the geographical redistribution of workers engaging in job turnover, these findings also raise two distinct issues. Firstly, in terms of the direction of migration, the orientation of involuntary inter-industry labour mobility is more likely to be urban-to-rural than rural-to-urban. Secondly, involuntary labour mobility may be highly correlated with return labour migration, whilst voluntary labour mobility tends to be associated with onward labour migration. In light of the substantial differences between economic sectors, such as wage levels and the subjects' career reputation, these findings implicitly suggest that workers involved in involuntary job turnover are less capable of acquiring the potential benefits associated with labour mobility. The inevitable result would seem to be that, in contrast to their voluntary counterparts, involuntary movers will be much more likely to suffer degradation of both their socioeconomic status and their wellbeing.

In conclusion, the findings of this research should help to shed some light on effective labour policy design. Since workers involved in involuntary job turnover are more likely to experience downward mobility, which would, in turn, lead to degradation of both their personal socioeconomic status and economic wellbeing, it is expected that in the near future, such workers will become an 'at-risk' group within the labour force, in terms of the probability of moving into the long-term unemployment pool. Furthermore, their geographical migration is more likely to be of a 'return' nature and, as the existing literature has widely confirmed, returnees often tend to be discouraged, leading to a lack of confidence in their search for new opportunities – the so-called 'once bitten, twice shy' effect – largely as a result of their prior unpleasant and unsuccessful experiences in the labour market (Morrison and DaVanzo, 1986; Long 1988; Lin and Liaw, 2000). As such, corresponding policy measures should aim to prevent further involuntary downward mobility and actively help those who are involuntarily placed in a position of having to change their jobs to reduce the potential difficulties arising from their need for continuous adjustment within the labour market.

REFERENCES

Barron, J. and S. McCafferty (1977), 'Job Search, Labour Supply and the Quit Decision', *American Economic Review*, **67**: 683-91.

Brenner, H. and A. Mooney (1983), 'Unemployment and Health in the Context of Economic Change', *Social Science and Medicine*, **17**: 1125-38.

Burdett, K. (1978), 'A Theory on Employee Job Search and Quit Rates', *American Economic Review*, **68**: 212-20.

Clark, K. and L. Summers (1979), 'Labour Market Dynamics and Unemployment: A Reconsideration', *Brookings Papers on Economic Activity*, **1**: 13-60.

DGBAS (1997-2001), *Manpower Utilization Surveys, 1997-2001*, Taipei: Directorate-General of Budget, Accounting and Statistics.

Diamond, P. (1981), 'Mobility Costs, Frictional Unemployment and Efficiency', *Journal of Political Economy*, **89**: 798-812.

Gallaway, L. (1963), 'Labour Mobility, Resource Allocation and Structural Unemployment', *American Economic Review*, **52**: 694-716.

Hall, R. (1972), 'Turnover in the Labour Force', *Brookings Papers on Economic Activity*, **3**: 709-56.

Jacobson, L.S., R.J. Lalonde and D.G. Sullivan (1993), 'Earning Losses of Displaced Workers', *American Economic Review*, **83**(4): 685-709.

Lee, J.S. (ed.) (2003), *Who Stole Away Our Jobs?*, Taipei: Commonwealth Publishing Company.

Lin, J.P. (2005), 'A Critical Review of the Problems Associated with Population and Labour Migration in Taiwan, 1980-2000', *Journal of Taiwan Sociology*, **34**: 147-209.

Lin, J.P. and K.L. Liaw (2000), 'Labour Migration in Taiwan: Characterization and Interpretation Based on the Data of the 1990 Census', *Environment and Planning*, **32**(9): 1689-1709.

Long, L. (1988), *Migration and Residential Mobility in the United States*, New York: Russell Sage Foundation

Malo, M.A. and F. Munoz-Bullon (2003), 'Long-term Effects of Involuntary Job Separation on Labour Careers', *Business Economics Series Working Paper No.03-42(11)*, Madrid: Universidad Carlos III de Madrid.

Marston, S. (1976), 'Employment Instability and High Unemployment Rates', *Brookings Papers on Economic Activity*, 1: 169-210.

Morrison, P.A. and J.S. DaVanzo (1986), 'The Prism of Migration: Dissimilarities between Return and Onward Movers', *Social Science Quarterly*, 67(3): 504-16.

Rhum, C. (1991), 'Are Workers Permanently Scarred by Job Displacements?', *American Economic Review*, 81(1): 319-24.

RuBarron, J. and S. McCafferty (1977), 'Job Search, Labour Supply and the Quit Decision', *American Economic Review*, 67: 683-91.

Samson, L. (1985), 'A Study of the Impact of Sectoral Shifts on Aggregate Unemployment in Canada', *Canadian Journal of Economics*, 18: 518-30.

Sicherman, N. and O. Galor (1990), 'A Theory of Career Mobility', *Journal of Political Economy*, 8(1): 169-92.

Stevens, A.H. (1997), 'Persistent Effects of Job Displacement: The Importance of Multiple Job Losses', *Journal of Labor Economics*, 15(1): 165-88.

Tsay, C.L. and J.P. Lin (1999), *Economic Restructuring and Labor Market Dynamics: Intra- and Inter-industrial Labour Mobility in Taiwan*, Taipei: Council for Economic Planning and Developments.

Turvey, R. (1977), 'Structural Change and Structural Unemployment', *International Labour Review*, 116: 209-15.

PART III

Labour Market Policies in the New Knowledge Economy

10 Employee Training Programmes and Sustainable Employability

Joseph S. Lee and Ping-Lung Hsin

INTRODUCTION

Given the persistently high level of structural unemployment in Taiwan over recent years, one of the government's primary policy goals which has continued to gain increasing importance throughout this period is the effective upgrading of the skills and knowledge of unemployed workers so as to enable them to secure reemployment. With the increasingly rapid globalization of the Taiwanese economy, constant upgrading of the skills and knowledge of the workforce is now a prerequisite to the maintenance of an acceptable level of sustainable employability for such workers. Formal employee training is clearly very important in terms of assisting the government to achieve this goal; indeed, its importance is evidenced by the significant proportion of GDP being spent on training in many industrialized countries. In 2002, for example, the government of Sweden spent 0.29 per cent of its GDP on employee training programmes, whilst the respective figures for Finland, the Netherlands and Denmark were 0.30 per cent, 0.60 per cent and 0.86 per cent (OECD, 2004).

Faced with growing unemployment and the need to move towards a knowledge-based economy, the government in Taiwan has been investing an ever-increasing proportion of its GDP into employee training. In 2001, for example, the government was spending only 0.03 per cent of the island's GDP on employee training, and although the figure had risen to 0.04 per cent by 2003, it nevertheless remained much lower than many of the western industrialized countries (Lee and Hsin, 2005). The government also introduced a three-year 'employability enhancement programme' (EEP) in 2002, injecting a total of NT$10.3billion (US$344 million) into employee training. On completion of the first phase, in 2004, the government injected a further NT$11.9 billion into the EEP, extending the programme for a further three years.

242   *Labour Market Policies in the New Knowledge Economy*

These first two phases of the EEP are regarded by the Taiwanese government as an experiment; nevertheless, if the programme proves to be effective in upgrading the skills and knowledge of the workforce as a whole (including those in employment, the unemployed and marginal workers) and thereby assists in establishing sustainable employability (thus alleviating the risk of unemployment even in times of rapid changes in technology and the industrial structure) the government is set to make the EEP a more permanent programme, and one which is destined to become a major component of current active labour market policy in Taiwan. Most importantly, however, given the proportion of GDP spent on employee training in Taiwan as compared to the expenditure in many European countries, the government is also fully aware that there is considerable room for improvement and expansion in this area.

Questions nevertheless arise as to whether such employee training programmes will have the effect that the government expects of them, helping workers to secure sustainable employability (thereby lifting the threat of unemployment and dislocation in a globalized economy where the economic structure and production technologies are constantly and rapidly changing) and effectively helping employees to improve their earnings ability (by raising wage rates, and thereby, not only raising the living standards of workers but also closing the income gap between the rich and the poor). Studies in other countries seem to provide positive answers to such questions, with many having demonstrated the positive relationship between employee training and the wage rates of participants (Hollenbeck and Wilkie, 1985; Lillard and Tan, 1986; Barron et al., 1989; Brown, 1989; Mincer, 1989; Lynch, 1992). Following a review of more than 20 such studies on employee training programmes, Ok and Tergeist (2003) concluded that in each case, a positive relationship existed between participation in employee training and the subsequent rise in wage rates, as compared to those of non-participants. These studies also found that, with age, there was a much slower erosion of skills amongst those workers who had participated in employee training programmes, thereby reducing their likelihood of unemployment or dislocation.

Other studies have found that employee training programmes can help participants to raise their overall level of employability which can significantly improve their chances of securing reemployment after having been laid off (Lynch, 1992; Kraus et al., 1997; Lynch and Black, 1998; Beneito et al., 2000; Barrett and O'Connell, 2001). These studies have also found that employee training programmes were effective in protecting employees from the wage diminution arising from job changes. However, the real question is whether employee training programmes can do the same for workers in Taiwan as they have done for workers in other countries, given the considerable differences in the established training system, as well as the comparative social and economic backgrounds.

This chapter therefore sets out to investigate the effectiveness of employee training programmes in assisting workers to rapidly secure reemployment, and in helping those in employment to secure sustainable employability, thereby facilitating a smooth transition into new jobs, as and when necessary.

EMPLOYEE TRAINING IN TAIWAN

As regards the current situation of employee training in Taiwan, although the government did promulgate the Employee Training Fund Act (ETFA) in the early 1970s, there is no national vocational training system currently in place because the ETFA was abolished during the 1975 recession so as to release employers from the burden of the employee training levy. The government has not reinstated this Act, nor has it enacted any other vocational training legislature since then; thus, as at 2006, no centrally coordinated employee training system exists in Taiwan.

Although the central government does, from time to time, formulate national training policies, no central government agency currently has responsibility for implementing these policies. It is therefore up to different government agencies to implement training policies as each of their individual budgets allow and to offer training courses as each agency sees fit. Furthermore, on completion of such training programmes, there are no established criteria, at central government level, for evaluating the effectiveness of these programmes; therefore, each agency decides what type of evaluation mechanism it requires, if indeed it recognizes any need for evaluation at all.

The Council for Economic Planning and Development (CEPD) is currently playing a rather loose and informal role in coordinating training programmes between different government agencies under the newly implemented EEP (Lee and Hsin 2005); however, given the lack of any central organization with overall responsibility for employee training, there is, at best, very limited information available on the current state of employee training in Taiwan. Nevertheless, the Council of Labour Affairs (CLA) did recently carry out a survey on current employee training in Taiwan, involving questionnaires mailed to a sample of 16,895 people, including those in employment, the unemployed and those outside the labour force (CLA, 2002). The survey results indicated that 14.2 per cent of respondents had received some job-related training during the survey year, with the greatest opportunities for receiving such training being amongst employees within the finance, insurance and real estate industry (46.4 per cent). The utilities industry, including electricity, gas and water, ranked second (41 per cent), followed by public administration (35 per cent). Less than 10 per cent of employees within the agriculture, construction, wholesale, retail and restaurants industries had participated in any training programmes (Table 10.1).

Table 10.1   Employee participation in job-related training, by industry, 2001

Industry	Total No. of Employees	Employee Participation in Job-related Training (%)	
		Yes	No
Agriculture, Forestry, Fisheries and Animal Husbandry	808,902	2.2	97.8
Mining and Quarrying	17,568	14.4	85.7
Manufacturing	2,547,578	12.5	87.6
Electricity, Gas and Water	53,737	41.3	58.7
Construction	733,972	5.0	95.0
Wholesale, Retail and Restaurants	2,147,711	7.7	92.3
Transportation, Storage and Communications	452,439	16.2	83.8
Finance, Insurance and Real Estate	378,668	46.4	53.7
Business Services	333,552	21.5	78.5
Social, Personal and Related Community Services	1,567,794	21.2	78.8
Public Administration	320,152	35.1	64.9
Total	9,362,073	14.2	85.8

Source: CLA (2002).

For most participants in such training programmes, the immediate benefits came from learning skills that were useful for their job performance (74 per cent of participants cited this particular benefit), whilst 45 per cent of participants indicated that the rules and regulations learned from attending these training courses were useful within their jobs. We can see that, in general, it is only within larger establishments that a greater proportion of employees have their training costs paid for by their employers (Table 10.2).

The CLA had conducted an earlier survey, in 2001, of 7,865 establishments, with particular focus on their employee training activities. From the results of this survey, the CLA estimated that only 13.8 per cent of all establishments in Taiwan were making such training programmes available to their employees, with the greater proportion of courses being made available by the larger establishments. For those establishments with more than 500 employees, training programmes were made available to 90 per cent of their employees, whilst in those establishments with 50 to 99 employees, the proportion was 53 per cent, and in those with less than 29 employees, the figure was as low as 12 per cent (CLA, 2002).

Table 10.2   Disbursement of employee training programme costs, 2001[a]

Types of Training Courses	Costs Borne by Employer (%)	Costs Borne by Trainee [b] (NT$)	(%)	Costs Shared between Employer and Trainee [b] (NT$)	(%)
Professional and Technical	84.5	12,512	11.4	6,083	4.5
Language	54.9	15,047	29.4	5,663	14.7
Computer-related	76.9	17,101	18.5	6,810	4.5
Managerial	86.3	20,714	8.0	6,100	6.7
Certification	57.6	13,512	35.2	8,020	7.2
Others	78.1	13,665	18.9	1,500	3.0

Notes:
[a]   Column totals may exceed 100 per cent since multiple selections were permitted.
[b]   Training course costs are average costs (in NT$).

Source: CLA (2002).

The CLA survey found that it was employees in public, rather than private, establishments who were provided with far greater opportunities for attendance on training programmes (75 per cent for the former, as compared to just 13.7 per cent for the latter). The average annual expenditure on employee training programmes for each establishment was found to be around NT$110,000 (US$3,437); however, as expected, considerably more was spent on employee training in public establishments, at about NT$1,245,000 (US$38,906), than in private establishments, at about NT$97,000 (US$3,031) on average (CLA, 2002).

In order to encourage private establishments to start offering more training courses to their employees, the government introduced a policy of partial or total subsidies to those public and private establishments which were prepared to set up training programmes for their employees. In general, however, it was the larger establishments which received the much greater proportion of the government training grants for such programmes, with 15 per cent of all establishments with more than 500 employees receiving government training subsidies, whereas 6.7 per cent of those with 200 to 299 employees received subsidies and only 1.9 per cent of those with less than 29 employees received any form of government assistance for training (Lee and Hsin, 2003; Table 3.9).

Clearly, therefore, the question arises as to why such government training subsidies are being consumed by the larger establishments. The main reason is largely because, since the larger establishments invariably have extra capacity, their employee training programmes are often set up to accept not only their own employees, but also trainees referred to them by government agencies. Thus, given that these large establishments are, in a sense, providing public training services, it may be quite logical for the government to subsidize part of their training expenses. The larger establishments also account for a far greater proportion of government training subsidies because under current government policy, only those establishments with annual expenditure on employee training in excess of NT$300,000 are eligible for such subsidies.

As regards the effectiveness of government subsidies – in terms of providing an appropriate incentive for establishments – according to a survey carried out in 2002 on a total of 201 establishments, the subsidies were found to have very little impact on the decision as to whether or not a training programme would be set up, but they did have a considerable impact on the size of the training programmes (Lee and Hsin, 2003). For example, only 5 per cent of the employers in the survey said that they would cancel their training programmes if subsidies were not available, whereas 65 per cent said they would reduce the size of their training programmes; the remaining 29 per cent indicated that government subsidies affected neither their decision to set up employee training programmes nor the size of these training programmes. However, as one might expect, the absence of such subsidies would have much more significant impacts on smaller establishments than on larger ones (Lee and Hsin, 2003; Table 3.24).

When setting up their employee training programmes, employers will often utilize more than one approach, the most popular being on-site training programmes managed and delivered by the company's own staff. According to the 2001 CLA survey, 54 per cent of the 210 establishments surveyed were utilizing such on-site training programmes. The second most popular approach was to send employees out to private institutes specializing in the development and delivery of training (43 per cent), whilst a relatively small proportion of employers (17 per cent) utilized off-site public training programmes set up and managed by public training institutes. The relative lack of popularity of the latter is because these institutes do not usually have the most up-to-date facilities or training instructors.

In-house training programmes (i.e., on-site programmes which are managed and delivered by outside instructors or institutes) do not seem to be a popular form of employee training in Taiwan, since this occurred in only 9 per cent of all the private establishments in the 2001 CLA survey (CLA, 2002). The survey also found that training in sales and clerical work were the most common contents of these employee training programmes (38 per cent) followed by production and technical training (32 per cent), legal training (25 per cent), R&D (21 per cent), general management (22 per cent) and computer-related training (15 per cent). The survey revealed that only 3 per cent of all establishments offered language training courses, which is, in fact, to be expected, given that language is a general skill. Very few employers would actually want to offer such general training because once those attending had completed such training courses, this would add to their overall attractiveness to other companies, to whom they could easily switch for higher pay (CLA, 2002).

Employee training programmes are clearly not so popular in Taiwan. For employers, this may be because of the high costs involved and the difficulties in finding a convenient time for a particular employee to participate in such training. There is also an indication that some employers believe that many of these training programmes are irrelevant to their needs; this is also the case in many private sector companies which do not recognize any need to train their employees. Thus more than two-thirds of all employers in the private sector who responded to the CLA survey indicated that they had no requirement for employee training.

Unfortunately, we find that this general apathy towards employee training programmes in Taiwan is often exacerbated by employees themselves, many of whom fail to appreciate the benefits of participating in training programmes, whilst others may argue that they do not have the time to attend such training. The CLA survey revealed that 24 per cent of the employed workers cited the irrelevance of these programmes to their immediate job as the main reason for not participating in them, whilst 74 per cent of all the employed workers in the sample, along with 58 per cent of all unemployed respondents, indicated that the main reasons for not wishing to participate in such training were that they were 'too busy with work' or had 'too much work at home'.

A further major reason for the unemployed respondents not wishing to participate was that these training programmes were seen as providing no direct assistance to them in terms of finding suitable jobs on completion of their training (CLA, 2002). On the whole, the lack of time and the irrelevance of the training programmes to their current area of work were found to be the main reasons behind the unwillingness of workers in Taiwan to attend such training programmes.

THE ECONOMIC EFFECTS OF EMPLOYEE TRAINING PROGRAMMES

The Effects of Training on Increases in Wages

It would appear that both employers and employees alike in Taiwan are of the opinion that the vast majority of employee training programmes currently being offered are of no use whatsoever, essentially because they have no relevance to their current work' this is therefore clearly an issue which is in need of some investigation. In attempting to undertake such an investigation, an opportunity arises to assess the relevance of employee training programmes from two aspects; firstly, whether the wages of training participants were subsequently any higher than those of non-participants, and secondly, whether unemployed training participants were able to secure reemployment any quicker than similar unemployed workers who were not participating in training.

In 2003, in an attempt to determine the level of these effects, a comprehensive questionnaire survey was set up for delivery to a sample of 11,130 employees who had previously participated in retraining or upgrading programmes organized and operated by private enterprises and training institutions. The programme providers were both privately and publicly owned and were either partially or wholly subsidized by the government. Of the total of 11,130 targets for the study sample, only 1,564 usable questionnaires were returned (Lee and Hsin, 2003). Details of the ultimate sample are provided in Table 10.3.

A comparison of the demographic characteristics between the returned and non-returned questionnaires was conducted so as to check whether there was any sampling bias caused by the low return rate; however, the comparison revealed no discernible bias. The demographic characteristics of those respondents who did return questionnaires were as follows.

Age and education levels

The young and better educated represented the largest proportion of those participating in government-subsidized training programmes, with those aged between 25 and 34 years accounting for 36.1 per cent of all participants. A further 29.9 per cent of trainees were aged between 35 and 44 years, whilst 23.3 per cent were 45 years old or older.

In terms of their better education, 29.4 per cent of those participating in the various training programmes had completed junior college education, 31.4 per cent had at least a further four years of college education, 31 per cent had 12 years of formal education, and only 8.3 per cent had nine years of education, or less.

Table 10.3   Sample characteristics of the 2003 study

Characteristics	No. of Persons	%
Sex		
Male	790	50.5
Female	774	49.5
Age		
24 years	167	10.7
25-34 years	565	36.1
35-44 years	468	29.9
$\geq$45 years	364	23.3
Educational Attainment		
Junior High School (or below)	130	8.3
Senior High School	484	31.0
Junior College	459	29.4
4 years College and University	406	26.0
Graduate Studies	84	5.4
Marital Status		
Married (Spouse Present) or Cohabiting	863	55.7
Single	597	38.5
Widowed, Separated or Divorced	89	5.7
Total	1,564	100.0

Source: Lee and Hsin (2003).

Skill levels of trainees
In order to carry out our analysis more effectively, those within the sample who were attending the various training programmes were divided into three groups, according to their particular level of skill. The three groups were categorized as: (i) the high-level manpower (HLM) group, which comprised of professional and managerial workers; (ii) the middle-level manpower (MLM) group, which included clerical and technical workers; and (iii) the low-level manpower (LLM) group, which comprised of service sector workers, sales staff and skilled production workers.

Employment status during the period of training
A considerable proportion (49.35 per cent) of all those attending the various training courses were in gainful employment at the time of their attendance, with a considerable number of these workers attending the courses for the purpose of upgrading their production knowledge and skills. The majority (64 per cent) of the HLM group was in employment at the time of their

training and in many cases, their attendance on the various employee training programmes had been facilitated by their employers. A further 32.29 per cent of those attending the training programmes were unemployed at the time of their training, and 18.3 per cent were not involved in any way in the labour force (Table 10.4).

Table 10.4　Employment status of programme participants, by skills levels

Employment Status	Skills Levels							
	HLM [a]		MLM [b]		LLM [c]		Totals	
	No.	%	No.	%	No.	%	No.	%
Employed	422	64.62	124	41.47	212	36.30	758	49.35
Unemployed	161	24.66	108	36.12	227	38.87	496	32.29
Not in the Labour Force	70	10.72	67	22.41	145	24.83	282	18.36
Total	653	100.0	299	100.0	584	100.0	1,536	100.0

Notes:
[a]　Professional and managerial workers.
[b]　Clerical and technical workers.
[c]　Sales, services and skilled production workers.

Source:　Lee and Hsin (2003).

Although one might be excused for thinking that these non-labour force participants were 'discouraged workers' who had enrolled in the training programmes with the aim of returning to work after completion of their retraining, sadly, as we later discovered, many of these trainees were not there for the purpose of learning new skills to facilitate their reemployment at all, but were simply attending because, by doing so, they were entitled to collect training allowances!

As the figures in the right-hand column of Table 10.5 show, most of the workers attending the training programmes (83.2 per cent) had made the decision to attend on their own initiative, and indeed, the largest proportion of those attending the courses on their own initiative were those with the lower skills levels. We find that self-initiated participation was cited by 93.36 per cent of the trainees in the LLM group. Although quite a small proportion of trainees (only 14.53 per cent) had been sent for training by their employers, the majority of those making up this category (25.72 per cent) were in the HLM group. The main reason for this difference is simply that most of the trainees in the LLM group were unemployed at the time of their enrolment in the training programmes.

Table 10.5   Reasons for participating in training programmes, by skills levels

Employment Status	Skills Levels							
	HLM [a]		MLM [b]		LLM [c]		Totals	
	No.	%	No.	%	No.	%	No.	%
Sent by Employer	169	25.72	27	9.06	28	4.77	224	14.53
Self-initiated	470	71.54	265	88.93	548	93.36	1,283	83.20
Sent by Govt Agency	17	2.59	2	0.67	7	1.19	26	1.69
Others	1	0.15	4	1.34	4	0.68	9	0.58
Total	657	100.0	298	100.0	587	100.0	1,542	100.0

Notes:
[a]   Professional and managerial workers.
[b]   Clerical and technical workers.
[c]   Sales, services and skilled production workers.

Source: Lee and Hsin (2003).

Responsibility for training costs

A considerable proportion of the participants in the HLM group (29.95 per cent) had all of their training costs covered by their employers, whereas only 10.7 per cent of participants in the MLM group, and 5.1 per cent of those in the LLM group, were receiving the financial support of their employers. We also find that, irrespective of their skills levels, approximately one-third of all training programme participants were sharing the costs of their training with their employers. Conversely, a much higher proportion of those in the LLM group had their full training costs covered by the government, which is quite understandable since a much larger proportion of these trainees were either unemployed or not in the labour force at the time of their attendance. As such, they had no employer on whom they could rely to cover their training costs, and it would of course be highly unlikely that they could afford to cover the costs of their training themselves (Table 10.6).

In an effort to determine whether participants in employee training programmes were having more success than non-participants, particularly in terms of securing higher wages, those who were in employment both prior to and after the successful completion of their training were selected for further analysis; as Table 10.7 shows, there were a total of 535 such trainees in this category. To facilitate the effective assessment of the wage rate for all training programme participants, a reference group was selected from the 1998-2000 Manpower Utilization Survey files, comprising of employed workers who had not participated in any training over the study period.

Table 10.6   Disbursement of training costs, by skills levels

Bearer of Training Costs	Skills Levels							
	HLM [a]		MLM [b]		LLM [c]		Totals	
	No.	%	No.	%	No.	%	No.	%
Trainees	98	15.05	41	13.71	60	10.33	198	13.00
Trainees and Employers/Govt	207	31.80	107	35.79	228	39.24	542	35.40
Employers	195	29.95	32	10.70	30	5.16	257	16.79
Government	151	23.20	119	39.80	263	45.27	533	34.81
Total	651	100.0	299	100.0	581	100.0	1,531	100.0

Notes:
[a]   Professional and managerial workers.
[b]   Clerical and technical workers.
[c]   Sales, services and skilled production workers.

Source: Lee and Hsin (2003).

Table 10.7   Characteristics of the trainees and the reference group

Characteristics	Trainees	Reference Group
Sex		
Male (%)	60.19	57.87
Female (%)	39.81	42.13
Educational Attainment (Years)	14.32	11.45
Working Experience (Average Years Seniority)	6.79	6.36
Industrial Distribution		
Manufacturing Industries (%)	40.93	38.74
Non-manufacturing Industries (%)	4.67	10.78
Service Industries (%)	54.39	50.48
Occupation		
Management and Professional (%)	54.02	10.66
Admin, Clerical and Sales (%)	12.90	34.65
Others (%)	33.08	54.69
Average Increase in Hourly Wage (NT$)	2.75	5.43
Total Number of Cases	535	12,698

Source: Data on programme participants is taken from the survey undertaken for this study; data on the reference group is taken from DGBAS (1998, 1999, 2000).

As the figures in Table 10.7 reveal, there were a total of 12,698 workers in this category with very similar demographic characteristics to those in the trainee sample, particularly in terms of gender distribution and average years of working experience; however, the average educational attainment was higher amongst the trainees than the reference group, and a much higher proportion of the trainee sample were managers and professional workers.

Wage increases were found to be higher for the reference group (5.4 per cent) as compared to those workers in the trainee sample (2.7 per cent), a finding which is at odds with human capital theory and which therefore implies that we need to control for a number of other factors if we are to effectively isolate the influence of training. In order to do this, the files on these two groups of workers were merged; thereafter an OLS regression analysis was carried out, as follows:

$$
\begin{aligned}
\text{D\_Wage} = \quad & 1.65 + 1.35 \text{ Sex} + 0.25 \text{ Ed} - 0.05 \text{ Ten} \\
& (1.78)^* \quad (3.27)^{**} \quad (3.10)^{**} \quad (1.56) \\[6pt]
& + 2.41 \text{ HLM} + 2.12 \text{ MLM} - 0.96 \text{ Ind1} - 1.33 \text{ Ind2} - 4.01 \text{ Train} \\
& (3.16)^{**} \quad (4.12)^{**} \quad (-2.23)^{**} \quad (-1.91)^{**} \quad (-3.81)^{**}
\end{aligned}
\tag{1}
$$

where D_Wage is the change in wages; Sex takes a value of 1 for male workers, otherwise 0; Ed is educational attainment measured in years of formal education; Ten is the labour market experience of workers measured in years; LM is the manpower quality level, where HLM is the 'high-level manpower' group (comprising of managerial and professional workers), MLM is the 'middle-level manpower' group (comprising of clerical and technical workers) and LLM is the 'low-level manpower' group (comprising of sales and skilled production workers); the LLM group is included in the control group; Ind is industry attachment, where Ind1 refers to manufacturing industry workers, and Ind2 are workers in other industries (workers in finances and service are included in the control group); Train represents the training status of workers, with training participants taking the value of 1, and non-participants taking the value of 0. The data in Equation 1 reveals that those workers with higher educational attainment levels, those from the financial service industries and those in professional, managerial, clerical and technical occupations, all enjoyed higher wage rate increases; conversely, the wage rate increases for females and poorly educated workers, and those in sales, production and service occupations, were all lower.

After controlling for individual characteristics, the coefficient of the Train variable in Equation 1 was found to be negative, which means that wage increases for those participating in training were lower than those for workers who had never participated in any form of employee training programme. Such a finding again stands in direct contradiction to human capital theory; however, our finding is not unique, since several European studies have reported similar outcomes.[1]

There are two possible explanations for this negative effect of employee training programmes on participants' wage increases, the first of which is that some of the participants in these training programmes may well have been preparing themselves for transfer to other industries or occupations. This would be motivated by a desire, upon completion of their training, to move away from declining occupations, or industries, towards those gearing up for expansion. During this process, these workers would of course lose some of their earlier accumulated human capital, and would therefore end up with lower wage increases than workers who had not participated in training programmes but who had nevertheless remained within the same job. Indeed, a recent study found that those participants in employee training programmes who did tend to change their jobs upon completion of their training, usually ended up with a net reduction in human capital over a short period, particularly where the change had been into a completely different field; however, in the long run, the training programme participants were still better off than those who did not participate in any form of employee training (Ok and Tergeist, 2003).

This may not, however, be the main reason for the lower wage increases for trainees in Taiwan because, according to a report by the Bureau of Vocational Training (BVT) on all of the training programmes conducted by the BVT on behalf of private employers, those changing their jobs on completion of their training courses, involving a move between different industries, accounted for a mere 10 per cent of all trainees (BVT, 2004). Therefore, the negative sign of the Train variable may also be explained by current practices in industrial relations and human resource management in Taiwan.

The 'seniority wage' system continues to represent a predominant form of remuneration in Taiwan, with performance-based wage systems being practised by only a few employers, and usually in either high-tech or foreign-owned firms; clearly, therefore, a very weak relationship exists between job performance and wage levels in Taiwan. This does not, however, mean that employers do not benefit from their attendance on the various training programmes. When asked whether these training programmes would have any bearing on wage increases, the majority response from employers was generally negative; however, when asked whether these training programmes were helpful in improving the job performance of trainees, 20 per cent said they were 'very helpful', 70 per cent said they were 'helpful' and 8 per cent said they were 'somewhat helpful'; there were no 'not helpful' responses whatsoever.

The Effects of Training on Reemployment

One of the main objectives of all employee training programmes undertaken in Taiwan is to help unemployed workers to find jobs as quickly as possible; that is, to attempt to reduce the overall duration of the period of unemployment. In order to determine whether the programmes have this effect, we compare the reemployment rates of the unemployed workers in the trainee sample with those of the unemployed workers in the Manpower Utilization Survey who had not participated in any form of employee training programmes.

So as to ensure that the comparison was undertaken between two groups of workers with similar backgrounds, that is, comparing like for like with the only difference being their participation or non-participation in employee training programmes, the criteria selected for this comparison were characteristics of age, educational attainment and average work experience prior to their period of unemployment (Table 10.8).

Table 10.8   Characteristics of unemployed training programme participants and unemployed non-participants

Characteristics of Unemployed Workers	Participants in Training Programmes	Non-participants in Training Programmes
Average Age (Years)	35.69	34.51
Average Educational Attainment (Years)	13.41	12.25
Average Work Experience Prior to Unemployment (Years)	2.99	3.95
Sex		
Male (%)	42.49	63.76
Female (%)	57.51	36.24
Work experience		
Yes (%)	73.14	94.08
No (%)	26.86	5.92
Unemployment Caused by Company Closure or Workforce Reduction		
Yes (%)	24.28	33.88
No (%)	75.72	66.12
Total No. of Sample	659	608

Source: Lee and Hsin (2003).

As the figures in Table 10.8 reveal, the demographic characteristics of these two groups of workers are very similar, with the only major difference being that a smaller proportion of workers had become involuntarily unemployed in the programme participants sample than in the reference group. Details on the reemployment rates for these two groups of workers are provided in Table 10.9.

Table 10.9   Reemployment rates for unemployed workers, by duration of unemployment [a]

Duration of Unemployment (weeks)	Non-participants in Training Programmes (%)	Training Programme Participants (%) [b]	
		Including Period of Unemployment Prior to Training	Excluding Period of Unemployment Prior to Training
Less than 4	12.66	21.20	28.86
4-8	11.36	11.30	10.54
8-12	10.94	8.24	11.48
12-16	9.60	4.34	3.76
16-20	7.17	4.60	4.74
20-24	5.69	3.65	3.73
24-28	7.20	5.60	2.79
28-32	4.67	4.32	2.61
32-36	3.85	5.14	1.81
36-40	4.82	2.15	2.52
40-44	4.70	1.72	0.40
44-48	4.96	2.71	3.87
48-52	8.59	2.78	3.08
52-56	4.50	3.33	0.00
56-60	5.15	3.23	1.75
60 and over	30.12	16.54	5.00
Average Monthly Wage Following Reemployment	NT$ 24,352.43 (8,979.334) [c]	NT$ 23,912.85 (9,531.141) [c]	

Notes:

[a]   Reemployment rates for the different periods are determined by the number of workers gaining employment, divided by the total number of unemployed workers; the number of unemployed workers in the different periods is determined by the total number of unemployed workers, less the total number of unemployed workers for the previous period, less 'censored workers' (workers who remain unemployed having dropped out of the available labour force).

[b]   Includes only unemployed workers who participated in training programmes and employed workers who left their employment to participate in training programmes.

[c]   Figures in parentheses are standard errors.

As the figures in Table 10.9 reveal, more than twice as many of those who were unemployed, but who had participated in the various training programmes, were able to find employment much quicker than those who had not participated in training; 28.8 per cent of training participants found jobs within a four-week period, as compared to 12.6 per cent of non-participants. Nevertheless, the benefits of participating in training programmes seemed to end here, since beyond this point, training programme participants did not appear to have any higher rate of reemployment than non-participants.

Surprisingly, it was in fact the case that non-participants appeared to have a better chance of gaining reemployment than those who had participated in training once the unemployment period went beyond 12 weeks. This is another finding which requires further explanation; we therefore run a further regression analysis of these two groups of workers, controlling for certain demographic characteristics, such as sex, age and educational attainment, as well as reasons for unemployment, training status and work experience. The results are presented in Table 10.10.

Table 10.10   Determinants of duration of unemployment prior to reemployment

Determinants	Including Period of Unemployment Prior to Training		Excluding Period of Unemployment Prior to Training	
	Coeff.	S.E.	Coeff.	S.E.
Constant	3.621 **	0.38	3.663 **	0.41
Sex (Male = 1)	−0.168 *	0.01	−0.207 **	0.10
Age (Years)	0.049 **	0.01	0.051 **	0.01
Educational Attainment (Years)	−0.113 **	0.02	−0.120 **	0.02
Prior Work Experience (Years)	0.001	0.001	0.002	0.001
Reason for Unemployment (Redundancy = 1, Voluntary = 0)	0.060	0.11	0.031	0.12
Labour Market Status (New Labour Market Entrant = 1)	0.243 *	0.14	0.366 **	0.15
Training Status (Participated in Training = 1)	0.411 **	0.10	0.102	0.11
Log Likelihood	−1539.90		−1706.14	

Note: ** indicates statistically significant at the 5 per cent level; and * indicates statistically significant at the 10 per cent level.

Source: Lee and Hsin (2003).

As the figures in Table 10.10 reveal, amongst all unemployed workers, the better-educated, younger, experienced and male workers needed less time to secure reemployment than older workers, female workers, new labour market entrants and workers with lower levels of education. Nevertheless, after controlling for all of these demographic factors, the figures in Tables 10.10 and 10.11 continue to demonstrate that the overall job search period is invariably longer for those participating in training programme than for non-participants.

Table 10.11   Determinants of duration of unemployment by type of training institution and skills level of participants

Determinants	Including Period of Unemployment Prior to Training		Excluding Period of Unemployment Prior to Training	
	Coeff.	S.E.	Coeff.	S.E.
Constant	2.41**	0.70	2.55**	0.82
Sex (Male = 1)	−0.20	0.15	−0.31*	0.17
Age (Years)	0.05**	0.01	0.05**	0.01
Educational Attainment (Years)	−0.05	0.04	−0.06	0.04
Prior Work Experience (Years)	0.01	0.02	−0.00	0.03
Laid-off Through Establishment Closure or Business Shrinkage	−0.12	0.18	−0.18	0.21
No Prior Work Experience	0.16	0.18	0.14	0.21
Unemployed	0.12	0.15	−0.47**	0.18
MLM	0.53**	0.18	0.64**	0.21
LLM	0.82**	0.18	0.97**	0.21
Public and Privately Operated Training Programmes	−0.29	0.23	−0.28	0.28
Non-government and Publicly Operated Training Programmes	0.46**	0.17	0.57**	0.20
Log likelihood	−802.34		−814.63	

Note: ** indicates statistically significant at the 5 per cent level; and * indicates statistically significant at the 10 per cent level.

Source: Lee and Hsin (2003).

One possible reason for training programme participants needing more time to get back into employment is that the figures in column 1 of Table

10.10 refer to the entire period of unemployment; clearly, however, some participants may have been unemployed for a considerable period of time prior to their attendance on the training programme. In order to correct this, we excluded any period of unemployment prior to enrolment into the training programme, and counted only the period required to find a new job on completion of the training. However, as the figures in the right-hand column of Table 10.11 show, following this adjustment, although no longer statistically significant, even at the 10 per cent level, the sign of the training variable remains positive. An alternative explanation is therefore required as to why trainees need a longer period than non-trainees to secure reemployment.

A similar finding of lower reemployment rates for training programme participants was found in a study of unemployed workers in Demark with this phenomenon being explained in terms of both 'lock-in' and 'post-programme' effects (Rosholm 2003). The 'lock-in' effect referred to the inability of trainees to engage in job search activities during the training period as extensively as their non-trainee counterparts, resulting in lower rates of reemployment amongst trainees.

The 'post-programme' effect referred to the tendency for those attending the various training programmes to adopt a belief that they had acquired certain new and specific skills which should be targeted at specific jobs. This perspective subsequently resulted in them narrowing the scope of their job search to specific areas and ignoring other reemployment opportunities, despite the fact that they may also have been able to utilize such skills and knowledge in these alternative positions. A person who had just completed a course in bus driving, for example, may look for jobs only as a bus driver, ignoring other jobs which, although not using all of his bus-driving skills, may, nonetheless require other skills gained from his training. He may not, therefore, even consider a job as a truck driver, heavy equipment mover or chauffeur, and will clearly reduce the possibility of success in his ongoing job search.

In the case of Taiwan, the 'lock-in' effect does not appear to be of such significance, because higher reemployment rates were achieved by all of those participating in training immediately on completion of their training. However, the 'post-programme' effect also demonstrates that training participants may tend to set up unrealistic reserve wage rates, since they believe that by participating in training they have successfully raised their human capital and therefore deserve higher wage rates. This effect, along with the effect of narrowing the focus of job search activities, as described above, indicate that the 'post-programme' effect does appear to be a more important contributor to the lower reemployment rates amongst training participants in Taiwan.

THE EFFECTIVENESS OF THE EEP AND THE DISTRIBUTION OF THE EEP BUDGET

We can apply the earlier findings on the effectiveness of existing training programmes to the assessment of the effectiveness of the EEP in general, and thereby provide guidance on the most appropriate allocation of the EEP budget. In order to do this, we must begin by determining exactly what the purposes of the EEP are, that is: (i) the upgrading of skills amongst workers currently in employment; (ii) the retraining of unemployed workers as a means of providing them with new skills and thereby equipping them for reemployment; and (iii) the retraining of those who, although not currently in the labour force, would like to return to the labour market once they are equipped with up-to-date skills. The costs per trainee for these three groups of workers, within each of the three skills levels, are presented in Table 10.12.

Table 10.12   EEP training budget, by different skills level and employment status, 2002-2004

Training Provided	Skills Levels		
(by Employment Status)	HLM	MLM	LLM
Employed			
Total No. of Trainees	214,159	121,311	853,620
Total Training Costs (NT$,000)	2,630,240	2,207,026	1,861,027
Costs per Trainee (NT$,000)	12.28	18.19	2.18
Unemployed			
Total No. of Trainees	27,760	20,940	144,022
Total Training Costs (NT$,000)	1,372,802	563,457	2,689,320
Costs per Trainee (NT$,000)	49.45	28.91	18.67
Not in the Labour Force			
Total No. of Trainees	990	2,880	10,350
Total Training Costs (NT$,000)	404,139	83,510	61,800
Costs per Trainee (NT$,000)	408.21	29.00	5.97

Source: Lee and Hsin (2003).

As the figures in Table 10.12 indicate, the costs of providing such upgrading training are highest for the MLM group (NT$18,190), followed by the HLM group (NT$12,280), and the LLM group (NT$2,180). As regards training costs for unemployed workers, the highest costs are found in the HLM group (NT$49,450), followed by the MLM group (NT$28,910), and finally, the LLM group (NT$18,670).

The figures previously presented in Table 10.11 demonstrated that the coefficients of the MLM and LLM groups were both positive, although larger for the LLM group than the MLM group. This indicates that the retraining programmes can help those in the HLM group to secure reemployment much more rapidly than those in the MLM group, whilst also helping those in the MLM group to secure reemployment more rapidly than those in the LLM group.

As has already been shown in the previous sections, there are no significant differences in wage increases between training participants at different levels of skills, and between trainees and non-trainees; therefore, if we use wage increases as an efficiency indicator for such upgrading training programmes, it is apparent that the government should be targeting upgrading training for the LLM group as the first priority, followed by the HLM group, and finally, the MLM group.

The remaining issue yet to be tackled, therefore, is the policy decision on which groups are targeted as the highest and lowest priorities for training. Unfortunately, this has to remain an unresolved issue for the time being, because additional data will be required if we are to effectively deal with the issue. The main reason for this is that no detailed information is currently available to show exactly how much quicker, on completion of their employee training programmes, the HLM group can secure reemployment as compared to the MLM group, and likewise, how much quicker the MLM group can secure reemployment as compared to the LLM group. Clearly, without such information we are unable to complete an effective cost-benefit analysis.

However, the one thing that is very clear is that unemployed workers participating in employee training programmes did not secure reemployment as quickly as those who had not participated in the training programmes, largely due to the 'post-programme' effects; thus, in addition to providing instructions on skills and work-related knowledge, any organization tasked with the responsibility for administrating training programmes should also attempt to provide accurate and up-to-date labour market information as part of the training course. Through such provision, trainees may be able to gain a better understanding of how to avoid the negative 'post-programme' effects, through the adoption of a more realistic job search plan, on a wider scale, and through setting more realistic reserve wage rates.

In summary, the coefficient of the variable 'unemployment' in Table 10.11, at −0.47, indicates that unemployed workers need less time to secure reemployment than those outside the labour force. Furthermore, the figures in Table 10.12 also indicate that the government should afford higher priority to the provision of retraining for the unemployed over those not currently in the labour force. Of these two groups, within each of the three skills levels, the costs of retraining are lower for the unemployed.

CONCLUSIONS

It is clear that as Taiwan's economy has become more globalized, and as the pace of change, with regard to the structure of the Taiwanese economy, has accelerated, increasing numbers of employees are in danger of falling into the category of 'structurally unemployed' workers unless the government, and employers, can provide wide-ranging training programmes, so as to provide continuous upgrading of the skills and working knowledge of these employees. The recent decision by the government to increase the number of employee training programmes supported by government funding, the implementation of the EEP, along with the expansion of the scope of this programme, all represent movements in the right direction.

However, from the results of the study upon which this chapter is based, we can see that the highest priority for this training effort must be given to upgrading training for those in employment, with training for the unemployed being afforded the second highest priority and training for those outside the labour force being given the lowest priority. The reason for the lower prioritization of the last of these groups is partly because of the higher training costs involved for those not currently in the labour force, and partly because, as we have regrettably found in this study, many of those who participate in these programmes attend solely for the purpose of collecting training allowances and not for the purpose of preparing themselves for employment.

Our study reveals several major deficiencies in Taiwan's current employee training system, with government action being necessary if these shortcomings are to be fully addressed. Neither employers nor employees currently have any significant level of interest in employee training programmes, largely because employers cannot find the time for their employees to participate in such training programmes, and also because employers and employees alike consider that these programmes are of no help to them in their current jobs. As our 2005 study has revealed, most of the training courses are designed by programme instructors without any input from employers, and without any survey having been undertaken on the training needs of either employers or employees (Lee and Hsin, 2005). It is therefore suggested that the central government should set up appropriate guidelines and requirements, so that when training institutes apply for government training subsidies they must first of all form a committee comprising of both vocational education experts and local employers. The role of this committee should be to design training course content, to select appropriate teaching materials and methods of instruction, and to ensure the quality of instructors, so that the content and the training methods are brought more into line with the needs of both employers and employees.

Despite having allocated considerable resources in the form of subsidies for employee training programmes, the central government in Taiwan currently has no means of evaluating their effectiveness; as a result, there is very little feedback. The government should, therefore, attempt to set up some form of standardized evaluation mechanism and criteria, so that regular evaluation can be undertaken of all employee training programmes based upon exactly the same criteria. This information can then be used to formulate labour market policies, indicating which type of training programmes should be subsidized and promoted. This information should help employers to decide which programmes their employees should attend, and, based upon the same information, employees can determine which programmes may be most useful to them, thereby altering the current perception that training programmes are irrelevant to the needs of both employers and employees.

Strong incentives should be provided by the government to encourage employers to set up appropriate employee training programmes, and to encourage employees to participate in these programmes. There are several ways in which the central government may provide such incentives so as to ensure that employee training programmes become more widespread and more popular. This chapter concludes with a few such examples.

1. Amend the current Fair Labour Standards Act to make working hours more flexible and enable employees to take time off for training without being penalized, financially or otherwise;

2. Disseminate information to employees on financial rewards for training;

3. Encourage enterprises to set up human capital accounts, through taxation and other fiscal policies, listing employee training programmes in their financial returns. This should lead to a move away from the tendency to regard employee training as a cost, or an element of employee welfare, towards the evaluation of these training programmes as investment items;

4. Establish a learning passport system so that the type, level and hours of employees training can be accurately recorded. Employers can use these passports to more accurately assess the competence of both current and prospective employees; and

5. Establish a national occupational standards system, so that employees will know what types of competences are required for certain jobs and what training is required to acquire the necessary skills and knowledge. Australia, New Zealand and several European countries currently have such systems, which have proven helpful in ensuring both the relevance and the effectiveness of training programmes, to employers and employees alike.

The government in Taiwan is currently taking some action, such as the establishment of a national employee training evaluation system, a national occupational standards system and a learning passport system (currently quite limited in scope). It is to be hoped that once these systems are firmly established, employers will feel more inclined to set up employee training programmes for their employees, and employees will be more willing to participate in such training programmes. This would ultimately lead to a more balanced demand and supply of labour in Taiwan.

NOTE

[1]   For example, using socio-economic panel data on Germany covering the period from 1990 to 1996, Lechner (1999) found that upgrading training had no positive effects on workers in East Germany. Similar results were also reported by Cockx (2003) on upgrading training programmes amongst Belgian workers.

REFERENCES

Arulampalam, W., A.L. Booth and M.L. Bryan (2003), *Training in Europe*, Geneva: IZA Discussion Paper, No.933.

Becker, G., (1964), *Human Capital*, Columbia: University of Columbia Press.

Barrett, A. and P.J. O'Connell (2001), 'Does Training Generally Work? – The Returns to In-company Training', *Industrial and Labour Relations Review*, **54**(3): 647-62

Barron, J., D.A. Black and M.A. Loewenstein (1989), 'Job Matching and On-the-job Training', *Journal of Labour Economics* (January): 1-19

Beneito, P., J. Ferri, M.L. Molto and E. Uriel (2000), 'Over/Under-education and Specific Training in Spain', in H. Heijke and J. Muysken (eds.), *Education and Training in a Knowledge-based Economy*, New York: St. Martin's Press, pp.191-214.

Bishop, J.H. (1991), 'On-the-job Training of New Hires', in D. Stem and J. Ritzen (eds.), *Market Failure in Training*, New York: Springer Verlag, pp.61-96

Bishop, J.H. (1996), 'What We Know About Employer-provided Training: A Review of the Literature', *Cornell University Working Paper, No.96-09.*

Booth, A.L. (1991), 'Job-related Formal Training: Who Receives it and What is it Worth?', *Oxford Bulletin of Economic Journal*, **112**(June): F.181-8.

Bowers, N. and P. Swaim (1992), *Probing (some of) the Issues of Employment-related Training: Evidence from the CPS*, Washington, DC: US Department of Agriculture, Economic Research Service.

Brown, J.N. (1989) 'Why do Wages Increase with Tenure: On-the-job Training and Life-cycle Wage Growth Observed within Firms', *American Economic Review*, **79**(5): 971-91.

BVT (2004), *Vocational Training Needs Survey Report in the Taiwan Area, ROC*, Taipei: Bureau of Vocational Training.

CLA (2002), *Report on Employee Vocational Training*, Taipei: Council of Labour Affairs.

Cockx, B. (2003), 'Vocational Training of Unemployed Workers in Belgium', *IZA Discussion Paper, No.682.*

DGBAS (1998-2000), *Manpower Utilization Survey, 1998, 1999, 2000*, Taipei: Executive Yuan, Directorate-General of Budget, Accounting and Statistics.

Eijs, P.V. and H. Heijke (2000), 'The Mismatch between Occupation, Education and the Costs and Benefits of Job-related Training', in H. Heijke and J. Muysken (eds.), *Education and Training in a Knowledge-based Economy*, New York: St. Martin's Press, pp.159-90.

Grubb, N.W. and P. Ryan (2004), *The Role of Evaluation in Vocational Education and Training*, Geneva: International Institute for Labour Studies.

Heckman, J., R.J. Lalonde and J.A. Smith (1999), 'The Economics and Econometrics of Active Labour Market Programmes', in O. Ashenfelter and D. Card (eds.), *Handbook of Labour Economics*, Vol.3, pp.1865-2097.

Hollenbeck, K. and R. Wilkie (1985), 'The Nature and Impact of Training: Evidence from the Current Population Survey', in J. Bishop (ed.), *Training and Human Capital Formation*, Ohio: Ohio State University, National Centre for Research in Vocational Education.

Kraus, F., P. Puhani and V. Steiner (1997), 'Employment Effects of Publicly-financed Training Programs – The East German Experience', *ZEW Discussion Paper, No.97-33.*

Langager, K. (1996), 'The Unemployed in Classroom Training', *Socialforsknings Instituttet, No.96.*

Lechner, M. (1999), *An Evaluation of Public Sector Sponsored Continuous Vocational Training Programs in East Germany*, Geneva: IZA Discussion Paper, No.93.

Lee, J.S. and T.J. Hwang (1998), *Sources of Skill for Employees in High-tech Industries*, Taiwan: National Central University, Human Resource Management Institute.

Lee, J.S. (2000), 'The Rise of Involuntary Unemployment and Unemployment Insurance Programmes in Asian Countries: The Case of Taiwan', in J.S. Lee (ed.), *Recent Developments in Involuntary Unemployment in Asian Countries: Causes and Policies*, Taiwan: National Central University, Research Centre for Taiwanese Economic Development, pp.45-70.

Lee, J.S. and P.L. Hsin (2003), *The Role of Human Capital in a Knowledge-based Economy*, Taipei: Council for Economic Planning and Development.

Lee, J.S. and P.L. Hsin (2005), *Strengthening the Vocational Training System in Taiwan*, Taipei: Executive Yuan, Council for Economic Planning and Development.

Leuven, E. and H. Oosterbeek (1999), 'Demand and Supply of Work-related Training: Evidence from Four Countries', *Research in Labour Economics*, **18**: 303-30.

Lillard, L. and H. Tan (1986), *Private-sector Training: Who Gets it and What are its Effects?*, Monograph, Santa Monica, CA: Rand Corporation.

Lynch, L.M. (1992), 'Private-sector Training and its Impact on the Earnings of Young Workers', *American Economic Review*, **82**(1): 299-312.

Lynch, L.M. and S. Black (1998), 'Beyond the Incidence of Employer-provided Training', *Industrial and Labour Relations Review* (October), **52**: 64-81.

Mincer, J. (1989), 'Job Training: Costs, Returns and Wage Profiles', *Working Paper*, Columbia: University of Columbia, Department of Economics.

Ok, W. and P. Tergeist (2003), 'Improving Workers' Skills: Analytical Evidence and the Role of Social Partners', *OECD Social, Employment and Migration Working Papers, No.10*.

OECD (1997), *Literacy Skills for the Knowledge Economy*, Organization for Economic Co-operation and Development, Paris: OECD Publications.

OECD (2004), *OECD Employment Outlook, 2004*, Organization for Economic Co-operation and Development, Paris: OECD Publications.

Richardson, K. and G.J. van den Berg (2002), *The Effects of Vocational Employment Training on the Individual Transition Rate from Unemployment to Work*, IFAU Working Paper Series 2002, No.8.

Rosholm, M. (2003), *Is Labour-market Training a Curse for the Unemployed?: Evidence from a Social Experiment*, IZA Discussion Paper, No.716.

11 Employment Insurance and Unemployment in Taiwan

Yang Shih

INTRODUCTION

The implementation of effective measures aimed at keeping unemployment down to an absolute minimum has become an important and ongoing policy goal for all governments around the world, in both developed and developing economies alike; however, it is quite clear that no government has ever totally succeeded in eradicating unemployment. It is, therefore, highly unlikely that the 'holy grail' of full employment, as was often promised in the past by various administrations, will ever be achieved; indeed, as demonstrated by the figures for selected countries since the late 1970s, unemployment is part of everyday life for some proportion of the population in every country (Table 11.1).

Thus, many governments have come to recognize that dealing with unemployment is an integral part of their administrative functions, and in their efforts to maintain unemployment at manageable levels they have gone on to formulate a variety of wide-ranging measures aimed at ensuring that whilst unemployed workers are appropriately cared for, they are also provided with the assistance they require in order to secure gainful employment. Of the various measures adopted, a system which incorporates unemployment insurance has the advantage of protecting the economic welfare of the unemployed whilst simultaneously encouraging them to seek work.

From a perspective of employment security, an employment insurance system can be combined with vocational training and employment services to create a comprehensive set of labour policies, whilst from an alternative perspective of social security, it is also quite feasible for employment insurance to be combined with retirement insurance, health insurance, occupational accident and injury insurance and long-term care insurance, to create a comprehensive social safety net. What is clear, however, is that most governments now regard the establishment of an effective employment insurance system as a key policy goal.

267

Table 11.1 Unemployment rates, by selected countries, 1978-2004

Unit: %

Year	Taiwan	Hong Kong	Japan	South Korea	Singapore	US	Canada	Germany	UK	France
1978	1.67	2.80	2.20	3.20	3.60	6.00	8.40	4.30	5.70	5.20
1979	1.28	2.90	2.10	3.80	3.40	5.80	7.50	3.80	5.30	5.90
1980	1.23	3.80	2.00	5.20	3.00	7.00	7.50	3.80	6.80	6.40
1981	1.36	3.60	2.20	4.50	2.90	7.50	7.60	5.50	10.40	7.40
1982	2.14	3.60	2.40	4.40	2.60	9.50	11.00	7.50	10.90	8.10
1983	2.71	4.50	2.60	4.10	3.20	9.60	11.90	9.10	11.70	8.40
1984	2.44	3.90	2.70	3.80	2.70	7.50	11.30	9.10	11.60	9.80
1985	2.91	3.20	2.60	4.00	4.10	7.20	10.50	9.30	11.80	10.20
1986	2.66	2.80	2.80	3.80	6.50	7.00	9.60	9.00	11.80	10.40
1987	1.97	1.70	2.80	3.10	4.70	6.20	8.90	8.90	10.60	10.50
1988	1.69	1.40	2.50	2.50	2.60	5.50	7.80	8.70	8.40	10.00
1989	1.57	1.10	2.30	2.60	1.80	5.30	7.50	7.90	6.30	9.40
1990	1.67	1.30	2.10	2.40	1.80	5.60	8.10	7.20	5.90	8.90
1991	1.51	1.80	2.10	2.30	1.80	6.80	10.40	7.20	8.10	9.30

Table 11.1 *(Contd.)*

Unit: %

Year	Taiwan	Hong Kong	Japan	South Korea	Singapore	US	Canada	Germany	UK	France
1992	1.51	2.00	2.20	2.40	2.00	7.50	11.30	8.20	9.90	10.20
1993	1.45	2.00	2.50	2.80	1.90	6.90	11.20	9.90	10.40	11.50
1994	1.56	1.90	2.90	2.40	2.00	6.10	10.40	10.00	9.40	12.10
1995	1.79	3.20	3.20	2.00	2.00	5.60	9.50	10.20	8.30	11.40
1996	2.60	2.80	3.40	2.00	2.00	5.40	9.70	11.20	7.60	12.00
1997	2.72	2.20	3.40	2.60	1.80	4.90	9.20	12.50	5.70	12.10
1998	2.69	4.70	4.10	6.80	3.20	4.50	8.30	11.40	4.70	11.50
1999	2.92	6.20	4.70	6.30	3.50	4.20	7.60	11.20	4.30	10.80
2000	2.99	4.90	4.70	4.20	3.10	4.00	6.80	10.00	3.80	9.50
2001	4.57	5.10	5.00	3.80	3.30	4.80	7.20	10.00	3.20	8.70
2002	5.17	7.30	5.40	3.10	4.40	5.80	7.70	10.90	3.10	9.00
2003	4.99	7.90	5.30	3.40	4.70	6.00	7.60	10.50	3.00	9.70
2004	4.44	6.80	4.70	3.50	4.00	5.50	7.20	–	2.80	–

Source: DGBAS (2006).

269

As a result of the steadily worsening unemployment rate in Taiwan since 1996, on 1 January 1999, the government eventually decided to add unemployment benefits to the island's labour insurance system; in reality, however, provisions for unemployment benefits had been made as far back as 1968 in the first revision of Article 74 of the Labour Insurance Act, which stated that the Executive Yuan would set the premiums for unemployment insurance, the regions it which the programme would be implemented and the date and method of such implementation; however, for a variety of reasons, no less than three decades had elapsed before unemployment insurance was eventually implemented in Taiwan, with the new Employment Insurance Law finally coming into force on 1 January 2003.

Under the original Labour Insurance Law, unemployment benefits were a subsidiary element of the labour insurance system; thus, they did not constitute an independent social security system. By contrast, under the new Employment Insurance Law, the system of unemployment insurance operates independently, with its own premium rates and fund-management provisions. The enactment of the new Employment Insurance Law thus represents an important milestone in the development of the employment insurance system in Taiwan.

The government subsequently embarked on the creation of a system of social insurance, using both the old and new unemployment insurance systems, in order to provide for the economic well-being of all unemployed workers, whilst simultaneously seeking to prevent other workers from joining the ranks of the unemployed, reducing the amount of time that any workers losing their jobs remained unemployed, and encouraging such unemployed workers to find alternative work. As a result, significant changes were made to government policy in this particular area between 1999 and 2003. The aim of this chapter is therefore to explore the main objectives behind the implementation of the new employment insurance policy in Taiwan over recent years, and to examine the results achieved by such implementation.

The Importance of Employment Insurance

The term 'unemployment insurance' is normally used to refer to a system of compulsory social insurance, the aim of which is to guarantee a minimum standard of living for all unemployed workers during their period of joblessness. In other words, it is a system which uses compulsory insurance to provide a guaranteed minimum income, for a set period of time, to workers who have suffered involuntary unemployment, resulting in some loss or absolute termination of their income. Such a system aims to protect workers whilst also protecting the country's labour force as a whole (Rejda,

1999). As a general rule, all persons applying for unemployment benefits must meet three major qualifications; that is, they must be: (i) involuntarily unemployed; (ii) willing to work; and (iii) actively looking for work. Furthermore, unemployment insurance is intended to guarantee only a very basic standard of living during the period of a worker's unemployment (Butler, 1999); thus, unemployment insurance provides temporary assistance for workers, each of whom are expected to make every effort to find alternative work as quickly as possible.

Unemployment and employment insurance systems are very similar to each other in terms of the way the systems operate, although employment insurance does place greater emphasis on providing practical help to the unemployed. Taking as an example the Canadian 'Employment Insurance Act' (an Act which came into effect in 1996, replacing the existing Unemployment Insurance Act and National Training Act); this Act was intended to strengthen the incentives for the unemployed to find a new job and to enable them to make the necessary adjustments in response to the changing economic environment. In essence, it was hoped that the new system would do more to help the unemployed to rejoin the workforce. The types of unemployment benefits that became available in Canada as a result of the Act included temporary income support, active reemployment benefits and a family income supplement.

If the employment insurance policy adopted by the government of any country is to be implemented with maximum effectiveness, it is vital that it should be properly coordinated with the country's vocational training and employment service systems.[1] These systems should be used to help those who become involuntarily unemployed to find alternative jobs, whilst also providing them with important vocational training; if the government is unsuccessful in its efforts either to help unemployed workers to find jobs or to retrain them, then it should provide unemployment benefits to help such workers to meet their most basic economic needs. Whilst workers are in receipt of unemployment benefits, the government should continue to provide them with the means of participating in vocational training and with the assistance necessary to find gainful employment; clearly, the ultimate objective is to get unemployed workers back into work as quickly as possible.

There is still some considerable debate as to just how beneficial unemployment insurance is to those who become unemployed. Viewed in terms of social function theory, the mere fact that a social system exists shows that there is a need for such a system and that it contributes to the normal functioning of society; however, there is the question of welfare dependency, since excessive provision of welfare benefits may lead to a weakening of the ability of people to solve their own problems, and may, in some cases, even reduce their willingness to lead a normal life. The basic concept of unemployment insurance was to enable unemployed workers to concentrate their efforts on either participating in vocational training or actively looking for work without having to worry about where their next meal was coming from.

The provision of unemployment benefits can also, on the one hand, boost the purchasing power of unemployed people, thereby helping to stimulate economic growth; on the other hand, however, studies have shown that in some regions, the introduction of unemployment insurance can actually lead to an increase in unemployment. Indeed, there is some concern that the unemployed can become dependent on unemployment benefits, leading to an increase in the average length of time that unemployed workers remain within the benefits system; many scholars are therefore cautious about the economic benefits of unemployment insurance (Atkinson and Micklewight, 1984; Burtless and Munnel, 1990). In order to get around this problem, work requirements are incorporated into the unemployment insurance systems of many countries; in the UK, for example, alongside conventional unemployment benefits, the government also provides a 'workfare' system, where those in receipt of unemployment benefits may be required to perform work assigned to them by the government; the main purpose behind this particular scheme is to prevent unemployed workers from becoming 'welfare dependent'.[2]

A number of empirical studies have found that when workers are unemployed for periods in excess of 15 weeks, their main source of support and assistance comes from family and friends, rather than the government or private charities (Williams, 1979). Such studies have also found that the longer a person remains unemployed, the more difficult it becomes for that person to rejoin the workforce (Addison and Blackburn, 1997). Any workers spending lengthy periods of time unemployed will gradually become accustomed to their existence and will often become unwilling to make the major changes to their life that going back to work will require. Under such circumstances, the provision of vocational training by the government and appropriate assistance in job-seeking can be even more helpful in getting such workers back into the workforce.

Over recent years, a much greater share of total unemployment has become attributable to involuntary unemployment; as such, in the design of their unemployment insurance systems, the governments of many countries are now increasingly using measures aimed at discouraging employers' casual termination of workers. In the US, for example, the unemployment insurance system uses an 'experience rating', whereby the unemployment insurance premiums which employers are required to pay vary according to their company's layoff rates (Anderson and Meyer, 2000); the aim of this system is clearly to enhance employment stability and reduce the number of people becoming unemployed in the first place.

Unemployment benefits are normally paid only to those workers who were previously in regular employment and who became unemployed involuntarily; thus, those workers with no regular employer are ineligible for unemployment benefit, essentially because of the difficulties involved in determining whether such workers are in fact unemployed and whether their unemployment was involuntary or otherwise. Other groups normally ineligible for unemployment benefits include school leavers looking for their first job, agricultural (and seasonal) labourers, and government employees;[3] some countries do, however, make special provisions for school leavers. If any employment insurance system is to achieve its aim, in terms of providing assistance for the unemployed as well as ensuring that the benefit payment structure is properly designed, a further key issue involved is the thorough integration with vocational training services and employment services; only then will the employment insurance system be able to function as an effective economic stabilizer.

Employment services play a vital role in helping unemployed workers to rejoin the labour force; therefore, the agencies responsible for providing employment services need to have a thorough understanding of the skills of the individuals for whom they are trying to find jobs, and they also need to operate efficiently in terms of collecting information on job vacancies from potential employers. Vocational training plays an important role in the cultivation of human talent; therefore, training plans must be carefully designed to meet the needs of the job market, so that the unemployed can be equipped with the skills they need to find suitable work. Without such ancillary systems, the employment insurance system cannot provide meaningful protection for the unemployed.

DEVELOPMENT OF THE EMPLOYMENT INSURANCE PROGRAMME IN TAIWAN

The new unemployment insurance system was implemented in Taiwan, in accordance with the 'Rules for the Implementation of Unemployment Benefits under the Labour Insurance Act', on 1 January 1999. The premium rates, which were initially set at 1.0 per cent, were extracted from the 6.5 per cent accident insurance premium of the island's labour insurance system; this social insurance system was the first of its kind in Taiwan, having been established in 1950. Initially, the labour insurance system had provided for only five types of payments: childbirth, injury/sickness, disability, old age and death; despite the Labour Insurance Act having made provisions for the establishment of unemployment benefits, these provisions had never been implemented.

Several factors lay behind the implementation of the unemployment insurance system in Taiwan in 1999. There had been a steady rise in the influence of labour organizations since the 1980s, with workers' rights having become a key issue for the Democratic Progressive Party (DPP), which was then in opposition. The pressure of public opinion therefore forced the ruling Kuomintang (KMT) administration to implement an unemployment insurance system; however, the process of formulating the new system was accompanied by fierce debate. One of the main questions on which this debate focused was whether unemployment insurance should constitute a separate, independent system, or whether it should be a subordinate element of the existing labour insurance system. There was also the question of the categories of worker to which the system should apply, and, in particular, whether the self-employed, as well as those workers with no regular employer, should be eligible to participate in the system. Both of these issues led to extensive debate.

At the end of 1998, the government opted for the more conservative strategy of adding unemployment benefits to the existing labour insurance system and also decided that workers with no regular employer should not be covered by the system. The government further stipulated that any person wishing to apply for payment of unemployment benefits had to meet a number of requirements, which were: (i) their unemployment must be involuntary; (ii) they must be willing and able to work; (iii) they must register with a public employment services agency; and (iv) payment of benefits would commence only if the government failed to arrange employment or vocational training for the individual within 14 days. Furthermore, following the commencement of unemployment benefit payments, if an unemployed person managed to find a part-time job which paid more than the minimum wage (NT$15,840 per month), payment of the benefits would cease.

Benefit payments were initially made every two weeks at a rate equivalent to 50 per cent of the salary level at which the unemployed individual had been registered for labour insurance purposes. In order to continue receiving benefits, recipients were required to present themselves in person to the offices of a public employment services agency to verify that they were still unemployed. The maximum periods for which an unemployed worker could receive unemployment benefits were linked to the number of years that they had made labour insurance contributions. Those workers who had contributed for less than five years could receive unemployment benefits for a total cumulative period of six months, with the maximum period for consecutive benefit payments being set at three months. For those who had contributed to the labour insurance system for five to ten years, the respective periods were 12 months (cumulative payments) and six months (consecutive payments), whilst for those who had contributed for more than ten years, the maximum period of payment was 16 months (cumulative) and eight months (consecutive). The system was designed to make it clear that there were rights and obligations on both sides, and to avoid giving the impression that unemployment benefits constituted a 'free lunch'.[4]

Two major revisions followed the implementation of the unemployment benefits system in January 1999. The first of these was on 30 July 1999, when the level of benefits paid was raised from 50 per cent of the worker's registered monthly salary to 60 per cent; at the same time, the interval between payments was increased from two weeks to one month, and the restriction on the maximum period for which application for benefits could be made was abolished. The second revision came on 13 December 2000, when the waiting period before payment of benefits would commence was reduced from 14 days to seven days, and the maximum consecutive period for which benefits could be paid was fixed at six months.

Although the government had gone to some lengths to allay concerns amongst the general public over unemployment benefits, making it easier to apply for benefits and raising the total amount of benefits paid, labour organizations were still uneasy with the fact that unemployment insurance had been established under the labour insurance system, that it lacked its own independent source of financing and that it had not been integrated with the necessary ancillary measures for helping unemployed workers to secure reemployment. It therefore became clear that the government would need to set up an independent employment insurance scheme; and indeed, the Executive Yuan immediately set to work on drafting the Employment Insurance Law. Having passed its third reading in the Legislative Yuan, the new Act was implemented on 15 May 2002 and came into force on 1 January 2003. The main objective of the new Employment Insurance Law was to reduce unemployment by making it easier for unemployed persons to find work, whilst at the same time guaranteeing a basic standard of living for the unemployed during the period in which they were either seeking work or participating in vocational training.

The most significant feature of the Employment Insurance Law was the expansion of the scope of unemployment insurance to cover all workers of Taiwanese nationality between 15 and 60 years of age (recall that enterprises with less than five employees had been excluded from the scheme under the old labour insurance regulations), whilst increasing the length of time that the unemployed had to wait for their first payment, from seven days to 14 days. The Employment Insurance Law provided for four types of payment: unemployment benefits, early re-employment awards, a vocational training living allowance and subsidies to cover unemployed workers' National Health Insurance (NHI) contributions. These four types of payment are discussed separately below.

Benefits Provided under the Employment Insurance Law

Unemployment benefits

Any worker covered by employment insurance for a period of at least one year during the three-year period prior to becoming unemployed is automatically eligible to receive unemployment benefits provided they are willing and able to work and have been registered as unemployed with a public employment services agency; unless the government has succeeded in helping them to find work or to join a vocational training scheme, payment of unemployment benefits begins 14 days after the worker registers as being unemployed.

Benefits are set at 60 per cent of the worker's average 'registered salary' in the six months prior to the date on which they became unemployed (this is the salary level at which they were registered with the labour insurance scheme, which may well differ from the worker's actual salary in his last job). The receipt of unemployment benefits can continue for a maximum of six months, after which the unemployed person must again accumulate the required period of time in employment in order to be eligible to receive further unemployment benefits.

Early reemployment award

Unemployed workers eligible to receive unemployment benefits can also apply to the Labour Insurance Bureau for payment of an early reemployment award if they secure gainful employment and subsequently accumulate a record of at least three months' employment insurance contributions prior to the expiry of their time limit for receipt of unemployment benefits. The size of the award is set at 50 per cent of the total amount of unemployment benefits that they were otherwise entitled to receive (up to the maximum of six months) but did not receive as a direct result of finding work. The aim of this measure is to encourage the unemployed to find work again as quickly as possible and to keep welfare dependency to an absolute minimum.

Vocational training living allowance

After becoming involuntarily unemployed, unemployed workers covered by the employment insurance system can register with a public employment services agency which can then go on to arrange a full-time vocational training programme for that person. Such persons then become eligible to apply for a vocational training living allowance during their period of vocational training. The allowance is paid at a rate equivalent to 60 per cent of the unemployed worker's average registered salary in the six-month period prior to the date on which they became unemployed. This allowance may be claimed for a maximum period of six months.

NHI contribution subsidies for unemployed workers

A comparison between the old and new employment insurance systems in Taiwan reveals that the new system incorporates a substantial number of additional payment items (also with higher payment levels), whilst the eligibility requirements for applicants are more relaxed. For example, during the period when an unemployed person is in receipt of either unemployment benefits or a vocational training living allowance, the government will subsidize the NHI contributions that the unemployed worker would normally have been required to pay if in gainful employment; however, this subsidy is available only for the unemployed workers themselves, and does not provide cover for the NHI contributions of the unemployed workers' dependants. On the other hand, the period of time for which applicants are required to wait prior to receiving their first payment has been increased from seven to 14 days.[5] Details of the major differences between the old and new employment insurance systems are provided in Table 11.2, whilst Figure 11.1 provides an illustration of the application process under Taiwan's current employment insurance system.

The introduction of employment insurance within any country generally comes in response to pressure from the general public under conditions of high unemployment, and given such circumstances, both the employment insurance policy and the proposed methods of implementation are often formulated within a very short period of time. However, since the government in Taiwan has traditionally taken a rather passive attitude towards unemployment, despite the island's first social insurance system (labour insurance) having been introduced in 1950, plans for unemployment insurance were not put forward until 1968, following which it took a further three decades before the system actually came into effect.

The period during which the 'Rules for the Implementation of Unemployment Benefits under the Labour Insurance Act' were being drafted was accompanied by intense debate, with the draft versions prepared by the Council of Labour Affairs (CLA) being subsequently rejected three times by the Executive Yuan, essentially as a result of the concerns amongst a number of government officials that the introduction of unemployment benefits would lead to welfare dependency amongst workers. The eventual introduction of the rules, which came into effect in 1998, was largely attributable to the continuing pressure and deep concerns of the general public over the problem of unemployment in a changing social and economic climate. However, even when unemployment benefits were eventually provided under the labour insurance system, not only was there no independent funding source for these benefits, but the absence of the necessary ancillary and support measures also made it difficult to achieve the goal of getting unemployed workers back into work as soon as possible.

Table 11.2 Comparison of unemployment benefit provisions under the Labour Insurance Act and Employment Insurance Law

Legal Provisions and Requirements	Unemployment Benefit Provisions			
	Labour Insurance Act 1999			Employment Insurance Law 2003
	Promulgated 28 December 1998	First revision: 30 July 1999	Second revision: 30 December 2000	Promulgated 15 May 2002
Scope of Application	1. Industrial employees in publicly or privately owned factories, mines, salt works, farms, ranches, forestry or tea plantations with five or more employees, and workers employed in the transport sector or by public utilities companies. 2. Employees at companies with five or more employees. 3. Employees in media, cultural, charitable or cooperative sector companies with five or more employees. 4. Government agency, public or private school and college workers, prohibited by law from participating in public or private school insurance schemes. 5. Employees in the fishing industry.	1. Workers in any industry/business category other than those listed in the original regulations. 2. Workers in any business with fewer than five employees.		All workers of Taiwanese nationality 15-60 years of age, with the following exceptions: 1. Workers covered by Public Employee Insurance or Military Personnel Insurance. 2. Workers already in receipt of Labour Insurance/Public Employee Insurance retirement benefits. 3. Workers whose employers or organizations are exempt from business registration requirements and not required to issue uniform invoices.
Requirements	Minimum of two years Labour Insurance contributions.	Minimum of two years Labour Insurance contributions.	Minimum of one year Unemployment Insurance contributions.	Minimum of one year Employment Insurance contributions.

Table 11.2 (Contd.)

Legal Provisions and Requirements	Unemployment Benefit Provisions			
	Labour Insurance Act 1999			Employment Insurance Law 2003
	Promulgated 28 December 1998	First revision: 30 July 1999	Second revision: 30 December 2000	Promulgated 15 May 2002
Waiting Period	14 days	14 days	7 days	14 days
Special Provisions	Benefits not available to those earning more than 80% of the minimum wage from part-time work whilst unemployed.	Benefits not available to those earning more than the minimum wage from part-time work whilst unemployed.		Benefits not available to those earning more than the minimum wage from part-time work whilst unemployed.
Amount and Method of Payment	50% of average monthly salary prior to period of unemployment; payment made every two weeks.	60% of average monthly salary prior to period of unemployment; payment made monthly.		1. Unemployment benefits: 60% of average monthly salary prior to unemployment; payment made monthly. 2. Early reemployment award: 50% of unpaid portion of the unemployment benefit to which the worker was entitled (single lump-sum payment). 3. Vocational training living allowance: 60% of average monthly salary prior to unemployment; payment made monthly. 4. NHI contribution subsidy for unemployed persons: covers that part of the unemployed worker's NHI contributions that the worker would normally have been required to pay if in employment.

Table 11.2 (Contd.)

Legal Provisions and Requirements	Unemployment Benefit Provisions			
	Labour Insurance Act 1999			Employment Insurance Law 2003
	Promulgated 28 December 1998	First revision: 30 July 1999	Second revision: 30 December 2000	Promulgated 15 May 2002
Maximum Period of Receipt of Benefits	1. Max. consecutive period of 3 months and cumulative period of 6 months for workers who had paid Labour Insurance contributions for less than 5 years. 2. Max. consecutive period of 6 months and cumulative period of 12 months for workers who had paid Labour Insurance contributions for 5-10 years. 3. Max. consecutive period of 8 months and cumulative period of 16 months for workers who had paid Labour Insurance contributions for over 10 years.	The overall maximum limits remained the same, but the restrictions on the maximum consecutive period for which a claimant could be in receipt of benefits were abolished.	The maximum period for which a claimant could be in receipt of benefits was set at 6 months, regardless of the number of years that the claimant had made Labour Insurance contributions.	1. The maximum period for which a claimant could be in receipt of either unemployment benefits or early reemployment awards was set at 6 months. 2. Vocational training living allowance could be paid for a maximum of 6 months per training programme.
Verification of Unemployed Status	Unemployed status to be verified every two weeks.	Unemployed status to be verified once a month.	–	Unemployed status to be verified once a month.

Source: DGBAS (2006).

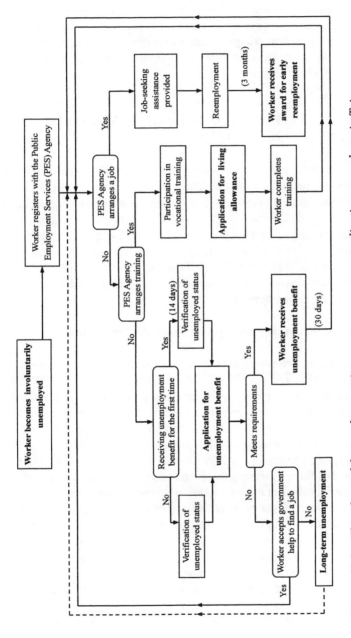

Figure 11.1   Flowchart of the employment insurance programme application procedures in Taiwan

Four years after the unemployment insurance system had been adopted in Taiwan, the government decided to switch over to a new policy of employment insurance, reflecting a more active approach to the problem of unemployment. The following section analyses both the original unemployment insurance policy and the subsequent employment insurance policy, and then goes on to compare the results achieved.

THE EFFECTIVENESS OF TAIWAN'S EMPLOYMENT INSURANCE PROGRAMME

In order to gain an understanding of the effectiveness of Taiwan's employment insurance programme in terms of tackling recent unemployment problems, we need to examine: (i) whether the implementation of the programme was carried out in a timely manner; (ii) how effective the programme has been in providing protection for unemployed workers, both in terms of the adequacy of the coverage for all unemployed workers and whether the payments made have been sufficient; and (iii) how effective the programme has been in assisting unemployed workers to obtain the necessary skills to prepare themselves for reemployment.

Implementation of the Employment Insurance Programme

There have been two waves of high unemployment in Taiwan in recent years, the first of which was in 1996 when the unemployment rate rose to 2.60 per cent from the 1.79 per cent of the previous year. The government did not, however, introduce any concrete measures in response to this rise in unemployment until 1999, when it implemented the unemployment insurance programme. When the second wave of high unemployment began, in 2001, the unemployment rate rose from 2.99 per cent in that year to 4.57 per cent in 2003; at that time, however, the government was already in a position to immediately implement the employment insurance system.

The old unemployment insurance programme that was already in place had proved to be inadequate in terms of protecting the welfare of the unemployed, largely because, aside from the provision of unemployment benefits, the government had no system in place aimed at helping unemployed workers to search for jobs or to engage in the sort of vocational training that would raise their overall employability. If we look at the UK, for example, the Jobseeker's Act was integrated into the existing system of unemployment support in 1995, with the Jobseeker's Allowance (JSA) subsequently being added into the unemployment benefits programme in 1996. Thus, when workers in the UK become unemployed, they immediately become entitled to job search assistance, with the government employment service advisers providing jobseekers with information on vocational training opportunities and ensuring that they receive appropriate training.[6] It was as a direct result of this additional service that the Jobseeker's Act led to a pronounced decline in the unemployment rate in the UK, from 7.60 per cent in 1996 to 5.70 per cent in 2001.

A similar situation is discernible in Canada, where a steady and continuous increase in unemployment was experienced throughout the 1990s. The payment of unemployment benefits and other associated benefits became a serious drain on federal government resources, leading to a steady worsening of the country's budget deficit. The government was faced with the need to make cutbacks in its overall level of expenditure on social welfare programmes and even to reduce the role of the government in welfare provision. On 7 March 1996, a bill was submitted to Canada's House of Commons proposing the replacement of the existing system of unemployment insurance by a new system of employment insurance. The new system subsequently proved more successful than the old one in terms of providing overall support and assistance to the unemployed, and particularly with regard to helping them to quickly return to the labour force. At the same time, the federal government delegated responsibility for the provision of vocational training to the provinces, although it did agree to provide the provincial government employment service centres with funding and access to relevant information so as to help them to perform their intermediary role between jobseekers and employers with maximum effectiveness (DHRSD, 2006). As a direct result of the implementation of the Employment Insurance Act, along with the integration of unemployment insurance with employment services, the unemployment rate in Canada fell from 9.20 per cent in 1997 to 8.30 per cent in 1998.

The experiences of both the UK and Canada clearly demonstrate the need for unemployment insurance to be integrated with employment services and vocational training if it is to have any meaningful impact on unemployment. As for the case of Taiwan, as the figures in Table 11.3 show, the unemployment rate continued to rise throughout the turn of the century, despite the introduction of the unemployment insurance system in 1999; this was largely because of the absence of the necessary employment services and vocational training provision. The government had, nevertheless, learned a valuable lesson from the failure of the unemployment insurance programme, as it subsequently went on to introduce training allowances and job-seeking assistance into the 2003 employment insurance programme, and, as a result, the unemployment rate did begin to fall. Thus, it is once again clear that employment insurance must be accompanied by appropriate support measures if it is to provide appropriate assistance to the unemployed.

Table 11.3 Unemployment rate in Taiwan, 1994-2005

Year	Official Unemployment Rate [a] (%)	Employed Persons [b] (x 1,000 Persons)			Unemployed Persons [c] (x 1,000 Persons)			Unemployment Rate (3) = (2)/(1) x 100
		Sub-total (1)	Private-sector Employees	Government Employees	Sub-total (2)	Former Private-sector Employees	Former Government Employees	
1994	1.56	6,160	5,159	1,001	89	85	4	1.44
1995	1.79	6,260	5,257	1,003	106	100	6	1.69
1996	2.60	6,286	5,259	1,027	167	160	7	2.65
1997	2.72	6,423	5,400	1,023	176	169	6	2.74
1998	2.69	6,555	5,580	975	178	171	7	2.71
1999	2.92	7,567	5,663	1,904	198	192	6	2.61
2000	2.99	6,745	5,790	955	212	206	6	3.14
2001	4.57	6,727	5,766	961	341	332	9	5.07
2002	5.17	6,771	5,825	946	396	384	13	5.85
2003	4.99	6,898	5,910	988	378	364	14	5.48
2004	4.44	7,131	6,137	994	337	314	23	4.73
2005 [d]	4.15	7,325	6,364	961	321	295	26	4.38

Notes:

[a] Refers to the unemployment rate announced by the government, and includes all new labour force entrants and experienced workers.

[b] Refers to all paid employees in private or government enterprises, but excludes all employers, the self-employed and unpaid family workers.

[c] Includes all persons previously employed in private or government enterprises, but excludes employers, the self-employed and unpaid family workers.

[d] The rates given for 2005 refer to the average for the first three quarters of the year.

Source: DGBAS (2006).

Coverage of the Employment Insurance Programme

Following the implementation of the unemployment insurance programme which, for the very first time, incorporated the provision of unemployment benefits into the labour insurance system, the programme was initially applicable only to enterprises with at least five employees; however, as a result of several revisions of the 2003 Employment Insurance Act, all employees in regular employment were ostensibly covered by the employment insurance system by 2005. Nevertheless, as can be seen from Table 11.4, at that time only around 72 per cent of the available workforce in Taiwan was effectively covered by the system. The problem lay in the fact that coverage was available only to workers aged 15-60 years, and that the system continued to exclude government employees, teachers, agricultural workers, those with no regular employer and school leavers looking for their first job. Clearly, therefore, the scope of the employment insurance provision still needs to be expanded if it is to provide more meaningful protection for all workers.

Table 11.4   Total number of persons covered by employment insurance in Taiwan, 1999-2005

Year	Total No. of Employees (x 1,000) (1)	No. of Employees Subscribing to Labour Insurance (x 1,000) (2)	Proportion (%) of Employees Subscribing to Employment Insurance (3) = (2)/(1)
1999	7,567	4,436	58.62
2000	6,745	4,879	72.33
2001	6,727	4,872	72.42
2002	6,771	4,827	71.28
2003	6,898	5,025	72.84
2004	7,131	5,242	73.51
2005	7,325	5,270	71.94

Note: * The figures for 2005 refer to the first three quarters of the year.

Sources: DGBAS (2006); BLI (2006).

Unemployment benefits are generally seen as a temporary protective measure; indeed, in providing such benefits, the hope is that the unemployed will be able to better concentrate their efforts on looking for work without having to worry about how they will be able meet their living expenses.[7] It is generally assumed that providing such benefits will reduce the overall duration of unemployment; however, when the government was planning the unemployment insurance system in 1998, the economic growth rate was high and the average duration of unemployment in Taiwan was only around 22 weeks. As a result, restrictions were set on the maximum period of eligibility for unemployment benefits according to the number of years the individual in question had been making Labour Insurance contributions; at that time, the maximum period for which benefits could be received was set at 24 weeks.

In 2003, when the new employment insurance system came into effect, the regulations were simplified, creating a uniform maximum benefit payment period of 24 weeks for all workers. However, as can be seen from Table 11.5, the average duration of unemployment was higher than 24 weeks in 2001; and indeed, subsequently rose to over 30 weeks. Thus, the maximum benefit payment period of 24 weeks was clearly no longer appropriate. Furthermore, Taiwan currently provides no support for those whose unemployment benefits have expired; thus, with the number of long-term unemployed persons growing steadily, some form of additional provision needs to be introduced, for example, through an extension of the maximum benefit payment period.

Table 11.5   Economic growth rates and average duration of unemployment in Taiwan, 1996-2005

| Year | Economic Growth Rate (%) | Types of Employment | | Average Duration of Unemployment (weeks) |
		First-time Jobseekers[a]	Experienced Workers	
1996	6.10	21.41	20.16	20.45
1997	6.59	21.87	21.21	21.36
1998	4.55	21.22	21.96	21.79
1999	5.75	22.02	22.65	22.52
2000	5.77	23.16	23.83	23.70
2001	-2.17	26.20	26.12	26.13
2002	4.25	28.23	30.64	30.26
2003	3.43	28.95	30.86	30.54
2004	6.07	27.01	29.95	29.40
2005	3.28[b]	27.85	27.74	27.62

Notes:
[a]   Includes school leavers and housewives re-entering the labour market.
[b]   The economic growth rate given for 2005 refers to the average for the first three quarters of the year.

Source: DGBAS (2006).

Payments to Unemployed Workers

Details of the value of the payments provided under the unemployment and employment insurance programmes in Taiwan over recent years are provided in Table 11.6, which shows that the average monthly unemployment benefit payment was equivalent to just over 60 per cent of the average registered salary, whilst the average monthly payment of living allowances for vocational training was a little under 60 per cent of the average registered salary; both of these figures appear to represent reasonable benefit payment levels. The minimum wage in Taiwan is currently set at NT$15,840 per month, and as can be seen from Table 11.6, the average monthly payments of unemployment benefits and vocational training living allowance both exceed this figure. Taiwan's unemployment insurance system does, therefore, appear to make adequate provisions with regard to meeting the basic economic needs of the unemployed; thus, the benefits provided should be sufficient to enable the unemployed to concentrate on job-seeking activities.

The level at which the provision of unemployment benefits is set will naturally have important impacts on the efforts of the unemployed workers with regard to looking for new jobs. If the 'income replacement rate' (IRR) is particularly high, then unemployed workers may be content to continue to claim unemployment benefits each month without expending any serious effort looking for work; and indeed, a deficiency of the current employment insurance programme lies in the fact that the average monthly unemployment benefit payment is higher than the average monthly living allowance for vocational training.[8] Despite the fact that vocational training can help the unemployed to acquire new skills, this could actually have the effect of encouraging them to collect unemployment benefits as opposed to encouraging them to participate in such training; and indeed, this is clearly evidenced by the small number of applications for vocational training living allowance and the extremely large number of applications for unemployment benefits.

In recent years, governments throughout the world have been struggling with worsening budget deficits and rising social welfare expenditure, with many countries responding by reducing the total amount of unemployment benefits payable and tightening the eligibility conditions for such benefits. However, this is not the case in Taiwan. As Table 11.7 shows, although the total amount of benefit applications approved in 1999 was relatively low, the approval rate has exceeded 93 per cent for each year since 2000, and this is a continuing trend. The vast majority of benefit applications are approved in cases of involuntary unemployment, which reflects a situation whereby the government is relying on unemployment benefits as its mainstream provision of assistance to the unemployed, with relatively little effort being focused on job-seeking assistance or vocational training for the unemployed.

Table 11.6 Unemployment insurance and employment insurance benefit payments in Taiwan, 1999-2005

	1999	2000	2001	2002	2003	2004	2005 [a]
Unemployment Benefit							
No. of Cases	39,471	105,227	485,851	611,646	325,340	212,097	228,206
Average Monthly Payment (NT$)	13,082	15,818	16,107	16,683	16,779	17,351	17,577
Total Amount Paid (NT$ Millions)	516.37	1,664.52	7,825.44	10,204.12	5,458.73	3,680.16	4,011.13
Early Reemployment Award							
No. of Cases	–	–	–	–	5,793	12,496	15,574
Average Monthly Payment (NT$)	–	–	–	–	33,698	35,772	37,995
Total Amount Paid (NT$ Millions)	–	–	–	–	195.22	447.00	591.74
Vocational Training Living Allowance							
No. of Cases	–	–	–	–	12,768	12,340	11,860
Average Monthly Payment (NT$)	–	–	–	–	15,959	16,426	16,881
Total Amount Paid (NT$ Millions)	–	–	–	–	203.77	202.70	200.20
Subsidized NHI Contributions							
No. of Cases	–	–	–	–	215,086	237,106	215,992
Average Monthly Payment (NT$)	–	–	–	–	534	540	550
Total Amount Paid (NT$ Millions)	–	–	–	–	114.91	128.12	118.73
Average Salary [b]	24,013	24,554	25,001	25,227	27,455	27,592	26,139

Notes:
[a] The figures for 2005 refer to the first three quarters of the year.
[b] The 'Average Salary' figures for the years 1999-2002 are taken from labour insurance statistics; the figures for 2003 onwards are taken from employment insurance statistics.

Source: BLI (2006).

Table 11.7 Unemployment benefit payments in Taiwan, 1999–2005 [a]

	1999	2000	2001	2002	2003	2004	2005
Total No. of Benefit Applications Received							
All Applications (x 1,000 Cases)	43,101	107,701	494,396	615,157	336,833	221,510	254,582
Initial Applications (x 1,000 Cases)	12,950	24,991	118,422	105,462	68,680	49,506	59,094
Further Applications (x 1,000 Cases)	30,151	82,710	375,974	509,695	268,153	172,004	195,488
Total No. of Benefit Applications Approved							
All Applications (x 1,000 Cases)	39,471	105,227	485,851	611,646	325,340	212,097	250,641
Initial Applications (x 1,000 Cases)	11,341	24,018	114,859	103,260	64,537	46,154	57,387
Further Applications (x 1,000 Cases)	28,130	81,209	370,992	508,386	260,803	165,943	193,254
Proportion of Initial Applications Approved (%) [b]	87.58	96.11	96.99	97.91	93.97	93.23	97.11

Notes:

[a] Figures prior to 2003 refer to unemployment benefit payments made under the labour insurance system; figures for 2003 onwards refer to unemployment benefit payments made under the employment insurance system.

[b] Proportion of initial applications approved = (No. of initial applications approved/No. of initial applications received) × 100.

Source: CLA (2006).

289

The Effectiveness of Vocational Training

If there is to be any hope of the employment insurance system in Taiwan achieving a significant reduction in the overall unemployment rate, in addition to providing adequate unemployment benefits, the government also needs to ensure that the appropriate employment services are being created and properly implemented. Furthermore, the effective matching of jobseekers to job vacancies is also crucial if both welfare dependency and unemployment are to be reduced.

Details of the provision of employment services in Taiwan between 1990 and 1998 are provided in Table 11.8, whilst similar details for the period from 1999 onwards (the time when unemployed workers were provided with unemployment benefits under the Labour Insurance system) are provided in Table 11.9. Prior to 1998, when unemployment in Taiwan was still relatively low, the proportion of jobseekers who had succeeded in finding work had remained at 40 per cent or higher. By 1998, however, labour market conditions had already begun to deteriorate, and by 2003 the proportion of jobseekers who were successful in finding work had declined to just 28.05 per cent.

Table 11.8   Employment service provisions in Taiwan, 1990-1998

Year	Total No. of Vacancies	Total No. of Jobseekers*	Total No. of Persons Finding Jobs through Government Assistance	Reemployment Rate (%)
	(A)	(B)	(C)	(C)/(B)×100
1990	509,393	185,589	91,839	49.49
1991	563,632	195,337	102,660	52.56
1992	559,635	173,974	77,174	44.36
1993	511,388	144,960	70,390	48.56
1994	410,099	136,850	73,099	53.42
1995	352,227	165,034	68,557	41.54
1996	323,150	174,090	75,588	43.42
1997	413,060	167,036	71,419	42.76
1998	427,495	174,262	68,015	39.03

Note: * The total number of jobseekers includes school leavers and unemployed persons not eligible for unemployment benefits.

Source: CLA (2006).

Table 11.9 Employment service provisions for recipients of unemployment benefits in Taiwan, 1999-2005

Year	Total No. of Vacancies (A)	Total No. of Jobseekers (B)	Total No. of Persons Finding Jobs through Government Assistance (C)	Reemployment Rate (%) (C)/(B)×100	Total No. of Unemployment Benefit Recipients (D)	Proportion of (D) Finding Jobs through Government Assistance (%) (D)/(C)×100
1999	365,629	248,679	69,644	28.01	554	0.80
2000	470,278	288,680	104,265	36.12	360	0.35
2001	405,637	439,489	128,205	29.17	1,653	1.29
2002	471,888	442,573	125,713	28.41	4,849	3.86
2003	720,746	450,079	126,229	28.05	6,456	5.11
2004	949,918	547,745	228,395	41.70	10,364	4.54
2005	1,008,307	580,020	263,403	45.41	10,237	3.89

Note: * The total number of jobseekers includes school leavers and unemployed persons not eligible for unemployment benefit.

Source: CLA (2006).

Following the introduction of the new employment insurance system in 2003, the proportion of the unemployed who succeeded in finding new jobs returned to the pre-1996 levels; however, this data was now inclusive of school leavers and workers with no regular employer. In fact, those in receipt of unemployment benefits whom the government had successfully helped to find work stood at only around 5.0 per cent, and this figure was falling steadily. Clearly, therefore, as opposed to just providing jobseekers with unemployment benefits and then leaving them to their own devices, greater effort is required by the government to match these jobseekers to job vacancies. Details of the benefit payments made in the years since the introduction of the unemployment insurance system are provided in Table 11.10.

In addition to helping to match jobseekers with job vacancies, another important policy element of employment insurance is the upgrading of the skills of unemployed workers, so as to improve their overall employability. When workers in Taiwan become involuntarily unemployed, they are not entitled to begin receiving unemployment benefits immediately, since they must first register with a public employment services agency so that the agency can either provide them with assistance to find a job or arrange a vocational training programme for them. Such workers will not be considered eligible for unemployment benefits until the agency has failed to either find them a job or to place them on an appropriate vocational training course.

'Orientation training' involves the provision of new skills to unemployed workers, whilst 'upgrading training' involves providing workers who are currently in work with additional training, either to develop their potential or to give them an additional set of skills so as to reduce the likelihood of them becoming unemployed. As the table shows, following the introduction of unemployment insurance in 1999, there was a pronounced increase in the number of persons participating in vocational training, with the increase being particularly marked in the case of 'orientation training'; however, following the implementation of the new employment insurance system in 2003, there was a steady fall in the number of people undergoing vocational training.

Following the introduction of the new employment insurance system, although there was an increase in participation in vocational training amongst those who had been in receipt of unemployment benefits, this group still accounted for less than 20 per cent of all vocational trainees (Table 11.11). Indeed, although there was an overall rise in the proportion of people in receipt of unemployment benefits who were also participating in vocational training, the vocational training system was having only limited impact in terms of combating unemployment, given that in absolute terms, the number of people participating in vocational training was actually falling. Much closer coordination between the employment insurance system and vocational training is therefore necessary if the unemployed are to be provided with comprehensive and effective support.

Table 11.10 Vocational training and unemployment benefits, 1991-2005

| Year | No. of Vocational Trainees | | | No. of Vocational Trainees Receiving Unemployment Benefits | Unemployment Benefit Recipients as a Proportion of all Vocational Trainees (%) |
	Orientation Training	Upgrading Training	Total Vocational Training		
1991	8,270	13,251	21,521	–	–
1992	9,652	14,141	23,793	–	–
1993	8,670	14,113	22,783	–	–
1994	8,608	12,863	21,471	–	–
1995	8,013	13,025	21,038	–	–
1996	8,582	16,075	24,657	–	–
1997	10,916	17,337	28,253	–	–
1998	10,354	19,469	29,823	–	–
1999	9,428	17,637	27,065	150	0.55
2000	10,992	19,038	30,030	128	0.43
2001	10,675	22,667	33,342	317	0.95
2002	20,705	19,705	40,410	2,075	5.13
2003	21,425	13,922	35,347	7,004	19.81
2004	15,136	13,699	28,835	5,227	18.13
2005	16,396	11,712	28,108	6,350	22.59

Source: CLA (2006).

Table 11.11   Unemployment benefits and the provision of vocational training under the employment insurance system in Taiwan, 1999–2005

Year	Total No. of Unemployment Benefit Applications (A)	No. of Applications Approved (B)	No. of Applicants for whom:			Proportion of Applicants for whom:		
			Jobs were Arranged (C)	Vocational * Training was Arranged (D)		Unemployment Benefit Payments were Approved (B)/(A) ×100 (%)	Jobs were Arranged (C)/(A) ×100 (%)	Vocational Training was Arranged (D)/(A) ×100 (%)
1999	43,101	39,471	554	150		91.58	1.29	0.35
2000	107,701	105,227	360	128		97.70	0.33	0.12
2001	494,396	485,851	1,653	317		98.27	0.33	0.06
2002	615,157	611,646	4,849	2,075		99.43	0.79	0.34
2003	336,833	325,340	6,456	7,004		96.59	1.92	2.08
2004	221,510	212,097	10,364	5,227		95.75	4.68	2.36
2005	254,582	250,641	10,237	6,350		98.45	4.02	2.49

Note: * Those persons who enrolled directly onto vocational training courses without having first applied for unemployment benefits were not included in the total for 'No. of Applicants for whom Vocational Training was Arranged'.

Source: Unemployment Payments under the Employment Insurance Law.

Whilst the Taiwanese government does seem to be providing greater assistance in the area of vocational training (as compared to the assistance provided through its current provision of employment services), this may well reflect the fact that those participating in vocational training are eligible to receive vocational training living allowances, as opposed to any reflection of a highly proactive attitude towards securing gainful reemployment amongst the unemployed. Under Taiwan's employment insurance system, if an unemployed worker applying for benefits fails to receive such benefits, this will normally be because the employment service agency has either arranged a job for the individual, or has arranged attendance on vocational training. Although there has been a significant increase since 2004 in the number of unemployed workers for whom the government's employment service agencies were able to arrange jobs, there has, nevertheless, been no significant increase in the number of people participating in vocational training programmes.

Under the current situation in Taiwan, over 95 per cent of the unemployed are receiving unemployment benefits, whilst only around 2.0 per cent are participating in vocational training programmes, and less than 5.0 per cent have jobs arranged for them. Details of those receiving unemployment benefits, those participating in vocational training courses and those for whom jobs were arranged each year since 1990, are provided in Table 11.11. Since these figures are largely in line with the analysis presented above, it is clear that there remains considerable room for improvement in employment policy in Taiwan, in terms of the provision of employment services and vocational training. These are the areas on which government focus is required in order to achieve significant improvements in the current unemployment situation.

CONCLUSIONS

Given that the establishment of the employment insurance system began much later in Taiwan than in many other countries around the world, one might reasonably expect that the Taiwanese government would have been able to absorb, and learn from, the experiences of other nations, thereby facilitating the establishment of a first-rate employment insurance system. In reality, for various reasons, rather than being established as an independent system in its own right, the unemployment insurance system was initially introduced as part of the existing labour insurance system. Although in 2003, the new employment insurance system was set up as an independent system, the influence of the old labour insurance system remained strong, in terms of both the regulatory framework and the agencies to which implementation was entrusted.

Employment insurance systems are invariably characterized by some degree of conflict between the different aspects of employment and insurance. Governments will usually place some effort into the implementation of effective care for the unemployed, which will often involve the provision of a limited living allowance so as to ensure a minimum standard of living, along with the simultaneous provision of vocational training to help them acquire new skills and secure reemployment. However, achieving an appropriate balance between 'self-help' and 'outside assistance' is not easy. If the level of unemployment benefits is too high, this may result in welfare dependency, undermining the willingness of the unemployed to look for work; if the level of benefits is too low, then such benefits will be insufficient to meet the basic living needs of the unemployed. Similarly, if the period for which unemployed workers can receive benefits is too long, this will encourage welfare dependency, whereas if the period is too short, then the system will fail to provide meaningful economic support to the unemployed. Clearly, the challenge for governments is to get the balance right.

In its role as an integral part of overall employment security policy, employment insurance needs to be integrated with vocational training and employment services if it is to succeed in reducing unemployment, whilst in its role as an element of social security policy, the emphasis has to be on protecting the economic well-being of every unemployed worker in line with the government's responsibilities towards all citizens. In reality, social security and employment security are two sides of the same coin; it is not really possible to divide employment insurance into those aspects relating to social security and those relating to employment security. In Taiwan's case, the goals that one would expect employment insurance to meet include both helping the unemployed to find work and providing them with economic security during their period of unemployment.

From the analysis presented in this chapter, it is clear that the current policy on employment insurance in Taiwan has tended to place the emphasis on the provision of economic assistance to the unemployed. The unemployed are entitled to receive unemployment benefits, whilst those participating in vocational training receive a living allowance, and unemployed workers who secure reemployment before the six-month benefit payment period expires can apply for an early reemployment award. The average monthly payments of both unemployment benefits and the vocational training living allowance amount to more 60 per cent of the average registered salary, with both of them exceeding the minimum wage (NT$15,840).

Given that 97 per cent of all applications for unemployment benefits are currently being approved, the economic protection provided by Taiwan's employment insurance system appears reasonably adequate; however, the proportion of unemployed workers who have jobs arranged for them by the various employment service centres, as well as the proportion who are enrolled in vocational training schemes, are both very low, at around 5.0 per cent and 2.5 per cent, respectively. There is therefore considerable room for improvement in assisting the unemployed to acquire the skills they need to secure reemployment, and matching jobseekers with job vacancies in the employment market. As things stand, with such an overemphasis on the provision of economic security, there is clearly a risk of welfare dependency becoming a serious problem; however, in the design of an employment insurance system, as with other types of social insurance systems, preventing the problem from developing in the first place is just as important as curing the problem once it has emerged.

The ultimate goal of employment policy should be to minimize the occurrence of unemployment, and, when it does occur, to help the unemployed to secure reemployment as quickly as possible. Taiwan's future employment insurance policy should place greater emphasis on the provision of vocational training and employment services; only then will Taiwan's employment policy be truly effective in helping to rescue all labour force participants from the nightmare of unemployment.

NOTES

[1] A total of 69 countries currently have some form of unemployment insurance system, with the classifications used for these systems varying widely, as do the methods of operation. The system used in Taiwan is based upon the Employment Insurance Law, as in Japan, whilst in the US, the Social Security Law authorizes state governments to enact their own unemployment insurance legislation; the UK has a Jobseeker's Allowance and Germany has an Employment Protection Law.

[2] In order to deal with the issue of 'welfare dependency', the periods for which benefits are provided in various countries are: 90-300 days in Japan; 4-30 weeks in the US; up to six months in the UK; 4-27 months in France; and 6-32 months in Germany. Under the current system of employment insurance in Taiwan, unemployment benefit is available for a maximum of six months.

[3] In France, those working in the government or other parts of the public sector are excluded, whilst Germany excludes temporary employees and Japan excludes seasonal workers unemployed for less than four months. In the UK, those not covered by the system include the self-employed, widows paying reduced social insurance premiums and certain categories of married women. The US excludes agricultural workers, those employed by religious organizations, temporary employees, domestic servants and the self-employed. The employment insurance system in Taiwan excludes those workers who have no regular employer. It is therefore clear that in most countries, employment insurance coverage is not extended to the entire working population.

4   Under the new employment insurance system in Taiwan, the implementation of which began in 2003, the maximum period for which unemployment benefits are payable is no longer linked to the number of years the worker has made Labour Insurance contributions. This is in contrast to many other countries, including the US, Germany, Japan and France, which continue to link the maximum period of benefit payments to the number of years for which contributions have been made; in the UK, the maximum period of benefit payments is linked to the recipient's age.

5   Taiwan imposes a waiting period of 14 days, whilst the US and Japan have a waiting period of seven days; the waiting period in the UK is just three days.

6   In accordance with the provisions of the Jobseeker's Act, an unemployed person is required to complete and sign a Jobseeker's Agreement to be eligible for the allowance (DWP, 2006).

7   Some countries continue to provide some form of assistance even after an unemployed person is no longer eligible to receive unemployment benefits; such assistance may be means-tested (SSA, 2006). The system in the UK integrates social insurance with social welfare; however, whilst eligibility for the Jobseeker's Allowance is based upon having made national insurance contributions, Jobseeker's Income Benefits are means-tested.

8   In Taiwan, the average monthly unemployment benefit payment is 60 per cent of the average salary. In Japan, the equivalent figure is 60-80 per cent (or 50-80 per cent in the case of workers aged 60-65 years). The situation in the US varies from state to state, but in most cases unemployment benefit is around 50 per cent of the worker's previous salary. In Germany, the figure is 67 per cent for workers with dependent children and 60 per cent for those without children. In the UK, the percentage varies according to age, with the payments normally being in the range of GBP28.85 to GBP50.35. Unemployment benefits in France are set at 57.4 per cent of the worker's previous salary (SSA, 2006).

REFERENCES

Addison, J.T. and M.L. Blackburn (1997), 'A Puzzling Aspect of the Effects of Advance Notice on Unemployment', *Industrial and Labour Relations Review*, **50**(2): 268-88.

Anderson, P.M. and B.D. Meyer (2000), 'The Effect of the Unemployment Insurance Payroll Tax on Wages, Employment, Claims and Denials', *Journal of Public Economics*, **78**(1-2): 81-106.

Atkinson, A.B. and G.J. Micklewight (1984), 'Unemployment Benefit, Duration and Incentives in Britain: How Robust is the Evidence?', *Journal of Public Economics*, **23**: 3-26.

BLI (2006), *Employment Insurance*, Bureau of Labour Insurance, Council of Labour Affairs, at website: http://www.bli.gov.tw.

Burtless, G. and A.H. Munnel (1990), 'Does a Trend Towards Early Retirement Create Problems for the Economy?', *New England Economic Review*, (November/ December): 16-33.

Butler, R.J. (1999), *The Economics of Social Insurance and Employee Benefits*, Boston: Kluwer Academic Publishers.

BVT (2006), *Employment Security Dictionary*, Bureau of Vocational Training, Council of Labour Affairs, Executive Yuan, ROC.

CLA (1998), *Employment Security Dictionary*, Bureau of Employment and Vocational Training, Council of Labour Affairs, Executive Yuan, ROC.

CLA (2005), *International Labour Statistics*, Council of Labour Affairs, Executive Yuan, ROC.

CLA (2006), *Employment Insurance*, Council of Labour Affairs, Executive Yuan, at website: http://www.cla.gov.tw.

DGBAS (2006), *Statistical Yearbook*, Directorate General of Budget, Accounting and Statistics, Executive Yuan, at website: http://www.dgbas.gov.tw.

DHRSD (2006), *Employment Insurance*, Canadian Department of Human Resources and Skills Development, at website: http://www.hrsdc.gc.ca.

DWP (2006), *Jobseeker's Allowance*, Department for Work and Pensions, at website: http://www.dwp.gov.uk.

Ministry of Labour (2006), *About the Unemployment Insurance System*, Ministry of Labour, South Korea, at website: http://edi.work.go.kr.

Rejda, G.E. (1999), *Social Insurance and Economic Security*, 6th edn., Upper Saddle River, NJ: Prentice Hall.

SSA (1999), *Social Security Programs Throughout the World, 1999*, US Social Security Administration, Office of Policy, Research, Evaluation and Statistics.

SSA (2006), *Social Security Programs Throughout the World, 2006*, US Social Security Administration, Office of Policy, Research, Evaluation and Statistics, at website: http://www.ssa.gov/policy/docs/progdesc/ssptw.

Williams, C.A. (1979), 'Meeting the Risk of Unemployment: Changing Societal Responses', *Annals of the American Academy of Political and Social Science* (May) **443**: 12-24.

12 Evaluating Taiwan's Public Service Employment Programme

Chao-Yin Lin and Mei Hsu

INTRODUCTION [1]

The alarming and continuing growth trend in the unemployment rate in Taiwan, from less than 2 per cent in 1995 to 5.2 per cent by 2002, clearly has serious negative social and economic impacts upon all workers within the island's labour market. Despite the Taiwanese government's implementation of a number of programmes aimed at solving the severe unemployment problem, the rate has nevertheless remained unacceptably high.[2] In the aftermath of the 1997 Asian financial crisis, the government of South Korea introduced a range of public works projects aimed at dealing with its own high unemployment rate. Thereafter, at the end of 2002, in an attempt to emulate the success of the Korean projects, the Taiwanese government introduced the 'Public Service Employment Programme' (PSEP) to be operated jointly by the Council for Economic Planning and Development (CEPD) and the Council of Labour Affairs (CLA).

The PSEP, a NT$20 billion programme, has created more than 85,000 jobs for the unemployed since its inception and can be regarded as one of the most important employment policies to be implemented by the Taiwanese government over recent years. A total of 16 governmental ministries and departments have taken part in the PSEP, providing a variety of public works projects for the unemployed, such as the creation and maintenance of databases, cleaning and beautification of public environments, checking and repairing of public facilities, as well as care for the young and the elderly within various communities around the island.

The introduction of the programme was approved by the Legislative Yuan in Taiwan, and carried out between 2003 and 2004. This chapter investigates such implementation, as well as its impact on the unemployment situation in Taiwan, with our evaluation of the programme focusing on both economic and social impacts.

BACKGROUND TO THE PUBLIC SERVICE EMPLOYMENT PROGRAMME

The rising unemployment problem in Taiwan has been characterized as a form of structural unemployment resulting largely from the transition in the overall industrial structure of the island which has been taking place since 1996. The net effect of this major transition was evidenced by large numbers of employees not only being made redundant, but also finding it extremely difficult to secure alternative gainful employment within the labour market, particularly in the short term (Lin, 2003).

The cumulative effect of this wave of transition was to ultimately push the unemployment rate up to 5.2 per cent, which, in numerical terms, meant that by 2002 there were a total of 515,000 unemployed workers on the island. According to one study, the general nature of the unemployed was characterized by middle-aged, low-skilled and poorly educated male workers, with many of these unemployed workers being heads of households; therefore, their sudden transition into unemployment brought with it both personal and family difficulties (Jiang, 2003). Furthermore, with the advent of such unemployment numbers, there was clearly the potential for the difficult economic conditions to further trigger associated social problems, such as family violence, community crimes and suicides.

Given such difficulties faced by the growing numbers of unemployed workers, the Taiwanese government adopted several economic measures, essentially aimed at simultaneously boosting the overall investment environment and accelerating the further transformation of the island's industrial structure. However, as was pointed out at that time by S.C. Hu, the Chairman of the CEPD, there was no possibility of these long-term economic measures solving the immediate personal and family difficulties confronted by the growing ranks of the unemployed; there was, therefore, an urgent need for reemployment programmes capable of providing effective short-term assistance for the unemployed (Hu, 2003).

If we examine closely the experiences of other Asian countries and their attempts to deal with their own unemployment problems at that time, it is clear that South Korea can be regarded as a model from which Taiwan could learn a great deal. In the aftermath of the Asian financial crisis of 1997, the South Korean government had introduced a number of 'public works projects' aimed at tackling the rising level of unemployment. Within just five years (1998-2003), the unemployment rate had been dramatically reduced from 6.8 per cent to 3.1 per cent (Lee, 2001; Lee, 2003). In spite of other factors troubling Korea, the projects did seem to be of use in terms of reducing the unemployment rate, and indeed, this Korean experience inspired the Taiwanese government to implement its own similar scheme, the PSEP.

Programme Content

The legal foundation of the PSEP was established in January 2003 with the promulgation of the PSEP Act; thereafter, the programme was officially implemented from July 2003 to June 2004. In accordance with the PSEP Act, an extra-governmental budget of NT$20 billion was allocated, with a cross- ministry working committee being appointed to administer the introduction of the programme. As specified within the PSEP Act, the programme had fourfold purposes, the first of which was to promote the employment of middle-aged and disadvantaged workers, lest they should become excluded from society as a result of long-term unemployment. The second purpose was to reduce the dependency of unemployed workers on unemployment benefit claims and related assistance, the third was to transfer certain public service works into the newly developed industries (such as care for the elderly and resource recycling), and the fourth was to improve the quality of people's lives and strengthen the island's infrastructure through the provision of public works projects. In terms of practical targets, the programme aimed to create 75,000 jobs within a year and to reduce the unemployment rate to 4.5 per cent by the end of 2003.

The PSEP was targeted primarily at both unemployed and disadvantaged workers, with the general criteria for programme participants being those aged between 35 and 64, possessing working experience of more than six months over the previous three-year period, and having registered with the government as unemployed; however, 'special cases', such as female breadwinners, disabled people, aboriginal workers and those with low-income status, were not necessarily confined within the aforementioned general criteria. Those who qualified and were interested in joining the programme could register with local CLA job centres, with all participants being required to complete forms containing their personal data, such as age, gender, education, working experience, duration of unemployment, and so on; this information was required in order to match the applicants to suitable job openings provided by the ministries or departments. It is estimated that between 2002 and 2004 around 120,000 people had registered for the programme at CLA job centres. The administrative data recorded by the job centres proved to be a valuable means of analyzing the characteristics of unemployed workers in Taiwan, and indeed, a random sample from this administrative database was used as the basis of our survey of PSEP participants.

The jobs provided by the PSEP should, in principle, prove to be valuable, both to those involved and to society as a whole. These jobs were planned to complement the 'Challenge 2008 National Plan' and were regarded as the direct responsibility of the government. The PSEP works were initially divided into 20 different types and later regrouped into six categories, including 'computerization of public files', 'improvements to public construction works', 'beautification of living environments', 'community services', 'enhancement of tourism' and 'others'. Most of these works required limited knowledge and skills and were extremely labour intensive.

As regards the working conditions for PSEP jobs, each participant was allowed to take part in the programme for a maximum of two phases (with each phase lasting six months); that is, the maximum any unemployed worker could remain within any given project was one year. The monthly wages for PSEP jobs ranged between NT$16,720 and NT$22,000, depending upon the features of the project. The wages for PSEP works had been set at slightly above the minimum wage in Taiwan (NT15,840 at that time), and once unemployed workers became PSEP workers, they would automatically be covered by the social insurance programmes, such as the Labour Insurance and National Health Insurance schemes; however, they would not be allowed to claim unemployment benefits whilst working within the PSEP.

Implementation of the PSEP

The PSEP was implemented in a top-down, cross-ministerial fashion, with the PSEP Board organized by heads of departments, along with relevant experts, and chaired by the Prime Minister. The administrative tasks of the programme were carried out by a cross-ministerial working committee, comprising of staff members from the CEPD, CLA, Directorate-General of Budget, Accounting and Statistics (DGBAS) and the Research, Development and Evaluation Commission (RDEC). At the start of the programme, the working committee reviewed proposals submitted by the ministries and departments and granted manpower quotas for each PSEP project, along with corresponding budgets. The departments and ministries had the options of implementing PSEP projects on their own, devolving them to local authorities or contracting them out to private companies and organizations.

The PSEP comprised of a total of 120 projects, as proposed by the various departments and ministries. There were also two special projects, one of which was a local, temporary and seasonal project within which there were a further 15 sub-projects, whilst the other involved a wage subsidy scheme for small and medium-sized enterprises (SMEs).[3] According to the data available in December 2003, a total of 127 PSEP projects had been implemented at that time (comprising of 118 major projects and nine sub-projects), with the largest proportion of these (apart from the category of 'others') being in the category of 'computerization of public files', at 15.75 per cent of the total. A further 14.17 per cent of these projects came under the heading of 'community services' (Table 12.1).

Table 12.1   Type of works, by number of projects

Type of Works	Total No. of Projects	% Share of Total
Computerization of Public Files	20	15.75
Improvements to Public Construction Works	7	5.51
Beautification of Living Environments	15	11.81
Community Services	18	14.17
Enhancement of Tourism	14	11.02
Others	53	41.73
Total	127	100.00

Source: Compiled from RDEC (2003).

Nevertheless, the category of 'beautification of living environments' accounted for the largest share of programme participants, employing 23,075 people, with 'community services' ranking second, employing 14,334 people (Table 12.2).

Table 12.2   Type of works, by number of workers

Type of Works	Expected No. of Employees	Actual No. of Employees	% Share of Total
Computerization of Public Files	8,349	8,472	11.62
Improvements to Public Construction Works	9,382	9,028	12.39
Beautification of Living Environments	22,820	23,075	31.66
Community Services	14,739	14,334	19.67
Enhancement of Tourism	2,685	2,643	3.63
Others	15,571	15,336	21.04
Total	73,546	72,888	100.00

Source: Compiled from RDEC (2003).

In terms of duration, 48 per cent of projects were implemented for one year, and 39 per cent for six months. In other words, most projects operated in accordance with PSEP regulations, taking six months as a unit, and two units as the maximum, with almost 50 per cent of the programmes being implemented for a one-year period (Table 12.3). As regards the department or ministry responsible, the Ministry of the Interior (MOI) is the biggest employer of PSEP workers, having employed 23,666 workers and implemented 26 projects in all categories except 'enhancement of tourism' (Table 12.4). The Council of Agriculture also employed a significant number of workers (10,150), mainly in forestation projects and the management of rivers and reservoirs.

Table 12.3   Period of duration of works, by number of projects

Duration of Project	No. of Projects	% Share of Total
6 months	49	38.58
7-11 months	17	13.38
12 months	61	48.03
Total	127	100.00

Source: Compiled from RDEC (2003).

Table 12.4   PSEP provision, by sponsoring agencies

Sponsoring Agency	No. of Projects	% Share of Total
Ministry of the Interior	26	20.47
Ministry of Education	7	5.51
Ministry of Economic Affairs	14	11.02
Ministry of Transportation and Communications	11	8.66
Department of Health	4	3.15
Environmental Protection Administration	3	2.36
Research, Development and Evaluation Commission	5	3.94
Council of Agriculture	16	12.60
Council of Labour Affairs	5	3.94
Council of Indigenous Peoples	11	8.66
Others	25	19.69
Total	127	100.00

Source: Compiled from RDEC (2003).

Most PSEP workers tended to be concentrated within a few ministries and on a few projects; however, despite being extremely labour-intensive, these projects tended to make little contribution towards improving the employability of the PSEP workers. According to group interviews undertaken with responsible PSEP staff members, given that the PSEP was required to be implemented within a very short timeframe, they had insufficient time to plan appropriate and innovative jobs for programme participants. Furthermore, due to a lack of effective coordination, public works proposed by different ministries and departments were not systematically integrated, and thus tended to overlap. In our subsequent evaluation, based on the empirical data, we will examine whether the type of project was a determinant of the reemployment of programme participants.

RESEARCH METHODOLOGY

Data Collection

The empirical data for this chapter is taken mainly from an earlier study carried out by the authors; however, whilst that study investigated the particular effects of the PSEP on programme participants, employers and the general public, in this chapter we concentrate solely on the effects of the programme on those participating, with the opinions of programme participants having been collected through telephone interviews during April-May 2004.

All of those who had taken part in PSEP projects, in any way, were regarded as the survey population (comprising of around 95,000 people). A systematic and stratified sampling was taken from this sample based upon a categorization of 25 cities and/or counties and 22 project types, with a survey sample list of 7,948 respondents subsequently being constructed. Of these, a total of 2,414 participants had been successfully interviewed by the end of the survey, giving a survey response rate of around 34 per cent. Since the population data used in the study was taken directly from the PSEP registration database, with a large random sample having been created, the survey data analysed here is regarded as both representative and reliable.

Methodology

Econometric models were constructed as a means of examining the determinants for both satisfaction with, and the reemployment effects of, the PSEP. The level of satisfaction with the PSEP was categorized within the questionnaire into four levels: (1) 'very well', (2) 'well', (3) 'not very well' and (4) 'not at all'. A Probit model was set up, both to determine whether a respondent was satisfied with the job creation project and to investigate the determinants of such satisfaction. The 'very well' and 'well' responses were therefore grouped together and defined as 'satisfied' with the PSEP, whilst the 'not very well' and 'not at all' responses were defined as 'not satisfied' with the PSEP.

Let I^*, a latent variable, represent the tendency towards being 'satisfied' with the PSEP, with I being a binary variable indicating that a respondent's satisfaction level was located either in the 'very well' or 'well' responses; thus I is set at 1. The latent variable I^* cannot be observed, but $I=1$ if, and only if, $I^* > 0$ and satisfaction with the PSEP is either 'very well' or 'well'; otherwise, if $I^* \leq 0$, then $I = 0$. Given the assumed normality of the errors, I and I^* are linked by the Probit model; thus, the Probit model of satisfaction can be expressed as:

$$P(I=1) = P(I^* > 0 | X_1, X_p, X_c) = X_1 \cdot \gamma_1 + X_p \cdot \gamma_p + X_c \cdot \gamma_c + \eta_1, \qquad (1)$$

where the vector, X_1, reflects the observable explanatory variables, including individual characteristics, such as 'Age', 'Gender' and variables indicating educational levels, as well as other socio-economic variables which affect the probability of satisfaction with the PSEP (at either the 'very well' or 'well' level).

The explanatory variable vector, X_p, indicates the six different types of PSEP projects, which are 'computerization of public files', 'improvements to public construction works', 'beautification of living environments', 'community services', 'enhancement of tourism' and 'others'. The variable vector, X_c, represents the subjective opinions of some of the respondents with regard to PSEP job characteristics, such as whether the PSEP job was a high-paying job (Wage_more), whether the wage was an exact match for the job characteristics (Wage_exact), or whether it was a low-paying job (Wage_less). The variable, 'Training', indicates whether or not the training provided by the programme was sufficient, whilst the 'Match' variable indicates whether the PSEP job characteristics matched the respondent's original job specialty and the 'Learn' variable indicates whether the respondents were able to learn more about their new job during their time with the programme. Finally, the coefficients γ_1, γ_p and γ_c are the corresponding parameters for estimation. The term η_1 reflects the unobservable determinants of the level of satisfaction, which is assumed to be normally distributed with mean zero and variance σ_1^2. A Probit model is similarly adopted as a means of evaluating the reemployment effect, investigating the determinants of the probability of the PSEP participants securing gainful reemployment on completion of the programme; the model set up for the reemployment effect is similar to that in Equation (1).

EMPIRICAL RESULTS

Basic information was collected on the prior working experience of the PSEP participants in order to carry out our analysis of their perceptions, as well as the factors motivating their efforts. In light of the information gained from this data collection, there were some concerns about whether the participants had received sufficient training for work on the PSEP projects. Analysis of the positive and negative effects of the PSEP was also undertaken, in terms of social inclusion, social capital and economic dimensions. Those factors explaining the degree of satisfaction and the probability of reemployment for PSEP participants were also investigated using regression analyses.

Data Description

Characteristics of the respondents

Table 12.5 presents the characteristics of the respondents from a sample population distribution of 51 per cent males and 49 per cent females. About 45 per cent of the respondents were aged 50 or above, indicating that the PSEP projects were complying with one of the main policy directions of the programme, that of employing middle-aged and older unemployed workers in the first instance. As to the educational level of participants, the majority were either high school or vocational school graduates, accounting for 60 per cent of the sample. About a quarter of the sample had either elementary education or no formal education at all, whilst only one in six were college or university graduates. This distribution of the sample indicates that the respondents' overall educational levels were not particularly poor, considering that this was an average educational level amongst the middle- and older-aged section of the island's population.

Table 12.5   Characteristics of the respondents

Variables	No. of Respondents	Total Sample	% Share of Total
Gender			
Male	1,027	2,014	51.0
Female	987		49.0
Age			
<35	89		5.0
35-49	874	1,773	49.3
50-64	761		42.9
65≥	49		2.8
Educational Level			
Elementary School (or below)	473		23.6
High School	1,185	2,005	59.1
College (or above)	347		17.3
Prior Work Experience			
Yes	1,439	2,014	71.45
No	575		28.55
Occupation (prior to participating in the PSEP)			
Management, Professional and Administration	124		9.61
Sales and Clerical Workers	487		37.75
Manual Workers	474	1,290	36.74
Self-employed	120		9.30
Casual Workers	85		6.59

It must also be considered, however, that participants with much lower educational levels may well find it difficult to get through the selection and recruitment process to get a PSEP job in the first place. Almost 30 per cent of the respondents had never worked before participating in the PSEP, a figure which indicates that the scheme did result in drawing more people towards active participation in the labour market. Clearly, those people who had not participated in the labour market as a result of a disadvantaged background may well have found the PSEP jobs attractive, especially as the working requirements were lower; therefore, the PSEP scheme could well have served to increase the overall labour market participation rate.

As regards the prior working experience of those who had worked before joining the scheme, 37 per cent were manual workers, with a further 38 per cent having been in sales or clerical work, whilst the combined group of managers, professionals and administrators represented less than 10 per cent of the whole sample. Generally speaking, the vast majority of PSEP participants had been neither technical nor professional workers prior to joining the programme, which may be the unavoidable result of low-skilled workers being more vulnerable to job losses in the advancing tide of unemployment. The PSEP would therefore have tended to target this particular section of the working population.

The effects of the PSEP on the economic status of the respondents
As Table 12.6 indicates, more than half of the respondents were primary breadwinners, with less than one in ten of the sample having no share of the burden of household expenditure. The majority of those participating in the PSEP reported that they spent their wages on personal and family needs, a finding which does indicate that the wages paid by the scheme have succeeded in providing essential help directly to the families of most of the respondents. More than half of the respondents agreed that the main benefit of participating in the scheme was 'improving personal/family income'. In this regard, the PSEP has achieved one of the important aims of its policy goals, that of reducing the financial burden of unemployed workers and their families.

The survey clearly demonstrates the importance of the PSEP to the participants, in terms of valuable economic support; however, as discussed above, the PSEP jobs were temporary and most of them were non-technical or non-professional. Furthermore, the wages were unattractive and future career prospects were limited. It seems clear that if they had not been constrained by economic difficulties, most of the participants might not have taken the PSEP jobs. Hence, the PSEP seemed to function as a programme based more on social policy than on labour market policy. This programme did provide a stable source of income to those participating during the period of our study, many of whom could not find any unsubsidized jobs in the regular labour market and yet continued to bear the burden of family responsibility. To these people, the PSEP scheme also served as a means of alleviating poverty.

Table 12.6   Economic status of the respondents

Questions	Responses	Total No.	% Share of Total
Are you the main breadwinner of the family?	Yes	1,102	54.72
	Not main breadwinner but share financial responsibility	715	35.50
	No	196	9.73
How do you spend the money earned from the PSEP?	Personal expenditure	226	11.22
	Family expenditure	1,629	80.88
	Pay debts and loans	120	5.96
	Saving	27	1.34
	Other	9	0.45
	Don't know	2	0.10
What is the major benefit from participating in the PSEP?	Saying goodbye to joblessness	230	11.42
	Improving personal/family income	1,119	55.56
	Sense of achievement	88	4.37
	Having a focus of life	164	8.14
	Expanding personal network	143	7.10
	Learning knowledge and techniques	175	8.69
	Others	90	4.47

Considering that more than half of the respondents were breadwinners, whilst a further third had some share of the burden of family responsibility, many of the participants would clearly have been placed under severe economic strain prior to taking part in the PSEP. Although the PSEP jobs were temporary in nature, they provided direct support to those participating, and to their families, during their transitional period of unemployment. It was of course hoped that by the time they had completed the course of their PSEP project, the economic environment would have improved considerably and that the participants could then return to the regular labour market.

The effects of the PSEP on social inclusion
As the counterpart to social exclusion, social inclusion is a social value which has been strongly emphasized within many of the European countries in recent years, since the unemployed are regarded as being amongst the highest-risk groups facing such exclusion. As Table 12.7 shows, the PSEP did lead to improvements in the social inclusion of respondents, from a perspective of social protection.

During their period of unemployment, about one-eighth of the respondents did not join the National Health Insurance (NHI) scheme, the island's universal social security scheme, which implies that because of the failure to pay the necessary contributions, their unemployment also led to a loss of eligibility for NHI treatment. Furthermore, less than 40 per cent of the respondents were covered by labour insurance prior to participating in the PSEP. However, in accordance with the PSEP regulations, ministries or departments were to act as employers, sharing the NHI and labour insurance contributions of PSEP workers. As a consequence, the PSEP did achieve the aim of including programme participants within society under the various social protection systems.

Table 12.7 indicates that the majority of respondents reported that they were more willing to participate in social activities after joining the PSEP; it was clear that they also paid more attention to the ongoing events of society in general. In other words, the respondents' participation in the PSEP may have enhanced their level of social interaction, as well as their motivation for political participation, which in turn, would have enhanced their level of social inclusion.

Table 12.7   The effects of the PSEP on social inclusion

Questions	Responses	Total No.	% Share of Total
Did you participate in the Labour Insurance programme prior to joining the PESP?	Yes	771	38.28
	Occasionally	106	5.26
	No	1,128	56.01
	Don't know	8	0.40
Have you become more willing to participate in social activities since joining the PESP?	Strongly agree	591	29.34
	Agree	739	36.69
	Disagree	435	21.60
	Strongly disagree	125	6.21
	Don't know/no opinion	122	6.06

The effects of the PSEP on social capital

Social capital is conceptualized as (i) quantity and/or quality of the resources that individuals can access, or use, through (ii) their location within a social network; the general proposition is that social capital enhances the likelihood of instrumental returns, such as better jobs (Lin, 2000). In this regard, the PSEP had positive effects on promoting the social capital of those participating. As shown in Table 12.8, the majority of the participants agreed that taking part in the PSEP had improved their relationships with relatives, with most of them also agreeing that joining the scheme was helpful in terms of expanding their network for finding future work.

Table 12.8   The effects of the PSEP on social capital

Statements	Responses	Total No.	% Share of Total
The PSEP has improved my relationships with my relatives	Strongly agree	507	25.17
	Agree	773	38.38
	Disagree	422	20.95
	Strongly disagree	114	5.66
	Don't know/no opinion	194	9.63
The PSEP has helped me to build up a useful network for finding jobs	Strongly agree	374	18.57
	Agree	748	37.14
	Disagree	468	23.24
	Strongly disagree	293	14.55
	Don't know/no opinion	130	6.45

The effects of the PSEP on reemployment

One of the main objectives of the PSEP was to improve the employability of participants thereby assisting them in their attempts to return to the regular labour market. However, the survey results show that the effects of the PSEP scheme on the reemployment of those participating have not been significant. Since most of the participants (67.7 per cent) were still working in the PSEP projects at the time of the survey, the reemployment effects could only be measured according to the one-third of respondents who had left the PSEP at the end of their contracts, or for other reasons. As can be seen from Table 12.9, amongst those who had left PSEP jobs, only about 33 per cent had found an unsubsidized job.

Table 12.9   The effects of the PSEP on reemployment

Questions	Responses	Total No.	% Share of Total
Have you had any job since leaving the PSEP?	Yes	213	32.77
	No	437	67.23
State the main reason for not being reemployed*	I do not intend to work again	25	8.72
	Lack of employment information	8	1.83
	Don't like the job opportunities	22	5.03
	No job opportunities	316	72.31
	Others	65	14.87

Note: * Follow-up question posed to those who had not become reemployed.

It is apparent that the main reason for the remaining two-thirds being unable to find an unsubsidized job after leaving the PSEP was simply that no suitable jobs were available for them within the depressed labour market. Their disadvantaged socio-economic status left the participants in an extremely vulnerable position within the labour market as a whole. In addition, it was unrealistic to expect that under such severe labour market conditions the disadvantaged situations of the most vulnerable workers could have ever been solved through the provision of temporary jobs. Prerequisites for dealing with this problem are various anti-cyclical measures, including both social and macro-economic policies.

The narcotic effects of the PSEP

Apart from the positive effects discussed above, the PSEP also had negative impacts on participants. The narcotic effect, which refers to the participants' continuous dependence on, or expectation of participating in, these kinds of schemes, is well observed amongst the respondents. As can be seen from Table 12.10, participants displayed a strong desire to rely upon PSEP projects for their long-term employment, with more than 90 per cent of the participants indicating that, if it were possible, they would like to participate in the scheme on a continual basis. By contrast, only 2.6 per cent of the respondents expressed no intention at all of staying with the PSEP. These figures clearly demonstrate the narcotic effect of the PSEP, which may not be conducive to promoting the reemployment of programme participants.

When broken down by respondent characteristics, this narcotic effect shows no significant difference between male and female participants; however, those in the older age groups did demonstrate a stronger desire towards staying in the PSEP projects, as did those with lower educational qualifications. This is understandable, since the people in these groups were generally more disadvantaged within the labour market and were more likely to be in need of state intervention if they were to succeed in returning to work. Hence, their inclination toward staying in public works was stronger than amongst younger participants, or those with higher educational levels.

The fact that the less-advantaged workers need greater state intervention poses a severe challenge to the PSEP. On the one hand, the PSEP projects need to target the most vulnerable groups, those who would otherwise find it very difficult to secure unsubsidized jobs in the labour market; on the other hand, however, the PSEP has to minimize the dependency of these participants on public work programmes and push them back into regular work. Therefore, both design and duration are vital elements of the programme. Participating in public works is useful in terms of helping participants to accumulate the necessary working skills and experience as well appropriate working attitudes; however, the public work contracts should not be too long, so as to avoid the heavy reliance of participants on such programmes. As a result, they may try to return to the regular labour market on completion of the programme.

Table 12.10   The narcotic effects of the PSEP

Variables	If possible, would you like to participate continuously in PSEP jobs?							
	Very much		Somewhat		Not really		Not at all	
	No.	%	No.	%	No.	%	No.	%
Gender (n = 2,007)								
Male	759	74.1	175	17.1	60	5.9	30	2.9
Female	746	75.9	164	16.7	50	5.1	23	2.3
Age (n = 1,425) ***								
35-44	284	70.1	80	19.8	25	6.2	16	4.0
45-49	263	70.5	69	18.5	27	7.2	14	3.8
50-54	245	78.5	48	15.4	17	5.4	2	0.6
55-59	141	81.5	29	16.8	3	1.7	–	–
60-66	141	87.0	14	8.6	4	2.5	3	1.9
Educational attainment (n = 1,998)***								
Primary School (or below)	401	85.1	56	11.9	11	2.3	3	0.6
Junior High School	319	78.6	70	17.2	11	2.7	6	1.5
Senior High School	577	74.3	137	17.6	45	5.8	18	2.3
College (or above)	201	58.4	76	22.1	42	12.2	25	7.3
Totals	1,505	74.7	339	16.8	110	5.5	53	2.6

Note: *** P<0.001.

The economic effects of the PSEP

Economic evaluations of the PSEP effects, derived from the empirical data, are provided in Tables 12.11 and 12.12. Table 12.11 presents the regression results of the determinants of satisfaction with the PSEP, whilst Table 12.12 presents the determinants of reemployment for the programme participants; all of the results are in accordance with the theoretical model specified earlier in this chapter.

We find, from Table 12.11, that age has no significant effect on the level of satisfaction for those participating in the programme. Even when the participants within the study were separated into three age cohorts, there was still no evidence of any significant age effect. However, we can determine the relative magnitudes and signs of the effects on the age cohorts from the satisfaction regressions, whilst controlling for the 45-54 age group as the reference group. As a result, we find that the 55-64 age group tends to be more satisfied with the PSEP than their younger counterparts. Conversely, as compared to their older counterparts, the 35-44 age group has a lower likelihood of satisfaction with the programme.

Furthermore, where the programme participants were well-educated males, receiving good training, learning various skills from the public service job and also receiving the help of their colleagues during their period of participation in the programme, then there was a greater likelihood of them being satisfied with the programme than their female counterparts. Moreover, if the PSEP job matched the specialities of the male participants, they were also more likely to be satisfied with the programme than their female counterparts. Finally, we find that, with the exception of 'enhancement of tourism' projects, the project types generally had no significant effect on the level of satisfaction with the programme. Those participating in 'enhancement of tourism' projects were less likely to be satisfied with the public service programme than their counterparts in the category of 'others'.

The empirical reemployment regressions, presented in Table 12.12, show that the programme participants were more likely to gain reemployment if they were unsatisfied with the programme, whereas those who were satisfied with the programme may run the risk of becoming highly dependent on the work, and thereby, being locked into the programme. Younger, male participants with higher educational levels were significantly more likely to find gainful employment than their female counterparts on completion of their temporary job; however, the results also indicate that being a household breadwinner had no significant effect on the probability of reemployment.

Basically, with the exception of 'enhancement of tourism' projects, the project type had no significant impact on the probability of reemployment, which implies that those participating in 'enhancement of tourism' projects would be more likely to find a job following their completion of the programme.

Table 12.11 Determinants of satisfaction for PSEP participants

Variables	Model Estimations [a]					
	Model 1 [b]		Model 2 [b]		Model 3 [b]	
Personal Characteristics						
Age	0.002	(0.39)	0.001	(0.22)	–	–
Age 35-44	–	–	–	–	-0.045	(0.18)
Age 45-54 (Reference group)	–	–	–	–	–	–
Age 55-64	–	–	–	–	0.078	(0.56)
Gender (Male=1)	0.139	(2.69)*	0.132	(2.34)*	0.123	(2.00)*
Primary Education (Reference group)	–	–	–	–	–	–
Junior High School	-0.229	(2.95)*	-0.226	(2.70)*	-0.207	(2.21)*
Senior High School	-0.282	(5.53)**	-0.262	(4.14)**	-0.243	(3.42)*
Junior College	-0.425	(8.81)***	-0.385	(6.04)***	0.366	(5.41)*
University	-0.572	(9.51)***	-0.540	(7.46)***	-0.526	(7.00)**
Project Types						
Computerization of Public Files	–	–	-0.070	(0.26)	-0.067	(0.24)
Improvements in Public Construction Works	–	–	0.144	(0.75)	0.141	(0.72)
Beautification of Living Environments	–	–	0.104	(0.71)	0.104	(0.71)
Community Services	–	–	0.110	(0.79)	0.106	(0.73)
Enhancement of Tourism	–	–	-0.468	(6.04)***	-0.461	(5.85)**
Others (Reference group)	–	–	–	–	–	–

Table 12.11 (Contd.)

Variables	Model Estimations [a]					
	Model 1 [b]		Model 2 [b]		Model 3 [b]	
Job Characteristics						
Wage_more	−0.031	(0.00)	−0.080	(0.02)	−0.056	(0.01)
Wage_exact	0.354	(3.03)*	0.355	(3.01)*	0.366	(3.19)*
Wage_less	−0.008	(0.00)	0.006	(0.00)	0.019	(0.01)
Training	0.446	(28.01)***	0.454	(28.02)***	0.454	(28.05)***
Match	0.323	(14.08)***	0.331	(14.45)***	0.332	(14.58)***
Learn	0.345	(15.34)***	0.350	(15.47)***	0.354	(15.81)***
Help	0.468	(18.36)***	0.471	(18.46)***	0.471	(18.52)***
Intercept	0.576	(4.63)**	0.535	(3.53)*	0.564	(5.39)**
Log Likelihood	−585.645		−580.012		−579.639	
Pseudo R^2	0.1303		0.1387		0.1474	
Sample size	2,014		2,014		2,014	

Notes:

[a] Figures in parentheses are the asymptotic *t*-ratios.

[b] *** indicates significance at the 1% level; ** indicates significance at the 5% level; and * indicates significance at the 10% level.

Table 12.12 Determinants of reemployment

Variables	Model Estimations[1]					
	Model 1[2]		Model 2[2]		Model 3[2]	
Personal Characteristics						
Age	-0.006	(6.4)**	-0.006	(6.37)**	-0.006	(6.09)***
Gender (Male = 1)	0.171	(4.18)**	0.192	(5.12)**	0.212	(6.08)***
Primary Education (Reference group)	–	–	–	–	–	–
Junior High School	0.057	(0.18)	0.038	(0.08)	0.008	(0.00)
Senior High School	0.273	(5.66)**	0.236	(3.69)*	0.206	(2.77)*
Junior College	0.334	(5.62)**	0.284	(3.46)*	0.231	(2.24)*
University	0.741	(18.89)***	0.689	(14.36)***	0.601	(10.55)***
Head of Household	0.017	(0.04)	0.012	(0.02)	0.019	(0.05)
Satisfaction	–	–	–	–	-0.583	(26.45)**
Project types						
Computerization of Public Files	–	–	0.187	(2.09)*	0.178	(1.85)
Improvements in Public Construction Works	–	–	-0.215	(1.56)	-0.181	(1.11)
Beautification of Living Environments	–	–	0.007	(0.00)	0.014	(0.01)
Community Services	–	–	0.050	(0.19)	0.058	(0.24)
Enhancement of Tourism	–	–	0.403	(4.05)**	0.316	(2.39)*
Others (Reference group)	–	–	–	–	–	–

318

Table 12.12 (Contd.)

Variables	Model Estimations[a]					
	Model 1[b]		Model 2[b]		Model 3[b]	
Job Characteristics						
Training	0.157	(3.58)*	0.171	(4.12)**	0.104	(1.43)
Match	0.329	(15.98)***	0.334	(16.17)***	0.287	(11.55)***
Learn	0.137	(2.68)*	0.135	(2.56)*	0.074	(0.73)
Too_old	-5.881	(0.00)	-5.940	(0.00)	6.057	(0.00)
Intercept	-0.937	(27.35)***	-0.944	(2.22)***	-0.528	(5.93)**
Log Likelihood	-625.863		-621.311		-608.557	
Pseudo R^2	0.1800		0.1861		0.216	
Sample size	2,014		2,014		2,014	

Notes:

[a] Figures in parentheses are the asymptotic *t*-ratios.

[b] *** indicates significance at the 1% level; ** indicates significance at the 5% level; * indicates significance at the 10% level.

319

In Models 1 and 2 of Table 12.12, receiving training and learning within the period of the programme did have positive effects on the probability of reemployment. Finally, the study upon which this chapter has been based indicated that if the requirements of the PSEP jobs could be matched to the learning speciality of participants gained from formal education, then they would be more likely to gain reemployment. In summary, personal and job characteristics had significant effects on the probability of an individual gaining reemployment, whereas the project type had no role to play with regard to the subsequent reemployment of programme participants.

CONCLUSIONS

In contrast to the policy goals specified within the PSEP Act, the programme did lead to short-term improvements in the employment of middle-aged and disadvantaged workers. The empirical results of our study indicate that in both social and economic terms, programme participants were better off during their period of employment in PSEP projects. It is, however, difficult to demonstrate the long-term employment effects simply by examining the reemployment rate, since only one-third of the programme participants found unsubsidized jobs after leaving the PSEP; furthermore, details of their period of stay in their new jobs were not available from the survey data. Hence, more follow-up studies on the programme participants should be conducted, in order to ascertain the employment effects of the programme in the long run. The determinant factors for reemployment tended to be more personal as opposed to being programme related, with personal characteristics including gender, age and educational level being significant in explaining the level of satisfaction and the probability of reemployment.

With the exception of 'enhancement of tourism', the type of project had almost no role to play in explaining either satisfaction or reemployment rates, although, to some extent, the project implementation methods did matter. Whether programme participants were interested in their jobs and whether they received proper training and help from employers had impacts on both the level of satisfaction and the likelihood of reemployment. Finally, although the PSEP has had some positive effects, certain negative effects, such as the narcotic effect, are inevitable. Despite this, the PSEP can achieve better results through improved implementation; the design and implementation of public works, for example, is a vital consideration. Constraints on the overall employment duration should prevent participants from becoming reliant on public works and encourage them to find unsubsidized jobs on completion of the PSEP. The provision of proper training and assistance would also help participants to find jobs after leaving the programme.

NOTES

[1]   This chapter is based upon data collected during the Evaluation Study of the Public Service Employment Programme, conducted in 2004, and sponsored by the Council for Economic Planning and Development (CEPD) in Taiwan. Following completion of this chapter, the CEPD published an omnibus book for the PSEP and gave it a new official name, the 'Public Works Employment Programme'. Hence, the titles 'Public Service Employment Programme' and 'Public Works Employment Programme' should be regarded as interchangeable.

[2]   Examples include a range of 'Sustainable Employment Programmes' and similar 'Diverse Employment Development Programmes'.

[3]   The PSEP actually includes two types of employment programmes; job creation in which workers are employed directly by the government, and wage subsidies aimed at encouraging private employers to hire unemployed workers. The wage subsidy scheme for SMEs alone, which was responsible for getting 48,000 workers back into work, accounts for around 15 per cent of the total PSEP budget. Since the fundamental principles behind these two programmes are quite different, this chapter deals only with the evaluation of the public works programme.

REFERENCES

Hu, S.-C. (2003), 'Conclusions', in J.S. Lee (ed.), *Who Stole Our Jobs?: The Unemployment Problems in Taiwan Since 1996*, Taipei: Commonwealth Publishing (in Chinese), pp.373-90.

Jiang, F.-F. (2003), 'Middle- and Old-age as an Employment Barrier for Workers', in J.S. Lee (ed.), *Who Stole Our Jobs?: The Unemployment Problems in Taiwan Since 1996*, Taipei: Commonwealth Publishing (in Chinese), pp.193-230.

Lee, J.-H. (2001) 'Income Assistance and Employment Creation through Public Works in Korea', in F.-K. Park, Y.-B. Park, G. Betcherman and A. Dar (eds.), *Labour Market Reforms in Korea: Policy Options for the Future*, Seoul: World Bank and Korea Labour Institute, pp.175-95.

Lee, J.S. (2003), 'Is the Public Service Employment Programme the Right Solution to the Unemployment Problems in Taiwan?', in J.S. Lee (ed.), *Who Stole Our Jobs?: The Unemployment Problems in Taiwan Since 1996*, Taipei: Commonwealth Publishing (in Chinese), pp.265-86.

Lin, J.-P. (2003), 'Labour Migration: A Way to Improve the Reemployment of the Unemployed', in J.S. Lee (ed.), *Who Stole Our Jobs?: The Unemployment Problems in Taiwan Since 1996*, Taipei: Commonwealth Publishing (in Chinese), pp.339-72.

Lin, N. (2000), 'Inequality in Social Capital', *Contemporary Sociology*, **29**(6): 785-96.

RDEC (2003), *Report of the Implementation of the PSEP by the End of 2003*, Taipei: Research, Development and Evaluation Commission (in Chinese).

Index